THE HOUSE BOOK

Phaidon Press Limited
Regent's Wharf
All Saints Street
London N1 9PA

Phaidon Press Inc
180 Varick Street
New York, NY 10014

www.phaidon.com

First published 2001
© 2001 Phaidon Press Limited

ISBN 0 7148 3984 1

A CIP catalogue record for
this book is available from
the British Library.

Printed in Hong Kong

Note

The houses are arranged
in A–Z order by architect,
patron or designer. In the
case of the vernacular and
traditional dwellings, we
have used the name of the
tribe or people who built
them. The dates given for
a house refer to the year
of completion or where
appropriate an extended
period of construction or
different construction phases.

Abbreviations

b = born
c = circa
d = died

AFG = Afghanistan
ARG = Argentina
ASL = Australia
AUS = Austria
BAR = Barbados
BEL = Belgium
BEN = Benin
BER = Bermuda
BR = Brazil
BZE = Belize
CAM = Cameroon
CAN = Canada
CH = Chile
CHN = China
CI = Canary Islands
COL = Colombia
CRO = Croatia
CU = Cuba
CZ = Czech Republic
DK = Denmark
EG = Egypt
EST = Estonia
FIN = Finland
FKN = Federation of St
Kitts and Nevis
FIJI = Fiji
FR = France
GER = Germany
GR = Greece
HUN = Hungary
ICE = Iceland
IN = India
IND = Indonesia
IR = Iran
IRE = Ireland
IRQ = Iraq
IS = Israel
IT = Italy
JAP = Japan
KAZ = Kazakhstan
KEN = Kenya
KYR = Kyrgyzstan
LX = Luxembourg
MALAY = Malaysia
MAU = Mauritania
MEX = Mexico
MLI = Mali
MNG = Mongolia
MON = Monaco
MOR = Morocco
NIG = Nigeria
NL = The Netherlands
NOR = Norway
NZ = New Zealand
PE = Peru
PNG = Papua New Guinea
POL = Poland
POR = Portugal
ROM = Romania
RUS = Russia
RWA = Rwanda
SA = South Africa
SAM = Samoa
SAU = Saudi Arabia
SL = Sri Lanka
SLO = Slovenia
SP = Spain
SW = Switzerland
SWE = Sweden
SYR = Syria
TAN = Tanzania
TKM = Turkmenistan
TRK = Turkey
UK = United Kingdom
USA = United States of
America
VEN = Venezuela
VIET = Vietnam
YEM = Yemen

THE HOUSE BOOK is a global survey of 500 houses, covering an astonishing array of architects, cultures, styles, materials and design movements. The selection ranges from mud huts to Baroque palaces, and Arts and Crafts houses to today's contemporary icons. Every notion of the house is explored – the visually astounding, iconic houses, architect-designed houses, as well as the homes and dwellings of diverse cultures around the world. The house is perhaps mankind's most enduring invention. Built originally to serve as shelter from the elements, the house in recent times has become a showpiece for architects to challenge our perceptions and display their prowess as designers and builders. Arranged in A–Z order by architect, patron, tribe or people, each house is illustrated by a key image revealing the diverse nature of the environment we call home. The architect and house is discussed concisely and placed in a broader, historical context. **THE HOUSE BOOK** is an accessible and informative source book for all those interested in the practical, decorative and complex construction that has such an enormous influence on all our lives.

Φ

Aalto Alvar

Summer House

One hour by boat from the nearest railway station, in a forest overlooking a lake in north-central Finland, this summer house was both a retreat and a test-bed where one of the most important twentieth-century architects developed his own particular contribution to Modernism. Under the influence of this sylvan, Scandinavian setting, the house marks a decisive shift away from the more familiar Modernist planar, abstract surfaces towards consciously varied tactile and aesthetic effects, a principal feature of the Finnish tradition in which Aalto was pre-eminent. The composition of the house is simple: two equal wings at right angles enclose the courtyard, with a separate guest annex. Fifty different types of brick and ceramic tile line the courtyard, while the walls frame stunning yet contrived views through a large, white-painted timber grid. Sensibility to site and manipulation of surface are hallmarks extending to Aalto's large public commissions.

☛ Holscher, A Jacobsen, Pietilä, Sirén, Wright

Hugo Alvar Henrik Aalto. b Kuortane, nr Jyväskylä (FIN), 1898. d Helsinki (FIN), 1976. **Summer House**, Muuratsalo (FIN), 1953.

Abelam

Haus Tambaran

Soaring above the other houses of an Abelam village is the *haus tambaran*, or ceremonial house, with its decorated front and peaked gable, which can be up to 25 m (80 ft) high. But even the much smaller, ordinary dwelling houses, next to and opposite it, are built to a similar design. They are 'all roof', having an 'A-frame' frontage made of leaning bamboo poles, and a ridge which slopes down to the ground at the rear, to which the side poles are lashed. Drawn in black and white and richly painted in red and blue, the upper facade of the *haus tambaran* (seen here) has rows of giant symbolic faces, cassowaries and flying foxes in bold, oval shapes. The lower part of the facade is covered by a plaited mat and has a low tunnel-like entrance.

The Abelam people live between the Sepik River and the Alexander mountains in northern New Guinea, where they grow taro, a root crop with succulent leaves, and yams – up to 2.5 m (8 ft) in length – which they display at festivals.

☛ **Sa'dan Toraja, Samoan, Toba Batak**

Abelam. Active (PNG), present day, earliest origins unknown. **Haus Tambaran**, East Sepik province (PNG), c1960, still built today.

Acayaba Marcos   Residencia Olga

A modern, inverted ziggurat forms the daring structure of the Residencia Olga. Built on a steeply-sloping site, the project was conceived by Acayaba as a prototype of standardized housing for highly uneven hill sites common in Brazilian cities. Six concrete columns, sunk into the ground, provide the support for an industrialized wooden structure which is tied to the slope higher up for further stability. Three regular bays are divided into four levels of accommodation: the bottom three levels contain bedrooms, while the top level is an open-plan spacious living, dining and kitchen area. The house is entered from the top of the cliff at this level, giving an illusion of walking into open space, and the grounds here are landscaped with a swimming pool, terrace and garage. By using a modular system of bays, reinforced by cross-bracings, the cost and use of material is minimized, while the owners benefit from an uninterrupted view across the city.

☛ Banta, Botta, Poole, Scott Tallon Walker

Marcos Acayaba. b São Paulo (BR), 1944. **Residencia Olga**, São Paulo (BR), 1989–91.

Adam Robert

Syon House

A meticulously applied Roman Doric order, a diagonally ribbed ceiling echoed by a fretted black and white marble floor, and copies of antique sculpture transformed the entrance hall of Syon House in the 1760s, when Robert Adam converted the Elizabethan house into the epitome of Neo-Classical taste. While the exterior – replete with turrets – is the result of an Elizabethan conversion of the cloister of a fifteenth-century nunnery, this hall and the suite of rooms that open from it were rebuilt and decorated by Adam for the first Duke of Northumberland. Adam's richly inventive series of rooms, set around a rectangular courtyard, use every plan imaginable; some chastely detailed like the hall, others more fancifully 'Etruscan', his representation of the less formal Roman domestic style, and all designed to show how classical taste could be recreated as though Syon House were a grand Roman mansion adapted for the Duke's own day.

☛ **Burlington, Cameron, I Jones, Terry**

Robert Adam. **b** Kirkcaldy, Scotland (UK), 1728. **d** London (UK), 1792. **Syon House**, Brentford (UK), 1762–9.

Airstream Co.

Airstream Trailer

Dubbed 'Airstream' because the trailer rode the highways as smoothly as a stream of air, the 1947 model shown in this promotional photograph moves along under the cycling power of French racing champion, Monsieur Latourneau. The picture was later stylized to serve as a logo for the company, to more graphically suggest that the aluminium-clad 'land yacht' – first launched in 1936 by Wally Byam as the Airstream Clipper – was (and still is) strategically designed to be light, manoeuverable and sturdy. A fully and artfully equipped home, it accommodates comfortable living on and off the road. Following Byam's creed to limit exterior changes to the functional rather than the fashionable, today's Airstream is still highly recognizable and its now iconic streamlined profile and aircraft-like construction have been attracting owners for seven decades. Thousands of vintage Airstreams are still seen at caravan rallies, on movie sets or on view in museums.

☞ Berglund, D Greene, Horden, Suuronen, M Webb

8

Airstream Company. Established Los Angeles, CA (USA), 1932, now located in Jackson Center, OH (USA). **Wally Byam.** b Baker, OR (USA), 1896. d CA (USA), 1962. **Airstream Trailer** (USA), 1947.

Aitchison Jr George Leighton House

Despite its unpretentious classical exterior, the interior of Leighton House is an unexpected Aladdin's cave of exotic delights. George Aitchison Jr designed the house in 1866 for his friend, the artist Frederic Leighton, who was known for his eccentric and eclectic tastes. These culminate in the Arab Hall, pictured here, which Leighton added in 1877–9 to house

his collection of oriental tiles that cover its walls. A fountain lies at its centre with recessed bays on each side, framed by shafts with alabaster capitals carved with birds; overhead, a small dome glows with coloured glass, some of it from Damascus. The windows in the upper part of the recesses contain *mashrabiyya* fretwork from Cairo. The frieze of

mosaics in the Persian style is the work of artist Walter Crane (1845–1915), and Aitchison designed the brass corona that hangs above the pool.

☛ Morgan, Roy, Vaux & Church, Walpole

George Aitchison Jr. b London (UK), 1825. d London (UK), 1910. **Leighton House**, London (UK), 1866, with later additions, 1877–9.

Akbar

Raja Birbal's House

Red sandstone has seldom been employed to such perfection as by the Mughals, who erected exquisite structures from it, sliced it to clad arches, walls and domes, and chiselled elaborate geometries into its porous surface. Built by local craftsmen, but devoid of their Hindu pantheon, this was an Islamic architecture in name only. It represented the syncretism propagated by Akbar, in whose court the Hindu Birbal was a minister. Contemporary politics and the folkloric popularity of Birbal's wit may explain the house's present attribution, but it is unlikely that he resided here. Located within the imperial harem in Akbar's citadel, Fatehpur Sikri near Agra, 'Birbal's house' may actually have housed two senior queens. A diagonal symmetry of square rooms (four below and two domed ones above), with two staircases, two hipped-roof porches and two terraces is indeed a functional interpretation of equality and co-existence.

☛ **Amar Singh II, Jai Singh I, Kamath, Mehmed II, Shah Jahan**

10

Emperor Akbar. Reigned (IN), 1556–1605. **Raja Birbal's House**, Fatehpur Sikri, nr Agra (IN), 1572.

Alberti Leon Battista   Palazzo Rucellai

Alberti's design for the Palazzo Rucellai was the first consistent attempt of the Renaissance to apply the Classical Orders to a palazzo frontage. Rising from a low basement, Tuscan, ornate Corinthian and plain Corinthian pilasters are applied in shallow relief, each correctly proportioned, to articulate the facade into three distinct storeys. In fact, the building has an additional mezzanine floor, delineated by a row of small, square windows with grilles, so the plinth and the storey it supports actually accommodate the ground floor and mezzanine. The ground floor was in fact semi-fortified and provided guardroom quarters and stabling necessary for the violent political climate of the times. Above this is the *piano nobile*, containing the ceremonial apartments, and above the top storey is an attic, concealed behind the large cornice. The perfect symmetry of this double-entrance facade was not realized as the final eighth bay was never completed.

☛ **Laurana, Maiano, Michelozzi, Sangallo**

11

Leon Battista Alberti. **b** Genoa (IT), 1404. **d** Rome (IT), 1472. **Palazzo Rucellai**, Florence (IT), 1446–57.

Aldington Peter

Turn End

An assembly of monopitched, white roughcast forms, Turn End and its associated pair of houses are both Modernist and timeless. Their careful massing and setting in an intricately worked garden show a much gentler face of Modernism than the hard concrete-and-glass which prevailed in the early 1960s. Using traditional materials, such as timber and tiles, the buildings meld with the neighbouring walls and plants. Outdoor spaces weave around the houses and ancillary structures, with intriguing glimpses always inviting further movement. Aldington designed these houses while he was researching construction techniques, which allowed him to keep the design simple enough for much of the work to be done by family and friends, yet still achieve a complex form. Myriad lighting effects create an internal counterpart to the exterior's richness of colour and texture. This mastery of construction became a hallmark of Aldington's practice.

☛ Aalto, Kahn, Lubetkin, Rogers

Peter Aldington. b Preston (UK), 1933. **Turn End**, Haddenham (UK), 1964.

al-Haddad Abd al-Qadar — House of Abd al-Qadar the Smith

This traditional Islamic house was created in the early seventeenth century by grafting the House of Abd al-Qadar (shown here), onto an older house built in 1540, known as Bayt Amna bint Salim. The houses have been unified to create one large dwelling linked by a covered walkway. The Abd al-Qadar villa became the *haramlik* (women's quarters), and the older villa served as the *salamlik* (men's quarters). From this central open courtyard, a staircase leads up to the *maq'ad*, or open air sitting room. The indoor reception rooms, guest rooms and harem quarters are situated around the courtyard, following the traditional Islamic house plan. These rooms are screened with *mashrabiyya*, wooden lattice-work – a typical feature of Cairene domestic architecture – and many overlook the secluded central courtyard garden below. Built of thick Helwan sandstone blocks, these interior spaces provide a cool and quiet escape from the clamouring dusty streets of the city.

☞ Bawa, El-Wakil, Fathy, Nasrid Dynasty

13

Abd al-Qadar al-Haddad. b c1600. Active (EG), seventeenth century. **House of Abd al-Qadar the Smith**, Cairo (EG), 1631.

Amar Singh II

Bari Mahal

The City Palace of Udaipur, the largest palace complex in Rajasthan, is composed of eleven *mahals* (palaces) successively added over a 300-year period. It is a maze of courtyards, apartments and decorated halls in which every wall has been embellished with inlaid Chinese tiles, jewel-coloured mosaics and figurative paintings of the *maharanas* and their courtiers.

The Bari Mahal, or Garden Palace, is set on the hillside overlooking the rest of the palace complex and, beyond that, Pichola Lake. Here, the *maharana* would lie in the water and enjoy the comforts of his position; but it was also the place of ceremonial and pious acts. This painting depicts a *maharana* worshipping the goddess Shiva beneath the colonnades while,

in the courtyard, dancers and musicians perform. The square pool in the centre is surrounded by white marble baluster columns with cusped arches, while small pavilions with ornate trellis screens are arranged along the raised storey.

☛ **Akbar, Jagat Singh II, Jai Singh I, Kamath**

Amar Singh II. Reigned (IN), 1698–1710. **Bari Mahal (Garden Palace)**, City Palace, Udaipur, Rajasthan (IN), c1703. *Rani Ari Singh in the Garden Mansion*, watercolour on paper, c1765.

Amsterdam Merchants

Houses on Prinzengracht

The two medieval quarters of Amsterdam had reached bursting point by the seventeenth century and the start of the city's golden age. Concentric rings of canals were planned in 1609 to encompass the old town, and these were extended in the 1660s. Moving outwards along the radial Leidsegracht and Reguliersgracht, which link them, the outermost ring is the Prinzengracht. The canals are lined with merchants' houses, workshops and warehouses, which are mostly squeezed into narrow plots, so they are four or five times as deep as their frontage is wide. Most houses have four storeys with sash windows of decreasing size as they rise, and garrets in the roof space. Their individual architectural emphasis is therefore mainly confined to the gables. The more ornate houses have gables comprising carved volutes or even exotic representations of fish, supporting a centrepiece capped by a shell; yet others have curved scrolls or are simply stepped.

☛ **Brussels Guildsmen, Fortrey, Henri IV**

Amsterdam Merchants. Active (NL), late sixteenth and seventeenth century. **Houses on Prinzengracht**, Amsterdam (NL), circa seventeenth century.

Anchorites

Tufa-Pinnacle Houses

Cappadocia, in central Turkey, is an area remarkable for its volcanic rock formations. Two now extinct volcanoes have deposited a deep layer of tufa across the region, which has eroded to leave a fantastic landscape of eccentric phallic obelisks. These obelisks are often topped with fragments of a harder black basalt layer, and they are known locally as 'fairy chimneys'. For centuries, Cappadocians have been excavating the soft rock and enlarging crevices to form houses, as well as churches and even monasteries. Fireplaces and furniture are often carved directly from the rock, and multiple window openings contribute to the resemblance to huge honeycombs or dovecotes. In some cases, the 'buildings' can be sixteen storeys high, with upper floors reached by rope ladders. In the seventh century AD, 30,000 anchorites lived in the area, and although this number is now much reduced, many of the cone-houses are still inhabited.

☛ **Gitano, C Johnson, Loess Han, Pueblo Indians**

Anchorites. Active (TRK), circa AD 300 to AD 1000. **Tufa-Pinnacle Houses**, Uchisar, nr Urgup, Cappadocia (TRK), 600 BC to twentieth century.

Ando Tadao

Koshino House

This interior view of the main living area shows the extreme abstraction of this two-level house, composed of two concrete boxes embedded in a sloping site. Ando, one of the most renowned contemporary Japanese architects and a winner of the Pritzker Prize, challenges the emotions and the senses through a minimalism that, in many ways, alludes to the Zen tradition. He is concerned with the individual's confrontation with space and resistance to seduction through an attentiveness to the essential. The play of light and shadow and bare spatial asceticism, where the outside world and its distractions are erased, give a sense of psychological isolation and inward reflectiveness. This mood is emphasized by the blank window, which forces the observer to look deeper into one's relationship to the space. The house reflects the principles of the minimalist movement of the 1960s, and its reaction against commercial vulgarity and the commodification of culture.

☞ **Chipperfield, Kikutake, Pawson Silvestrin, Shinohara**

Tadao Ando. b Osaka (JAP), 1941. **Koshino House**, Ashiya (JAP), 1979–81.

Andresen O'Gorman

Mooloomba House

A two-storey deck house in the bush by the ocean's edge, Mooloomba House has rightly been described as 'less a house, more an inhabited landscape'. Nestling between the banksias and box trees on North Stradbroke Island, a short boat ride from Brisbane, the holiday home has a seductively open, easy relationship with its surroundings. Built from Australian hardwoods – a recurring feature in Brit Andresen and Peter O'Gorman's architecture – the house comprises a two-storey main wing with four bed alcoves, a shower room and toilet, and terminating in a belvedere overlooking the Pacific. Peeling off at right angles are the living spaces – a summer North Room and a winter South Room, separated by a courtyard onto which they both open. Although Andresen is Norwegian and O'Gorman studied in America, their work is among the more compelling of a new generation of practices trying to forge a contemporary but distinctly Australian style.

☛ Clare Design, Edmond & Corrigan, Klotz, Poole

18

Andrews John

Andrews Farmhouse

On first sight, there is something slightly alien about the Andrews Farmhouse; the curious tower and strange drums at its corners lend the impression more of a research station than a home. In fact, the house is both – a reworked traditional farmstead that employs the latest energy-efficient techniques. Andrews built this square, low-slung house for his family in Eugowra, 210 miles north-west of Sydney, its overhanging roof a deliberate take on local farmsteads. Rooftop solar panels and a wind vane generate electricity that heats water in winter and, in summer, pumps water from the rainwater vats to sprinklers on the roof, the evaporating water cooling the house. Andrews is best known for his work in America, such as the Scarborough College (1962–3) which established his architectural reputation at a young age. Returning to his native Australia in 1979, his work continued to seek solutions appropriate to particular situations and settings.

☞ **Grose Bradley, Herzog + Partner, Jackson, Murcutt, Vale**

John Hamilton Andrews. b Sydney, NSW (ASL), 1933. **Andrews Farmhouse**, Eugowra, NSW (ASL), 1981.

Annamese

Floating Houses

Houses built over water on piles are common throughout south-east Asia. However, these Annamese houses differ in that they are built on rafts, essentially as houseboats. Most floating dwellings are found on the rivers and canals of towns where land is scarce, but these houses belong to the inhabitants of the Annam Mountains, who are far more isolated than coastal dwellers. These inland people are traditionally itinerant, so the idea of a house that can be removed from one side of a mountainous lake to the other both suits their temperament and their economic need to exploit the lake's resources of fish. The tropical climate provides an abundance of excellent fine-grained hardwood, suitable both for building and for resisting rot. The framed construction, allied to a light, overhanging roof, reduces the effects of glare and high humidity internally, while forming a strong structure that can take the strain of being moved.

☞ Dai, Kyrgyz, Maori, Toffinou

20

Antrim Labourers

Sod-Roofed Cabin

The under-roof of this cabin in the north-east of Ireland is made from cut sods of turf, upon which a thatched roof of a locally gathered material – rushes, marram grass or flax – would be laid and tied down with a network of ropes. The walls are made of cut turf which is dried out and laid like bricks before being white-washed. Such a dwelling could be constructed within a day to provide shelter for an itinerant population, and abandoned when the inhabitants moved on in search of work. Before the Irish Famine of the 1840s, the single-room cabin was the most common housing type, and the linear plan goes back to at least the 1600s. The widespread persistence of the sod-roofed cabin form until at least the mid-nineteenth century is due in part to the geographical and political isolation of the country. Because Ireland was beyond the reaches of Roman occupation, elements of Celtic and pre-historic culture were preserved beyond the Dark Ages.

☛ **Breton, Finistère Farmers, Hebridean Crofter**

Antrim Labourers. Active (IRE), seventeenth to nineteenth century. **Sod-Roofed Cabin**, Co Antrim (IRE), circa seventeenth century to mid-nineteenth century.

Apyshkov Vladimir   Chaev Residence

Both the client and the architect for this house had engineering backgrounds, and the simple, clear-cut detailing of the rigorous forms have an engineered air, made more picturesque by later surrounding trees. Chaev's wealth came from the Trans-Siberian railway and his city residence of 1906, also by Apyshkov, was an ingenious composition in Jugendstil, the German interpretation of Art Nouveau. However, by 1910 most Russians turned away from this 'foreign' style, leading to a revival of Neo-Classicism which became so all-pervading in the nineteenth century that they regarded it as their own style. Here on the Neva estuary, Chaev chose again to follow fashion, in an area where many classical waterside houses were being created. Apyshkov is best known for his 1905 book, *The Rational in the Latest Architecture,* which discussed the modernity and democratic basis of Jugendstil, but his career was mainly in military buildings and as a teacher.

☛ **Cameron, Geisler & Guslisty, Nash, Schinkel**

Vladimir Petrovich Apyshkov. b 1871. **d** Leningrad (RUS), 1939. **Chaev Residence**, Kameny Island, St Petersburg (RUS), 1913–15.

Amiga House

This house was designed to make innovative use of boat-building technology to allow radical new forms and largely off-site prefabrication. From the garden side, the model shows an uninterrupted concrete slab at ground floor level, extending as a terrace over the swimming pool. The lower of the two composite carbon-fibre shells has a double-height living space and the taller one a dining area, with a box containing two bedrooms above it, and the master bedroom at the top. The shells were designed to give a feeling of enclosure and privacy, whilst allowing views through the house. Although it failed to get planning permission and was never built, this house was widely published. Its rejection in a London neighbourhood once renowned for liberal thinking shows how conservative British views on architecture had become. London-based Ron Arad is best known as a furniture designer, whose robust work ranges from one-off metal chairs to mass-produced plastic bookshelves.

☞ **Berglund, Chipperfield, Future Systems, Grimshaw**

Ron Arad. b Tel Aviv (IS), 1951. **Amiga House**, London (UK), project, 1997.

Architecture Studio

Maison rue Robert Blache

The unexpected intrusion of the rising curved facade of this house – evocative of the traditional mansard roof – into an otherwise mundane street in Paris produces an enigmatic, though arresting 'urban episode' characteristic of the work of the Architecture Studio. With four storeys built above a narrow existing ground floor, the tower-like house consists of two 100 sq m (1,076 sq ft) units which are set around a central exposed steel-cage staircase. The affrontive presence of this house reflects the architects' self-avowed espousal of Kierkegaard's maxim that it is necessary 'to leave open the wounds of possibility'. The Studio's production, described once as 'cryptic buildings that possess an unimpeachable logic', tries to remain free of every preconceived style and technique, embracing the urban context with technologically advanced buildings whose process of evolution is 'not complete with the delivery of the building'.

☞ Holl, Lescaze, Rudolph, Williams & Tsien

24

24

Architecture Studio. Rene-Henri Arnaud. b Saint-Chamond (FR), 1958. **Jean-François Bonne. b** Saint-Mandé (FR), 1949. **Alain Bretagnolle. b** Vichy (FR), 1961. **Laurent-Marc Fischer. b** Paris (FR), 1964. **Marc Lehmann. b** Rabat (MOR), 1962. **Martin Robain. b** Paris (FR), 1943. **Rodo Tishado. b** Cajamarca (PE), 1940. **Maison rue Robert Blache**, Paris (FR), 1997.

Arquitectonica Pink House

This is a house of layers, pink upon pink, with gradations from powder-pale to vibrant rose. Designed between 1976 and 1979 by Laurinda Spear and Bernardo Fort-Brescia, the husband-and-wife team behind Arquitectonica, this house grew to define a new era in Miami, ending the long period in which architects spurned the vibrant colours of the tropics.

The Pink House is an unconventional modernist form that draws on the dual traditions of Art Deco and the Bauhaus, both predominant in Miami; its primary building materials are stucco-clad concrete inset with glass block. The setting, on the shore of Biscayne Bay, reinforces its tropicality, as does the central feature, a long, narrow internal swimming pool that

runs along the entire north-south axis of the building. Founded in 1977, this Miami-based firm has gained an international reputation for its daring use of colour and boldly innovative geometric forms.

☞ **Barragán, Israel, Koning Eizenberg, Legorreta**

Arquitectonica (ARQ). **Bernardo Fort-Brescia**. b Lima (PE), 1951. **Laurinda Spear**. b Rochester, MN (USA), 1950. **Pink House**, Miami Shores, FL (USA), 1976–9.

Ashburnham Roger

Scotney Castle

A fragment of a moated castle with a machicolated tower is all that remains of the fortifications built by Roger Ashburnham in the late fourteenth century in response to French raids on the Kent coast that resulted from the Hundred Years War. The castle was little more than a small manor house of mellow sandstone ashlar sheltering within the shadow of the surviving tower. Once the French threat had receded, subsequent owners, the Darell family, largely rebuilt Scotney Castle in the 1630s, retaining the earlier round tower and adding ranges of their own. However, in 1836 these too were replaced by a new house further up the hill, built from stone quarried from around the castle, while the old castle was left to fall into a picturesque ruin. The quarry, now filled with mature shrubs and trees, forms a perfect backdrop to enhance the setting of what is one of Kent's most romantic castles.

☛ **Burges, Compton, Ishikawa, Ludlow, Moreton Family**

Roger Ashburnham. Active (UK), mid to late fourteenth century. **d** 1392. **Scotney Castle**, Lamberhurst (UK), 1378–80, with later additions and renovations.

Asplund Gunnar   Villa Snellman

Asplund's serene Neo-Classicism, combined with a regional, almost monastic simplicity, is already evident in the Villa Snellman, his first major work. The solemnity of the house derives from a Nordic rendering of the Greek temple, with organizing, compositional elements from traditional sources, yet with a clear Modernist influence. The classical details of the shutters, windows, minimal garlands and *baldachino* above the entrance bestow a reverential tone amid the high, planar walls, while the house is thoughtfully sited in its environment. This seminal project by Asplund, who was one of the most significant architects working in Sweden in the early twentieth century, bears all the characteristics of his work. Often considered a transitional figure between traditional and modern architecture, he almost always exhibits a debt to Classicism, united with a Modernist purism, rooted in an indigenous Scandinavian architecture.

☛ **Aalto, Behrens, Erskine, Hoffmann, Muthesius, Sirén**

Erik Gunnar Asplund. b Stockholm (SWE), 1885. **d** Stockholm (SWE), 1940. **Villa Snellman**, Djursholm, nr Stockholm (SWE), 1917–18.

Atelier 5

Merz House

Beneath the pervasive vines that cover this house lies a concrete structure, built as a solitary object in the tradition of Le Corbusier. It was designed by a group of Swiss architects who self-consciously continued exploring the formal language of their architectural mentor and fellow countryman in the post-war period. The two-storey house, with large picture windows facing onto a lake, rests on *pilotis* and is contained within a governing frame. The living, dining, kitchen and bedroom areas are on the raised first floor, with a guest room and sun terrace on the second floor. Since its inception in 1955, Atelier 5 has strived towards achieving an 'anonymous architecture' in a truly mutual, collaborative process, with housing as a theme and central mission, and is best known for its Halen housing estate near Berne (1955–60). It seeks not to follow current trends, but to create new didactic prototypes which fulfill the atelier's basic functionalist orientation.

☛ Ando, Herzog & de Meuron, Le Corbusier, Mies van der Rohe

Atelier 5. Erwin Fritz. b Wädenswil (SW), 1927. **d** (SW), 1988. **Samuel Gerber. b** Langnau (SW), 1932. **d** (SW), 1998. **Rolf Hesterberg. b** Zurich (SW), 1927. **Hans Hostettler. b** Wahlern (SW), 1925. **Alfredo Pini. b** Biasca (SW), 1932. **Merz House**, Môtier (SW), 1958–9.

Atelier 66

Vacation House

The solid forms of this imposing hilltop belvedere appear to rise up out of the rocky slope on which it stands. Built in 1973, the house exploits its dramatic setting, giving commanding views over the sea and the village of Oxylithos, Euboea. The building is skilfully adapted to the varied climate and topography of the region; the solid walls protect its interior courtyards from prevailing easterly winds and have a high thermal mass to moderate the extremes of seasonal temperatures. Living areas are organized into a series of zones of internal, semi-covered and external spaces that flow into one another, allowing for maximum flexibility of use, under different weather conditions. Established in 1965, the Antonakakis's practice, Atelier 66, is probably best known for this modernist interpretation of the vernacular courtyard house typology, which has ancient antecedents in the region.

☛ Eldem, Fathy, Issaias & Papaioannou, Konstantinidis

Atelier 66. **Dimitris Antonakakis. b** Chania, Crete (GR), 1933. **Suzana Maria Antonakakis. b** Athens (GR), 1935. **Vacation House**, Oxylithos, Euboea (GR), 1973–4.

Azuma Takamitsu Tower House

Built on an irregular-shaped site roughly the size of two car parking spaces, the five-level, exposed concrete Tower House is a masterpiece of the minimal urban dwelling. Designed for the architect and his family, the rooms of this house are stacked on top of each other, connected only by a winding open stair as a continuous space with no interior doors. The compact interior space is opened up visually by a large picture window between the second and third floors. The house is situated on a boulevard created in preparation for the 1964 Tokyo Olympics, and expresses the architect's 'desire to remain steadfast in the middle of the city', to embrace the chaotic and contradictory city head-on and overcome its high land values. While buildings constructed adjacent to the house have risen and fallen, the house continues to stand, strong as a monument to the commitment of a very individual architect.

☞ Ando, Bolles & Wilson, Kishi, Raymond

Takamitsu Azuma. b Osaka (JAP), 1933. **Tower House**, Tokyo (JAP), 1966.

At first glance, this sitting room, with its low ceilings, timber beams and inglenook, has a medieval feel, but two details place it firmly in the twentieth century – the innovative free-flowing space and the considered use of materials. It is a complex room which manages to combine formal axial routes (between the dining and sitting rooms, and the front and garden doors, not visible in this picture), large gathering areas and small intimate spaces, all with deceptive ease. In true Arts-and-Crafts tradition, materials are finished according to their use – compare, for example, the rough, tree-like quality of the timber beams to the smooth finish of the ingle settle, which is finely planed to reveal the grain of the oak. This is one of the many individual house commissions that Baillie Scott undertook, but he also did speculative work, such as Waterlow Court, a housing scheme in Hampstead Garden Suburb, which set new standards in house planning.

☞ **Lutyens, Morris, Parker & Unwin, P Webb, Voysey**

Mackay Hugh Baillie Scott. **b** Ramsgate (UK), 1865. **d** Broughton (UK), 1945. **48 Storey's Way**, Cambridge (UK), 1912–13.

Ban Shigeru   Curtain Wall House

Built in a traditional district of Tokyo, this steel-structured house opens up to its neighbourhood in an extraordinary manner. The first-floor deck extends on two elevations, and is mirrored by the roof slab above, from which are suspended double-height fabric curtains. According to Ban, the curtains soften the daylight and, with internal sliding doors, insulate the interior space from the cool night air, especially in winter. The curtains not only create a space that obscures the boundary between inside and outside, but they also allow a connection between the open and free atmosphere of *Shitamachi* (old downtown) and the interior of the house. Educated at the Cooper Union in New York, Ban's designs express his exploration of the use of various materials in building (particularly recycled cardboard tubes) to reveal the alternative character of the site and the building – as clearly demonstrated by the Curtain Wall House.

☛ **Azuma, Fujimori & Oshima, Ito, Ogawa, Reynolds, Sejima**

Shigeru Ban. **b** Tokyo (JAP), 1957. **Curtain Wall House**, Tokyo (JAP), 1995.

Banta Philip

XYZ House

Sited on a steep, almost unbuildable slope, the XYZ House was part of a reconstruction programme in the Oakland Hills, California, after a disastrous natural fire in 1991. Four stacked floors on a small, rectangular footprint create a 'vertical working volume'. This crisply-detailed, orthogonal block is animated by two free-curving balconies and a large, detached overhanging roof plane, further enhanced by steel earthquake-bracing structural members, attached at acute angles from each other to 'spell out' the letters X-Y-Z. The principal facade is mainly constructed from large windows framed by thin aluminium trims to maximize the spectacular view. The bottom two floors house a painting studio and master bedroom, while the top two comprise a kitchen, dining area, study and an airy, double-height living room. The latter is an outdoor-indoor space, with glass corners giving a panoramic view of Oakland below and, in the far distance, San Francisco Bay.

☛ **Acayaba, Botta, Israel, Koenig, Lautner, Meier**

Philip Banta. b Boston, MA (USA), 1950. **XYZ House**, Oakland, CA (USA), 1993.

Baracco Juvenal   Gezzi House

On the edge of the Peruvian desert sands, overlooking the South Pacific Ocean, this beach house was designed to provide the Gezzi family with an escape from city life. In using inexpensive local materials, washing the walls with cheerful vernacular colours and focusing on the informal openness of the home, Baracco has created a refreshing weekend retreat.

As one of Latin America's leading architects, Baracco is a major proponent of contextual buildings and is committed to reviving Peru's rich architectural heritage; his use of balconies, open rooftop terraces and bright colours are clear reminders of pre-Columbian and Spanish building traditions. Light and shade are artfully manipulated for decorative as

well as functional purposes. The open lattice-work cane walls and railings and the soaring bamboo terrace roof provide shady relief from the sun, natural ventilation and dramatically frame panoramic views.

☞ **Bawa, Dewes & Puente, Jourda Perraudin**

Bardwell Thomas   Bardwell House

With its symmetrical front facade and asymmetrical roof sloping to the rear, the Allen House is typical of its time (colonial America) and place (New England). Historians believe this house to have been built by Thomas Bardwell in 1722, later passing on to a succession of his family members. The Saltbox has long been considered a purely American house form, but it was actually an evolution of the English Tudor cottage with an added lean-to. Rectangular in plan with two floors and an attic, the roof would be steeply-pitched to the rear, sloping down almost to the ground floor. The central doorway, generally on the south-facing side, was usually flanked by two double-hung windows with a row of five windows on the first floor above. Inside, there were typically just four rooms, two per floor, each with its own hearth. Subtle regional differences exist in these generally wood-frame and clapboard houses, and in the southern states, the same form was termed a Catslide house.

☞ **Gallén-Kallela, McKim Mead & White, Roland Family, Rossi**

Thomas Bardwell. b (USA), 1691. **d** (USA), 1781. **Bardwell House (Allen House)**, Deerfield, MA (USA), 1722.

Barnes Edward Larrabee   Heckscher House

The Heckscher House takes the traditional American shingle style and reduces it to the pure simplicity of geometric forms placed gently in the landscape. Edward Larrabee Barnes designed this vacation house to sit delicately amid the spruce trees on a coastal site in Maine. It consists of four separate geometric structures, each recalling traditional vernacular forms without reiterating them, connected by a wooden deck with views to the coastline beyond. An outdoor eating area is shaded, appropriately to its coastal setting, by a sailboat spinnaker set to adjust to the sun's path. As was typical of his work, Barnes – the designer of several important American museums in Dallas and Minneapolis – kept the detailing to a minimum, thus allowing the spaces to have an elegant, abstract simplicity. Barnes was hugely influenced by his teachers, Walter Gropius and Marcel Breuer, after they had left the Bauhaus in Germany to teach at Harvard University.

☛ Breuer, Gropius, Gwathmey, Moore, Richardson

Edward Larrabee Barnes. b Chicago, IL (USA), 1915. Heckscher House, Mount Desert Island, ME (USA), 1976.

Barragán Luis   San Cristobal

Barragán's spare, planar compositional style is evident in this compound of family house with equestrian stables and a pool. The blue expanse of sky is reflected in the pool, juxtaposed with the solidity and texture of the pink walls behind; the ascetic stillness of the compound is complemented by the gushing water. Recalling the aqueducts of Barragán's own childhood village of Mazamitla, the troughed water is an example of how he drew inspiration from the vernacular of his native country. This complex, designed with his student, Andrés Casillas, is an interplay of human habitation and animal shelter, sunlight and shadow. Although the self-taught Barragán built relatively little, he has had an impact on three generations of Mexican architects as a revered mystic of architecture, and on minimalist architecture worldwide. As Barragán himself has summarized: 'Any work of architecture which does not express serenity is a mistake'.

☞ **Campo Baeza, Legorreta, Niemeyer, Pawson Silvestrin**

Luis Barragán. **b** Guadalajara (MEX), 1902. **d** Mexico City (MEX), 1988. **San Cristobal**, Egerstrom Residence and Stables, Los Clubes, Mexico City (MEX), 1967–8.

Baumschlager & Eberle

Häusler House

The tough concrete and crisp geometry of the Häusler House turns its back on the red-tiled, pitched-roof suburban architecture of its neighbours. Essentially introverted, the house is entered through a large opening in the solid concrete frontage, which is actually a passageway that splits the building in two and can be closed off with a sliding wooden gate to create a courtyard. A further internal courtyard is set within the larger half of the house, but here, in contrast to the exterior, the detailing is lighter and finely-scaled. The fortress-like appearance is re-emphasized at the rear (shown here), where a protective concrete grid is set beyond the glazed elevation of the louvred-timber house itself. A series of open-air terraces at varying levels are strictly contained within this gridded zone. The architects grew up and practice in this beautiful, but now heavily developed part of Austria, so their critique of its post-war development is well-informed.

☞ **Eames, Kada, Snozzi, Studio Granda**

Baumschlager & Eberle. Carlo Baumschlager. b Bregenz (AUS), 1956. **Dietmar Eberle. b** Hittisau (AUS), 1952. **Häusler House**, Hard (AUS), 1995.

Bawa Geoffrey

Bawa House

This central space of Geoffrey Bawa's own house echoes both a type of pillared hall found in ancient Sri Lankan Buddhist temples and the *impluvium,* or courtyard pool of a Roman villa; but he also cites sources as diverse as Italian hilltowns and the Alhambra in Granada as key influences. Built on the site of a row of four houses, the house intricately blends indoor and outdoor living spaces with a sequence of planted courtyards. It feels as if it has evolved naturally, but the modulation of bright light and restful shade is carefully orchestrated and the eye is led through a subtly contrived series of views. Bawa achieved an international reputation while remaining very much a regional architect, and has built almost entirely in Sri Lanka. His rootedness in his home country is shown both in the details of his buildings and in the arrangement of spaces, which reflect traditional building forms and a sensitive response to the local climate.

☛ al-Haddad, Fathy, Nasrid Dynasty, Pompeii Romans

Geoffrey Bawa. b Colombo (SL), 1919. **Bawa House**, Colombo (SL), 1969.

Behrens Peter

House at Mathildenhöhe

With its sensuously elongated gables, Behrens' house in the Darmstadt artists' colony betrays his connection with Jugendstil. Yet, its stark colours, lack of ornament and compositional discipline foreshadow the rational synthesis between design and industry he would achieve later as a leading figure of the Deutsche Werkbund. In 1901, Behrens was still transforming himself from a Jugendstil artist into an architect via interior decoration. Following the philosophy of Nietzsche, he and his contemporaries believed that art could address the huge social and economic questions of modern life which characterized Wilhelminian Germany. In 1907, at a time when life and art were synonyms and functionalism was not yet a pejorative term, Behrens was appointed as architect of the electrical company, AEG. His work melded design and industry, setting the tone for the Deutsche Werkbund and starting a theme which reverberated throughout the twentieth century.

☞ **Loos, Mackintosh, Morris, Muthesius, Olbrich**

Peter Behrens. b Hamburg (GER), 1868. **d** Berlin (GER), 1940. **House at Mathildenhöhe**, Darmstadt (GER), 1901.

Belize Campesino

'Baton Rouge'

In many parts of Central America – Belize, Costa Rica and Nicaragua – the tea and tobacco plantation workers and peasant farmers are termed *campesinos*. They build their own houses amid the plantations from whatever materials they can obtain. Usually the house has a framework of poles or rough timber, the vertical lengths being 'earthfast' (inserted into the ground), and the floor being raised to catch the breezes and avoid seasonal flood waters. The frame is covered with boards, sheet metal, or even grass. Discarded oil barrels are particularly useful when cut and beaten flat; being identical in size, they make effective wall panels. Corrugated iron sheets, painted to deter rust, may cover the single- or double-pitch roofs. Some houses have verandas and are brightened with plants in paint pots. The houses are often named, as with the 'Baton Rouge' shown here, which means 'red stick', once used as a territorial marker by Native Americans.

☛ **Droppers, Murcutt, Nevisian Creole, Rural Studio**

Belize Campesino. Active (BZE), from eighteenth century to present day. **'Baton Rouge'** (BZE), c1960s.

Berglund Staffan   Villa Spies

Rising like an elegant hemispherical spacecraft above the dramatic rocky coastline, the Villa Spies is a summer house designed by Staffan Berglund for the wealthy Danish visionary and business genius, Simon Spies. The villa's futuristic features include a circular dining space, which rises out of the ground at the press of a button, sound-proofed walls, electric shutters, electronically-controlled lighting and a heated outdoor swimming pool. With a band of windows in the place of an outer wall, the house has a 360-degree view to the sea and the archipelago that surrounds the city of Stockholm. Spies originally founded his business on tourism and set up a competition in 1967 to design an environment for leisure in the country that both visitors and residents could enjoy. Although Berglund's original entry won the 'Bubbles for Pleasure' competition, it was never built; however, his ideas inspired Spies to commission this villa.

☞ Arad, Future Systems, Lautner, Prouvé, Suuronen

42

Staffan Berglund. Active (SWE), mid-twentieth century to present day. **Villa Spies (Villa Fjolle),** Torö (SWE), 1969–70.

Bernese Farmers   Farmhouse

Although it might look ramshackle, this vernacular farmhouse is actually a highly-evolved building, perfectly suited to its uses and setting in a mountain climate with a long, cold winter and heavy snowfall. The single roof with broad eaves will carry any falling or melting snow away from the house; the few windows will help keep the house warm and reduce draughts; the timber is readily and locally available and constructed in a way suited to hand-tools and local craftsmen. The entrance to such farmhouses and most of the windows are usually south-facing to maximize sun and warmth, and under the overhanging eave, the farmer would dry crops and even make use of the protected space to socialize. The cold north side is reserved for storage or livestock. In each region of Switzerland, sometimes in each valley, the form and the exterior appearance of the house is slightly different, creating many regional variations.

☞ **Landaise Farmers, Shirakawa Farmers, Zumthor**

Bernese Farmers. Active (SW), circa twelfth century to present day. **Farmhouse**, Saanenland (SW), circa twelfth century to present day.

Berringer Colonel Benjamin   St Nicholas Abbey

St Nicholas Abbey is the oldest house in Barbados and one of only three remaining Jacobean mansions in the western hemisphere. Colonel Benjamin Berringer, a plantation owner and member of the aristocratic elite that dominated the social and political life of Barbados, began the building of this stone and timber mansion in the 1650s. The Jacobean style, at the time so fashionable in Britain, was religiously applied to the house – distinctive Dutch ogee gables, coral stone finials, a Chinese Chippendale staircase and even a herb garden created according to a medieval design; however, a Georgian portico was later added to the main facade during the eighteenth century. To demonstrate the dominance of the colonists' own culture, the design does not veer from the proscribed canon, and went so far as to include fireplaces in the bedrooms and an enormous Dutch chimney stack – even though the tropical climate rendered them unusable.

☛ **Carter, Cecil, Fortrey, Nevisian Creole**

Colonel Benjamin Berringer. d Speightstown (BAR), 1661. **St Nicholas Abbey**, St Peter (BAR), c1650–60.

Berthelot Gilles Château d'Azay-le-Rideau

The Château d'Azay-le-Rideau was conceived by the French financier Gilles Berthelot, one of a group of influential men who built imposing country houses for themselves in the Loire Valley early in the sixteenth century, and, in doing so, established Italian Renaissance taste in France. Romantically sited on the banks of the River Indre, Azay-le-Rideau retains some of the outline of a castle, but its plan is regular and its details attempt to pay court to the order and symmetry of Renaissance classicism. A courtyard doorway is adorned with a profusion of half-columns, pilasters and pinnacles in the form of candelabra; however, there is more restraint on the elevation overlooking the water. Built in 1518–27, its designer is unknown, but both Berthelot and his wife, Philippa Lesbahy, were closely involved in its finished form; indeed, it was Madame Berthelot who directed its construction.

☛ J le Breton, Cortona, L'Orme, Le Breton, Traquair

Gilles Berthelot. Active (FR), early sixteenth century. **d** (FR), 1529. **Château d'Azay-le-Rideau**, nr Tours, Indre-et-Loire (FR), 1518–28.

Bigio Nanni di Baccio   Villa Medici

Famous now as the home of the *pensionnaires* of the French Academy at Rome, the Villa Medici stands on the Pincian hill – known in antiquity as the 'Hill of Gardens' – stretching east to the Aurelian wall and looking west over the city of Rome spread beneath it. The slope of the hill means that the rather stern main entrance, on the opposite side to the garden facade shown here, is two storeys below the *piano nobile*. This more decorative garden facade, with its open loggia – flanked by spiral stairs rising to twin belvederes – leads from the gardens to a three-bayed, double-height salon. Begun in the 1560s by Nanni di Baccio Bigio for Cardinal Ricci, and continued by his son Annibale Lippi, the villa took its present form when Cardinal Ferdinando de' Medici bought it in 1576. He employed Bartolomeo Ammanati (1511–92) and, possibly, Giacomo della Porta (1532–1602), to remodel the garden facade to incorporate his collection of ancient statues and reliefs.

☛ **Henri IV, Laurana, Porta, Vasari, Vaux & Church**

46

Nanni di Baccio Bigio. **b** Florence (IT), c1512. **d** Rome (IT), 1568. **Villa Medici**, Rome (IT), 1564–85.

Bijvoet & Duiker

Aalsmeer House

The asymmetrical, single-pitched roofs of the Aalsmeer House, although antithetical to the then contemporary trend of flat roofs, exemplifies the peculiar economical approach of the Dutch Modern movement. The timber-frame construction, with exterior wood cladding, is also inconsistent with the acknowledged Modern building materials, although it does enable an open plan and a free facade, both hallmarks of early Modern architecture. The architects exploited the building method of column construction to full effect, particularly in the use of corner windows. In plan, the house is a simple square with the addition of a garden shed and a circular stairwell along one side. Both of these features are clearly delineated on the elevations, form following function. The seemingly aberrant materials and dynamic composition, although unusual at the time it was built, became prominent features in the later seminal architecture of 1950s and 60s California.

☞ **Brinkman & van der Vlugt, Doesburg, Hoff**

Bijvoet & Duiker. **Bernard Bijvoet**. b Amsterdam (NL), 1889. d Haarlem (NL), 1979. **Johannes Duiker**. b The Hague (NL), 1890. d Amsterdam (NL), 1935. **Aalsmeer House**, Aalsmeer (NL), 1924.

Blackfoot

Tipi

Originally an agrarian people, the Blackfoot adapted quickly to the imported culture of guns, which revolutionized buffalo hunting. The tipi, meaning 'dwelling', afforded them absolute freedom of movement, which was vital on the Northern Plains in order to hunt the migratory buffalo. Its conical structure was formed by placing four foundation poles into the ground, then lashing about twenty poles together at the apex and covering it with buffalo hides held down with stones and pegs. An interior skin was used for insulation and waterproofing. Inside, a hide curtain formed an ante-chamber to separate the children from their parents. While they had earned a reputation for bellicosity, the Blackfoot were, conversely, among the most highly-skilled of the native American artists. Dreams, visions and symbolic representations of their cosmology of three parallel universes, as well as colourful scenes of animals or skies cast with thunder, embellished the exterior of their tipis.

☛ **Kyrgyz, Moors, Sami, Tihama Farmers**

Blackfoot. Active (USA), sixteenth century onwards. **Tipi**, Northern Plains, MT (USA), c1900.

Bo Bardi Lina

Glass House

Designed by Bo Bardi early in her career for herself and her husband, the Glass House has been described as elegant and poetic by its many visitors; however, it would not meet today's building regulations. The remarkably slender columns which support the building, and elevate it above the sloping ground, are complemented by thin horizontal sections of reinforced concrete and fully-glazed facades, resulting in a high degree of transparency and lightness. The main living space is arranged on first-floor level around a central atrium full of lush tropical plants, underscoring the close relationship of the house with the surrounding Brazilian forest, which was once visible on all sides, but has since given way to development. In her subsequent commissioned work, Bo Bardi avoided working on private houses, stating, 'I have a horror of designing homes for madams,' and mainly concentrated on public buildings in which she could achieve an expression of collective identity.

☛ Ellwood, P Johnson, Koenig, Mies van der Rohe, Neutra

Lina Bo Bardi. b Rome (IT), 1914. **d** São Paulo (BR), 1992. **Glass House**, São Paulo (BR), 1951.

Bofill Ricardo

Emilio Bofill House

This vacation home, built for the architect's father around the ruins of an older house, is composed of seven individual sections orientated towards a pool. The central, red pavilion encloses the dining area, while other more private sections contain the living space, bedrooms and kitchen. Like Mies van der Rohe's Barcelona Pavilion, the house sits on a rectangular platform, yet Bofill has adopted a deliberate de-functionalizing aesthetic which emphasizes geometrical organization, proportion and enclosure. The house seeks to embrace its natural setting; the high windows in the interior courtyard mimicking the pointed cypress trees and the brown earthen tones of the walls visually connect the house to the rock outcroppings which surround it. Bofill is perhaps better known for his huge socialist housing complexes, but this private house shows his ability to work on an intimate scale using both modern and classical historical precedents.

☛ Coderch, Corrales & Molezún, Graves, Schweitzer

50

Ricardo Levi Bofill. b Barcelona (SP), 1939. Emilio Bofill House, Montras (SP), 1972–6.

Bohlin Cywinski Jackson   Ledge House

Built on a rocky and forested hillside in the Catoctin Mountains of Maryland, this house derives its name from the manmade ledge on which it has been constructed. It replaces a traditional log cabin that had been built on this ledge in the 1940s, which set the precedent for the form of the building that was to follow. The architects – an American firm known for its work using natural materials – used white cedar logs, heavy Douglas fir timbers, galvanized roofing metal and a quartzite stone brought in from New York's Lake Champlain. This stone, while similar to the local stone, was chosen for its structural and aesthetic superiority. The features of the Ledge House include a massive fireplace constructed of the quartzite, a forecourt which provides an outdoor gathering space and, surprisingly, an indoor pool. The logs and timbers are used to reinforce the concept that the house is an organic part of the forest.

☛ **Edmond & Corrigan, Mockbee Coker, Yoshimura**

Bohlin Cywinski Jackson. Peter Bohlin. b Mt Vernon, NY (USA), 1937. **Bernard Cywinski. b** Trenton, MJ (USA), 1940. **Jon Jackson. b** McKees Rocks, PA (USA), 1952. **Ledge House,** Catoctin Mountains, MD (USA), 1996.

Bolles & Wilson Suzuki House

This small, exposed concrete house, located on a 5.5 x 7 m (18 x 23 ft) corner site in Tokyo, and supported by fork-like legs, was designed for an editor and his family. The four-storey interior, an obsessively compressed and sealed space, is packed with functional elements. A child's bedroom and sleeping platform are cantilevered above the double-height living/dining area, efficiently connected by ladders and staircases, which affords an illusion of space. A small car fits into one half of the ground level as if it were part of the house. This dense and complex arrangement of minimal dwelling functions offers an intimate, human-scale environment where the inhabitants can conduct their everyday lives. As anticipated by his earlier work, Wilson here proposes the house as 'a shadow of the city' that complements a missing part of a life conducted in a bright public realm.

☞ Azuma, Ito, Kishi, Stein, UN Studio, Ushida Findlay

Bolles & Wilson. Julia Bolles. b (GER), 1948. Peter Wilson. b Melbourne (ASL), 1950. Suzuki House, Tokyo (JAP), 1995.

Botta Mario
House at Riva San Vitale

The perilous-looking iron bridge emphasizes the isolation of this square-plan tower house, set on the hillside of Monte San Giorgio. Its pure form is typical of Botta's interest in 'ideal' geometries, and he was one of a group of architects who looked back to the abstract forms of 1930s Italian Rationalism, seeking to create a contemporary monumentalism. His work is often based on the simple forms of cube and cylinder found in ancient architecture, rather than on specific historical references. The bridge penetrates the tower and leads to a studio on the top floor, where stairs lead down to the other levels. The austere, steep site does not permit the luxury of a garden, but there is a porch on the lowest level providing spectacular views over the snow-capped peaks above Lake Lugano. Other Swiss architects were influenced by Botta's 'interventionist' rather than contextual architecture, which also had its roots in *rocoli,* tower-like buildings traditional to the area.

☛ Le Corbusier, Kahn, Rossi, Scarpa, Snozzi, Vacchini

Mario Botta. **b** Mendrisio (SW), 1943. **House at Riva San Vitale**, Ticino (SW), 1971–3.

Breton

Fisherman's Penty

The peninsula of Brittany, today a flat plateau, is formed by some of the oldest mountains in Europe. Five times older than the Alps, its peaks have been eroded by greater age. But nowhere is the ancient igneous bedrock, together with man's practical use of it, more endearingly revealed than in this fisherman's *penty*, lodged between gigantic granite boulders.

The word *penty* today means cottage, but it used to refer to a labourer's or fisherman's one-roomed dwelling, often attached to a larger property. This *penty's* pleasing cubed proportions are typical, the steep roof slope suggesting an earlier tradition of thatch. Slates, not used until the nineteenth century, though available locally, usually came from neighbouring Anjou. The

loft, lit here by two dormer windows, was used for storage of crops or tackle; the floor, by tradition, would be beaten earth. Breton granite is normally grey, but here it is a rosy pink peculiar to the *Côtes d'Amour* on Brittany's north coast.

☛ **Antrim Labourers, Finistère Farmers, Hebridean Crofter**

54

Breton. Active (FR), circa AD 500 to present day. **Fisherman's Penty,** Plougrescant, Brittany (FR), as built nineteenth century.

Breton Jean le   Château de Villandry

Against a square and embattled medieval castle keep, Jean le Breton, secretary of state to François I, built a new courtyard formed by three ranges of apartments set over an arcade, and rising directly from the water of a broad moat. Although the steeply-pitched roofs of the terminal pavilions and exuberantly decorated dormers, characteristic of earlier Loire châteaux, have their place, the classical detailing is far more restrained and well ordered in accordance with the latest Renaissance taste. Over the arcades, for instance, flat pilasters frame the windows and articulate the facades in a precise, clearly defined way. For all this demonstration of fashionable architecture, Villandry is as well known today for its gardens which, following restoration by Dr Joachim Carvallo (1869–1936), are a model of French taste, its parterre terraces laid out with yew trees and low box hedges forming interlocking patterns of hearts.

☛ Berthelot, Cecil, Cortona, L'Orme, Le Breton

Jean le Breton. Active (FR), early to mid-sixteenth century. **Château de Villandry**, nr Tours, Indre-et-Loire (FR), 1532.

Breuer Marcel

Breuer House II

The controlled simplicity of this Breuer house – essentially two rectangular forms, one of natural timber cantilevered over another of white-washed concrete – demonstrates his direct and rational design method. Such a disarmingly simple organization, stemming from a very straightforward idea, is characteristic of both Breuer's architecture and his furniture designs, such as his famous tubular chrome and black leather Wassily armchair (1925) from his time at the Bauhaus School. Built into a hillside, this house is relatively small but very open, with large banks of windows and an overhanging balcony suspended by thin, steel cables; a workshop is contained within the concrete base. His attention to detail, as in the diagonal boarding of the cantilevered portions of the house, help to define the importance of each element. Breuer's iconic housing designs have often been used as a prototype for practical solutions to domestic design.

☞ **Gropius, P Johnson, Mies van der Rohe, Muche, Seidler**

56

Marcel Breuer. b Pécs (HUN), 1902. **d** New York, NY (USA), 1981. **Breuer House II**, New Canaan, CT (USA), 1947–8.

Brinkman & van der Vlugt

Sonneveld House

Floating above its recessed base, the main body of this steel-framed house is supported on *pilotis*, the slim structural columns that can be seen at the two front corners. Despite its strict geometry, the interior space was flexible with living rooms on the first floor and a flat roof that allowed the family to enjoy an open-air terrace. Built at the same time as their famous Van Nelle Tobacco Factory (1926–30), this house was commissioned from the architects by Van Nelle's General Manager, Albertus Sonneveld. They were asked not only to design the exterior of the house, but also everything inside, from the choice of furniture and appliances to a series of ingenious devices for 'modern' living, including a small lift that brought wood for the somewhat un-modern open fireplace in the library. The house was so completely equipped that the family was able to move into its new environment without any remnants from their previous lives.

☛ Bijvoet & Duiker, Doesburg, Lubetkin, Luckhardt, Žák

Brinkman & van der Vlugt. **Johannes Andreas Brinkman**. b Rotterdam (NL), 1902. d Rotterdam (NL), 1949. **Leendert Cornelius van der Vlugt**. b Rotterdam (NL), 1894. d Rotterdam (NL), 1936. **Sonneveld House**, Rotterdam (NL), 1933.

Browne Enrique

Casa Caracola

As its Spanish name suggests, the Casa Caracola was built in the form of a *caracol* or seashell. The house is a large oval inscribed into a square parcel of land, separated from its close neighbours by a protective boundary wall. Starting at the street entrance, a continuous wall winds inward in a spiral, creating a narrowing circulation route as it curves in on itself, and terminates at a waterfall into the swimming pool. Common areas are situated towards the core of the plan with the dining room, unexpectedly painted yellow, providing the nucleus. The rest of the house is a cool white, and the living room (seen here) has exposed wooden beams radiating out towards glass walls. Private rooms are located in the area between the boundary wall and the oval form of the house. As well as houses, this prolific young architect has designed important commercial buildings in Santiago, such as the Edificio Consorcio Vida, with its 'cascading garden' facade.

☛ Barragán, Groote, Klotz, Niemeyer, TEN Arquitectos

Enrique Browne. b Santiago (CH), 1942. **Casa Caracola**, Las Condes, Santiago (CH), 1987.

Bruder Will

Townsend Residence

Previously pseudo-Spanish in style, this house in Arizona was totally remodelled and now reveals itself in a series of five curved, organic volumes. Clad in galvanized metal, aluminium and perforated stainless steel with sandblasted concrete block masonry, the house is illuminated by the desert light as it sits comfortably against its mountainside backdrop, amidst extensive desert vegetation. Gallery-like spaces with breathtaking views across Paradise Valley display the owners' collections of contemporary art, crafts and modern furniture. Bruder was trained as a sculptor before starting his career as an architect under the tutelage of Gunnar Birkerts and Paolo Soleri. Since 1974, he has earned a reputation for architecture which is sensitive to the unusual character of the American desert landscape. His largest project is the Phoenix Central Library of 1995, which opened to widespread acclaim from visitors and the architectural community alike.

☞ **Fehn, Mockbee Coker, Neutra, Predock, Schweitzer**

Will (William) Bruder. b Milwaukee, WI (USA), 1946. **Townsend Residence**, Paradise Valley, AZ (USA), 1997.

Brussels Guildsmen   Guild Houses

Wartime destruction followed by restoration has never had so extraordinary a result as in the Grand Place. In 1695, the French Marshal de Villeroy bombarded the centre of Brussels and most of the famous mid-sixteenth century guild houses of the Grand Place were destroyed. Just a few remained, De Zak, on the left, which was built for the Coopers' Guild, and De Kruiwagen (The Wheelbarrow), on the right, for the Tallow Merchants. These follow the style of the times with very large windows separated by ornate piers or pilasters – De Zak has herms instead in its upper storey. The gables are finished in fantastic fashion with curves and double curves, swags and broken pediments, candelabra-like finials, balls and shells.

When the remainder came to be restored, this fantasy continued and it takes a trained eye to spot the change in taste from an enthusiastic but untrained Classicism to the exuberance of full-blooded Baroque.

☞ **Amsterdam Merchants, Fortrey, Le Breton, Pöppelmann**

Brussels Guildsmen. Active (BEL), late fifteenth to sixteenth century. **Guild Houses**, Grand Place, Brussels (BEL), built mid-sixteenth century, partly rebuilt after 1696.

Bulfinch Charles   Harrison Gray Otis House

This was the third townhouse that Bulfinch designed for his patron within the space of thirteen years. Otis was of the new, post-Revolutionary American aristocracy, a natural client for America's first native-born professional architect. Working from English models, and a nudge from Jefferson, Bulfinch set the pattern for both public and private Federal architecture, developing a national brand of Neo-Classicism that was modest yet elegant. Loftier than the earlier houses, here Bulfinch clearly separates the public area from the domestic by emphasizing the principal floor with triple-hung windows; the first to be seen in America. Bulfinch introduced architectural concepts in Boston that eventually travelled south and then west with the new nation. Most significantly, he broke the box mould of the colonial house, creating oval rooms, spiralling staircases and varying room heights, bestowing a style that came to be called 'Bulfinchian'.

☛ Hoban, Jefferson, Nash, Roper

Charles Bulfinch. b Boston, MA (USA), 1763. d Boston, MA (USA), 1844. Harrison Gray Otis House, Boston, MA (USA), 1805–8.

Burges William

Castell Coch

The fairy-tale conical roofs to the round towers of Castell Coch are a clear indication that this is a late Victorian recreation, rather than an authentic medieval Welsh castle. It was designed by Burges as a restoration of the medieval ruin that occupied the site, in order to provide a summer house for the landowner, Lord Bute. The exterior is austere, yet romantic, with an entrance approached by a drawbridge and equipped with a portcullis. The work on the interior was mostly carried out after the architect's death in 1881, but the profusion of richly-detailed painted decoration, tiling and panelling is typical of his approach. Burges was a passionate and romantic medievalist, a friend of artists Rossetti and Swinburne, who reacted against the inevitable advances of industrialization. He played an important part in reviving the Gothic style in architecture, of which Castell Coch and the earlier Cardiff Castle restoration are primary examples.

☛ **Ashburnham, Ludlow, Morris, Pugin, Traquair**

William Burges. b London (UK), 1827. **d** London (UK), 1881. **Castell Coch**, Glamorganshire, Wales (UK), 1875–91.

Burlington Lord   Chiswick House

Lord Burlington's passion for the Palladian style of architecture inspired this villa whose natural habitat might be the banks of the Brenta in Vicenza, where many of Palladio's villas sit. Instead, it overlooks an ornamental stream and gardens laid out in the developing English Picturesque tradition. Built to adjoin Burlington's Jacobean house (now demolished) at Chiswick, the villa was meant to be seen as a statement of correct Classicism, fired as a broadside against the licentiousness of English Baroque. Its portico leads into a fine series of rooms of varying shape, based on a central octagon, and each proportioned to the others. These could accommodate the aesthetic needs of a connoisseur for a weekend retreat, while the main house served the domestic needs. Now standing in isolation, the villa more clearly shows off its parentage and indebtedness to the first British Classical architect, Inigo Jones.

☛ Cameron, Jefferson, I Jones, Kent, Palladio

Lord Burlington (Richard Boyle, 3rd Earl of Burlington). b London (UK), 1694. d London (UK), 1753. **Chiswick House**, London (UK), 1726/7–9.

Burnett Micajah

Center Family Dwelling House

The US Federal style, with its subdued ornamentation and symmetrical facade, was adopted by the religious Shaker sect which sought an architecture based on harmony and essential practicality. Shaker dwelling houses were built to accommodate hundreds of adherents, known as families, organized along spiritual rather than blood lines. While men and women lived under one roof with a communal dining room, there were separate dormitories, entrances and staircases in this environment designed to instil the tenets of their religion. Burnett, a skilful builder, applied raised mortar to the brick coursing, which added depth to the facade, while improving its impermeability. Perfection was paramount: the effulgence of light and air, the permanence of limestone and the simplicity of carved wood reflect the Shakers' asceticism, anticipating the Modernist aesthetic in design, as evidenced by the continued popularity of the style.

☛ Bulfinch, A J Davis, Leverton, Roosevelt

Micajah Burnett. b Pleasant Hill, KY (USA), 1791. d (USA), 1879. **Center Family Dwelling House**, Pleasant Hill, KY (USA), 1824–34.

Calrow James   Brevard-Mmahat House

The Brevard-Mmahat House is a tall, narrow building with a double-storey front portico supported by Corinthian columns. A cast-iron gallery, one of the first built in the area, runs along the side garden. Although officially an antebellum house, built before the outbreak of the American Civil War, a library wing was added after the war in 1869. The New Orleans Garden District was created in 1825 when a plantation was subdivided to form the town of Lafayette, later annexed by New Orleans in 1852. The houses of this now gracious neighbourhood are typified, as is seen in Brevard-Mmahat House, by galleries, broad porches and outdoor garden 'rooms'. They are, unusually, open houses with only louvred shutters protecting them. The Brevard-Mmahat House holds an additional literary distinction in that it appears as Mayfair House in several of bestselling author, Ann Rice's books, including *Witching Hour*.

☛ **Dyckman, Kavanaugh, Marmillion, Roper, Weeks**

James Calrow. Active (USA), early to mid-nineteenth century. **Brevard-Mmahat House**, Garden District, New Orleans (USA), 1857.

Cameron Charles

Pavlovsk Palace

In creating Pavlovsk, Cameron brought the rural idyll of English Palladianism to Russia. Nature, controlled but rustic, laps at the walls of rationality and intellect. The palace is square with sequences of classical rooms of differing colour schemes and great refinement around a circular central hall, which rises to the light under a flat dome. As the palace stands on rising ground above the little Slavyanka river, the dome is hardly visible from the park side, but dominates the opposite facade and the great circular colonnade which creates the entrance. Cameron was a Scot trained in London and Rome, who came to Russia in 1779 at the invitation of Catherine the Great: Pavlovsk Palace was created for her son, the Grand Duke Paul. Its picturesque park with classical pavilions, temples and bridges, reflects Catherine's passion for English culture; Cameron had already created several elegant embodiments of this on her own estate at Tsarskoe Selo.

☛ Burlington, I Jones, Kazakov, Palladio, Rastrelli, Terry

Charles Cameron. b London (UK), 1745. d St Petersburg (RUS), 1812. Pavlovsk Palace, nr St Petersburg (RUS), 1782–6.

Campen Jacob van   Mauritshuis

Giant, two-storey Ionic columns and pedimented centrepieces topped by a typically Dutch hipped roof are the defining features of this mature Classical house in The Hague. Jacob van Campen's house for Prinz Johan Maurits van Nassau did for Dutch architecture what Rembrandt's *Night Watch* (1642) did for Dutch painting: suddenly a small nation briefly became Europe's leader, economically, scientifically and culturally. Pieter Post executed the design with fine brickwork and stone detailing. The compact, square plan, without wings, was entirely suited to a small city site and accommodates two main formal storeys set over a basement for services and attics for secondary bedrooms. The design came to be much copied, its details and plan being quickly taken up in England following the Restoration of Charles II. Today, the building houses the Royal Picture Gallery and Rembrandt's paintings can be seen here in suitably contemporary surroundings.

☞ **Amsterdam Merchants, I Jones, Le Vau & Hardouin-Mansart**

Campen Jacob van   Mauritshuis

Jacob van Campen. b Haarlem (NL), 1595. **d** Amersfoort (NL), 1657. **Mauritshuis**, The Hague (NL), c1633–5.

Campo Baeza Alberto   Casa Gaspar

The Casa Gaspar's high exterior walls, forming a perfect 18 m (60 ft) square, are unfenestrated despite its spectacular setting in an orange grove in southern Spain. The introspective plan is divided into three equal parts – two courtyards on either side of the central, generously-proportioned house – all of which emphasize a deft control of direct and reflected light. Although the all-white planar architecture recalls the Purist movement of the early twentieth century, the house's simple plan and stark geometry is indebted to Mies van der Rohe's courtyard house studies of the 1930s, as well as to the work of Luis Barragán. Campo Baeza's affinities to the sparse yet luxuriously detailed aesthetics of minimalism are evident, rather than an allegiance to the geometric gymnastics of his Spanish contemporaries, Torres & Lapeña. The Gaspar house sums up Campo Baeza's goal of 'achieving everything with almost nothing: more with less'.

☛ **Ando, Barragán, Laan, Pawson Silvestrin**

Alberto Campo Baeza. **b** Valladolid (SP), 1946. **Casa Gaspar**, Cadiz (SP), 1991.

Carrère & Hastings

Frick Residence

With its loggia, refined stonework and the clear delineation of its precinct from the public street, the Frick Residence exudes Neo-Classical grandeur, even though more recent neighbours overshadow it. Carrère & Hastings proved they were able to satisfy American plutocratic taste nearly as well as their more original rivals, McKim Mead & White. In its prime location on New York's Fifth Avenue, overlooking Central Park, it followed a convention at least a generation old for the very wealthy to live uptown; but domestic arrangements were not Henry Clay Frick's priority. Built towards the end of his life, when he had long been one of America's richest citizens, Frick intended the house to become a museum after the death of both himself and his wife, for his expensive and increasingly refined art collection. The interior, despite its fabulous artworks, is almost as inscrutable as the exterior: part institution, part tomb, part museum – but almost nothing to do with domesticity.

☛ Delano & Aldrich, Hoffman & Chalfin, Rousseau

Carrère & Hastings. John Merven Carrère. b Rio de Janeiro (BR), 1858. d New York, NY (USA), 1911. Thomas Hastings. b New York, NY (USA), 1860. d New York, NY (USA), 1929. Frick Residence, New York, NY (USA), 1913–14.

Carter Christopher

Carter House

In the early seventeenth century, English settlers spread their hybrid vernacular houses throughout the Bermuda islands. The Carter House is typical of the English cottage tradition, adapted to suit the tropical, stormy climate of Bermuda. The walls and roof are constructed from the soft local limestone, which is then sealed and lime-washed. The same stone is used for the two main architectural elements, also typical of Bermudian architecture, the porch and the broad, stone stepped chimney. Aside from adding character to the building's simple form, the massive bulk of the masonry helps to buttress the house against the strong prevailing winds. As important as protection against storms is the collection of water, which is always in short supply on the islands; rain water is directed from the roof via a series of gutters straight into storage tanks below. At the other climatic extreme, hinged, white-painted timber shutters protect against the sun.

☞ Berringer, Breton, Hebridean Crofter, Nevisian Creole

70

Christopher Carter. Active (BER), seventeenth century. Carter House, St David's Island (BER), 1640.

Cauchie Paul

Maison Cauchie

The strong vertical facade of this Brussels house, decorated with Art Nouveau murals, is unified by its sgraffito surfaces – incised patterns revealing a different coloured layer beneath – which give it an essentially pictorial character. The murals, painted by Cauchie himself, depict eight female figures symbolizing the Arts. Inside, the house is also elaborately decorated; sgraffito is again used to great effect on the wood panelling and furniture. Cauchie, a painter, architect and interior designer, built this house and studio for himself, in collaboration with the architect Edouard Frankinet (1877–1937), to showcase his talents as a mural artist. The perfect unity between its architecture and interior decoration makes it one of the finest examples of Belgian Art Nouveau. Mackintosh, Hoffmann and the Wiener Werkstätte influenced Cauchie's geometric interpretation of the style, although he produced few other buildings, preferring to concentrate on painting.

☞ **Hoffmann, Mackintosh, Morris, Schönthal, Strauven**

Paul Cauchie. **b** Athens (GR), 1875. **d** Brussels (BEL), 1952. **Maison Cauchie**, Brussels (BEL), 1905.

Cecil Robert

Hatfield House

Hatfield House, one of the best surviving Jacobean houses in England, displays French, Italian and Flemish influences, arranged on a medieval-inspired H-plan. It was built by Robert Cecil – the first Earl of Salisbury and Chief Minister to both Elizabeth I and James I – as his private residence, and to accommodate the visiting royal court. The two wings contain separate private apartments for the King and Queen. It is a curious agglomeration, probably due to the number of hands involved, including the carpenter Robert Lyming, the Surveyor General of the King's Works, Simon Basil, and even Inigo Jones. The central elevation is notable for its three-storey facade with Doric, Ionic and Corinthian orders, and the two-storey hall with mullioned windows and modelled plaster ceiling – a Jacobean version of a medieval hall. Today, the house is occupied by the 6th Marquess of Salisbury who takes a particular interest in the gardens, planting them with sixteenth-century specimens.

☛ Berringer, Fortrey, I Jones, Le Vau & Hardouin-Mansart

Robert Cecil, 1st Earl of Salisbury. b Westminster, Salisbury (UK), 1563. d Marlborough (UK), 1612. **Hatfield House**, Hatfield (UK), 1607–11.

Cerceau Jean du   Hôtel de Sully

In the aftermath of the Religious Wars in the early seventeenth century, Henri IV, assisted by his minister, Sully, implemented a programme of political, social and economic reform which returned stability to France. The reforms also resulted in changes to urban and architectural design, especially in Paris where vast swathes of the city were being rebuilt. An important domestic architect of the time, Cerceau was responsible for some of the most celebrated houses, including the Hôtel de Sully, which was purchased by Sully five years after its completion. Famous for his inventive use of ornament, he provided the hôtel with rich decorations in a style not previously seen. The court facades are ornamented with allegorical figures, and the window surrounds are covered with sculptural friezes and pediments. Cerceau was born into a family of great French architects; his grandfather was the eminent architect Jacques Androuet du Cerceau (c1515–85).

☛ Henri IV, Le Breton, Le Vau & Hardouin-Mansart

Jean Androuet du Cerceau. b Paris (FR), c1585. d Paris (FR), 1649. Hôtel de Sully, Paris (FR), 1625.

Chareau Pierre   Maison de Verre

The translucence of the Maison de Verre's glass blocks, and the precision of its black steel framing and red oxide accents, are reminiscent of an inlaid black-lacquered Japanese box. This three-storey house, built as a doctor's residence with a surgery at ground floor level, is inserted into the void of an eighteenth-century courtyard, and is one of the canonical works of the twentieth century. Diffused light filters into the open-plan interior via the two glass facades, and the framing device of the exterior steel ladder is continued inside in the slender, black steel vertical forms that punctuate the constantly shifting horizontals of the floor plan. Collaborating with the Dutch architect, Bernard Bijvoet, Chareau created a house with a sensual urbanity, unique for its inventive handling of standard ready-made materials, its deployment of suspended and sliding components, and a density of form and refinement of details.

☞ Gray & Badovici, Le Corbusier, Rietveld & Schröder

Pierre Chareau. b Bordeaux (FR), 1883. d East Hampton, NY (USA), 1950. **Maison de Verre**, Paris (FR), 1928–31.

Chatterjee Inni & Wheaton Samir

Poddar House

Capitalizing on the natural slope of the site, Inni Chatterjee has created a multi-level family home that opens onto airy, light-filled interior spaces. Dramatically crowning the design is the undulating, wave-like copper-clad roof set atop a broad cantilever, supported by cement columns. Terraced levels, patios and interlinking wide corridors are reminiscent of the imperial Mughal palace and courtyard gardens at Fatehpur Sikri. Wheaton's large interior courtyard pool is showcased on the ground floor and viewed through walls of plate glass from the surrounding rooms. Thin, decorative grit-wash and cement bands punctuate the exterior greystone brick and concrete blocks. These striated surfaces accentuate the elegant horizontal spread of the home. In the Poddar House, we see the synthesis of contemporary building materials and Post-Modern design elements with India's imperial Hindu and Mughal stone palace architectural traditions.

☞ **Amar Singh II, Correa, Gandhi, Graves, Jai Singh I, Rewal**

Inni Chatterjee. Samir Wheaton. Both active (IN), late twentieth century to present day. **Poddar House**, Delhi (IN), c1990s.

Chermayeff Serge   Bentley Wood

This two-storey, long-fronted house stands in a broad landscape, stretching out an arm to one side where, as if held in the hand, a majestic stone carving by Henry Moore surveys the distant scene. Completed shortly before World War II, Bentley Wood was recognized as the most mature of English modern houses of the 1930s. Chermayeff integrated its white-painted, timber-frame structure and cladding with its grid-like visual form, using timber unsentimentally, as if it were steel. The plan, a model for relaxed weekend living, was designed for the architect and his family, with furnishings chosen to complement the abstract paintings by John Piper and Ben Nicholson. Frank Lloyd Wright visited in the summer of 1939, remarking, 'It'll take a little time for God to make it click', but contemporary critics recognized Bentley Wood's aristocratic poise and the effortless convergence of modern ideas of space with older themes in landscape design.

☞ Connell, Fry, P Johnson, Lubetkin, Mendelsohn

Serge Ivan Chermayeff. b Grozny, Chechnya (was Azerbaijan) (RUS), 1900. **d** Wellfleet, MA (USA), 1996. **Bentley Wood**, Halland (UK), 1937–8.

Chilote Islanders

Palafitos

The remarkable *palafitos* (house on stilts) is the indigenous coastal form of domestic architecture to be found on the Chilean archipelago of Chiloé. It is a distinctive expression of the islands' sea-based economy, designed to sit in the water at high tide in order to provide a landing-stage for sea vessels, while at low tide it is left high and dry over the sands where the locals glean the leftovers of the ocean's harvest. The houses were traditionally constructed by the islands' expert joiners, in conjunction with friends, family and neighbours, on special days of collective labour known as *mingas*. When a government ordinance of 1975 threw these traditions into jeopardy, by stating that all new building works must be supervised by trained professionals, Taller Puertazul – a team of architects, engineers, historians and anthropologists – was formed to promote the continuity of the local vernacular and achieved a striking revival of the form.

☞ **Annamese, Dai, Isabella I & Ferdinand II, Toffinou**

Chilote Islanders. Active (CH), sixteenth century to present day. **Palafitos**, Chiloé (CH), sixteenth century to present day.

Chipperfield David   Knight House

'Spatial character' is the idea behind the straightforward composition of this 'non-ideological' house. Describing himself as an architect who seeks a relation between form, figure and material, Chipperfield experiments continually with space, striving to achieve compositions rather than collages. In this house, solid and transparent planes interact to produce a network of open and closed spaces in an abstraction of form, volume and void. While the ground floor, seen from this angle through an expanse of glass, seems entirely open to the garden, the upper floor appears to be opaque; and both interiors are in contrast to the framed void of the exterior terrace. A one-time student of Norman Foster and Richard Rogers, Chipperfield eschews what he calls their technological determinism, concentrating instead on the nature and quality of space itself: 'we should be able to deal with the past without parody, and look to the future without whimsy.'

☛ Ando, Mather, Pawson Silvestrin, Rogers

David Chipperfield. b London (UK), 1953. **Knight House**, Richmond (UK), 1987–9.

Clare Design   Clare House

With its industrial-looking, corrugated-iron cladding and open-plan living arrangements, the Clare House feels utterly contemporary; at the same time, it has strong links to traditional Queensland architecture. Built in 1991 by Kerry and Lindsay Clare – the Australian husband-and-wife architect team – as a family home for themselves, its robust yet lightweight timber-frame structure, raised above its sloping site, takes on ideas developed in the Redicut homes of the 1900s. This timber housing system is seen by some as the closest thing Australia has to a vernacular design. Like Redicut homes, the Clare House combines an economy of materials with generous spaces. Built for just AU$160,000, the house accommodates the seven-strong family, with sleeping quarters in the loft-like upper storey and living areas in the open-plan ground floor where verandas extend outwards on either side to embrace the surrounding landscape.

☞ Andresen O'Gorman, Grose Bradley, Murcutt, Poole

Clare Design. **Kerry Clare**. b Sydney, NSW (ASL), 1957. **Lindsay Clare**. b Brisbane, QLD (ASL), 1952. **Clare House**, Buderim, QLD (ASL), 1991.

Coderch José Antonio   Casa Ugalde

Coderch was a founding member of the Grupo R, a group of Modernist architects active in Barcelona in the 1950s, whose aim was the renewal of Catalan architecture. His Casa Ugalde is perhaps the single, most important piece of architecture in Catalonia since Mies van der Rohe's German Pavilion of 1929. But whereas Mies employed a universal grid to delineate the Modernist concept of interiority/exteriority, the Casa Ugalde, built on the coast as a weekend home, takes its cue from the undulating terrain and lush landscape to define the internal and external spaces. No plans can explain these interweaving spaces, and indeed Coderch made extensive revisions to the layout of the building as the construction progressed in order to finely-tune the house to its complex site. The result is a sequence of interior spaces that are tailored to specific vistas, gradually opening up the house through a series of angled and undulating planes to the spectacular ocean-scape beyond.

☛ A Jacobsen, Patkau Architects, Siza, Torres & Lapeña

José Antonio Coderch. b Barcelona (SP), 1913. d Barcelona (SP), 1984. Casa Ugalde, Caldes d'Estrac, Barcelona (SP), 1951.

Compton Sir William   Compton Wynyates

Compton Wynyates lies in an enclosing valley guarded by topiaried bushes that look as though they have marched out of the surrounding woodland. These add to the wonderfully picturesque effect of what must have been a rather old-fashioned courtyard house when built between 1500 and 1520 for Sir William Compton, a courtier and close companion of Henry VIII. The great Perpendicular-style chapel window in the centre is still medieval in spirit, as are all the various windows, even those added in later centuries. Its crenellations and turrets, designed to give an air of courtly chivalry rather than defensive capability, show no sign of the impending symmetry and order that would invade British architecture in the sixteenth century. Even the surrounding moat, which was drained in the Civil War, was designed to demonstrate status. With its happy disregard for fashion, it is unashamedly a house for show.

☛ **Ashburnham, Henry VIII, Ludlow, Wolsey**

Sir William Compton. b (UK), c1482. **d** Warwickshire (UK), 1528. **Compton Wynyates**, nr Tysoe, Warwickshire (UK), c1500–20.

Connell Amyas

High and Over

Perched on the hillside above Amersham, Connell's first major commission has three cubic wings forming a Y-shaped plan around a hexagonal hall, and is orientated to make the most of spectacular views. Corridors are almost completely eliminated and spaces flow elegantly yet informally into one another, while still clearly segregating different areas. The long bands of windows and roof-top sun terrace show the influence of Le Corbusier, but the house also reflects the interest in Classical proportion of both the architect and the client, Bernard Ashmole, director of the British School in Rome where Connell studied. High and Over has been viewed both as the last great British country house and as the first modern house in the English countryside. In 1933, Connell formed a partnership with fellow New Zealander, Basil Ward, and English architect, Colin Lucas; as Connell Ward Lucas they built what are considered by many to be the best inter-war modern houses in Britain.

☛ Chermayeff, Fry, Le Corbusier, Lubetkin, Tait

Amyas Douglas Connell. b Eltham (NZ), 1901. d London (UK), 1980. **High and Over**, Amersham (UK), 1929.

Contarini Marin

Cà d'Oro

The unique tradition of Venetian Gothic architecture reached its pinnacle with the Cà d'Oro, or House of Gold, patrician Contarini's most lavish of palaces. The canal-side arcade entrance, via the lower level storerooms, is surmounted by two superimposed *piani nobili* with the intricate floral tracery loggia so characteristic of Venice, here the work of mason Matteo Raverti. The practical purpose of these recessed balconies was to introduce much needed light into the deep plan of the house. The remarkable crenellation and rare delicate pendant tracery above were the work of Giovanni Bon and his son, Bartolomeo, who went on to create the magnificent entrance to the Ducal Palace. Gilded friezes, ornamental merlons and golden pinnacles surmount the palace, but the pursuit of lavishness is most evident in the facade, which was adorned elaborately with precious materials, including vermilion, ultramarine and no less than 23,000 sheets of gold leaf.

☛ Laurana, Maiano, Michelozzi, Sangallo

Marin Contarini. b (IT), 1386. d (IT), 1441. Cà d'Oro, Venice (IT), 1421–36.

Coober Pedy Miners   Dugout Houses

Coober Pedy, an opal mining town in one of Australia's arid desert regions, is perhaps most notable for the underground homes created by more than half of its 3,500 inhabitants. The name of the town, from the aboriginal *kupa-piti* meaning 'white man in a hole', exemplifies the inhabitants' practical response to the hostile environment. Aside from the benefits of creating an ambient temperature without the need for mechanical cooling, the dugouts are extremely cost effective, with no need for building materials. There is also no limit to the size of the houses, as new rooms are simply carved out of the rock, either by hand or machine, depending on the desired shape and finish. Following the discovery of the first opal in 1915, many soldiers returning from World War I came to try their luck at opal mining. Local legend has it that after the trenches of France, these soldiers initiated the now ubiquitous custom of underground living.

☛ **Anchorites, Gitano, Loess Han, Pueblo Indians**

Coober Pedy Miners. Active Coober Pedy, SA (ASL), early twentieth century to present day. **Dugout Houses**, Coober Pedy, SA (ASL), c1915 to present day.

Cook Marshall   Pascual House

The client for the Pascual House wanted a spacious two-bedroom house. However, the small site and a restrictive budget meant a creative architectural solution was required. Marshall Cook's approach was to design three contrasting elements: a southern enclosure of precast concrete panels, a northern, glazed living area and, in between, a timber utility structure, all of which are left exposed to reduce finishing and maintenance costs. The interior is defined by a mezzanine overlooking the light-filled living room, a simple steel-framed box infilled with windows and cedar louvres. The north-facing glazing heightens the close connection with the garden and enlarges the room by borrowing exterior space. This thoughtfully designed house illustrates the on-going relevance of the principles of the California Case Study Program, in which low-cost industrial building technology provided the basis for innovative and intelligent design.

☞ Bo Bardi, Eames, Koenig, Neutra, Poole

Marshall Cook. b Napier (NZ), 1940. **Pascual House**, East Tamaki, Auckland (NZ), 2000.

Cormier Ernest   Maison Cormier

Amid the strong concrete volumes and rich play of light and shadow lie the seductive sculptural details that invite the visitor into the house and world of architect Ernest Cormier. The Muse of Artistic Inspiration, sculpted by the architect himself, serenely guards the entrance to this Art Deco house, whose five storeys cascade down the southern slope of Mont Royal. With an interior as opulent as its exterior is refined, the house is quite fitting for an architect who was as much an artist as he was an engineer. While studying at the Ecole des Beaux Arts in Paris, Cormier mingled and worked with those who were to become the pioneers of the Modern Movement, such as Le Corbusier. The influence of these two schools of thought – seen here in the use of Beaux-Arts ordered proportions and Modernist volumes – can be found in all of Cormier's works and became a definitive characteristic of the Art Deco style he brought back to eastern Canada.

☞ **Gray & Badovici, Hoffmann, Lauterbach, Mallet-Stevens**

Ernest Cormier. b Montreal, QC (CAN), 1885. d Montreal (CAN), 1980. **Maison Cormier**, Montreal, QC (CAN), 1930–1.

Corrales & Molezún
Casa Huarte

This suburban house in Madrid has a strong presence around the perimeter of its site and a very private internal space. The steel-framed house is clad with large areas of dark bricks which have been softened by the growth of Virginia creeper. Two landscaped courtyards at its centre are separated by a monopitched tiled roof (to the left) that rises up to the entrance

tower of the house. With terraces of grass and planting rising up to the rear of the house, the lower courtyards, one with a swimming pool, have a high level of privacy and sense of enclosure. Sliding doors and large areas of glazing surrounding the courtyards allow for a seamless flow of space between exterior and interior. Corrales and Molezún have collaborated

on a number of works since 1957, when they worked together on the Spanish Pavilion at the Universal Exposition in Brussels, while maintaining individual offices.

☞ Bofill, Coderch, Fehn, Gunnløgsson

Corrales & Molezún. José Antonio Corrales Guttierez. b (SP), 1921. Ramón Vázquez Molezún. b (SP), 1921. d (SP), 1993. Casa Huarte, Puerta de Hierro, Madrid (SP), 1966.

Correa Charles House at Koramangala

When Correa designed his own house, the open courtyard was a natural point of departure – an organizing principle for the interior spaces as well as an ecological device for controlling light and ventilation. The entrance promenade – a street-side gateway, a covered path and a vestibule guarded by a carved wooden gatekeeper – culminates in this sudden fullness. Across lies the living room, and beyond, the garden. Correa's house and studio make a *yin-yang* interlock around this architectural centrifuge, from where energy permeates into every other space. It is the contradictory *shoonya* (nothingness) prescribed in the *Vastu Sastras*, Hindu treatises on architecture, and occupies the central square of a nine-square mandala. From the early 1980s, the mandala and the courtyard have been recurrent tricks in Correa's repertoire. They further his inquiry of tradition and modernity, and embody the simplicity of means and expression for which he is justly famous.

☛ **Barragán, Bawa, Doshi, Patwon, Rewal**

Charles Mark Correa. b Secunderabad, Andhra Pradesh (IN), 1930. **House at Koramangala**, Bangalore (IN), 1985–9.

Cortona Domenico da   Château de Chambord

Neither the symmetry nor the defensive castellated outline of the Château de Chambord are quite what they seem, for both are far from absolute – rather, they are just an impression. In 1519, the French King, François I, wanted to build a hunting lodge, but it had to reflect up-to-date taste and regal power. Although he may have gone to the fashionable Italian architect Domenico da Cortona for a design, he insisted on having the features of a traditionally French château. If Cortona indeed made plans, the masons adapted them when they began work. The impressive round towers differ extensively from each other, and terminate in a fantastic array of turrets, dormers and chimneys, liberally adorned with Classical motifs in un-Classical profusion. Thus medieval castle and Renaissance style combine to provide the setting for both the royal hunt and extravagant entertainment.

☞ Berthelot, Henry VIII, L'Orme, Le Breton, Wolsey

Domenico da Cortona. b Florence (IT), 1484. d Rome (IT), 1546. **Château de Chambord**, Chambord (FR), 1519–47.

CZWG

Street-Porter House

The spiky, angular forms of Piers Gough's house for Janet Street-Porter are deliberately designed to look like its owner – a well-known TV presenter with distinctive spectacles. It is an eclectic, referential building with an upside-down *piano nobile* – the main reception rooms are one floor down from the top. The triangular-windowed, rooftop-eyrie is a study entered via an external spiral staircase – to keep work and home separate – and is vaguely suggestive of a bohemian Paris garret. Below, diamond 'spectacle' screens enclose one balcony, while another balcony, incorporating seating, projects from the kitchen to hold up the end of a table. The bedroom takes up the entire first floor, while the ground floor includes a billiards room. A staircase rises through the house, with a mesh-floored dining room projecting over it. The brickwork gets lighter in colour the higher up the facade: a visual trick copied from New York. In 1998, Gough was awarded a CBE for his services to architecture.

☛ **Aitchison, Gehry, Tigerman, Venturi**

CZWG (Campbell, Zogolovitch, Wilkinson & Gough). **Piers Gough**. **b** Brighton (UK), 1946. **Street-Porter House**, London (UK), 1986–8.

Dai

Bamboo Houses

One of over fifty minority ethnic groups in China, the Dai live in the sub-tropical southern Yunnan, near the border of Thailand, with which they share similarities in climate and culture, as well as proximity to the mighty Mekong River. Buddhist farmers who have ploughed the rice fields for over a thousand years, the Dai build large bamboo houses raised high above the ground on wood pillars. The open lower floor is used for raising domestic animals and storage. Steps lead up to a veranda, which may be open-sided to provide a space for relaxing, preparing food or drying clothes. Beyond this is the living space with a floor of bamboo matting on which the family eat, rest or receive guests. This is separated from the bedroom by a wall of bamboo strips. The houses have high gabled thatched or tiled roofs with overhanging eaves. Bamboo is used extensively throughout Dai houses for ventilated screen walls and much of the furniture, including tables, chairs and beds.

☞ Annamese, Chilote Islanders, Maori, Toffinou

Dai. Active Yunnan (CHN), from 109 BC. **Bamboo Houses**, Xishuangbanna, Yunnan (CHN), from circa AD 1000 to present day.

Davis Alexander Jackson   Henry Delamater House

One of more than a hundred picturesque villas designed and popularized by Davis, this eager little country house exhibits the gingerbread brackets, board-and-batten siding and bulging bays that are the signature of his Americanized reading of the 'English cottage style'. Fully realized by the mid-nineteenth century, the fashion for ornamental, romantic summer homes and village dwellings had spread across the land, their form and decoration largely influenced by, if not directly copied from, the architect's exacting drawings reproduced in contemporary pattern books and magazines. Philosophically grounded in the revolt against Classicist domestic architecture, Davis pioneered charm in its stead, creating family houses as welcoming as their verandas were elaborate. The Delamater House, its overly pronounced gable at an equal height to neighbouring treetops, is tailored to its immediate landscape and orientated towards Nature.

☞ Gartman, McCoskrie & Greenfield, Potter

Alexander Jackson Davis. **b** New York, NY (USA), 1803. **d** West Orange, NJ (USA), 1892. **Henry Delamater House**, Rhinebeck, NY (USA), 1844.

Davis John

Pioneer Farmstead

Set amidst the dense woodland of this North Carolina forest, John Davis' early American log and fieldstone farmstead draws on Swedish vernacular log-building traditions. Log cabin house design originated in the northern countries of Europe and was first constructed in America by Swedish settlers in Delaware in the late 1630s; later pioneers were to build log cabins further and further west. Many Americans still lived in these primitive-type dwellings as late as 1800. Early log cabins were built as temporary dwellings, to be replaced once the pioneer community was better established and permanent building materials, such as stone, were procured. Here, like other farmsteaders, Davis utilizes easily obtainable local woodland materials, aiming for minimal building costs. This pioneer-style house is sustainable organic architecture in the purest sense, reflecting economic and ecological common sense and cultural relativism.

☛ Bohlin Cywinski Jackson, Roland Family, Sirén

John Davis. Active (USA), nineteenth century. **Pioneer Farmstead**, Great Smokey Mountains, NC (USA), c1830s.

Day Christopher

Ty-cwrdd Bach

The curving turf roof, the thick stone walls and the windmill generator against the open sky indicate that this is a house built in the pioneering spirit. Christopher Day's first building project, for occupation by himself, his wife and their child, was a protest against modern consumer culture and a bid to return beauty to the landscape. Using the foundations and tumbled stonework of a 250-year-old chapel, unroofed in 1916, Day actually built the structure with friends, lifting stones by hand, digging a well and making all the joinery. Inside, a large central room is flanked by bedrooms, a kitchen and a bathroom, with varying ceiling heights and a sense of intimacy, based on principles derived from the teachings of Rudolf Steiner. The experience taught him not only about design but about the link between building and human relationships, especially when 'gift work' is involved, as described in Day's influential book *Building with Heart*, 1990.

☛ Antrim Labourers, H Greene, Reynolds, Vale

Christopher Day. **b** Portsmouth (UK), 1942. **Ty-cwrdd Bach**, Pembrokeshire (UK), 1971–4.

Delano & Aldrich

Kykuit

Kykuit has been the home to America's Rockefeller family since 1913, the year it was completed as a country retreat for John D Rockefeller Snr. The architects, Delano & Aldrich, were prominent society architects, trained in the Beaux-Arts tradition. A study in symmetry with its tall, elaborately carved facade, Kykuit, like many American Beaux-Arts buildings, draws architectural inspiration from several European sources, including the Italian Renaissance and the French Norman house. It is situated to overlook magnificent gardens (by landscape architect, William Welles Bosworth) with fountains and stone terraces, as well as to enjoy the panorama of the Hudson River beyond. The gardens and the interiors (designed by Ogden Codman) were influenced by the publication of Edith Wharton's book, *Italian Villas and their Gardens*, of 1904. The house today provides a showcase for the Rockefeller collections of ceramics, furniture, paintings and sculpture.

☞ **Bigio, Hunt, McKim Mead & White, Raphael, Vignola**

Delano & Aldrich. **William Adams Delano**. b New York, NY (USA), 1874. d New York, NY (USA), 1960. **Chester Holmes Aldrich**. b Providence, RI (USA), 1871. d Rome (IT), 1940. **Kykuit**, Pocantico Hills, NY (USA), 1913.

Denton Corker Marshall

Marshall House

There is not a hint of cosiness about this concrete bunker of a house cut into the dunes of Phillip Island, a windswept place near Australia's southernmost tip. Even its advocates admit that 'it lurks like a Stealth Bomber, hidden and subversive'. The house was designed by Barrie Marshall of Denton Corker Marshall, one of Australia's most successful architectural practices, as his own holiday home. Because of the environmentally-sensitive nature of the site, Marhsall built the house from concrete dyed to match the black rock base and banked grass-covered berms around it; all you see from the beach is a low black line. By contrast, the north elevation, where the black concrete wall opens onto a neatly manicured courtyard (a suntrap in winter), has an eerily artificial quality. The house is a provocative alternative to the conservative bungalows that more usually litter Australia's shoreline.

☛ Ando, Future Systems, Katsalidis, Souto de Moura

96

Denton Corker Marshall. John Denton. b Suva (FIJI), 1945. Bill Corker. b Melbourne, VIC (ASL), 1945. Barrie Marshall. b Melbourne, VIC (ASL), 1946. Marshall House (House at Phillip Island), Phillip Island, VIC (ASL), 1995.

Dewes Ada & Puente Sergio   La Casa del Ojo de Agua

Set in a densely tropical ravine above a spring-fed stream, this two-block house is described by its architects as a form of water architecture: 'It was the environment of a brook which we converted into the environment of a house.' Visible throughout the house, the water channel flows through the upper two-storey block creating a plunge pool, then passes below glass brick flooring in the lower main block (seen here), which houses a single bedroom and ensuite bathroom, and on into the Atongo River below. Mature trees on the site have been integrated into outdoor rooms and patios to provide shade and shelter, and three of the lower block's external 'walls' are simply mosquito nets. La Casa del Ojo de Agua takes the Barnsdale and Wrightian architectural landscape approach one step further by fully integrating the architecture into its natural surroundings. Said Dewes and Puente: 'We wanted to redefine nature as a force, not as an ornament.'

☛ Acayaba, Andresen O'Gorman, Bo Bardi, Wright

Ada Dewes. **b** Gronau (GER), 1944. **Sergio Puente**. **b** Mexico City (MEX), 1942. **La Casa del Ojo de Agua**, Tepoztlán, Morelos (MEX), 1987.

Diller & Scofidio Slow House

This conceptual model shows an experimental holiday house for an art dealer. It is conceived as the final stage of the journey which many wealthy New Yorkers make each summer weekend, out from Manhattan, along the length of Long Island to a seaside retreat. It has a curving funnel-shaped plan suggesting that the journey is continued through the house itself. The rooms broaden out towards the shore where there is a fantastic view, framed by an enormous picture window. This view is also displayed on a television monitor in front of the window, juxtaposing what the architects see as two equally artificial ways of looking at the landscape. Diller & Scofidio have built little, but are renowned for numerous projects which include video and art installations. Influential as both teachers and writers, they believe the advent of digital technology means 'the irreducible units of architecture are now bricks and pixels'.

☛ **Hariri & Hariri, Mather, Moss, RoTo Architects**

98

Diller & Scofidio. Elizabeth Diller. **b** (POL), 1954. **Ricardo Scofidio**. **b** New York (USA), 1935. **Slow House**, Long Island, NY (USA), project, 1989.

Doesburg Theo van   Studio House

This studio house is the culmination of van Doesburg's attempts to translate the tenets of Neo-Plasticism – a Modernist preoccupation with shifting volumes and sliding planes – into a built form. The artist/architect was best known as the incessant polemicist of the De Stijl movement, whose early endeavours at architecture were compelling,

unbuilt constructions of intersecting planes of primary colours, similar to the paintings of his colleague Mondrian. However, in this, his last built project, he moved away from spiritual constructions of De Stijl's earlier works towards a more objective, technical solution. Traces of the kinetic spirit of van Doesburg's early compositions can still be seen in the

composition of his studio house – the two cubic volumes seemingly pulling apart, the studio in the upper cube and the living quarters in the lower one. Also, his usual palette of primary colours is retained in the doors and openings.

☛ Brinkman & van der Vlugt, Hoff, Rietveld & Schröder

Theo van Doesburg (Christian Emil Marie Küpper). b Utrecht (NL), 1883. **d** Meudon, nr Paris (FR), 1931. **Studio House**, Meudon, nr Paris (FR), 1929–31.

Dogon

Ginna

In Mali, West Africa, the Bandiagara Escarpment has been the unlikely home of the Dogon people for over four centuries, and by the Tellem for as long before them. They built their dwelling compounds and granaries from earth and stone, with both circular and rectangular plans, raising them on the *talus* (debris of fallen rock) of the high cliff. Beyond the escarpment, the flat lands of the Seno plain were cultivated, and today many Dogon have relocated from the cliff to villages on the plain itself. Each village has a symbolically anthropomorphic plan, as does each compound within it. The headman of a Dogon lineage lives in a *ginna*, as shown here, where the compartments on the facade of the mud house are moulded to display votive objects. A shrine and a men's meeting house, or *togu na*, would be situated nearby. The Dogon are noted for the variety of masks used in their sacred dances and some of their shrines have a mask-like appearance.

☛ **Mousgoum, Ndebele, Syrian Farmers, Tiwa Indians**

100

Dogon. Active (MLI), fifteenth century to present day. **Ginna**, Bandiagara Escarpment (MLI), fifteenth century to present day.

Dollmann Georg von   Schloss Linderhof

When Ludwig II of Bavaria succeeded to power in 1864, he set about emulating Louis XIV and his seventeenth-century palace at Versailles with his own Schloss Herrenchiemsee (begun 1878). No less Revivalist, but prettier by far, was his later Schloss Linderhof, which adds the late Bavarian Baroque style of a century and half beforehand to the mixture.

Set in a wooded valley, deep in the Ammergau Alps, surrounded by a lake and formal gardens, it was built and decorated in 1870–86 with a suite of rooms that would have accommodated Louis and all his mistresses. Ostensibly designed by Georg von Dollmann, who may only have executed the design, the finely-executed Rococo interiors were the

creations of Franz von Seitz, director of the Munich State Theatre. Indeed the whole effect is theatrical and a counterbalance to Ludwig's Wagnerian fantasy which he realized at Schloss Neuschwanstein in 1869–81.

☞ **Le Vau & Hardouin-Mansart, Ludwig II, Pöppelmann**

Georg von Dollmann. b Ansbach (GER), 1830. **d** Munich (GER), 1895. **Schloss Linderhof**, nr Oberammergau (GER), 1870–8.

Doménech Lluís   Casa Morera

A confection of a house on a busy street corner in the heart of Barcelona, the Casa Morera does not, on first sight, appear the revolutionary building that it is. Designed by one of the leading figures of Modernisme – Spain's answer to Art Nouveau – the house is a political manifesto. Doménech was a member of La Lliga de Catalunya, an influential political movement seeking independence for Catalonia from Spain during the early part of the twentieth century. In returning to the architecture of medieval Barcelona – a period when the Catalan capital thrived – Doménech and his contemporaries, such as Antoni Gaudí, rediscovered a distinctively Catalan style which they felt served their ends. However, they were not wholeheartedly opposed to innovation. Behind its Gothic facade, the Casa Morera used materials such as steel and glass in wholly modern ways. The house was awarded the Town Hall prize in 1905 as the best new building in Barcelona.

☛ **Gaudí, Guimard, Hoffmann, Horta**

Lluis Doménech I Montaner. b Barcelona (SP), 1849. d Barcelona (SP), 1923. **Casa Morera**, Barcelona (SP), 1905.

Domenig Günther   Steinhaus

Günther Domenig's house, built on the site of his childhood holidays, is part house, part architecture school, part ongoing architectural expression. Working with the metaphorical expressive shapes used by Deconstructivists, it represents an ambiguous 'bird', and yet is built of materials so rough they can draw blood. The house, which is described extensively in a series of scribbled, irregular drawings, was developed as a manmade mound split into cliffs and a ravine, with expressive steel and concrete outcrops. The entrance is via a deep path, leading to a glass cylinder where the ground water level is visible. The building is organized around a spiralling plan where the formal organization of the rooms is deliberately disrupted. Along the route is sleeping accommodation, or 'baskets', a crooked cube meeting space, a wedge-shaped eating area, a path leading out to the sky and terminating in a take-off ramp for the apocryphal bird, aimed across the lake.

☛ Diller & Scofidio, Eisenman, Jersey Devil, Parent

Günther Domenig. b Klagenfurt, Carinthia (AUS), 1934. Steinhaus, Carinthia (AUS), begun in 1986.

Donovan Hill   C House

There is a distinctly foreign feel to the C House: the strong horizontal lines, the timber screens, its pagoda-like quality all suggest that this is no ordinary suburban Brisbane home. Concerned that the Australian suburbs are losing all 'sense of place', Donovan Hill have here turned to traditional Islamic architecture as a model for a new way of living. The C House reverses the suburban American pattern of the boxy house with front and rear lawns that Australia has, since the 1950s, so endlessly replicated. Instead, the house focuses inward with the rooms opening onto a central courtyard – an outdoor room at the heart of the building which, while open to the elements, is protected by the oversailing roof. In addition, the house is beautifully detailed – a feature which marks it out not just from the suburban norm, but also from the bush-style of so many young Australian architects.

☛ Andresen O'Gorman, Bawa, Correa, Dewes & Puente, Groote

104

Donovan Hill. Brian Donovan. b Emerald, QLD (ASL), 1959. **Timothy Hill. b** Brisbane, QLD (ASL), 1963. **C House**, Brisbane, QLD (ASL), 1998.

Doshi Balkrishna   Doshi House

This modernist house of exposed brick and concrete, inside as well as out, has an understated, almost austere presence which allows it to merge with its quiet surroundings. Yet, at the same time, it is designed to offer a rich, complex and dynamic living experience for the architect and his family, animated by distinctive contrasts in its spatial qualities, a lively visual and physical interaction of exterior and interior, and the use of stimulating colour schemes in the cool indoor areas. The house is characteristic of Doshi's work, which uses simple rectilinear geometries to build up complex building masses of open and closed spaces connected by a network of corridors, or ritual routes. Doshi worked in Paris for Le Corbusier on Le Corbusier's Indian projects of the 1950s, but subsequently, in his own practice, fused that rigorous modernist vision with his own experience and reading of traditional Indian temple city architecture.

☞ Bofill, Correa, Kahn, Le Corbusier, Rewal

Balkrishna Vithaldas Doshi. b Poona (IN), 1927. **Doshi House**, Ahmedabad (IN), 1959–61, with later additions, 1985–7.

Droppers

Drop City

In 1965, three artists bought land in southern Colorado and started what was to become one of the most famous (some say infamous) group communities of the 1960s. The Droppers – writers, painters, musicians and film-makers who made up the community – were determined to live free, creative lives outside the bounds of established society. They based the design of their distinctive shelters on polyhedral geometry using inexpensive locally available materials such as plywood, chickenwire, tarpaper, chopped up car bodies and windscreens. Each dome-shaped structure contained a separate function – the central cluster of domes, seen here, housed bathrooms and the kitchen, while peripheral domes were used as bedrooms, artists' studios and even a mixed-media theatre (seen here on the far left). Not surprisingly, the anti-establishment lifestyle of the Droppers attracted attention, and Drop City became an influential prototype for other co-operative communities.

☛ Day, Fuller, D Greene, Horden, Reynolds, Soleri

Droppers. Founded by **Gene Bernofsky**. **b** New York, NY (USA), 1941. **JoAnn Bernofsky**. **b** New York, NY (USA), 1942. **Clark Richert**. **b** Wichita, KS (USA), 1941. **Drop City**, nr Trinidad, CO (USA), 1965–70.

Duany Plater-Zyberk

Windsor House

The traditions of the Caribbean and Florida's oldest city, St Augustine, inform the architecture of Windsor, a 'new town' on the Florida Atlantic coast. Both the town and this house, were designed by Andres Duany and Elizabeth Plater-Zyberk, whose renown has come largely from their pedestrian-orientated town plans as a response to urban sprawl. The architecture of Windsor House relies on such Caribbean-inspired features as broad overhangs, wooden balconies and shutters, breezeways and large windows to permit cross-ventilation – all features of the tropical vernacular. An open loggia connects the main living spaces on the ground floor and, at the same time, borders the swimming pool. Duany Plater-Zyberk is among the leaders of a revived New Urbanist, neo-vernacular architecture in the USA and is also responsible for the planning of the famous New Urbanist resort of Seaside in Florida (1984–91).

☛ **Arquitectonica, Carter, Krier, Nevisian Creole**

Duany Plater-Zyberk. Andres Duany. b New York, NY (USA), 1949. **Elizabeth Plater-Zyberk. b** Bryn Mawr, PA (USA), 1950. **Windsor House**, Windsor, FL (USA), 1992.

Duchamp-Villon Raymond Maison Cubiste

Geometrical, stalactite-like forms are suspended from the underside of the balcony of this 'Cubist' house. Duchamp-Villon intended these, and other surface treatments of its otherwise traditional facade, to suggest a relationship between built and natural forms, motivated by his desire to relate a new architectural order to the existing environment, and to modern life. A sculptor and leading figure of the Cubist movement, he produced this design – which existed only as a model facade – for an exhibition of Cubist art at the 1912 Salon d'Automne. The result is an architecture of the eye that emphasizes the plastic effects of the facade; space defined by planes, rather than the spatial organization of the plan. At this time, the development of a new theory of form was just beginning in France. It was the Czechs who would develop the Cubist theories further and go on to produce a new expression of architectural form.

☞ Cormier, Janák, Mallet-Stevens

Pierre Maurice Raymond Duchamp-Villon. **b** Damville, Eure (FR), 1876. **d** Cannes (FR), 1918. **Maison Cubiste**, Salon d'Automne, Paris (FR), facade model, 1912.

Dyckman States Morris   Boscobel

Long considered an important Federal period work of Palladian influence, Boscobel is a study in proportion and refinement. It is elegant in both its simplicity of design and its adornment, most particularly the carved wooden swags along the portico and the graceful balustrades. A descendant of the early Dutch settlers and a staunch British Loyalist, States

Morris Dyckman dreamed of building an English manor house in the Hudson River Valley. Little did he know that the house would, in fact, become an outstanding example of American architecture of the period. While in London in 1800, he bought all that he would need to furnish such a house – china, crystal and silver – before the first foundation stone was even laid.

But, sadly, he died quite suddenly soon after the building work started, and was never to see his dream realized. It was left to his widow, Elizabeth, to complete Boscobel, with the help of William Vermilyea, a master builder and a relative.

☛ Burlington, Hoban, Palladio, Weeks

States Morris Dyckman. **b** New York, NY (USA), 1755. **d** New York, NY (USA), 1806. **Boscobel**, Garrison, Hudson Valley, NY (USA), 1806.

Eames Charles and Ray   Eames House (Case Study House No.8)

Lightweight, steel-and-glass, and in the perpetual sunshine of southern California, the Eames house presented an enticing image to other architects, but especially to British architects: Norman Foster, Richard Rogers, John Winter and Michael Hopkins have all paid tribute to it. If one building launched British 'high tech', this is it. The husband and wife team responded to the Case Study Program, initiated by the magazine *Arts and Architecture,* to demonstrate the applicability of modern design to domestic buildings. The house and its associated studio (visible beyond the house) create as much space as possible with minimal materials. Developing an identifiable aesthetic out of such practical construction gave it an enduring place in the canon of great architectural works. Elevating the ordinary, the everyday and 'found objects' became the Eames' hallmark, particularly in the eclectic mix of artfully ordered objects inside the house.

☛ **Ellwood, Koenig, Mies van der Rohe, Rogers, Soriano**

Charles Ormond Eames. b St Louis, MS (USA), 1907. d St Louis, MS (USA), 1978. **Ray Kaiser Eames**. b Sacramento, CA (USA), 1912. d Los Angeles, CA (USA), 1988. **Eames House (Case Study House No.8)**, Pacific Palisades, CA (USA), 1949.

Eaton Norman

Greenwood House

Rough stone and materials which look as if they have come from their surroundings were characteristic of Eaton's work. The carefully contrived siting, the corner window in the dining room, stone and timber finishes all show an affinity with the Arts and Crafts movement which had influenced Eaton while travelling in Europe in the early 1930s.

Meanwhile, several close contemporaries strove to make Modernism acceptable in South Africa – a quest boosted by the arrival of several refugees from Nazi Germany. Eaton's houses, however, developed a consciously African architecture, using local materials and skills, for instance in decorative paving. The servants' quarters in this house – the art of planning for

domestic staff lasted longer in South Africa than elsewhere – are an extraordinary composition of round forms and thatched roofs. His work bears comparison with Frank Lloyd Wright's, even if he lacks the master's formal inventiveness.

☞ Aalto, Fagan, E F Jones, Kahn, Wright

111

Norman Eaton. b Pretoria (SA), 1902. **d** Pretoria (SA), 1966. **Greenwood House**, nr Pretoria (SA), 1949–51.

Edmond & Corrigan

Athan House

With its razor-sharp lines and theatrical, pinstriped cladding, the Athan House makes a striking contrast to its surrounding eucalypt forest. 'The building in some ways represents an urban idea relocated to the Australian bush', say its architects, Edmond & Corrigan, a practice that bucks the 'outback' trend of much contemporary Australian architecture in favour of a more urbane approach. The house is an unofficial hotel of sorts where the clients' extended family of teenage and grown-up children can live together, yet privately. Designed like a medieval city or walled fortress, complete with its own entry bridge, the house is a labyrinth of strangely-angled rooms, twisting staircases and knife-edged balconies – a real maze of spaces that offer family members the option of getting away from each other or congregating.

☛ **Domenig, Patkau Architects, Scogin Elam & Bray**

112

Edmond & Corrigan. **Margaret Leone Edmond**. b Melbourne, VIC (ASL) 1955. **Peter Campion Corrigan**. b Melbourne, VIC (ASL) 1944. **Athan House**, Monbulk, VIC (ASL), 1986–8.

Eichler Joseph Eichler Home

This typical Eichler Home turns its back on the street and focuses all of its attention on the ample leisure area in the private back yard. Well-designed, inexpensive modern homes were hard to find in the San Francisco Bay area before businessman-turned-building contractor, Joseph Eichler, built his first housing development in 1950. While living in a rented Frank Lloyd Wright house, Eichler conceived of a new breed of affordable housing that would not sacrifice quality for cost. Although modest in scale, Eichler Homes have impressive features, such as open floor plans, high ceilings, exposed redwood beams and underfloor heating. Bedrooms and bathrooms are often on the street side to reinforce the private nature of the main living space. The characteristic rear glass facades create continuous views overlooking the yard and remain one of the most popular features of the homes. Today, 11,000 Eichler Homes still survive in the San Francisco Bay area.

☛ Breuer, Eames, Goodman, Koenig, Neutra

Joseph Eichler. b New York, NY (USA), 1900. **d** San Francisco, CA (USA), 1974. **Eichler Home**, various locations, San Francisco Bay area, CA (USA), as built 1950s and 60s.

Eisenman Peter   Frank House (House VI)

Peter Eisenman's iconic and elaborate Frank House is one of a sequence of highly theoretical, built experiments of new architectural forms which question the nature and use of family homes. This is achieved by twisting and manipulating the structural grid on which Modernist houses were based. The architectural games affect the occupants' use of the house itself:

the marital bed is split down the middle by a slot which cuts through wall, roof and floor – treating the gap as though it were a solid object. Elsewhere in the house, two staircases seem to mirror each other, but one of them is only an illusion – an unusable, red-carpetted form in the ceiling which leads nowhere making the house appear upside down, challenging

the viewer's concept of gravity. Eisenman remains the most formally complex of the New York Five, a group of American architects who experimented with and reinvented strict Modernist forms and beliefs before going their different ways.

☞ Domenig, Graves, Gwathmey, Koolhaas, Meier

114

Peter Eisenman. b Newark, NJ (USA), 1932. **Frank House (House VI)**, West Cornwall, CT (USA), 1972.

Eldem Sedad

Rahmi Koç Yali

Regarded as Turkey's greatest twentieth-century architect, Sedad Eldem began designing contemporary, innovative buildings grounded in the traditional Ottoman style in the 1930s. Overlooking the Bay of Tarabya, the Rahmi Koç Yali reflects Eldem's graceful use of contemporary linear simplicity to recreate a light and elegant Bosphorus riverside summer home. The design is dominated by a large glazed, cantilevered upper floor, its form echoed below in the windows at ground level. The interior is flooded with light, and opens onto a front terrace overlooking the river and a garden terrace overlooking the pool and marble peristyle. A stylized Turkish vernacular form is captured in the wooden coffered ceilings, the painted trim and the overall traditional symmetrical layout; the cruciform central salon, or *sofa*, is framed by four bedrooms, or *oda*, one at each corner.

☛ **Chatterjee & Wheaton, Erickson, Köprülü Family**

Sedad Hakki Eldem (Ömer Sedad). **b** Istanbul (TRK), 1908. **d** Istanbul (TRK), 1988. **Rahmi Koç Yali**, Tarabya (TRK), 1975–80.

Elliot Henry

Octagon House

The windows that punctuate the eight sides of this house, and its matching octagonal cupola, afforded panoramas beyond those possible in a traditional rectangular dwelling. This seems quite appropriate for a design that took the traditional clapboard house, veranda and all, and made it new. Although local in its use of materials, this house was one of many that arose from an explosive, although short-lived, trend of the mid-nineteenth century. The idea of octagonal building was suggested by a British phrenologist, Orson Fowler, in his book *A Home for All* (1848). He expounded the superiority of octagons for their functionality (greater floor area to total wall length ratio), as well as for the aesthetics of their form, which approached the ideal circle. His reasoning found favour with architect, Henry Elliot, and gave form to the many octagonal structures that can still be found in New England and eastern Canada today.

☞ Bardwell, A J Davis, McCoskrie & Greenfield, Sloan

Henry Elliot. b (CAN), 1824. d (CAN), 1890. Octagon House, Dartmouth, NS (CAN), 1871.

Ellwood Craig   Rosen House

Ellwood, who came to prominence during the post-World War II expansion of Los Angeles in the 1940s, designed this elegant house for a banker. The pristine spareness of the steel frame, with its iconic, welded box details, the grey plate glass and brick infill panels, clearly dominates its economical expression. The plan, influenced by a Mies van der Rohe-educated associate in Ellwood's office, is made up of a nine-square-grid, the central square being an open courtyard. However, unlike Mies' Farnsworth House or Philip Johnson's Glass House – both of which were designed for one person – the Rosen House manages to comfortably accommodate the complexities of a five-bedroom, six-bathroom family home.

The house has a sense of spaciousness achieved through the use of large expanses of glass, which opens up the house both to the courtyard and the grounds, while providing a reflection of the landscape on the surface of the house itself.

☞ **Eames, P Johnson, Koenig, Lautner, Neutra**

Craig Ellwood. b Clarendon, TX (USA), 1922. **d** Pergine-Valdarno (IT), 1992. **Rosen House**, Brentwood, CA (USA), 1962.

El-Wakil Abdel Wahed   Halawa House

Light and shadow strike the white-washed limestone block exterior of this Egyptian seaside villa, highlighting its strong architectonic components. This home signifies the Utopian vision of Abdel Wahed El-Wakil, a loyal follower of fellow architect, Hassan Fathy, and his interest in the revival of the indigenous roots of Egyptian house architecture. Here, we can see his use of many traditional North African and Islamic villa motifs: vaulted arches, loggias, or open gallery rooms, low masonry courtyard benches, windcatchers, shallow domed spaces, public and private courtyards, and the oblique arrangement of entrances. Ornate open brickwork and wooden lattice-work window treatments (*mashrabiyya*) maximize natural ventilation sources and, at the same time, cast delicate silhouettes. Blending tradition, local conditions and materials, El-Wakil reinterprets International Modernism through a flavour of his vernacular roots.

☛ al-Haddad, Bawa, Correa, Fathy, Gandhi, Yazdi

Abdel Wahed El-Wakil. b Cairo (EG), 1943. **Halawa House**, Agamy (EG), 1972–5.

Erickson Arthur   Helmut Eppich House

Despite the immediate contrast between the structural geometry of this terraced concrete house and the fluidity of its natural surroundings, the ultimate unity achieved is perhaps the most distinctive and ubiquitous characteristic of the Eppich House. Every element of its design – whether it be the overhang of its lowest level or the rhythm of its flying concrete beams – bears a sensitive relationship to the details and subtleties of its surroundings. The fluid dissolution of the distinction between manmade and natural – house and setting – is a trademark of Arthur Erickson's designs. Working at a time when modern architecture was widely accepted, Erickson had the freedom to endow his works with the deep appreciation for nature and experience he had accrued over his lifetime. This sensitivity both gained him an international reputation and characterized his seminal contribution to the creation of a north American 'West Coast' architectural style.

☛ **Corrales & Molezún**, **Domenig**, **P Johnson**, **Kahn**, **Rudolph**

Arthur Charles Erickson. b Vancouver, BC (CAN), 1924. **Helmut Eppich House**, West Vancouver, BC (CAN), 1972.

Erskine Ralph

House and Studio

Erskine's house to the right and studio and garage to the left define a central open space, rather like a farmyard. This English-born architect, who emigrated to Sweden in 1939, had learnt how to cope with snow and ice, and incorporated a double roof with an airspace, seen on the gable end, which prevents melting and refreezing, the cause of dangerous icicles and blocked gutters. Walls are made of precast concrete panels, specially textured. In the courtyard garden, boulders gather the warmth of the sun in summer. The living quarters consist almost entirely of a single, open-plan room, with the kitchen as an enclosed 'pod' at midway point and a free-standing fireplace that can be turned in different directions.

Erskine has spent a large part of his career specializing in low-cost housing, but is more recently known for his extraordinary, boat-shaped office building, The Ark (1988–91), in Hammersmith, London.

☛ **Asplund, Fehn, Holscher, A Jacobsen, Pietilä**

Ralph Erskine. b London (UK), 1914. **House and Studio,** Drottningholm, nr Stockholm (SWE), 1963.

Eschwege Baron von   Palácio da Pena

Built on a rocky hilltop overlooking the city of Sintra, the Pena Palace follows the *castillos roqueros* tradition, where the inaccessibility of the natural site is used to the castle's defensive and strategic advantage. Throughout the complex, Moorish and Gothic architectural elements are fused with the Manueline style, a Portuguese highly decorative, late-Gothic style of the reign of King Manuel I (1495–1521). Islamic-Moorish interest in ornamental surface treatment is evident in the use of colourful glazed tilework, seen here on the arched entrance. From this perspective, the Pena Palace marks the beginning of a composite and Revivalist style in the Iberian peninsula. Dom Fernando II commissioned the German architect, Baron von Eschwege, to design and build the palace on the site of the ancient monastery of Nossa Senhora de Pena (Our Lady of Sorrow) after the disbanding of all religious orders in 1838. However, Eschwege did not live to see the entire palace completed.

☛ **Isabella I & Ferdinand II, Nasrid Dynasty, Tarifa**

121

Baron von **Wilhelm Ludwig Eschwege**. b Aue, nr Wanfried (GER), 1777. d Wolfsanger, nr Kassel (GER), 1855. **Palácio da Pena**, Estremadura, Sintra (POR), begun 1840, completed by Demetrio Cinnatti and Possidónio da Silva, 1885.

Esherick Joseph   Goldman House

Esherick, whose work has been termed Bay Region Style, made a conscious effort to depart from the white Modernism of his contemporaries to design houses that reflected more directly his clients' needs, the site, the climate and the historical urban context. The Goldman House, with its environmentally-conscious, L-shaped plan enclosing a shady east-facing garden, avoids the more common approach used in the Bay area, where the glazing is exposed to the elements. With this basic arrangement in place, Esherick employed natural daylight to modulate the internal environmental conditions throughout the high-ceilinged, sometimes double-height spaces. The glazing is broken up with a grid of mullions, making reference to the many Victorian houses in the San Francisco Bay area. The Goldman House exemplifies Esherick's rejection of formal concepts of purity and embraces humanity, nature and a Californian architectural tradition.

☞ Kavanaugh, Moore, Turnbull

Joseph Esherick. b Philadelphia, PA (USA), 1914. d San Francisco, CA (USA), 1998. **Goldman House**, San Francisco, CA (USA), 1951.

Fagan Gabriël

Fagan House

Situated in a valley where strong winds sweep down from Table Mountain, the street facade of Fagan House is closed and protective, while the living areas (seen here) open up to views of the ocean. Bedrooms are west facing and covered by a rippling laminated timber roof. Many features of the house respond to the dramatic climate, and its steeply sloping site. Massive white-painted brick walls allow for solar gain in cold weather, and sliding shutters keep out the harsh sun, yet admit strong light into the interior. The house is a testimony to the architect's craftsmanship and his deep understanding of the aesthetic, tactile and even audible qualities of materials. It evolved from the basement workshop, where all the joinery and metalwork could be made by Fagan and his family, into a large and informal house for communal living. The house is a modern take on a vernacular tradition – Fagan has been involved in the conservation of many Cape Dutch buildings.

☞ Eaton, Jourda Perraudin, Stel, Villiers

Gabriël Fagan. b Cape Peninsula (SA), 1925. **Fagan House**, Camps Bay, Cape Town (SA), c1963.

Hassan Fathy, while respecting the European traditions of his architectural training, also resented them for being part of the colonial legacy that had threatened Egypt's own identity. He decided to turn his back on the West and invented a style that incorporated the essence of his cultural heritage. The client Hamed Said and his wife, both artists, were also concerned with issues of national identity and required a simple house that would be in harmony with nature. The house, one of Fathy's most critically acclaimed works, was originally made up of a domed studio space with an adjoining sleeping area and open loggia. However, the Saids were so impressed with the result that they commissioned additional living quarters. Fathy wrapped the new component around a courtyard, creating a harmonious cloistered complex. The house became the meeting place for a group concerned with the need to establish a distinct Egyptian culture, and remains today a powerful symbol of their beliefs.

☛ **Bawa, Eldem, El-Wakil, Loess Han**

Hassan Fathy. b Alexandria (EG), 1900. d Cairo (EG), 1989. **Hamed Said House**, Cairo (EG), 1942–5.

Fehn Sverre

Villa Busk

Situated on rocky terrain along the Oslofjorden, the Villa Busk is anchored to the sloping ground with solid concrete walls, which give way to a lighter, timber-constructed roof. Sometimes called the 'poet of the straight line', Fehn plays on this theme in the rational plan of the house, built along the 'internal route' of a single corridor that runs its entire length.

The adjoining four-storey tower, reached by an enclosed, glazed bridge, has children's rooms on the lower level and a study above, connected by a spiral stair. Avoiding a sensationalist 'signature' style, Fehn's thoughtful use of such materials as wood and concrete is similar to that of Louis Kahn, creating a tension with the natural setting by the

undisguised human intervention. Noted as a regionalist architect, Fehn's work was cited by the 1997 Pritzker Prize jury for 'a fascinating and exciting combination of modern forms tempered by the Scandinavian tradition'.

☛ Aalto, Asplund, Kahn, Korsmo, Larsson

Sverre Fehn. b Kongsberg (NOR), 1924. **Villa Busk**, Bamble (NOR), 1987–90.

Fernau & Hartman

House in West Marin

Situated on a wooded hillside above a lagoon, this house was designed as a complete contrast to compartmentalized urban living. The architects took advantage of the idyllic setting to design a house that would function as a place for three simple activities – eating, playing and resting. The strength of the design lies in the negligible distinction between the interior and the exterior, which is reinforced in every aspect of the house. From the L-shaped courtyard plan that embraces the landscape, to the finely-detailed, vertically-folding doors that remove even the barrier of glazing, the space extends without limit into its surroundings. Only the road-side elevation has been constructed of solid, environmentally efficient straw-bale to create some degree of privacy. The filtered light of the forest canopy and glimpses of the lagoon beyond become the backdrop to the family's daily activities, unconstrained by the more usual four walls of a city dwelling.

☛ Clare Design, Holl, Poole, Rural Studio

Fernau & Hartman. **Richard Fernau**. b Chicago, IL (USA), 1946. **Laura Hartman**. b Charleston, WV (USA), 1952. **House in West Marin**, CA (USA), 1995–9.

Ferrater Carlos   Alonso-Planas House

Crisp forms, geometric regularity and sharp details reveal an architecture of restrained poetic formalism that is Ferrater's hallmark. By using a visually simple, but conceptually complex set of interlocking spaces, he seeks a richness of experience through simplicity of means. The house is sited perpendicular to the contours of a sharp slope, with three storeys of accommodation overlooking the valleys of Barcelona and the sea. Two low, L-shaped wings extend to form a tunnel entrance to one side and a submerged art studio on the other, lit by a strip of sloping clerestory windows. Large expanses of white walls block out the bright sun, with horizontal scoring on the surface to break the visual monotony, while fenestrations are covered with evenly-spaced *brises-soleil* running horizontally to echo the wall planes. The overall effect of the white planes under the intense blue sky is an ambiguity of scale and materials, adding a surreal effect to an otherwise quiet rationality.

☛ **Campo Baeza, Corrales & Molezún, Meier, Torres & Lapeña**

Carlos Ferrater. b Barcelona (SP), 1944. **Alonso-Planas House**, Barcelona (SP), 1998.

Feyferlik Wolfgang   Haus Feurer

The almost traditional farmhouse tile roof of the Haus Feurer dissolves, as if by magic or time, to bring a dappled light inside. The glass tiles provide a view upwards, and thus a relationship to the sky, while the arrangement of the rooms affords views in all directions. The connection of the house to its site is also made explicit in the kitchen, which sits 45 cm (17 in) below ground level to give the feeling of being part of the landscape. The house is built around a U-shaped courtyard, its three independent concrete frames ascending in size as they step around. The house is characteristic of the architect's design approach in its simple, rectangular spaces which are made special by their proportion and transparency to the outside and to each other. Feyferlik is one of several Graz architects who evolved a new Austrian avant-garde, displacing and reusing modern and traditional forms.

☛ Corrales & Molezún, Kada, Stern, Venturi

Wolfgang Feyferlik. b Hausham (GER), 1957. **Haus Feurer**, St Anna am Aigen (AUS), 1992.

Finistère Farmers

Menhir Cottage

Religion has always played a powerful part in Brittany's culture. Prehistoric menhirs (sacred standing stones) and dolmens (stone burial chambers) abound along Brittany's south coast, and menhir cottages strongly suggest that many of the ancient beliefs and superstitions surrounding them survived into the last century, woven into the dominant Catholic tradition. These remarkable dwellings originally derived from ancient megalithic chambers and may have used true menhirs in their construction. The grey granite slabs forming the walls of existing cottages however, are an imitation. Some 2.5 m (8 ft) high and about 0.3 m (1 ft) thick, the slabs are buried half a metre into the ground for support and the clay mortar filling the gaps between the stones gives the buildings a curious zebra-like effect. Earlier forms had a hipped roof with a central fireplace; however, by the mid-nineteenth century a gable was added at one end to support a rubble-stone chimney.

☛ Antrim Labourers, Breton, Hebridean Crofter

129

Finistère Farmers. Active (FR), nineteenth century. **Menhir Cottage**, Nevez, Finistère (FR), as built mid-nineteenth century.

Fischer von Erlach Johann Bernhard Schönbrunn Palace

When Fischer von Erlach published his first plans for a new imperial palace in Vienna, he combined the size of Versailles with the curved facade and opulent modelling that Bernini had proposed for the Louvre. This might have made what became the Schönbrunn Palace the most remarkable exemplar of absolute power in all Europe. Even in its modified form it is grand enough. Begun for Emperor Joseph I in 1696 on a different, lower site, it has an immensely long facade with a seven-bay, columnar centrepiece, stepped wings with giant pilasters, and seven-bay terminal pavilions. A wide staircase, curving round a large circular fountain in the forecourt, leads to the huge entrance hall of the centre block.

However, this was still not grand enough for the Empress Maria Theresa, who commissioned Nikolaus Paccassi to remodel the palace in 1744–9, resulting in two galleries, but a reduction in the overall interior architectural effect.

☛ **Hildebrandt, Le Vau & Hardouin-Mansart, Pöppelmann**

Johann Bernhard Fischer von Erlach. b Graz (AUS), 1656. **d** Vienna (AUS), 1723. **Schönbrunn Palace**, Vienna (AUS), 1696, remodelled 1744–9.

Fontana Giovanni & Schädel Gottfried

Menshikov Palace

With the choppy waters of the Great Neva splashing on its steps and the defensively walled land behind it, this palace of Peter the Great's closest associate, Alexander Menshikov, has the rugged sense of conquering nature that characterized both men. Ivan Zubov's engraving of 1717 shows the palace newly completed. This was one of the first significant masonry

buildings in Peter's new city, and its U-shaped plan, pilastered facades and magnificently tiled Dutch interiors made it grander than anything the Tsar created for himself. The Italian Fontana was brought to Russia in 1703 by Peter and worked on several commissions in Moscow for the powerful Menshikov before coming north to start this palace in 1710. Schädel

arrived in 1713 and joined him. Fontana played a key role in the Tsar's programme of Westernizing Russia by supervising the 1709 translation of Vignola's *La Regola delli Cinque Ordini d'Architettura*, originally published in Renaissance Italy in 1562.

☞ Cameron, Kazakov, Kent, Rastrelli, Shekhtel

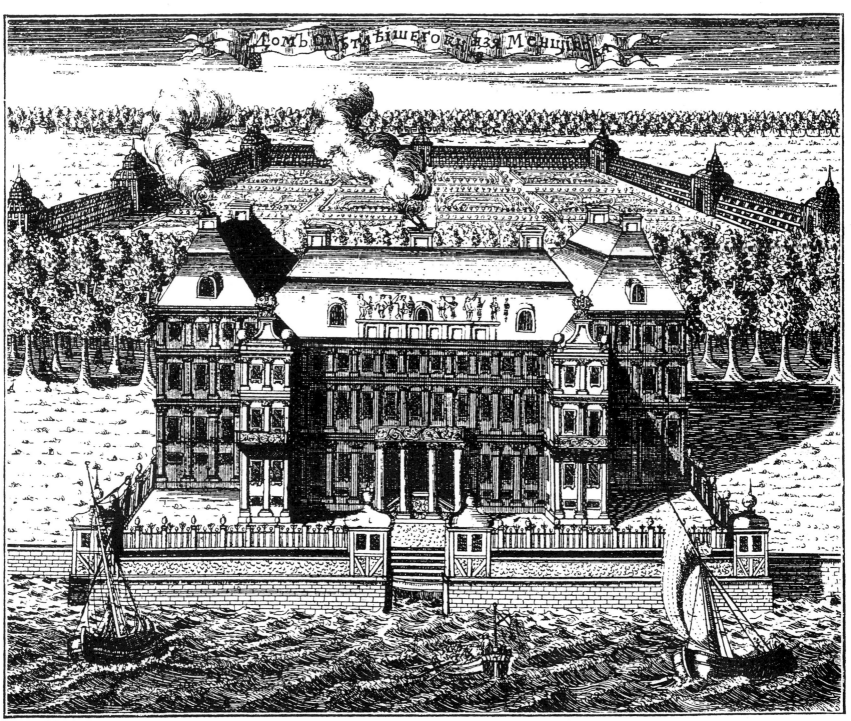

Giovanni Maria Fontana. Active (RUS), early to mid-eighteenth century. **Gottfried Johann Schädel**. **b** c1680. **d** 1752. **Menshikov Palace**, Vasilevsky Island, St Petersburg (RUS), 1711–16. Engraving by Ivan Fedorovich Zubov, 1717.

Fortrey Samuel   Kew Palace

Built in 1631 for Samuel Fortrey, a London merchant of Dutch descent, Kew Palace was not occupied by the royal family until the eighteenth century, when the interior was extensively remodelled so that King George III and Queen Charlotte, among others, could escape from the formalities of London and the grander royal palaces. Its original name, the Dutch House, better describes its style, which marries the traditional red brick of London (and Holland) with the new taste for curved and pedimented gables, then all the rage among Amsterdam's merchants. Kew Palace is hardly classical in the accepted sense of some of its contemporaries, but its symmetrical outline, pedimented windows, and the pilasters and columns of the central bay appealed to a conservative taste that found the style of Inigo Jones too daring, and did not contrive to disguise the batteries of chimney-stacks, rising where they were needed, rather than where symmetry might dictate.

☞ **Amsterdam Merchants, Brussels Guildsmen, Cecil, I Jones**

Samuel Fortrey. Active (UK), seventeenth century. **Kew Palace**, Royal Botanic Gardens, Kew (UK), 1631.

Fry Maxwell

Sun House

These white-painted, cement-rendered, reinforced concrete walls, though seldom seen so brilliantly against a deep blue sky, enshrine all the sun-worshipping, health-giving tenets of the Modernist manifesto. Sun House was built in 1934–5 with long bands of windows and a terrace, hidden on the roof, to provide the privacy for nude sunbathing. Cantilevered balconies supported by steel columns, a complete lack of decoration and a flat roof add up to 1930s Modern architecture at its most doctrinaire. The young Fry had set up practice and worked on a handful of buildings with Walter Gropius – former director of the seminal German design school, the Bauhaus – who emigrated to England as the Nazis consolidated power in Germany. However, Gropius disliked traditional British attitudes to architecture and moved on to the United States, leaving Fry (among others) to strengthen and develop the British Modern movement.

☛ **Connell, Goldfinger, Gropius, Loos, Lubetkin, Luckhardt**

Edwin Maxwell Fry. **b** London (UK), 1899. **d** Cotherstone (UK), 1987. **Sun House**, London (UK), 1934–5.

Fujimori Teronobu & Oshima Nobumichi

Nira-House

This house is named after the 1,000 *nira*, or chive plants, on the surface of the roof which, both metaphorically and literally, create an organic architecture. Inspired by farmhouses in northern Japan with vegetation growing on their thatched roofs, Fujimori and Oshima intended the slender green stems of the chives to contrast with the roof planks of sanded American pine. The chives are planted in small pots in the winter and bloom in the summer with white flowers. Built on a sloping site, 4 m (13 ft) below the road, the house is entered at the upper level by way of a bridge. This entry overlooks a double-height, covered terrace which divides the eastern living wing from the western wing containing a studio, library and tea room. Fujimori, who is also a noted architectural historian, is one of the few architects in Japan to successfully combine word and image with tactile architectural form.

☞ **Raymond, Shirakawa Farmers, Yoshimura**

Teronobu Fujimori. b Nagano Prefecture (JAP), 1946. **Nobumichi Oshima. b** Tottori Prefecture (JAP), 1960. **Nira-House (Chive House)**, Tokyo (JAP), 1997.

Fuller Richard Buckminster

Wichita House

This circular, aluminium, single-unit dwelling was a prototype for a mass-producible, lightweight house with premoulded, pre-installed services, capable of being transported and erected anywhere. It built on Fuller's visionary ideas first explored in his 1927 Dymaxion House project (dynamic plus maximum efficiency), which was technologically ahead of its time. The floors were to be laid on pneumatic bladders, suspended by tensile cables from a central mast anchored in a solid base which contained septic and fuel tanks. The external walls were to be of transparent plastic with curtains of aluminium sheeting, and the doors operated by photo-electric cells. Fuller was editor of the environmental magazine, *Shelter*, in the 1930s, and it was his commitment to industrialization of the building process as the key to 'solving total humanity's evolutionary shelter problems' while respecting the earth's resources, that underpinned his designs.

☞ Airstream Co., Droppers, Otto, Prouvé, Segal, Soleri

Richard Buckminster Fuller. b Milton, MA (USA), 1895. d Los Angeles, CA (USA), 1983. **Wichita House**, KS (USA), 1946.

Furness Frank

William H Rhawn House

Original, bizarre (and celebrated for being both), Furness was Philadelphia's architect of choice during the business and building boom following the American Civil War. He could impose his arsenal of mannerist eccentricities on the design of a suburban home as deftly as he could wield them on a downtown bank. The Rhawn house is evidence of his individualism at work: a unique, daring and personal composition of conventional architectural elements (columns, brackets, gables, arches) and ordinary materials (stone, brick, shingle, wood); his genius was in the mix. The great U-shaped porch supports and balances a pyramid of a roof that peaks in stages to a towering height. This house is different enough from the formalist nature of most contemporary houses to warrant the suggestion that his innovations prefigured the later, newer architecture of functionalism, as may be seen in the work of Louis Sullivan, who worked as a young man in Furness's office.

☛ **Greene & Greene, Potter, Pugin, Sullivan, Viollet-le-Duc**

136

Frank Furness. b Philadelphia, PA (USA), 1839. d Medea, PA (USA), 1912. **William H Rhawn House**, Philadelphia, PA (USA), 1881.

Future Systems Project 222

This house is all but invisible; only the ellipse-shaped glazed facade orientated towards the sea gives away the fact of human presence on the site. The facade has been described as a lens, cut into the landscape above the cliffs on the Welsh coastline, trained on the magnificent view west which gives the house its *raison d'être*. The rest of the structure, consisting of an arc-shaped retaining wall banked up with earth, and a plywood roof laid on a steel ring-beam, is camouflaged with grass. Inside, a single space is divided by free-standing service pods, containing the bathroom and kitchen, and is dominated by a large circular sofa. The architects have built their reputation on innovation, pushing their designs to the aesthetic and technical limits. This house represents a development of the 'unique language of curvaceous forms' which characterizes most of their work, not least the Media Centre at Lord's Cricket Ground (1999).

☛ Arad, Fuller, D Greene, Grimshaw, M Webb

Future Systems. Jan Kaplicky. b Prague (CZ), 1937. **Amanda Levette. b** Bridgend (UK), 1955. **Project 222**, St Bride's Bay, Wales (UK), 1994.

Gabriel Ange-Jacques   Le Petit Trianon

A 'simple' refuge from the pressures of court life in the Palace of Versailles, Le Petit Trianon is in studied contrast to the Baroque opulence of its neighbouring châteaux. The building, commissioned by Louis XV, gave Gabriel an opportunity to explore his emerging belief (reacting to the more elaborate architecture of his father, Jacques-Jules Gabriel) in the importance of classical proportioning, reason and discipline in architecture. This turn from sumptuous embellishment marks a transition from Rococo to Neo-Classicism, and toward the evolution of the 'Style Louis XVI'. Through such restraint, he achieved in this small counterpart to its seventeenth-century cousin, Le Grand Trianon, a refined simplicity. Square in plan with tripartite facades of restrained decoration, this attractive little house, in pale limestone and rose-pink marble, was a favourite retreat of Marie Antoinette.

☛ **Burlington, Campen, Le Vau & Hardouin-Mansart**

Ange-Jacques Gabriel. b Paris (FR), 1698. **d** Paris (FR), 1782. **Le Petit Trianon**, Versailles (FR), 1762–4.

Galician Celts

Palloza

This round, thatched-roof stone house, or *palloza*, is typically found along the north-west of the Iberian peninsula, in the foothills of the Galician and Asturian highlands. Often incorrectly compared to the rounded pre-Roman houses called *castrenas*, the *palloza* is different in terms of its size and layout. The design is, in fact, derived from the region's Celtic settlements. Oval or circular in shape, the huts have thatched, conical pitched roofs and usually an attached outhouse. The exterior is made of rough hewn granite or slate stone, and they range in diameter from 12 – 20 m (40 – 65 ft). The interior is divided into two levels; the upper level for the family's living area, the lower level to shelter livestock. Stone hearths at the centre of the living area were kept lit at all times to ward off evil spirits. Benches surround the hearth and were used for eating, story telling and sleeping. One of the *palozza* in this hamlet is now a museum of the region's Celtic heritage.

☛ **Finistère Farmers, Hebridean Crofter, Provençale Farmers**

Galician Celts. Active (SP), seventh century BC to present day. **Palloza**, O Cebreiro Hamlet, nr Lugo, Galicia (SP), c200 BC.

Gallén-Kallela Akseli   Kallela

Trained as a painter in Helsinki and Paris, Gallén-Kallela built this studio-house for himself and his young family after travelling through eastern Finland and Karelia to study folk art and vernacular architecture. During the period of the Grand Duchy of Finland (1809–1917), many artists looked to Finnish folk art and myth as a counter to the Russian, Neo-Classical culture of their political masters. When in Paris, Gallén-Kallela had started to paint scenes from the Finnish national epic, the *Kalevala*, which drew a great deal of attention when they were exhibited at the World's Fair in Paris in 1900. His timber-built studio-house inspired by Karelian farm buildings and set in woods sloping down to a lake, was an equivalent expression in architecture. This 'National Romanticism', as it came to be known, was further developed by such architects as Eliel Saarinen and Lars Sonck at the turn of the twentieth century.

☛ **Aalto, Gartman, Gesellius Lindgren & Saarinen, Vesnin**

140

Akseli Gallén-Kallela (Axel Waldemar Gallén). b Pori (FIN), 1865. d Stockholm (SW), 1931. **Kallela**, Ruovesi (FIN), 1894.

Gandhi Nari

House at Korjat

Cascading horizontal bands of red brickwork form a series of planted terraces and staircases leading up to this private residence. Set on an incline above a lake, the fortress-like entrance and facade appear to be concealed while the house comprises several separate pavilions which are linked by a walkway. Gandhi spent many years working for Frank Lloyd Wright in the US before returning to India in 1964. As a proponent of the organic architectural movement, Gandhi's buildings are sympathetic to their sites. Like other organic architects, he does not produce any drawings; construction is based on site markings that indicate how the building should grow, and details are developed *in situ*. Through utilizing local materials, drawing on historical Indo-Islamic architectural influences, and injecting modern-day forms and the sense of flowing space, he has created a harmonious, indigenous and contemporary Indian architectural style.

☛ **Chatterjee & Wheaton, Correa, Doshi, Wright**

Nari Gandhi. b Surat (IN), 1934. **House at Korjat**, Maharashtra (IN), c1993.

Gartman Victor   Artist's Studio and Guest House

The filigree carving on the cover-boards of this wooden house is so fine that it seems at odds with the rugged log walls. In fact, the patterns and hanging shapes are as much derived from peasant embroidery as from the traditional decoration of Russian peasant houses or *izbas*. This studio was the first new structure that the Moscow millionaire, Savva Mamontov, commissioned for the Abramtsevo estate after he bought it in 1871 and, inspired by William Morris, he decided to make it a centre for the revival of Russian peasant crafts. Gartman was then a leading figure in debates about how new architecture could encapsulate 'the spirit of the Russian people'. During this time, many countries in northern Europe were displaying a strong interest in Romantic Nationalism through the arts. Gartman's follower, Ivan Ropet, was commissioned to represent Russia in this nationalistic style at the International Exhibitions of Paris 1878, Copenhagen 1888 and Chicago 1893.

☛ **A J Davis, Morris, Nikitin, Peter the Great, Tolstoy, Vesnin**

Victor Alexandrovich (Eduard) Gartman. **b** St Petersburg (RUS), 1834. **d** Kireevo, nr Moscow (RUS), 1873. **Artist's Studio and Guest House**, Abramtsevo, nr Moscow (RUS), 1873.

Gaudí Antoni   Palau Güell

Gaudí, the most famous participant in the renaissance of Catalan culture, is celebrated for his extraordinary individualistic style. This was based on the ancient Spanish *Mudéjar* style and an innovative view of structure, using parabolic arches. The salon of the Palau Güell shows this in the ironwork of the screens, coiled lamp brackets, and the arches supporting the high lantern roof. This is studded with star-like openings, giving it a Moorish flavour and, outside, the appearance of a termite heap, speckled with peepholes. Opening off it is a small oratory and, on the left, a gallery overlooking the street. To the right, stairs rise to the private rooms, reached from the mezzanine behind the screen. The galleries above have carved screen shutters, so that members of the family may see without being seen. This extraordinary room, with its great height and variety of openings, works well at interlocking the spaces, making it very much the heart of the house.

☛ **Domènech, Guimard, Horta, Mackintosh**

143

Antoni Gaudí y Cornet. **b** Reus, nr Tarragona (SP), 1852. **d** Barcelona (SP), 1926. **Palau Güell**, Barcelona (SP), 1885–9.

Gehry Frank

Gehry House

This view of the entrance to Gehry's own house, on a quiet residential street, demonstrates his attempt to capture the quality of the existing gambrel-roofed, asbestos-shingled bungalow within an iconoclastic reconstructed shell, thus celebrating it as an *objet trouvé*. Constructed of fragmented forms made of cheap materials – such as chainlink fencing, plywood and corrugated metal – the house creates a shocking impression with its pierced and skewed forms caught as if in the midst of an earthquake, while acknowledging the iconic quality of the suburban house. Gehry, who won the Pritzker Prize, the lifetime achievement in architecture award, in 1989, was loosely associated with Deconstructivism and Post-Modernism, and went on from this early domestic scale to work on his renowned, large public buildings; in particular, the iconic, steel-clad Guggenheim Museum in Bilbao of 1997.

☛ CZWG, Eisenman, Israel, Moss, Stern, Venturi

144

Frank Owen Gehry. b Toronto (CAN), 1929. **Gehry House**, Santa Monica, CA (USA), 1978.

Geisler Mikhail & Guslisty Boris   Nabokov Residence

On the smart Bolshaya Morskaya street near the Winter Palace, one could easily pass by this house amidst the ponderous eclecticism around it, until the sunshine suddenly catches the gold of the frieze. The subtle synthesis of Art Nouveau with a light eclecticism suggests the tastes of an interesting and original client – establishment yet progressive – and that was precisely the case. The work of respectable but not famous architects, this was the city residence of the noble Nabokov family, enlarged from a two-storey house for the growing family of one of the Tsarist government's most intelligent and liberal-minded statesmen, Vladimir Dmitrievich Nabokov, who played a progressive political role right up to the October Revolution of 1917. His son, also Vladimir, grew up here and, in enforced emigration after 1917, became famous as a writer – author of the scandal-raising novel *Lolita*, amongst much else.

☛ **Apyshkov, Guimard, Horta, Rastrelli, Shekhtel**

Geisler Mikhail & Guslisty Boris

Mikhail Fedorovich Geisler. **b** 1861. **d** after 1930. **Boris Fedorovich Guslisty**. **b** 1871. **d** 1915. **Nabokov Residence**, St Petersburg (RUS), 1901–2.

Gesellius Lindgren & Saarinen

Hvitträsk

Sweeping roofs, shingle-hung gables and field stone recall the English Arts and Crafts movement and the Neo-Romanticism of H H Richardson. Hvitträsk is a romantic idea: a community where the architects could entertain their artist friends, including the composer, Jean Sibelius. Finnish artists found artistic-utopian ideals attractive because they sanctioned a national identity based around indigenous materials, folklore and language, without provoking political repression during a period when Finland was a Russian Grand Duchy. The grand scale of Hvitträsk – set around a courtyard above a lake – hints at an Arts-and-Crafts dichotomy. Artistic communities for the bourgeoisie would inevitably be larger buildings than the vernacular dwellings which were their supposed models. And the provocative composition, such as the relationship between the off-centre bay window and the gable, demands conceptual thinking that is the preserve of architecture rather than craft.

☛ Aalto, Morris, Richardson, Saarinen, Voysey, P Webb

Gesellius Lindgren & Saarinen. Hermann Gesellius. b Helsinki (FIN), 1874. d Kirkkonummi (FIN), 1916. Armas Lindgren. b Helsinki (FIN), 1874. d Helsinki (FIN), 1929. Eliel Saarinen. b Rantasalmir (FIN), 1873. d Bloomfield Hills, MI (USA), 1950. Hvitträsk, Kirkkonummi, nr Helsinki (FIN), 1901–3.

Geyter Xaveer de   House in Brasschaat

Glass walls loosely defining living spaces that open onto enclosed courtyards belie the private nature of this ultra-modern villa. Taking advantage of a natural forested hill on this small suburban site, the architect buries the front of the structure into a dune, leaving only the canopy of the rooftop garage and entry exposed to its neighbours. Inverting the example of Le Corbusier's *architectural promenade*, a ramp takes the visitor down towards the single-storey living quarters with their glass curtain walls. The ramp also acts as the divider between the private spaces, which open onto enclosed patios, and the communal living spaces, which open to the terrace and views of the garden beyond. The result is an open plan that still maintains a high level of privacy between the rooms. The architect successfully develops the concept of the airy Mies van der Rohe courtyard house, while gracefully, and originally, overcoming the site's suburban constraints.

☛ **Koolhaas, Le Corbusier, Mies van der Rohe, Rogers**

Xaveer de Geyter. **b** Doornik (BEL), 1957. **House in Brasschaat**, Antwerp (BEL), 1990–3.

Gill Irving & Mead Frank   Bailey House

Sitting high above the ocean in La Jolla, California, this curious house appears out-of-place in the stark landscape of the rock cliffs. Designed by Gill in 1907 during a short-lived partnership with Frank Mead, an American who had recently returned from North Africa, the house combines an eclectic mix of Arts-and-Crafts detailing, popular Spanish Mission motifs and Moorish features. At the request of the client, who was from the Midwest, this weekend home was designed to resemble a barn with a large, double-height living room and an open balcony hallway leading to the upstairs bedrooms. Gill was trained in the Chicago office of Louis Sullivan, along with the young Frank Lloyd Wright, before setting up his own practice in 1893. His progressive politics, his fight to improve building standards, and his pioneering use of cubic forms and architectural concrete have earned him a reputation as one of the unsung heroes of early American Modernism.

☞ **Greene & Greene, Maybeck, Raymond, Schindler, Sullivan**

148

Irving John Gill. b Syracuse, NY (USA), 1870. **d** Lakeside, CA (USA), 1936. **Frank Mead. b** Camden, NJ (USA), 1865. **d** (USA), 1940. **Bailey House**, La Jolla, CA (USA), 1907.

Girolamo II

Trulli

These conical stone houses, or *trulli*, are to be found in the rocky plateau area of Apulia, at the heel of the Italian 'boot', and give its central region, the Murgia of the Trulli, its name. A primitive method of building, developed to its current form in the early seventeenth century by the formidable Count Girolamo II, the *trulli* were constructed without mortar using a corbelling system. Doorways and larger openings are often arched, using the same technique, so as to make them stronger. When the King's tax collectors were due, they could easily be dismantled (and later rebuilt) so that no house tax was demanded. Built as clusters of square stone cells forming rooms, each one was spanned by a cone, the most important room having the highest roof. The conical roofs were coursed in rough tufa stone, usually with a finial like a golf ball on a tee at its pinnacle. The walls and corner chimneys are painted white, which contrasts attractively with the sea of grey roofs.

☛ **Galician Celts, Inuit, Santorini Islanders, Syrian Farmers**

149

Count Girolamo II. b Apulia (IT), c1600. **d** Barcelona (SP), 1665. **Trulli**, Alberobello, Apulia (IT), circa seventeenth century to 1950s, still lived in today.

Gitano

Excavated Dwellings

While one of the earliest forms of human dwelling, at least forty million people around the world today still live in caves, excavated or natural. Excavated dwellings are usually carved from soft rock which hardens on exposure to air, and provide dry, thermally comfortable and totally environmentally integrated accommodation. These *Gitano* dwellings in Andalucia, southern Spain, some up to 5 m (16 ft) wide, can be excavated in only a week, and may have first been carved by the Moors in the fourteenth century. A chimney is tunnelled vertically through the rock, and a vaulted ceiling gives strength to the dwelling. The windows and doors are carved as though a regular house had been inserted into the white-washed rock face. The collapse of some excavated dwellings after heavy rains has caused many *Gitano* to leave, but migrant workers and young people seeking a simple – and economic – life continue to maintain the tradition.

☛ Anchorites, C Johnson, Loess Han, Pueblo Indians

150

Gitano. Active (SP), from early sixteenth century to present day. **Excavated Dwellings**, Guadix (SP), sixteenth century to present day.

Giulio Romano

Palazzo del Tè

The single-storey Palazzo del Tè demonstrates the dexterity inherent in the work of Giulio Romano, one-time pupil of Raphael. Among the earliest buildings in, what was to become, the Mannerist style, the palazzo was originally built on an island as a summer retreat for Duke Federigo Gonzaga. Although influenced by Raphael's Villa Madama, Romano deliberately flouted Classical rules, and arranged four distinct wings around a central courtyard, with a garden to one side. The consciously juxtaposed and subtly irregular architectural elements create an air of unease – keystones appear to slip from the window arches, and smooth Serlian motifs contrast with excessively rough, rusticated facades. This unease is continued inside where heightened-perspectival frescos blur the edges of the walls and ceiling. From this, Romano went on to build authoritatively in an intellectual interpretation of the Classical vocabulary, combined with his own dissolute free expression.

☛ **Bigio, L'Orme, Raphael, Sangallo, Vasari**

Giulio Romano (Giulio Pippi or Giuliano Giannuzzi). **b** Rome (IT), 1499. **d** Mantua (IT), 1546. **Palazzo del Tè**, Mantua (IT), 1526–34.

'The most gaped-at new house in the US', said *Life* magazine of the Bavinger House, one of an extraordinary series of experimental houses designed by Bruce Goff. The house was self-built by the sculptor-client, Bavinger, with his family and his students. Sited on a small, rocky ravine – the bridge helps stabilize the house – a single mast, made of two oil-drilling pipes and old biplane wires, supports a copper-covered timber roof over a single, continuous spiral space. The kitchen and bathroom are tucked into the core of the spiral. Protruding into the main space are a series of open pods, for dining or sleeping, upholstered top and bottom, with separating curtains and netting. A rubble-stone wall wraps around this form, rising from 2 m to 15 m (6 ft to 50 ft) at the centre. While Goff's work had moved on from his early influences by Frank Lloyd Wright, he continued to develop the use of site, materials and programme as key elements.

☛   **Bruder, Day, H Greene, Prince, Reynolds, Wright**

Bruce Goff. **b** Alton, KS (USA), 1904. **d** Tyler, TX (USA), 1982. **Bavinger House**, Norman, OK (USA), 1950–5.

Goldfinger Ernö   Willow Road

Ironically, the protest that greeted plans for Goldfinger's houses at Willow Road was based on the mistaken belief that they were to be white concrete, like other Modern houses of the time. In fact, they were the most successful integration of pre-war Modernism into the powerful and much-loved British tradition of the Georgian terrace. Three houses are grouped into a single, elegantly proportioned terrace, the *piano nobile* visible through large first-floor windows. The proportions are Georgian, the brickwork contextual, but the language is clearly Modernist. The horizontal windows feature Goldfinger's first use of the 'photobolic screen', the horizontal plane at the top of the window which bounces light deep into the room. Inside, many of the walls fold away; on the top floor, the three children's bedrooms open to form a single playroom. Goldfinger's own house was the slightly larger, middle of the three, and is now a museum owned by the National Trust.

☞ Connell, Fry, Le Corbusier, Lubetkin, Luckhardt

Ernö Goldfinger. **b** Budapest (HUN), 1902. **d** London (UK), 1987. **Willow Road**, London (UK), 1937.

Goodman Charles Hollin Hills

Transparent and light, this flat-roofed and purposely simple prefabricated house was part of a grand experiment to provide efficient and economical housing. Begun in 1949, Hollin Hills was one of America's first post-war 'modern' communities and became a laboratory for Goodman's experiments in prefabrication. Over the course of a little more than two decades, 458 homes were built in this wooded suburb of Washington DC. Goodman went on to work as a consulting architect to the National Homes Corporation, a manufacturer of prefabricated houses, where at least 100,000 of his houses were produced. His work involved experimenting with new materials, such as aluminum, in an attempt to create light, open houses. A wall, he wrote, is 'a series of parts joined together... the opaque element and the transparent element which allows you to have privacy where you want it and openness where you want it'.

☛ **Eichler, Fry, Goldfinger, Prouvé, Segal**

Charles Goodman. b (USA), 1906. **d** (USA), 1992. **Hollin Hills**, Fairfax County, VA (USA), begun 1949.

Grataloup Daniel   Maison d'Anières

There is not a single right-angle nor symmetrical element in this house, according to the architect. Its form is the result of his in-depth study of functionality and movement expressed as a unity of shapes and materials and realized through high technology. It is the first sprayed concrete, double-skinned monocoque, or single shell, house of its kind in the world; its structure, walls, roof, chimney, furniture and fittings, benches and even storage bins are all formed from the double-skin layer of mesh sprayed with concrete. The house is spacious and luxurious; its free-form interiors, with curved benches, sofas and a sculptural fireplace, also feature an in-built hi-fi system and adjustable coloured lighting panels. The rooms are large, sometimes as high as 8 m (26 ft) and the windows can be up to 3 m (10 ft) in diameter. The house was built in five months and Grataloup claims construction costs for this form of building are 30 per cent lower than traditional construction methods.

☛ Arad, Hübner-Forster-Hübner, Keisler, Senosiain

155

Daniel Grataloup. b Lyon (FR), 1937. **Maison d'Anières**, Lake Geneva (SW), 1972.

Graves Michael   Plocek House

From its sloping wooded site, the Plocek House projects a firm, classical street-side facade, its three storeys divided into basement, *piano nobile* and attic. The house boasts a grand entrance intended both to reinforce its sense of scale and to imbue it with human proportions. A garden pavilion, set apart from the house, serves as a quiet study. With its reinterpreted, exaggerated classicism and muted palette, the Plocek House is the first of Graves' buildings to show this development in his style. Originally influenced by the Modernism of Le Corbusier, Graves became one of the New York Five architects or 'Five Whites', so named for the absence of colour in their work. Since then, however, he has moved towards designing witty and erudite buildings that have a human scale and exaggerated historical forms. Before the Plocek House, earlier works hinted at Graves' personal vocabulary, but it is with this residence that his distinguished style is revealed.

☛ Eisenman, Gwathmey, Meier, Stern, Venturi

Michael Graves. b Indianapolis, IN (USA), 1934. **Plocek House**, Warren, NJ (USA), 1982.

Gray Eileen & Badovici Jean   Villa E-1027

Built as a small vacation house on a spectacular, isolated site overlooking the Mediterranean, this house was designed with a 'minimum of space, maximum of comfort' in collaboration with its occupant, Jean Badovici. Its name corresponds to the coded initials of its creators: E=Eileen, 10=J, 2=B and 7=G. Composed of a regular, rectangular volume and adjoining terrace, the house – Gray's most famous work and an important example of Modernist architecture – is subdivided according to functional demands, and its sensuous yet practical furnishings contributed to its sense of intimacy. Le Corbusier also painted murals on the walls and built his own cabin nearby. As the designers wrote in a 1929 edition of *L'Architecture vivante* :

'This very small house thus has, concentrated in a very small space, all that might be useful for comfort and to help indulge in *joie de vivre*.' Gray built little and is today mainly known for her highly innovative furniture and interior design.

☞ Chareau, Le Corbusier, Mallet-Stevens, Perriand, Prouvé

Eileen Gray. **b** Enniscorthy (IRE), 1878. **d** Paris (FR), 1976. **Jean Badovici. b** Bucharest (ROM), 1893. **d** Monaco (MON), 1956. **Villa E-1027**, Roquebrune (FR), 1926–9.

Greene & Greene

Gamble House

One of the Greene brothers' 'ultimate bungalows', the Gamble House exhibits the plaited nature and superb craftsmanship of their aesthetic: an interweaving of textures, of timber shingles, clinker brick and wooden battening. The layered nature of this construction is also reflective of an interweaving of traditions: Gustav Stickley and the American Arts and Crafts movement,

and the Japanese tradition of wooden construction were both absorbed by the Greenes and seemlessly synthesized in a vernacular regionalist idiom shared by such other California architects as Bernard Maybeck and Julia Morgan. The house is less open on the interior than Frank Lloyd Wright's Prairie houses, but makes extensive use of verandas and balconies to

exploit the views over a riverbed and distant mountains. The rich interiors of mahogany and teakwood exude a sense of ease suitable to the relaxed, idyllic lifestyle of Pasadena at the turn of the century.

☞ **Mackintosh, Maybeck, Morgan, Sullivan, Wright**

Greene & Greene. **Charles Sumner Greene. b** Brighton, OH (USA), 1868. **d** Carmel, CA (USA), 1957. **Henry Mather Greene. b** Brighton, OH (USA), 1870. **d** Pasadena, CA (USA), 1954. **Gamble House**, Pasadena, CA (USA), 1907–9.

Greene David — Living Pod

This model of an experimental living pod combines an exploration of the contrasting demands of our daily lives (physical and functional needs) with the efficiency of a biologically determined organism. The interior is zoned into living areas for work, sleep and play, the space being modified with inflatable furniture or dividers as required. Machines attached to the exterior of the pod provide necessary services: such as an eating machine, wash capsule, clothing dispensers and climate control; being external, these elements can easily be adapted or replaced. The pod can be freestanding and self-contained, or plugged into a service structure, clustering together to create a community. David Greene was a member of Archigram, a group whose seemingly wild conceptual schemes were realized mainly through their influence rather than direct execution – the high-tech service pods of Richard Rogers' Lloyds Building being the most obvious example.

☛ Grataloup, Horden, Kiesler, Rogers, M Webb

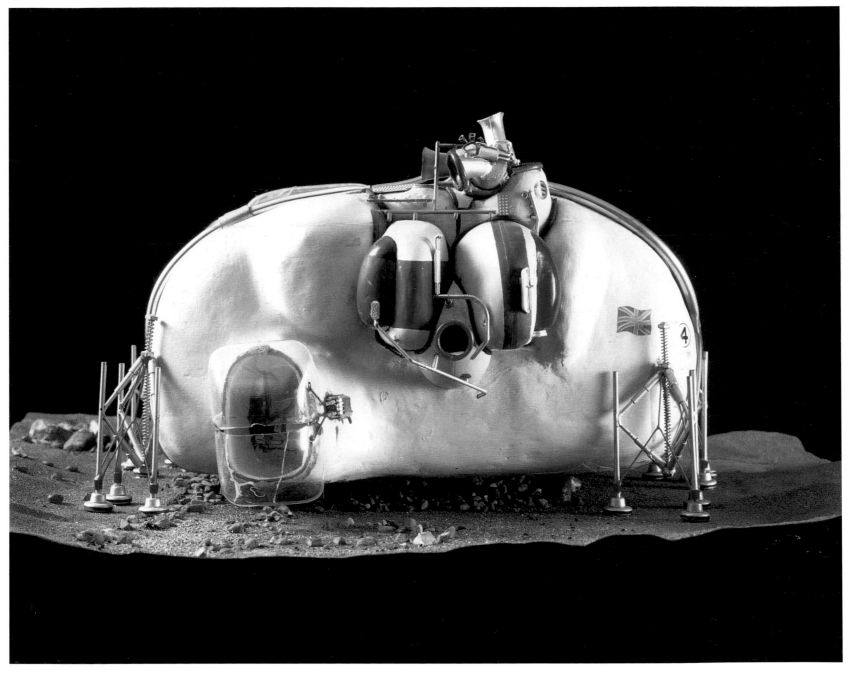

David Greene. **b** Nottingham (UK), 1937. **Living Pod**, project, 1965.

Greene Herb

Greene Residence

Herb Greene based the form of his house on that of the American buffalo, which used to roam the prairies of the Midwest in great numbers. He tried to inject a feeling of pathos into the 'looming, wounded creature' that is the house; but it also evokes a natural shelter, with the entrance under a metaphorical spreading wing, like that of a mother hen. There is a strong sense of accretion and collage, an organic gathering of form and materials to create a strong physical presence. Inside, the house is cave-like, the irregularly-layered wooden shingles creating comforting texture and rhythms; while the relation of the different levels and the expression of the exterior form internally are simultaneously dramatic and vertiginous. Greene was one of the most talented architects to study under Bruce Goff, whose eclectic expressionistic style has clearly influenced Greene's work, as well as his humanistic approach to organic architecture, expressive of life and feeling.

☛ Bruder, Droppers, Goff, Grose Bradley, Prince

160

Herb Greene. b New York, NY (USA), 1929. **Greene Residence (Praire Chicken House)**, Norman, OK (USA), 1961.

Grimshaw Nicholas   Housing at Grand Union Walk

The technology and materials of light-industrial units are an unusual choice for single-family housing in the heart of London. However, these houses were built as part of a planning requirement for Grimshaw's adjoining high-tech, hangar-like Sainsbury's supermarket – and they share its language. Limited to gaining light from its north facade, the first-floor, double-height living space, with split-level balconies, is lit by a high glass wall which slides up electronically to extend the living area onto the balcony. A curved metal wall billows out over the Grand Union Canal, inset with aeroplane-style windows, enclosing the more private areas. On the lower floor is a professional room for working at home, with direct access to the private canal-side deck. Grimshaw is better known for his larger-scale, high-tech industrialized assembly buildings (such as the Waterloo International Terminus of 1993), but here successfully applies these aesthetics to housing.

☞ **Architecture Studio, Chipperfield, Future Systems, Ritchie**

Nicholas Grimshaw. b Hove (UK), 1939. **Housing at Grand Union Walk**, London (UK), 1986–8.

Groote Christian de   Errazuriz House

This house is in communion with its setting, yet it has a dominant visual presence, emphasizing the verticality and layering of its structure. The Chilean architect, Christian de Groote, has designed some 400 individual houses, and each one has come from an instinctive response to the site and the needs of his client. He says, 'I always endeavour to make my work contextual; my idea of context cannot be reduced either to the geographic issue or the concept of place … [it is] like the constellation of data around the problem.' The challenge of this deeply-sloping site – with its breathtaking views to the Villarrica volcano – was to link it to the lake without destroying its natural beauty. The front facade is terraced, with projections defined by the retained surrounding trees. The raw qualities of materials – fair-faced shuttered concrete, rough hewn and substantial joinery – are expressed sculpturally throughout and there is a consistent rhythm in the geometry of the elements.

☞ Chilote Islanders, Donovan Hill, Edmond & Corrigan, Meier

162

Christian de Groote. b Valdivia (CH), 1931. Errazuriz House, Villarrica (CH), 1998.

Gropius Walter   Double House

White, cuboid forms, asymmetrical composition and fenestration which elevates function to expression – the tall windows light and denote stairwells, the large window an artist's studio – are hallmarks of European Modernism. And this 'double house', one of three pairs designed by Gropius for staff at the Bauhaus, comes from the heart of that movement.

Like the school itself, the form suggests equilibrium between dynamic forces rather than symmetrical balance; the two large blocks at either end almost strain to rotate around the central arm. Large, first-floor studios are the principal spaces, a device which shows its ancestry in late nineteenth-century artists' houses, such as those by Norman Shaw. Despite its

artistic intentions, there is also a room in the house for servants. Gropius had to meet the demands of bourgeois occupants – though they be artists – as Bauhaus staff included the likes of Kandinsky, Klee and Schlemmer.

☞ Breuer, Fry, Le Corbusier, Mies van der Rohe, Muche

Walter Gropius. **b** Berlin (GER), 1883. **d** Boston, MA (USA), 1969. **Double House**, Dessau (GER), 1926.

Grose Bradley Newman House

You would be forgiven for thinking the inspiration behind the Newman House was too many bad sci-fi TV shows; it looks like an early spaceship that has mistakenly landed in the Australian bush. In fact, the house at Balgownie draws on a long-standing Australian tradition – the steel-framed, corrugated iron-clad architecture of farm buildings and sheep stations. Although corrugated iron gets hot in the Australian sun, it is a good conductive material so the heat dissipates quickly. It is also cheap, light and durable – qualities that endear it to many contemporary Australian architects. Few use it, however, with such aplomb as Sydney-based architects, Grose Bradley (a husband and wife team). Pushing the shed analogy further still, they installed agricultural rotary ventilators along the roof edge to help keep temperatures inside the house cool. The Newman House is one of Grose Bradley's earlier projects and won the prestigious Wilkinson award for architecture in 1992.

☛ Andrews, Clare Design, H Greene, Murcutt, Poole, Ritchie

Grose Bradley. James Grose. b Brisbane, QLD (ASL), 1954. Nicola Bradley. b Kuala Lumpur (MALAY), 1956. Newman House, Balgownie, Woollongong, NSW (ASL), 1991.

Guarini Guarino — Palazzo Carignano

Undulating, convex-concave curves – so typical of Roman Baroque churches – ripple along the entire facade of the Palazzo Carignano linking two rectangular wings. The facades are made from unstuccoed terracotta that has been moulded to form elaborate window frames and a Baroque form of rustication. Behind the central curve, at *piano nobile* level, is the oval main salon of the palace. Vaulted up to an open oculus, the salon is top-lit by clerestory windows, with a cupola above concealing the source of this light. The processional route through the palace begins with a dark entrance hall which leads through to the oval undercroft of the salon. Here, twinned stairways lead back towards the street before returning to the central axis and the light of the salon. Guarini's architecture, which is mainly found in Turin, can be characterized by his interest in spatial experimentation and use of three-dimensional geometry.

☞ **Fischer von Erlach, Hildebrandt, Pöppelmann, Portoghesi**

Guarino Guarini. **b** Modena (IT), 1624. **d** Turin (IT), 1683. **Palazzo Carignano**, Turin (IT), 1679.

Guimard Hector   Hôtel Guimard

This flamboyant Art Nouveau townhouse was built by Hector Guimard for himself and his new wife, the American painter and heiress, Adeline Oppenheim. It shows Guimard's interest in a rich mix of materials; brick, cast stone, natural stone, faïence and terracotta, and his use of organic motifs, which also dominate his famous Paris Metro entrances. His office was on the ground floor and the large windows on the third floor light his wife's studio. Guimard always emphasized the intellectual rigour of his work, saying 'I have only applied Viollet-le-Duc's theory [of structural rationalism] but without being hypnotised by medieval forms'. Instead, he believed that, 'it is to nature that we must look for advice … for unity achieved by infinite variety.' Whereas Victor Horta had applied English wallpaper and fittings to his Hôtel Tassel interiors, Guimard designed everything himself, from carpets to table linens, featuring the whiplash curves which epitomize the Art Nouveau style.

☛ Doménech, Gaudi, Horta, Morris, Viollet-le-Duc

Hector Guimard. b Lyon (FR), 1867. d New York, NY (USA), 1942. Hôtel Guimard, Paris (FR), 1909–12.

Gunnløgsson Halldor   Gunnløgsson House

One of the protagonists of the 'new tradition' in post-war Danish architecture, Gunnløgsson imbued this simple house with his interpretation of a traditional Danish lifestyle. The house acknowledges the impact on Danish architecture of such influential figures as Mies van der Rohe and Frank Lloyd Wright. This can be seen in the rigorous modular plan laid out on a 2 m (6.5 ft) grid and the simple load-bearing timber structure with brick infill. In contrast to these influences, Gunnløgsson incorporated more traditional elements, such as the central fireplace and fir-board ceilings. Furniture and fittings designed by some of his well-known contemporaries and countrymen, such as Poul Kjaerholm, Kåre Klint and Arne Jacobsen, were selected to complement the open spatial quality of the house. With its simple, open plan and finely-detailed traditional timber, stone and brick, the house constitutes one of the finest Modern houses built in Denmark.

☛ Holscher, A Jacobsen, Mies van der Rohe, Wright

Halldor Gunnløgsson. b Copenhagen (DK), 1918. **d** Rungsted (DK), 1985. **Gunnløgsson House**, Rungsted, Strandjev (DK), 1958.

Gwathmey Charles

Gwathmey House and Studio

Set in a former potato field, this house and artist's studio were intended to appear sculpted, as though carved out of a solid block of wood. Charles Gwathmey, a leading Modernist and one of the New York Five, began work on the larger of the two structures, the house itself (in the foreground) in 1965, and completed the studio in 1967. The clients were his parents, a painter and a photographer, who commissioned their son just after he left his apprenticeship with Edward Larrabee Barnes. The interiors echo the geometries of the exterior: a workroom and guest bedrooms on the ground floor, and an external staircase leading up to a double-height living room on the first floor, with kitchen and dining areas. The studio block is positioned at an angle to the main house; the design intent was to create a sense of movement between the two. Gwathmey later went on to design the addition to a great, sculptural masterpiece, Frank Lloyd Wright's Guggenheim Museum.

☞ Barnes, Eisenman, Graves, Meier, Moore

Charles Gwathmey. b Charlotte, NC (USA), 1938. Gwathmey House and Studio, Amagansett, NY (USA), 1965–7.

Hadrian

Villa Adriana

One of the great pleasures of Roman Emperors was to build. Hadrian's biographer records that, in this sprawling complex, part-palace, part-administrative centre, he indulged himself by naming parts of it after famous places in Egypt and Greece to remind himself of his travels across the Empire. Amid this array of dining pavilions, towers, libraries, baths, gardens and walks, Hadrian also built himself an inner sanctum, surrounded by a circular enclosing wall and canal. Here, the standard plan of a Roman house – lobby, atrium, *tablinum* or large room – is reworked in a circular geometry; the sequence of curves and counter–curves transform it into a retreat fit for an Emperor. Heated baths to the left (which lead to the canal so that it can be used as a swimming pool), and a tiny library chamber to the right complete the ensemble. Beyond is a tower where guests could dine while enjoying an uninterrupted view of the setting sun.

☛ **Maiuri, Minoan, Pompeii Romans, Tiberius**

Emperor Publius Aelius Hadrian. b Italica, nr Seville (SP), AD 76. d Naples (IT), AD 138. **Villa Adriana (Hadrian's Villa)**, Tivoli (IT), AD 118–134, restored 1956.

Hara Hiroshi

Ito House

The Ito House consists of three discrete structures, with minimal openings, set in a forest in Nagasaki, Japan. Two exposed wood-shingle cubes – 6.4 m (21 ft) and 5.2 m (17 ft) – are designated as wings for the parents and children respectively, while a long corridor-like structure contains a study. Using cubes that progress in size in increments of 0.6 m (2 ft), Hara examines whether there is a connection between arithmetical progression and behaviour patterns of the inhabitants of the cubes. He also suggests an alternative future society where the idea of community – in this case, of family – is dissolved and each individual, equipped with information technology, must devise his or her own world. This building composition not only expresses Hara's opinion on the pathological aspects of houses in contemporary society, but also his intensive exploration of an alternative typology.

☛ Dewes & Puente, Lacaton Vassal, Ogawa, Sejima

Hiroshi Hara. b Kanagawa (JAP), 1936. **Ito House**, Nagasaki (JAP), 1998.

Hariri & Hariri
Barry's Bay Cottage

The sweeping thrust of the wooden deck draws the eye along the sensual facade of this cottage on its way to the expansive vistas and flow of the natural setting beyond. This effect is characteristic of Hariri & Hariri's manipulation of the inherent sensuality of the natural setting, materials and form. The design details of this new cottage speak to the existing elements of the site, including the original and now incorporated A-frame cottage which is just 1 m (3 ft) away: the horizontal slot windows referring to the markings on the bark of the surrounding birch trees; the fluid arc of the deck to the lakefront beyond; and even the pitched roof to that of the old cottage. Hariri & Hariri, as members of the Post-Modern era, have become known for their innovative play on natural and manmade, new and old. Their attention to the poetics of all form has differentiated their work and placed them at the forefront of a new generation of contemporary architects.

☛ Donovan Hill, Holl, Hølmebakk, Jersey Devil

Hariri & Hariri. **Gisue Hariri. b** Abadan (IR), 1956. **Mojgan Hariri. b** Aghajari (IR), 1958. **Barry's Bay Cottage**, ON (CAN), 1992.

Harvey Earl   Driftwood Tree Huts

When his son died in a boating accident in 1971, Earl Harvey built these two structures, perched in the top of two redwood trees, as a memorial. Constructed over a period of four years, the timber was salvaged from driftwood and the limbs of lumbered redwoods. The two huts are fixed precariously in the live, forked tree trunks, the leafy branches pushing up beneath giving them the appearance of having sprouted spontaneously from the trees themselves. The huts are accessed (mostly by local children) via a winding stair supported on steel reinforcing bars hammered into the tree trunk. One hut contains a fully-functioning wood-burning stove, while the other houses a more fanciful 'wishing well' – a piece of pipe that winds its way from the floor of the hut to the ground. Dropping coins into a slot in the floor, the children can listen to them rattle their way down to the ground while they make their wish.

☛ **Day, Goff, H Greene, Van der Merwe Miszewski**

Earl Harvey. Active mid to late twentieth century. **Driftwood Tree Huts**, Eureka, CA (USA), 1975.

Hasegawa Itsuko   House in Nerima

Itsuko Hasegawa based this house on the layout of the client's former home, which had been developed to reflect the family's lifestyle. It consists of two main parts: a two-storey residence for the parents and a detached unit for their daughter, connected by exterior staircases and terraces covered with undulating roofs. The metal staircases, which link two terraces and a belvedere with a moon-viewing platform, create a unique sequence of spaces that cannot be experienced as either completely exterior or interior. Perforated metal screens, together with the metal roof decks, contrast with the structural concrete elements; at the same time, their abstracted forms express patterns derived from natural elements. Developing on the abstracted geometric forms seen in her early works of the 1970s, Hasegawa here makes elaborate use of the dense urban conditions of Tokyo to create an alternative space where a poetic life is suggested.

☛ **Gehry, Ishiyama, Ito, Okada & Tomiyama, Shinohara**

Itsuko Hasegawa. b Shizuoka (JAP), 1941. **House in Nerima**, Tokyo (JAP), 1986.

Hausa

Merchant's House

The elaborately decorated facade of this Hausa townhouse, deeply moulded in mud plaster, depicts symbolic designs (such as the *dagi*, an endless knot signifying eternity), as well as those of personal significance which would also establish the status of the owner. The Hausa, a Muslim people of northern Nigeria, are mainly urban and many live in traditional cities, such as Kano and Zaria. The Hausa townhouse consists of a walled compound containing several separate one-room buildings within it. Each is constructed of pear-shaped earth bricks, called *tabali*, which are laid in mud mortar and then covered with a mud plaster. The flat roofs are constructed by arranging lengths of palm into a tight mesh, over which raffia mats and earth are laid. At the corners moulded pinnacles, of probable pre-Islamic origin, are raised. A platform seat beside the door is for visitors, who are seldom admitted beyond the *zaure* or entrance room.

☞ Dogon, Isidore, Tiwa Indians, Yazdi

Hausa. Active (NIG), from early nineteenth century to present day. **Merchant's House**, Kano (NIG), twentieth century.

Havana Creole

Casa del Conde de Lombillo

Standing out from its crumbling neighbours, this restored townhouse in Old Havana shows many of the typical details of Cuba's Spanish colonial architecture. The house – a palace of the Count of Lombillo in its heyday – overlooks the Plaza Vieja, one of the Cuban capital's oldest plazas, dating from the sixteenth century. Like many of the Plaza Vieja's houses, it would have been built of stone or brick, covered in stucco and painted in bright colours. At ground floor, a deep arcade joins those of neighbouring homes to create a covered sidewalk protected from the tropical sun. A monumental, classical portal, with a split pediment and high pedestal columns, leads inside the home, which is organized around a narrow central courtyard. On the first floor, a series of arched windows boast the fan-shaped, stained-glass panes typical of these colonial houses. Today, true to Cuba's prevalent communist ideology, the house has been converted into fourteen low-cost homes.

☛ **Bawa, Calrow, Mora, Tarifa**

Havana Creole. Active (CU), mid-sixteenth century to present day. **Casa del Conde de Lombillo**, Old Havana (CU), 1745, restored 1989.

Hawksmoor Nicholas

Easton Neston

Hawksmoor's first independent work was this great rectangular block for Sir William Fermor, completed in 1702. Its use of the Giant Composite order and tight vertical emphasis could be said to reflect the architect's personality – dour, proud and reticent. Hawksmoor learned the Baroque style while working for Sir Christopher Wren, whom he consulted on the design.

The slightly projecting central bay is the only emphasis on the garden facade, and the main entrance on the far side is much the same, except for the occasional curved pediment. However, these never interrupt the balustraded parapet, which seems to check the upward rush of pilasters and pulls the whole design together. Although this was the only country house

Hawksmoor designed, he helped his colleague Vanbrugh, whose houses echo this prototype. Wren said of Hawksmoor that there never was 'a more reasonable man, nor one so little prejudiced in favour of his own performance.' Here is the proof.

☛ **Fischer von Erlach, Talman, Tichborne, Vanbrugh, Wolsey**

Nicholas Hawksmoor. b East Prayton (UK), 1661. **d** London (UK), 1736. **Easton Neston**, Northamptonshire (UK), c1696–1702.

Hebridean Crofter

Crofter's Cottage

This is a traditional crofter's cottage, with two fireplaces, not the usual single one, but otherwise just as built for centuries in the Scottish Highlands and Islands where agriculture is devoted to hill-sheep. With little profit, crofters used to build with whatever the locality could provide – rubble-stone, earth, rough timber, straw and heather. Their single room might perhaps be partitioned so as to give one end some privacy; otherwise beds were set into cupboards under the low roof. The single hearth was usually set at one end beneath a 'hingin' lum' ('hanging chimney') – a kind of hood hung over the fireplace and supporting a chimney. In addition, thick clay walls would help keep out the cold. Because both these and rubble-stone walls had to be proofed against driving rain, they would be covered in limewash, and the roof thatched in straw or heather, which was sometimes kept in place against gales by rope nets.

☛ **Antrim Labourers, Breton, Finistère Farmers, Galician Celts**

177

Hebridean Crofter. Active Scotland (UK), late sixteenth century to present day. **Crofter's Cottage**, North Uist, Hebrides, Scotland (UK), late sixteenth century to circa eighteenth century.

Henri IV

Pavillon du Roi

When the Place Royale (now Place des Vosges) was conceived in 1603 by Henri IV, the guiding hand was that of his Queen, Marie de' Medici, who brought to Paris the Italian fashion for regularly laid-out squares with dominating features in key positions. So the centres of the north and south sides are marked out by taller houses set on triple-arched gateways, the Pavillon du Roi, shown here, and the Pavillon de la Reine. Arcaded at ground level, the upper storey follows the French fashion for brick elevations with rusticated stucco quoins and window surrounds, and separate steeply-pitched roofs for each house, with prominent dormers and tall chimney-stacks. This square was to be a gathering place for Parisians at times of public rejoicing, and for the rest of the seventeenth century it was occupied by the wealthier bourgeoisie. Following the French Revolution, however, all references to royalty were abolished and it became known as the Place des Vosges.

☛ **Amsterdam Merchants, Brussels Guildsmen, Fortrey**

Henri IV, King of France. b Pau (FR), 1553. Reigned (FR), 1589–1610. d Paris (FR), 1610. **Pavillon du Roi**, Place Royale (now Place des Vosges), Paris (FR), 1603.

Henry VIII

Nonsuch Palace

Two great octagonal corner towers and a smaller octagonal stair turret rising up into a fantastic array of pinnacles, are what this surviving picture can tell us of a long-vanished Tudor extravagance. The history of architecture is littered with such famous buildings that met an untimely end. Originally built in 1532 as a hunting lodge for Henry VIII, designed by his

Office of Works, it ended its days, 150 years later, being sold by Charles II's mistress, the Duchess of Cleveland, who needed the money. The palace was entered from the north through an imposing gateway into an outer court, and a second, even more imposing gateway led into an inner court. These were built of brick or timber, 'incomparably beautified' as John

Evelyn recorded in 1666, with 'timber-puncheons, entrelices, etc … that it seemed carved in the wood and painted …'. Indeed, the decoration was up-to-date, incorporating many Renaissance motifs into the largely medieval plan and outline.

☛ Berthelot, Compton, Smythson, Wolsey

Henry VIII, King of England. b Greenwich (UK), 1491. Reigned (UK), 1509–1549. d London (UK), 1547. **Nonsuch Palace**, Ewell (UK), 1538–47, demolished in 1682–3 and excavated in 1959. Watercolour by Joris Hoefnagel, 1568–9.

Herzog & de Meuron

Rudin House

One of the world's most influential architectural practices, Herzog & de Meuron designed this family dwelling which appears to mimic the iconic child's drawing of a house. However, while the simple form appears familiar, there are many details that confound expectations on closer inspection. For example, the 'front door' is accessed via a flight of steps from underneath the building, and the pitched roof joins the walls smoothly with no protective overhang. Although cast in concrete, the house appears, contradictorily, to float above its site. The Swiss architects, inspired by the fact that, unlike Switzerland, French building laws do not require a cellar, determined to clear away all that normally anchors a building to the ground. The flat plinth at ground level rests on concrete *pilotis*, projecting beyond the ends of the house to reinforce its lightweight appearance. With its wide, sliding floor-to-ceiling windows, the house opens up to the surrounding fields and orchards.

☞ Ando, Chipperfield, Kishigami, Koolhaas, Zumthor

Herzog & de Meuron. Jaques Herzog. b Paris (FR), 1950. **Pierre de Meuron. b** Basel (SW), 1950. **Rudin House**, Leymen (FR), 1997.

Herzog + Partner

House in Regensburg

The prominent German architectural practice, Thomas Herzog + Partner, designed this beautiful and constructionally stringent house in 1977 using early solar design principles, a recurrent theme in its work. The house has a prismatic structure on a fixed spatial grid, and is arranged around an existing tree which serves as the main shading device. The triangular cross-section of the building serves as a form of wind bracing. A sloping greenhouse construction is integrated into the overall form of the house, designed for passive energy gains. The internal layout is based on passive solar use, and is divided into four zones: access corridor (north side), services (east), principal rooms (west) and an intermediate temperature zone with the greenhouse to the south. However, these zones are variable as the internal walls have been designed to be moveable. External and internal walls are made of lightweight construction timber, heavily insulated with a rear ventilated pine-board cladding.

☞ Andrews, Otto, TR Hamzah & Yeang, Vale

Herzog + Partner. **Thomas Herzog. b** Munich (GER), 1941. **Verena Herzog-Loibl. b** Würzburg (GER), 1943. **House in Regensburg** (GER), 1977–9.

Hildebrandt Johann Lucas von   Upper Belvedere Palace

The summer palace of Prinz Eugen, the Belvedere Palace, was built by Hildebrandt in two stages. The first, the Lower Belvedere, was completed by 1715 and then, crowning the gardens, came the Upper Belvedere of 1721–2. This begins and ends with prominent corner pavilions, a traditional form descended from the corner towers of ancient castles, but here providing a theme picked up by the canted sides of the projecting centrepiece. Its tightly paired pilasters continue across the three-storeyed main range, but not the two-storeyed wings, and reappear again on the pavilions; a precise means of articulating the whole facade. This strict basis allowed Hildebrandt scope for rich ornamental detail, which, together with the interiors, took longer to complete. The glory of the interior is the spatially-integrated entrance hall, staircase and the rooms leading from it; the Sala Terrena and, above, a large salon overlooking the garden.

☛ **Fischer von Erlach, Oliveira, Pöppelmann**

Johann Lucas von Hildebrandt. **b** Genoa (IT), 1668. **d** Vienna (AUS), 1745. **Upper Belvedere Palace**, Vienna (AUS), 1721–2.

Hoban James

The White House

The White House has been home and workplace to every US President, with the exception of George Washington, who commissioned the open competition for the Presidential seat in 1792. James Hoban's winning Neo-Classical Georgian design, of which the central portion largely remains intact today, was based on Leinster Hall in Dublin and Plate 41 of James Gibb's *A Book of Architecture* (1728). Gutted by British soldiers during the war of 1812, the building was saved from utter destruction by a providential downpour. The familiar colonnaded north entrance and south portico, designed by Benjamin Latrobe, were faithfully reconstructed, while large-scale modernization in 1902 added wings containing offices.

The white stucco facade of this surprisingly compact house masks an interior containing four staterooms to receive VIPs, and bears witness to successive presidential additions, such as Roosevelt's Oval Office and Clinton's jogging track.

☞ Bulfinch, Cameron, Jefferson, Nash, Tichborne, Weeks

183

James Hoban. b Callan (IRE), 1763. d Washington DC (USA), 1831. **The White House**, Washington DC (USA), 1792–1801, rebuilt 1814–29.

Hoff Robert van't   Villa Nora

The horizontality of this flat-roofed house is emphasized by the grey lines painted around the edges of the concrete slabs. Designed just after van't Hoff had returned from a trip to meet Frank Lloyd Wright in Chicago, the house alludes to Wrightian overhangs, extended horizontals and sliding volumes, but here expressed in smooth reinforced concrete. The symmetrical plan is animated by a skylight that admits light to the interior of the house and a terrace that overlooks an artificial pond to the south. Publicity about the house brought van't Hoff to the attention of Theo van Doesburg, who invited him to contribute to the publication of the first issue of *De Stijl* (The Style), the magazine produced by the highly-influential Dutch group of Modern artists and architects of the same name. Although van't Hoff stayed with the group for two years, his interest in architecture waned and he built the last of his nine buildings at the young age of thirty-four.

☛ Doesburg, Loos, Raymond, Rietveld & Schröder, Wright

Robert van't Hoff. b Rotterdam (NL), 1887. d New Milton (UK), 1979. **Villa Nora (Villa Henny),** Huis ter Heide (NL), 1914–16.

Hoffman Jr Francis Burrall & Chalfin Paul   Vizcaya

Vizcaya is a palazzo built, not in the Venetto, but in Miami on the shore of Biscayne Bay. Its owner, James Deering, was an heir to a Midwestern American farm equipment fortune who, having travelled widely, chose to retire to the comparatively untamed subtropical wilderness that was Miami in the early twentieth century. He purchased 180 acres and his interior designer, Paul Chalfin, hired the young architect Francis Burrall Hoffman to design a house. Hoffman was constricted in his choice of form, given Chalfin's proposed recreations of Italian Renaissance interiors, often using original wall elements and treasures shipped over from Europe. Designed around a palazzo-style courtyard (unfortunately enclosed in the 1980s with a dark pyramid roof), the house became a virtual museum of the decorative arts. There are also Italian gardens designed by Diego Suarez, a quaint 'farm village', and just offshore, a stone barge designed by Sterling Calder.

☞ **Contarini, Morgan, Peruzzi, Sangallo**

Francis Burrall Hoffman Jr. **b** New Orleans, LA (USA), 1882. **d** Hobe Sound, FL (USA), 1980. **Paul Chalfin. b** (USA), 1873. **d** (USA), 1959. **Vizcaya**, Miami, FL (USA), 1914–17.

Hoffmann Josef   Palais Stoclet

The flat, white marble walls, elaborate bronze trimmings and part-romantic, part-industrial-style staircase tower of this house mark a watershed in architectural styles. It is both the most important house of the Secession movement (spawned in Vienna at the turn of the twentieth century) and the crossover point between nineteenth-century and Modernist architecture. The fifty-roomed mansion, designed for the Belgian industrialist Adolphe Stoclet, is a massive, total work of art, or *Gesamtkunstwerk*, where all furniture and furnishings are integrated into the design concept. Twinned Gustav Klimt mirror-image murals are features of the long, low dining room. The house is asymmetrical and comparatively free in its plan, dominated by the paradoxically plain tower, elaborately adorned with statues. Both old style palace and new-age industrial machine for living, the Palais Stoclet is one in a long line of great European townhouses.

☞ Cauchie, Horta, Loos, Mackintosh, Wagner

186

Josef Hoffmann. b Pirnitz (CZ), 1870. d Vienna (AUS), 1956. **Palais Stoclet**, Brussels (BEL), 1905.

Holl Steven

Stretto House

The pavilions and pools of this house overlap and combine in a rhythm based on a musical score. Holl cites Béla Bartók's *Music for Strings, Percussion and Celeste* as his inspiration; a *stretto* is the close overlapping of two voices or sounds. The architecture takes light and space as its equivalent to the instrumentation and sound in the four movements of the piece.

Four concrete dams between three ponds on the site also inform the flowing nature of the house and the subtle progression between different floor levels. These changes in level are also marked by changes in materials and surfaces; while white concrete blocks form the external walls, light curvilinear metal sheeting gently spans the roofs. Holl became known initially

for his light-filled and colourful interiors, and his major built works include the critically acclaimed Kiasma, the Museum for Contemporary Art in Helsinki (1998) and the Chapel of St Ignatius, Seattle University, Washington (1997).

☛ **Coderch, Kahn, Sirén, Siza, Torres & Lapeña**

Steven Holl. b Bremerton, WA (USA), 1947. **Stretto House**, Dallas, TX (USA), 1989–92.

Hølmebakk Carl-Viggo　　　Summer House

Carefully situated on a rugged, but popular site on the south coast of Norway, the Risor Summer House is built on an adjustable structural grid, which allows concrete stub columns to be cast where necessary so as not to disturb the long-established pines. Influenced as much by the local ship-building tradition as by vernacular architecture, Hølmebakk created a site-sensitive timber construction. The Summer House appears to ramble in between the trees and the huge, glacier-smoothed stone face, with roof levels adjusting to the various branches overhead, as well as the foundation points accommodating the tree roots. Taking cues from the trees that surround it, the house is built of, and clad in, Norwegian pine, spruce and oak, with different treatments of oil used to resist the effects of weather and wear and tear. The result is a visual recollection of the primitive hut, while the building technology that made it possible is unmistakably modern.

☛　Aalto, Fehn, Gunnløgsson, Peter the Great, Sirén

Carl-Viggo Hølmebakk. b Horten (NOR), 1958. **Summer House**, Risor (NOR), 1997.

Holscher Knud   Holscher House

Located near a forest north of Copenhagen, the Holscher House is defined by two protective, parallel masonry walls. Enclosed within these arms, spaces are arranged to make the most of the sun's path. The master bedroom is exposed to the rising morning sun, as is a terrace to the east which is used for eating breakfast and lunch. Another terrace to the west can be enjoyed in the late afternoon before the sun sets. The interiors are simply arranged around a two-storey central core of bathrooms, dressing room and sauna, recalling the traditional Danish farmhouse in which cooking, eating and sleeping were carried out in a single room. Holscher, an industrial designer as well as an architect, considered the house as a total work of art. He designed everything from the hand-made bricks and concrete ceiling panels, to the fixtures and fittings. The house, still owned by the Holscher family, has remained unchanged since its completion thirty years ago.

☛ Aalto, Erickson, Gunnløgsson, A Jacobsen, Mecanoo

Knud Holscher. **b** Rødby (DK), 1930. **Holscher House**, Holte (DK), 1971.

Horden Richard   Ski Haus

Horden's high-tech pod appears to have just landed on the slopes of this Swiss mountainside – and it quite probably has. The feet of its insect-like form are planted delicately on the snow and underneath one can just see the legs of skiers about to clamber inside. This modern interpretation of the alpine hut provides protection from extreme conditions for climbers and skiers, but unlike the traditional mountain refuge, it is designed to be entirely portable – a helicopter is used to transport it from one remote peak to another. Once inside, it is relatively spacious with bunks and seats providing a bare minimum of creature comforts. Telecommunications, heat and electricity are supplied by solar panels and vast aerials fixed to the roof. The pod is held within a braced frame that can be altered according to the slope. Its high-tech language has evolved from the prototype of Horden's earlier Yacht House, a distillation of Archigram's influence on Late Modernism.

☛ **D Greene, Future Systems, Grimshaw, Team 4, M Webb**

Richard Horden. b Leominster (UK), 1944. **Ski Haus**, various locations in Switzerland, 1991.

Horiguchi Sutemi Okada House

Okada House, which brings together traditional Japanese architecture and gardens with De Stijl-like compositional principles, has been described as the starting point of Modern architecture in Japan. It consists of a timber-frame Japanese wing, seen here, with a tea room and moon-viewing bamboo veranda recalling the seventeenth-century Katsura Imperial Villa, as well as a reinforced concrete living wing; the two volumes visually intersecting at the long, rectilinear reflecting pool. Horiguchi, a leader of the Japanese Secessionist movement *Bunriha* (1920–7), was one of the first Japanese architects to visit the Bauhaus. In 1924 he wrote an influential book on contemporary Dutch architecture. He also became a noted scholar of Japanese tea room architecture, thereby underscoring an inherent link between the modern and traditional *sukiya*-style. The house was demolished in 1995 – only photographs that were published around the world remain.

☛ **Rietveld & Schröder, Toshihito & Toshitada, Yamada**

Sutemi Horiguchi. b Gifu Prefecture (JAP), 1895. **d** Tokyo (JAP), 1984. **Okada House**, Tokyo (JAP), 1933.

Horta Victor

Hôtel Tassel

The luscious, Art Nouveau staircase of this private house demonstrates all the characteristics of the new style that swept Europe at the time: whiplash lines, abstracted botanical and zoological decorative forms, asymmetry, a rich palette of colour and materials – themes which unified the whole design. Although there was evidence of this new artistic style in Catalonia (particularly Gaudí's extraordinary regional architecture in Barcelona), this was the first building to crystallize the ideas being developed by European artists and express them in architectural terms. Horta went on to design many other buildings in this manner, notably the Hôtel Solvay (1895–1900), and the style was taken up by many others, including Hector Guimard (in his Castel Béranger). The Art Nouveau style was comparatively short-lived, but represents a major contribution to the extremely abundant creativity across Europe just before the birth of Modernism.

☛ Cauchie, Gaudí, Hoffmann, Mackintosh, Shekhtel

Baron Victor Horta. **b** Ghent (BEL), 1861. **d** Brussels (BEL), 1947. **Hôtel Tassel**, Brussels (BEL), 1892–3.

Hübner-Forster-Hübner
Casanova House

Hübner-Forster-Hübner is known for its prefabricated structures and self-build concepts; Casanova House was an early project for the firm and was constructed in one day (the 4th of November) in 1975. Comprised of twenty-three prefabricated, plastic Casanova room cells, all of 12 sq m (130 sq ft), the 'house' is in fact a cluster of dwelling and office units set on a one-time dump site in the countryside around Stuttgart. The spatial units were delivered to the site fully equipped with wiring, heating elements and plumbing, floors fully carpeted, walls lined with fabric by way of wallpaper and shelving. The units were then simply lifted into place and connected, the final assembly achieved in hours. The cubes are octagonal in plan for the main living areas and offices, and square for services and smaller units. The unusual setting of the inbuilt windows and throughways allow the interior to merge with the exterior, and provide dramatic daylighting.

☞ D Greene, Prouvé, Segal, Starck, Suuronen

Hübner-Forster-Hübner. Peter Hübner. b (GER), 1939. **Casanova House**, Neckartenzlingen (GER), 1975.

Hudson Featherstone

Baggy House

The pre-patinated copper roof of this house, flat from this view, in fact bulges to echo the forms of the nearby cliffs at Baggy Point. Below it, the huge, south-western windows overlooking the Atlantic coast drop electronically into slots in the ground. To the right, the white-rendered walls suggest the great Modernist steamship trope – and, at the same time, the chimneys of the local white-rendered Devon thatched cottages; the Baggy House is nothing if not inclusive. It is structurally elaborate, with one huge, central granite column tapering up to a point; another column of laminated maple tapers inversely. The sea room on the left is a small version of the house with its own slide-down windows. Materials in the lower levels are rough-hewn and riven; as you move up through the rooms, they become polished, turned and cast. The house bears a hybrid family relation to the Arts and Crafts movement, while drawing Modernism into the elaborate mass of materials used.

☞ Holl, Mackintosh, O'Donnell & Tuomey, Predock, Wright

194

Hudson Featherstone. Anthony Hudson. **b** Norfolk (UK), 1955. **Sarah Featherstone. b** Barnstaple (UK), 1966. **Baggy House**, Croyde (UK), 1995.

Hunt Richard Morris   Biltmore

A French Renaissance chateau built in the Blue Ridge Mountains of North Carolina, Biltmore holds the title as the largest private house ever constructed in the USA. Richard Morris Hunt had designed many grand mansions for some of America's richest families, but Biltmore, for George Vanderbilt (1862–1914), was by far his grandest. The house, with a 238 m (780 ft) Indiana limestone facade, has 250 rooms, of which thirty-four are bedrooms, and a swimming pool, bowling alley and gym in the basement. Hunt, who was instrumental in bringing the Beaux-Arts educational system to the USA, drew on precedents from French châteaux, including Blois, Chenonceaux and Chambord; distinct allusions to all three can be found in Biltmore's architecture, from the form of the house to the detailing of the windows. The house was fully electrified on its completion in 1895, and was among the first residences to use the new light bulbs invented by Thomas Edison.

☛ Cortona, Delano & Aldrich, L'Orme, Richardson

Richard Morris Hunt. b Brattleboro, VT (USA), 1827. d Newport, RI (USA), 1895. Biltmore, Ashville, NC (USA), 1889–95.

Hutu

Rondavel Thatched Hut

The great advantage of a round house is its inherent strength: lacking corners, the weight of the roof can be readily disposed over the walls, provided that a doorway is properly incorporated. The Hutu, farmers who live in scattered groups, build these simple *rondavel* huts, their walls made from poles with twin, narrow strips of wood roped to them, and the whole infilled with soil and plastered with mud. The conical roofs are similarly made and covered with banana leaves or grass. A group of such houses serves a family, each house acting as an individual room – a parent's room, a male children's room, a female children's room, a guest room, a work room, and so on. But the past is giving way to the future and, although harder to build, rectangular houses are starting to appear. These can be readily partitioned and sometimes use imported materials, such as the manufactured fired-clay tiles for the roof seen here.

☛ **Dogon, Ma'dan, Maasai, Mandan Indians, Maori, Zulu**

Hutu. Active (RWA), AD 600 to present day. **Rondavel Thatched Hut**, Gisenye (RWA), as built today.

Inuit

Iglu

The *iglu* dwelling of the Inuit people (more popularly, if incorrectly, known as Eskimo) is a fast disappearing habitat, and can only rarely be seen in the extreme north of Alaska and Canada, Labrador and the west coast of Greenland where the Inuit live. The domed *iglu* is built of blocks of snow, cut with a bone knife, laid in a continuous spiral of about 5 m (16 ft) diameter, each block resting against its predecessor; no other structure is necessary. A snow platform or *iqliq*, covered with animal skins, provides the bed, and draughts are prevented by cutting a section of the entrance tunnel into the ice floor to create a 'sink' which traps the cold air. Blubber lamps in stone bowls can raise the temperature inside to 15°C (60°F), and illumination during the day is provided by a clear ice block set in the dome, enhanced by a snow block acting as a reflector. Most Inuit now live in prefabricated huts, but the *iglu* is still occasionally used today on winter hunting trips.

☛ **Girolamo II, Provençale Farmers, Syrian Farmers**

Inuit. Active (CAN), Greenland (DK), (RUS) and Alaska (USA), c3000 BC to present day. **Iglu**, found today in Labrador, NF (CAN), NT (CAN), west coast of Greenland (DK) and Alaska (USA), as built late twentieth century.

Isabella I & Ferdinand II   Casas Colgadas

Imposing cantilevered balconies of this enchanting cliff top house afford spectacular views over the eastern precipice of Cuenca's wild and rocky gorge and the narrow Huécar river and valley below. Originally forming part of a fifteenth-century royal summer residence, this group of Casas Colgadas (Hanging Houses) reveal influences from Moorish fortified palace architecture. The strong *genius loci* of the site indicates the buildings' defensive hilltop positioning, so necessary throughout the tumultuous Christian conquests of the time. Cuenca was renowned for its ivory workshop, and the Muslim Taifa kings of Toledo were great patrons. The Taifa dynasty (1031–86) and succeeding rulers engaged architectural and decorative styles of caliphal Cordoba and Seville. The beautifully decorative timber eaves, balustrades and shutters are reminiscent of the multilevel balcony design seen at the Alhambra Palace and Generalife Residence in Granada.

☛ **Acayaba, Eschwege, Nasrid Dynasty, Tarifa**

Queen Isabella I. b Madrigal de las Attas Torres, Castile (SP), 1451. Reigned Castile, 1474–1504 and Aragon, 1479–1504. **d** Medina del Campo (SP), 1504. **King Ferdinand II. b** Sos, Aragon (SP), 1452. Reigned Aragon, 1466–1516 and Castile (as Ferdinand V), 1479–1516. **d** Madrigalejo (SP), 1516. **Casas Colgadas**, Cuenca, Castilla-la-Mancha (SP), mid-fifteenth century, restored 1926.

Ishii Kazuhiro   Sukiya-Yu

Sukiya is a Japanese residential style that first emerged in the early seventeenth century as a variation of the grandiose, formal *Shoin* style, which is often characterized by gorgeous ornamentation. By contrast, *Sukiya* emphasizes rustic simplicity, intimacy and caprice, and Ishii's interpretation of the style in this dwelling for a single woman creates an intrinsically relaxing place that cannot ordinarily be achieved in a homogeneous urban setting. The house consists of eight free-standing structures, linked by a corridor, which accommodate various residential elements. Each of them presents a refined and elaborate design referring to specific modern *Sukiya* houses of the 1920s and 1930s, but here reinterpreted to explore an alternative meaning of the style in the contemporary suburb. Their asymmetrical arrangement provides a circulation route along which various scenes of daily life unfold spontaneously.

☛ **Fuller, Kishi, Ogawa, Toshihito & Toshitada, Yoh**

Kazuhiro Ishii. b Okayama (JAP), 1944. **Sukiya-Yu**, Okayama (JAP), 1990.

Ishikawa Kazumasa & Yasunaga   Matsumoto Castle

Standing in the mountainous region of Nagano in central Japan, Matsumoto (also known as Fukashi Castle) is one of the country's twelve surviving castles with intact multi-storeyed donjons, or central fortified towers. Some of the other famous examples, such as the castles in Nagoya and Hiroshima, were destroyed by air raids during World War II. Matsumoto Castle comprises the main and secondary donjons, a turret and a moon-viewing pavilion, all constructed on top of a great stone foundation and surrounded by a moat. Its colour scheme of white walls and contrasting black lacquerwork and grey tile roofs is particularly striking. Developed during the sixteenth century, these castles originally served as mountain fortresses, but later came to symbolize military power and political authority for feudal lords; around them prosperous towns and cities, bustling with Samurai or warriors, merchants and artisans, would be established.

☛ Horiguchi, Tokugawa, Toshihito & Toshitada

200

Kazumasa Ishikawa. b Kawachi (JAP), c1535. d 1592. Yasunaga Ishikawa. b Okazaki (JAP), c1554. d 1642. Matsumoto Castle (Fukashi Castle), Nagano (JAP), 1591–4.

Ishiyama Osamu Fantasy Villa

This semi-cylindrical house, sunk into the ground at the bottom of a small basin in the cold climate of Ohmi, consists mainly of bent, corrugated steel sheets. Simple holes in the end facades, of various shapes and sizes, are glazed with colourful stained glass which suggest an astrological element while providing daylight to the interior space. The house has a straightforward circulation route: this begins with an open staircase on the southern entrance facade, which leads to an internal bridge that meets a mezzanine and ends with another staircase at the north entrance. The use of ubiquitous industrial materials in a simple manner leads one to believe that the house could have been self-constructed by the owner but in fact, the Fantasy Villa is one of a series of alternative low-cost housing which Ishiyama developed in the 1970s.

☛ Hasegawa, Ito, Segal, Starck

Osamu Ishiyama. b Okayama (JAP), 1944. **Fantasy Villa**, Ohmi, Aichi Prefecture (JAP), 1975.

Isidore Raymond

La Maison de Picassiette

Images of mosaic birds, trailing wisteria, church buildings and exotic scenes formed out of ceramics, glass and found objects cover every centimetre of Raymond Isidore's home. This shrine and artwork grew over thirty years from the small house he originally built in 1928. In 1937, he began to cover the outside walls with *objets trouvés* – perfume bottles, plates – using mortar tinted blue and ochre. He soon moved on to cover the interior and the furniture, mostly with religious iconography much influenced by the nearby Chartres Cathedral. Isidore retired from his job sweeping the local graveyard in 1956 and dedicated himself to his creation, building a chapel and a sculpture garden, which are the pinnacles of his artistic work.

His motivation came from a desire for 'a place where my spirit feels at home', rather than a house designed by an architect. He was nicknamed 'Picassiette' by a journalist – a play on Picasso and *pique-assiette*, a plate-picker or scrounger.

☞ Droppers, Larsson, Manrique, Reynolds, Senosiain

Raymond Isidore. **b** (FR), 1900. **d** Chartres (FR), 1964. **La Maison de Picassiette,** Chartres (FR), 1928–64.

Israel Frank

Drager House

Built in an area of the Berkeley Hills consumed by fire in 1991, the jagged form of this house expresses an awareness of California as a place of margins rather than centres, split in the middle, like the fault line which runs near to the site. One of Israel's last projects, this house shows his indebtedness to various California building traditions, including the dynamic formal disjunctions of Frank Gehry, the hillside architecture of Richard Neutra, the treatment of the exploded box begun by Rudolph Schindler, as well as a reverence for Japanese architecture as reinterpreted along America's west coast. In addition, Israel draws from the palette and materials of the Arts and Crafts movement, enfolding the house in a copper roofing, which spills down its side, replacing the traditional wooden shingles. Attentive to the steep slope of the site, the large corner windows are designed to frame the view.

☞ Gehry, Koning Eizenberg, Moss, Neutra, RoTo Architects

Franklin David Israel. b New York, NY (USA), 1945. **d** Los Angeles, CA (USA), 1996. **Drager House**, Berkeley Hills, CA (USA), 1994.

Issaias Dimitris & Papaioannou Tassis

Two-Family House

The brief for this house, which is situated at the foot of Mount Pendeli in Athens, was to provide accommodation for three generations in two separate units. Entered via a small courtyard, the house is developed over three levels; the grandparents inhabit the courtyard level, while the parents and children live on the upper two floors. The design is based on an analysis of the everyday activities taking place in a family home. There are internal and external vertical routes through the building, which playfully exploit the relationship between the inside and outside spaces, and the solid and void elements. An external route leads from the courtyard, via the first-floor terrace, to a belvedere on the top level. The use of materials, such as exposed concrete for the columns of the visually dominant structural grid and blockwork for the walls, illustrates the architects' concern with the use of building techniques that can be executed by local builders.

☛ Atelier 66, Botta, Lauterbach, Snozzi, O M Ungers

Dimitris Issaias. b Athens (GR), 1952. **Tassis Papaioannou**. b Athens (GR), 1953. **Two-Family House**, Pendeli, Athens (GR), 1989–92.

Ito Toyo   White 'U' House

This house, as its name implies, consists of a continuous U-shaped volume with an inward-sloping roof and a rectangular volume connecting its two ends. The continuous 45 m (147 ft) interior space contains a minimal number of enclosed rooms, leaving the rest for circulation and an open living area. Ito intended the house's interior to be a fluid zone where light distribution, air movement and human activities would be perceived as in flow. In addition, he experimentally arranged the elements in the curved area – including skylights, fluorescent cove lights and furniture – with their own corresponding curves. The phenomenological experience which this generated was meant to express a physical sense of rhythm which the inhabitants might exhibit during the course of daily living. Ito's experimental design demonstrated that a house can significantly affect human experience and, at the same time, it challenged conventional designs for a dwelling.

☞ **Ando, Hasegawa, Ishiyama, Sejima, Shinohara**

205

Toyo Ito. b Nagano (JAP), 1941. **White 'U' House**, Nakano (JAP), 1977 (since demolished).

Jackson Daryl

Jackson House

There is a loose informality to the Jackson house; the different materials and irregular shapes all contribute to a relaxed feel, but at the same time there is evidence of an exploration of architecture as a system of construction. However, Jackson's inspiration for this beach house for himself and his family was a very formal architecture indeed

– the traditional monastery. The house consists of a collection of rooms which wrap around the contoured hilltop site, creating an open courtyard at the centre reminiscent of the cloistered courtyards of medieval monasteries. At the same time, it responds to the climate and a need for almost constant outdoor living; rooms, like lean-tos, are set against the

boundary wall in a manner which evokes a temporary encampment. In 1965 Jackson founded an architectural practice which today has earned an international reputation for consistently high quality, diverse buildings.

☞ Andrews, Katsalidis, Morphosis, Ritchie

206

Daryl Jackson. b Clunes, VIC (ASL), 1937. **Jackson House**, Bermagui, NSW (ASL), 1992.

Jacobsen Arne   Summer House

The shed roof that gently attaches itself to the large wall, the outdoor fireplace that hangs on the chimney, the picture window and the patio, all exemplify the informality and relaxed relationship to the outdoors of much Scandinavian architecture of this period. Even the potentially monumental curved wall, that organizes the more casual components of the architect's own summer house in the country, is broken down through texture and horizontal articulation. But the whiteness and proportion of the house set it apart from nature, and this tension makes it a pivotal design in Jacobsen's career. One of the key figures in the development of Scandinavian Modernism, he was educated to balance new techniques and functions with tradition and culture, and later on his houses were closely attuned to a northern European climate. He was also a designer of tableware and furniture, and is possibly more well-known today for his cult-status *Egg Chair* (1957).

☛ Aalto, Asplund, Le Corbusier, Mies van der Rohe

Arne Jacobsen. **b** Copenhagen (DK), 1902. **d** Copenhagen (DK), 1971. **Summer House**, Gudmindrup Lyng (DK), 1938.

Jacobsen Hugh Newell   Johnson House

High up on a hill above the rolling grass of a thousand-acre stud farm is a house that abstracts southern US history and recasts it as modern. Hugh Newell Jacobsen was one of the first to experiment with vernacular forms in an era of straightforward structures, although this house does show a strong Modernist sentiment, and an equally strong penchant for Classicism. The Neo-Classical style was the traditional house form of the South, but this version of the 'house on the hill' suggests the aesthetic without the detail. Like the local architecture, Johnson House is white-painted brick; the columns have travertine at their base and rise to support wooden sunscreens and rafters. White birch trees are planted in the forecourt and echo the grid of the columns. Inside, the single-storey spaces flow into one another, a trademark of Jacobsen's houses which are often organized as processional experiences while, in this case, still fitting neatly within the constraints of the grid.

☞ Geyter, Graves, P Johnson, Stern, Venturi

Hugh Newell Jacobsen. b Grand Rapid, MI (USA), 1929. Johnson House, Lexington, KY (USA), 1980.

Jagat Singh II

Jag Nivas Lake Palace

The ultra-romantic Jag Nivas Lake Palace completely covers a small island in the manmade Pinchola Lake, giving the impression that it is floating, like a serene ocean liner. It was built as a complex of palaces from the mid-seventeenth century onwards (the artificial lake having been formed in the fourteenth century) interspaced with courts, fountains, trees and gardens. It was once the summer residence of the ruling Ranas of Mewar, and epitomizes the whimsy and elegance which characterized the pleasure palace architecture of the Rajputs. As members of the Hindu warrior caste, their reputation for chivalry was comparable with the knights of medieval Europe; and this is where they came to relax and enjoy life's pleasures. The most extensive building was carried out by Maharana Jagat Singh II during his reign in the eighteenth century. More recently, it was used as a film set for the James Bond movie, *Octopussy*.

☛ **Akbar, Amar Singh II, Jai Singh I**

Maharana Jagat Singh II. Reigned (IN), 1734–51. **Jag Nivas Lake Palace**, Udaipur (IN), c1746–54.

Jai Singh I

Amber Palace

Set upon a commanding hillside overlooking Lake Mauta, the Amber Palace was the stronghold of the Rajput rulers prior to the settlement of Jaipur. Begun in 1592 by Maharaja Man Singh its magnificence was conceived by Jai Singh I, under whose direction the palace assumed its aura of splendour. The exquisitely tiled, three-storey Ganesha Pol (as seen here) was the gateway to the three pleasure palaces built around the *Aram Bagh* – a Mughal-style pleasure garden. Each residence contained a special feature: the Sheesh Mahal – a windowless chamber with tiny mirrors embedded into its walls that give the illusion of a glittering night sky when a candle is lit; the Sukh Niwas, hall of pleasure, with its ivory inlaid sandalwood doors, and a water course running through it to cool the air. The skilled craftsmanship evident in the mosaics, the latticed windows, the glass inlay and the elegant alabaster reliefs, make Amber Palace one of the finest examples of Rajput architecture.

☛ **Akbar, Amar Singh II, Jagat Singh II, Patwon**

210

Jai Singh I. b 1623. **d** 1668. **Amber Palace**, Jaipur, Rajasthan (IN), 1592–1667.

Janák Pavel

Dr Fára's House

In this remodelling of a traditional Czech Baroque facade, the moulded sculptural surface of the building is evocative of its historic style, while at the same time creating a revolutionary architectural language of planes and folds. Designed by Pavel Janák, the most important theorist of Czech Cubism, this project was an early attempt to find an expressive architectural vocabulary that could capture the energy, motion and rhythm of modern life in three dimensions. Inspired in part by French Cubism and Duchamp-Villon's Maison Cubiste of 1912, Janák was also highly influenced by German art history and theories of artistic perception, as well as the legacy of the eighteenth-century Czech architect, Santini-Aichel, whose unusual work synthesized Gothic and Baroque motifs into a unique style similar in spirit to some work of the Czech Cubists. Janák, in addition to his work, wrote essays about cubist architecture, including the well-known article, 'Prism and Pyramid' of 1912.

☛ **Duchamp-Villon, Gaudí, Olbrich, Plečnik**

Pavel Janák. b Prague (CZ), 1882. **d** Prague (CZ), 1956. **Dr Fára's House**, Pelhřimov (CZ), 1913.

Jefferson Thomas   Monticello

Monticello is Thomas Jefferson's ode to the architecture he loved; that of Greece, Rome and Palladio's Italy. The third president of the USA, Jefferson was considered to be the country's first architect, and called Monticello his 'essay in architecture'. In the course of the forty years of its construction, he transformed the house from a one-room dwelling to a three-storey, 33-room mansion. Following the death of his wife in 1784 and a trip to France, he rebuilt the house on a grander scale, influenced by European architecture, with far more elegant rooms and adding the famous entrance portico. Inside, the house is filled with his labour-saving innovations, including automatic doors and a dumb waiter. Jefferson was the first major exponent of Palladian-influenced architecture in the New World and his passion for Classicism has influenced American architecture through the centuries. Even today his buildings still inform the art of American building.

☛ Burlington, Cameron, Hoban, I Jones, Palladio, Terry

Thomas Jefferson. b Shadwell, VA (USA), 1743. d Monticello, VA (USA), 1826. **Monticello**, nr Charlottesville, VA (USA), 1769–1809.

Jencks Charles & Farrell Terry   The Thematic House

Architectural critic, Charles Jencks, has described the works which he and architect friends (including Terry Farrell and Piers Gough) carried out on his 1840s Holland Park house as an 'attempt to face directly the question of meaning' in architecture. The garden elevation can be read as an abstract representation of his family: father, mother and two children, with their dog at the centre. Jencks, who influenced and defined the Post-Modern movement through works such as *The Language of Post-Modern Architecture* (1977), was interested in exploring the symbolic potential of architecture. He felt that subliminal anthropomorphism and a multilayered fusing of functional form and image were key to a more humane way of building. The interior of the house is a symbolic expression of time, completely restructured around a new concrete circular staircase, 'the sun well', and a two-storey 'moon well' with complex iconography incorporating science and philosophy.

☛ **CZWG, Duany Plater-Zyberk, Krier, Outram, Venturi**

213

Charles Jencks. b Baltimore (USA), 1939. **Terry Farrell.** b Manchester (UK), 1938.. **The Thematic House**, London (UK), 1978–84.

Jersey Devil

Red Cross House

At the core of this rugged and experimental house in the Florida Keys is a little block-and-stucco cottage, one of dozens erected by the Red Cross in 1935 after a very destructive hurricane swept through Florida. The architects, Jersey Devil – so named as they established their practice in the state of New Jersey – are nomadic, moving from site to site in their Airstream trailer, settling in for the duration of the project's construction. With the cottage as their starting point, they created a complex construction that provides accommodation for family living and work space. Using sturdy, commonplace materials, the building was assembled so as to withstand the sometimes fierce tropical weather – in particular hurricanes.

The result is a study in corrugated steel and glass; a house that affords long views out to the ocean and across the middle Keys from its tower lookout.

☞ Airstream Co., Clare Design, Grose Bradley, Saitowitz

Jersey Devil. Jim Adamson. b Ashbury Park, NJ (USA), 1948. **Steve Badanes. b** New York City, NY (USA), 1943. **Red Cross House**, Islamorada, FL (USA), 1991.

Johnson Charles   Boulder House

The look-out tower of this house rises from enormous, ancient granite boulders that it mimics in shape and texture, blending with the desert in Arizona. Built of stucco-covered masonry, the tower contains the master bedroom suite, located on the upper storey. On the first floor, the glass-enclosed living and dining rooms nestle among the rocks, but open on one side to a terrace with expansive desert views. Johnson roofed the living spaces and tower with *vigas,* protruding log beams, a building technique which supported the adobe dwellings once common in this region. The main fireplace mantle is covered in plaster, which the architect sculpted by hand to simulate the rustic, curvaceous appearance of adobe walls. The guest room fireplace, under a rock overhang incorporated into the house, was used as a fire pit by native people for many generations. Johnson says, 'I personally call the house "Whispering Boulders", because the rocks had so much to say'.

☞   Breton, Bruder, Schweitzer, Tiwa Indians, Wright

Charles Foreman Johnson. **b** Plainfield, NJ (USA), 1929. **Boulder House**, Carefree, AZ (USA), 1982.

Johnson Philip

Glass House

This structure, small in scale yet prodigious in terms of its influence, shows Johnson's indebtedness to the work of Mies van der Rohe: in the use of standard steel sections for a strong yet decorative finish of the facade, in the corner treatment and the relation of the column to the window frames. It was based on Mies' earlier 1945 sketches for the as yet unbuilt Farnsworth House, and is an iconic work in the International Style. But Johnson is working here almost as a landscape designer, treating the house as a frame for its natural environment; he uses the lawn, extended onto the raised platform, as a well-groomed carpet on which to place the architectural object. The house is externally symmetrical, and organized around an interior brick cylinder, which stands in contrast to the incorporeality of the glass envelope. The French architect, Auguste Perret, on visiting the house reportedly remarked, 'Trop de verre' (Too much glass).

☛ Cook, Gropius, Kahn, Mies van der Rohe, Neutra

Philip Cortelyon Johnson. b Cleveland, OH (USA), 1906. **Glass House**, New Canaan, CT (USA), 1949.

Jones E Fay

Parsons Residence

Built into a wooded hillside set among 240-acres in the Ozark Mountains, this sprawling house masks its size with a long profile and low-hipped roofs that blend harmoniously into the landscape. Inside, continuous spaces flow into one another – both horizontally and vertically – without fixed boundaries, creating an unanticipated sense of openness. The sparsely- furnished, spacious interior highlights the contrast between the textures and shapes of organic building materials, such as wood and stone, and the simple lines and solid colours of the furniture and textiles. An admirer of Frank Lloyd Wright, the young Jones befriended the architect in 1953 and later became an apprentice at the Taliesin West studio. Wright's vocabulary is apparent in the detailing of this house, and Jones cites him as the most important influence on his work. Intentionally remaining out of the public eye for most of his career, Jones continues to run a successful practice in his native Arkansas.

☛ **Goff, Moss, Sullivan, Wright**

Euine Fay Jones. b Pine Bluff, AR (USA), 1921. **Parsons Residence**, Springdale, AR (USA), 1966.

Jones Inigo

Queen's House

With its clear-cut, white-stuccoed lines, the Queen's House at Greenwich heralded a new order in British architecture, utterly different from the ornate Jacobean style of its day. Jones designed it in 1616 as a lodge for Queen Anne of Denmark, wife of James I, although she died before it was finished. The house was later completed in the 1630s. In the early 1600s, Jones visited Italy where he studied Palladio's Renaissance style, with its insistence on order, symmetry and proportion as the basis of Classical architecture. Jones brought this back to England, his plain detailing of the Queen's House recalling the villas of Palladio which relied on well-proportioned walls and windows with a classical portico to emphasize the entrance. Here, the portico acts as a loggia from which the Queen would have watched the hunt in Greenwich Park. However, the house was only finally occupied after the Restoration by Queen Henrietta Maria, wife of Charles I, as a dower house.

☛ Adam, Fortrey, Hawksmoor, Palladio

Inigo Jones. **b** London (UK), 1573. **d** London (UK), 1652. **Queen's House**, London (UK), 1616–35.

Jourda Perraudin
House in Vaise

This house and studio, designed by Françoise-Hélène Jourda and Gilles Perraudin, has a quality of lightness and transience that exemplifies the architects' preoccupation with rational systems based on nature. The house is built almost entirely of plywood, with a large glass-panelled facade, and covered by a massive fabric canopy that stretches across a web-like steel roofing system. Situated within the boundary of an old presbytery, the design is a reduction to essentials, emphasized by a floating effect as the house appears to hover lightly above the ground. The economical prefabricated steel structure was erected in less than a week, allowing the house itself to be installed underneath. Rooms are separated by plywood sandwich panels, and shallow barrel vaults delineate the living and dining areas. Each bay room, with its simple design and elemental construction, achieves the primary aims of a practical, economical and adaptable living space.

☞ Baracco, Fagan, Gandhi, Poole

Jourda Perraudin. Françoise-Hélène Jourda. b (FR), 1955. Gilles Perraudin. b (FR), 1949. House in Vaise, Lyons (FR), 1987.

Junquera Jerónimo & Pérez Pita Estanislao

House at Santander

Sitting atop a flat rise, boldly overlooking the Santander port, this house design clearly embraces the International Style. Junquera & Pérez have drawn their inspiration from the industrial glass building style developed by Mies van der Rohe, specifically from his Farnsworth House (1946–50) – the prototype for glass houses. The exterior expresses strict geometry in its modular component parts. Walls have been turned into window panels, thus exposing the traditionally private life of the home to the public. Virtually all structural and interior design components are visible. The upper-level gallery floor undulates diagonally above the sitting room on the ground floor. The high ceilings and glass walls of the living room flood the home with light, and add to the overall open feel of the home. The architects have fully adapted what would traditionally be industrial building materials and design for this residential habitation.

☛ Baumschlager & Eberle, Mies van der Rohe, Myers, Soriano

Jerónimo Junquera Garcia del Diestro. b Madrid (SP), 1943. Estanislao Pérez Pita. b Madrid (SP), 1943. d Madrid (SP), 1999. House at Santander, Santander (SP), 1982–3.

Kada Klaus

House Kada B.

A hundred-year-old house is made new and playfully reduced to kitsch when painted a shocking blue-green and placed next to a mute plywood box stained a complementary rust colour. These two complete opposites – one figurative, the other abstract – are connected by a two-storey, completely glazed stair hall which slides over, and in some places encompasses the tile roof. The entrance is boldly and simply marked by a suspended plane, which acts as a balcony for the room above. At the rear, the plywood box dissolves into full-height louvres, and the kitchen opens onto a raised terrace which is set across both the old and new parts of the house. One of the avant-garde Graz architects who rejected Miesian Modernism, and then classical Post-Modernism, Klaus Kada has a special affection for glass; he sees its transparency as psychologically liberating with connotations of openness and freedom.

☞ **Feyferlik, Stern, Studio Atkinson, Venturi, Zumthor**

Kanda Kada. b Graz (AUS), 1940. **House Kada B.**, Leibnitz (AUS), 1996.

Kahn Louis

Esherick House

In this building, Kahn endowed what is, in effect, a small suburban house – constructed in the stuccoed, timber-frame vernacular of countless such houses – with something of the monumentality of ancient architecture. He achieved this using two means. First, a plan of almost Palladian simplicity: two long, deep rooms either side of a staircase hall, one side a double-height living room, the other a dining room with a bedroom above it, and a service block to the side. Second, the facades onto the street and garden have deep alcoves – solid with bookshelves on the street side, and largely open on the garden side. Solid timber doors to the garden, set back the whole depth of the reveal, alternate with wider bays of glazing set flush to the outer face of the wall, forming full-height bay windows. In his later public buildings, Kahn would achieve a greater monumentality using more solid materials, but even in this modest house, the grandeur of his aim remains impressive.

☛ Eichler, Esherick, Sullivan, Wright

Louis Isidore Kahn. b Saarama (EST), 1901. d New York, NY (USA), 1974. Esherick House, Chestnut Hill, PA (USA), 1959–61.

Kamath Revathy

Nalin Tomar House

The rooms and terraces of this multi-level residence are orientated towards the west, where the windows and obelisks frame picturesque views of the medieval theological college and lake that give Hauz Khas its name. This historic Muslim quarter is Delhi's own little bohemia – teeming with haute couturiers and purveyors of 'designer' kitsch. The perforated metal dome over the five-storey high entrance elevation is a landmark for that *faux* landscape, while the cascading roofscape is a gesture of respect to the ruins. This crafted aesthetic has been Kamath's signature since the 1980s, when she joined the campaign for low-cost buildings inspired by traditional architectures and informed by Hassan Fathy's writings – a culturally specific alternative to (Post) Modernism. The Nalin Tomar house expresses Kamath's stand against what she sees as the thoughtless importation of Western models into a culturally rich but threatened urban environment.

☛ **Akbar, Bawa, Eldem, Fathy**

Revathy Kamath. Active (IN), mid-twentieth century to present day. **Nalin Tomar House**, New Delhi (IN), 1992.

Katsalidis Nonda   St Andrews House

More like a beached shipping container than a home, St Andrews House, says its architect, the acclaimed Australian designer Nonda Katsalidis, is a fusion of sentimental vernacular sources with the abstract traditions at the heart of Modernism. The house's rusty-looking, Corten steel and rough-hewn wood planking are reminiscent of traditional Australian building forms – the sort of rough and ready barns and outbuildings that you find in small settlements up and down the country. Yet here, Katsalidis has put them together with such knowing precision that they take on quite different connotations. The house has a straightforward arrangement: the heavy sections of recycled timber provide privacy for the bedroom wing; the living area is a large double-height space, glazed at ground-floor level, and clad above in Corten steel, the russet colour of which is echoed in the surrounding vegetation.

☛ **Denton Corker Marshall, Hara, Jackson, Klotz**

224

Nonda Katsalidis. b Athens (GR), 1951. **St Andrews House**, St Andrews Beach, Mornington Peninsular, VIC (ASL), 1991.

Kavanaugh Matthew   'Painted Ladies'

Inspired by the eighteenth-century terraced row houses of London, San Francisco's townhouses were built to accommodate the thriving middle class which emerged after the California Gold Rush. Highly ornamented and brightly painted, the timber-frame structures earned the name 'Painted Ladies'. Although some were designed by well-known architects, most were prefabricated and assembled by specialist builders. This row of iconic 'Painted Ladies' was built by the developer, Matthew Kavanaugh, in the San Francisco 'Queen Anne' style, noted for its use of asymmetry, pointed roofs, crenellated detailing and bay windows. Its wooden structure allows a variety of internal layouts based on a standard plan, although the rooms are often small and discrete. The use of the innovative and flexible balloon-frame construction is particularly suited to this location, prone, as it is, to tremors and earthquakes.

☛ Esherick, Furness, Pender, Potter, Richardson

Matthew Kavanaugh. Active (USA), late nineteenth century. **'Painted Ladies'**, San Francisco, CA (USA), 1894–5.

Kazakov Matvei   Petrovsky Palace

This eclectic confection in red brick with white stone details dominates a semi-circular courtyard which is entered between a pair of fortress-like towers. Catherine the Great had Petrovsky Palace built just outside Moscow's then boundaries as her last overnight staging point on the journey from St Petersburg before ceremonial entry into Russia's spiritual heart. Originally even more Gothic in style, it was one of several palaces in this manner, mixing Classical plan form with European Gothic and medieval Russian detailing, that were built for Catherine by Kazakov and his former master Bazhenov. However, while Petrovsky was finished, her more ambitious Tsaritsyno, south of Moscow, never was. After this early exotica, Kazakov became the founding architect of Moscow Classicism, giving the city a whole new scale and atmosphere through a vast number of refined and superbly graceful Classical ensembles, such as Moscow University and the Golitsyn Hospital.

☛ **Cameron, Fontana & Schädel, Rastrelli, Vanbrugh**

226

Matvei Fedorovich Kazakov. **b** Moscow (RUS), 1738. **d** 1812. **Petrovsky Palace**, Moscow (RUS), 1775–9.

Kent William

Holkham Hall

One of the earliest masterpieces of the new Palladian style, Holkham Hall owes its pedimented front, finely balanced, three-storey pavilions and outer ranges to the inspiration of Thomas Coke's Grand Tour of northern Italy with William Kent in 1714. On his return, Coke (the future Earl of Leicester) consulted the Palladian enthusiast Lord Burlington and began the design of his new house, employing draughtsman Matthew Brettingham to work on the classically-disciplined elevations he had in mind. By 1729, Kent was employed to design the overall plan and the details for the house. This resulted in the pedimented Saloon, the arcaded Stone Hall behind (not completed until 1764) and the flanking formal rooms in the central block. The outer ranges serve as a family wing, to the left, and a chapel wing, to the right. So great was the devotion to Classical architecture, even the locally-made yellow brick used for the facade was fashioned after antique Roman bricks.

☛ **Burlington, Hawksmoor, I Jones, Palladio, Vanbrugh**

William Kent. b Bridlington (UK), 1685. **d** London (UK), 1748. **Holkham Hall**, Norfolk (UK), 1729–34.

Kiesler Frederick   Endless House

Embryonic, biomorphic forms constitute Kiesler's unbuilt Endless House project. Inspired by the organic sculptural forms of the 1930s, especially the work of Constantin Brancusi, and the Surrealist movement, Kiesler pursued the notion of continuity – or 'endlessness' – throughout his career, in his many theoretical projects. The Endless House was to be built out of reinforced concrete as a single shell, with openings cast into place. In various schemes, the house consists of several levels containing all the spaces necessary for a conventional house, as well as unconventional rooms, such as the 'sound-proof study' and the 'seclusion chamber'. A single, vertical core contains all the necessary services, allowing the rest of the spaces to change and flow according to the individual needs of the inhabitants. In the Endless House, Kiesler says, 'all ends meet and meet continuously … as they meet in life.'

☛ **Fuller, Grataloup, D Greene, Okada & Tomiyama, Prince**

Frederick John Kiesler. **b** Czernowitz (AUS), 1890. **d** New York (USA), 1965. **Endless House**, project, 1958–9.

Kikutake Kiyonori   Sky House

This reinforced concrete house was designed by Kikutake for his family as an architectural structure open to change and growth – an idea at the heart of the Metabolist movement which he founded a year after this house was completed, with architects including Kisho Kurokawa and Fumihiko Maki. Originally, the main 10 sq m (107 sq ft) living volume rose above a sloping site on four concrete piers, like a bird's nest floating above the city. The house subsequently underwent a variety of plan configurations using a 'Movenett' system of kitchen and bathroom fixtures, and additional rooms were hung under the floor of the main structure as needed. Over time, Kikutake added three hanging units for his children, a second kitchen, bathroom and an experimental sunroom, and then finally removed the temporary units to reveal the original structure. Kikutake went on to design much larger-scale Metabolist works and visionary urban plans.

☛ Hasegawa, Ito, Rietveld & Schröder, TEN Arquitectos

Kiyonori Kikutake. b Fukuoka Prefecture (JAP), 1928. **Sky House**, Tokyo (JAP), 1959.

Kishi Waro

House in Nipponbashi

This minimal, 2.5 m (8 ft)-wide 'pencil' dwelling stands strong as a white geometric gem in this traditional urban district of Osaka. A steel-frame structure, 13 m (42 ft) deep with prefabricated concrete side panels, supports three compressed lower floors and a 6 m (20 ft) high upper dining space and adjacent open-air roof garden. The street facade's steel louvres, screens and stairs act as a semi-permeable interface between the city and the living-work spaces beyond. The more ample top floor floats high above the urban chaos below, recalling Le Corbusier's Beistegui apartment (1930) in Paris. Originally trained in architectural history, Kishi practices in the more traditional city of Kyoto and draws from many sources, including the California Case Study houses and the *sukiya* aesthetic, as expressed in the Katsura Imperial Villa. This is one of Kishi's many urban townhouses designed as prototypes of a new, aesthetic, industrial vernacular architecture.

☛ **Architecture Studio, Azuma, Ellwood, Le Corbusier, Lescaze**

230

Waro Kishi. b Yokohama (JAP), 1954. **House in Nipponbashi**, Osaka (JAP), 1990–2.

Kishigami Katsuyasu   Imazato House

This two-storey house is located in a residential suburb of Takamatsu, one of the provincial capitals of Shikoku Island. Its south and east facades make use of two very different materials – galvanized steel and translucent polycarbonate corrugated panels – to create subtle, contrasting textures. They are used to echo the internal arrangement of the house, which is focused around an interior courtyard that is lit by diffused daylight entering through the polycarbonate walls. The rooms, simply arranged in an overall box-like form with minimal openings, are visually connected only with the courtyard where lighting levels change over the course of the day. The inward-orientated living experience is emphasized by the translucent walls, which are sufficiently opaque to prevent observation from passersby. Kishigami's strict intention to reduce any external expression has resulted in this deliberately blank, minimal, yet finely-detailed house.

☛ Ando, Junquera & Pérez Pita, Katsalidis, Klotz, Ogawa

Katsuyasu Kishigami. b Kagawa (JAP), 1957. **Imazato House**, Takamatsu (JAP), 1999.

Klotz Mathias   Casa Klotz

This weekend retreat by Mathias Klotz is an exercise in abstraction, pure geometry and clean proportion. The house – a double-cube volume measuring 6 m x 6 m x 12 m (20 ft x 20 ft x 40 ft) – sits along the empty beach at Tongoy, a seaside town located some 400 km (248 miles) north of Santiago, Chile. The wall that faces onto the access road is left intentionally blank; in contrast, the rear elevation has full-height windows overlooking the bay. The first floor has two galleries: one containing stairs, a bathroom and a small bedroom, the other the main bedroom and double-height living and dining areas. Upstairs are additional guest rooms and terraces, all facing onto the ocean panorama. To emphasize its object-like quality, Klotz raised the house 30 cm (1 ft) off the ground on short stilts. Rough pine planks on the wooden structure's exterior give it the air of a rustic summer camp, more than a polished vacation home.

☛ **Baumschlager & Eberle, Katsalidis, Studio Granda**

Mathias Klotz. b Santiago (CH), 1965. **Casa Klotz**, Tongoy, nr Santiago (CH), 1991.

Kocher Lawrence & Frey Albert   Aluminaire House

Built for the Allied Arts and Building Products Exhibition in New York, the all-metal Aluminaire House was a pioneering structure when erected, in only ten days, in 1931. It was the first steel and aluminium house built in the USA, and one of the earliest examples of the budding International Style. The affordable, lightweight, three-storey house followed the development of the experimental prefabricated houses of Le Corbusier, who proposed the Dom-Ino House in 1914, and Buckminster Fuller's Dymaxion House in 1927. The client, architect Wallace K Harrison, purchased the Aluminaire House as a summer retreat and moved it from its original site to two further locations on Long Island, as if to demonstrate its adaptability. Preservationists fought successfully to save the aging structure and secure it as an historic landmark. The New York Institute of Technology later purchased it and is now restoring the structure to its original metallic glory.

☞ Fry, Fuller, Le Corbusier, Luckhardt, Prouvé, Tait

Lawrence Kocher. b San Jose, CA (USA), 1885. d Williamsburg, VA (USA), 1969. Albert Frey. b Zürich (SW), 1904. d Palm Springs, CA (USA), 1998. Aluminaire House, Syosset, NY (USA), 1931 (since relocated to the New York Institute of Technology, Central Islip, NY).

Koenig Pierre

Stahl House (Case Study House No.22)

'Los Angeles is their back yard' was the way the *Los Angeles Examiner* described the new house of the Stahls in 1960. Pierre Koenig's second house for John Entenza's Case Study Program is the epitome of the reductivist architecture of the 'Contemporary' style of 1950s California. With its welded steel frame and roof deck, overhanging eaves and open-air swimming pool, it still features regularly in many fashion and film shoots. Built on a relatively cheap site, due to its poor soil and steeply sloping aspect, the owners wanted to take full advantage of the impressive view. Koenig cantilevered the main living space of the steel-frame house out over the slope on massive reinforced concrete beams supported by huge caissons bored into the ground. In 1989, a Case Study exhibition, 'Blueprints for Modern Living', produced a full-scale mock-up of the house, using television screens to represent the lights of the city below.

☛ Cook, Eames, Ellwood, P Johnson, Neutra, Soriano

234

Pierre Koenig. b San Francisco, CA (USA), 1925. **Stahl House (Case Study House No.22)**, Los Angeles, CA (USA), 1960.

Koninck Louis Herman de   Villa Berteaux

Inspired in his early days by the Art Nouveau architecture of fellow Belgian, Victor Horta, de Koninck's interpretation of the Modern style was formally more creative and less rigid than many of his European contemporaries. This is shown at the Villa Berteaux in the interplay between horizontal and vertical windows; this playful composition also borrowed the porthole windows and metal handrails from ship designs, a favourite Modernist source. De Koninck was renowned for his technological innovation; he introduced the exterior reinforced concrete wall to Belgium. This house, built for an engineer, displays his mastery of construction techniques with smooth, rounded corners and elegantly composed volumes. De Koninck was best known internationally for the CUBEX kitchen, which was designed as a series of modular components that could be purchased separately and assembled in various configurations to fit a client's needs.

☛ Bijvoet & Duiker, Doesburg, Lauterbach, Rietveld & Schröder

Louis Herman de Koninck. **b** Brussels (BEL), 1896. **d** Brussels (BEL), 1984. **Villa Berteaux**, Uccle-Brussels (BEL), 1936–8.

Koning Eizenberg

Koning Eizenberg House

The end facade of this long, skinny house – 250 sq m (2,700 sq ft) but measuring only 5 m (17 ft) wide – reveals its designers' biggest concerns: blurring the boundaries between indoors and out, and playing with transitional elements, such as doors and windows. This Santa Monica house – designed by Australian-born, Los Angeles-based architects, Hank Koning and Julie Eizenberg, for themselves and their family – boasts oversized, ground-floor doors that slide open to seamlessly connect house (specifically the living room) and garden. Upstairs, tall, narrow French windows continue to blur the transition between open and closed areas. The diagonally-patterned, green stucco skin fulfills the designers' intention to conceal the house amid the surrounding landscape. In the end, the architecture becomes merely a backdrop to the outdoors – the epitome of informal living popularized in both southern California and Australia.

☞ **Gehry, Holl, Israel, Morphosis, Moss**

Koning Eizenberg. *Hank Koning*. **b** Melbourne (ASL), 1953. **Julie Eizenberg**. **b** Melbourne (ASL), 1954. **Koning Eisenberg House**, Santa Monica, CA (USA), 1993.

Konstantinidis Aris   Weekend House

Located on a small peninsula between Athens and Cape Sounion, this simple weekend house, consisting of three parallel stone walls unified by a flat concrete roof, contrasts dynamically with its Mediterranean setting. The house stands as an 'approximation of the essential', the roof protecting the living spaces from sun and rain, almost like a hand raised above the eyes to protect them from the light. A small portion of the space is enclosed, while the remainder is covered but open to the sounds and smells of the sea. The furnishings are minimal; sofas are used for beds and the dining area is simply defined by a table next to the fireplace. The clear and simple architectural language allows sun, light, darkness and shadow to play a primordial role in the act of dwelling. Konstantinidis is one of the most highly regarded post-war Greek architects, noted for successfully combining Modernist principles with regional Greek architecture.

☛ Atelier 66, Neutra, Raymond, Santorini Islanders

Aris Konstantinidis. **b** Athens (GR), 1913. **d** Athens (GR), 1993. **Weekend House**, Anavyssos, Attica (GR), 1961–2.

Koolhaas Rem/OMA   House near Bordeaux

The striking structure of this hillside house was intended to give it a feeling of 'launch'. The heavy concrete box forming the upper floor, containing the bedrooms, appears to float uneasily across the transparent, glazed middle level on which the main living space is situated. The equilibrium of the house is maintained by the steel beam overhead, anchored to the ground by a cable. The dramatized approach to the building structure suggests a deliberate flouting of the laws of rational expression enshrined in the modernist functionalist tradition. At the same time, the system of delicate balances creates a dynamic domestic landscape which, with an open elevator room at its heart, meets the wheelchair-user client's desire for a house which 'will define my world'. As such, it is very much a part of the OMA tradition of designing urban and suburban landscapes around intricate organizational narratives.

☛ **Future Systems, Le Corbusier, Mecanoo, UN Studio**

Rem Koolhaas/Office for Metropolitan Architecture. **Rem Koolhaas b** Rotterdam (NL), 1944. **House near Bordeaux**, Gironde (FR), 1998.

Köprülü Family   Köprülü-Yalisi Kösk

The shores of the Bosphorus are lined with summer mansions, or *yalis*, overlooking the strait; this pavilion, or *kösk*, belonged to one of the oldest, dating from the very end of the seventeenth century. The plan is cruciform: a domed central room, with a multifaceted marble fountain splashing in the centre, gives on to three timber bays which extend over the water, each lined with cushioned seats. The continuous strip of sash windows occupy only the lowest portion of the wall, which contributes to maintaining a high, cool interior. Complex systems of windows and wooden shutters were evolved for these pleasure pavilions. The sashes could slide completely out of sight, opening the rooms to the breeze and view, while shutters could be raised from above or below to give precise control over shading. The architecture of the Köprülü Yalisi, affording continuous views of its waterside setting, suggests the pleasures for which it was designed.

☛   Eldem, Hølmebakk, A Jacobsen, Mehmed II

239

Köprülü Family. Active (TRK), seventeenth and eighteenth century. **Köprülü-Yalisi Kösk**, Anadoluhisari (TRK), 1699.

Korsmo Arne   Villa Damman

In 1930, Axel Damman commissioned Arne Korsmo to design fourteen houses for the Havna neighbourhood in Oslo, including this, the developer's own house. With its strong plan and play of overlapping forms, the Villa Damman remains one of Korsmo's most important works, and an expression of his commitment to Norwegian Modernism. The street front of the house is dominated by a long walkway leading from the garden to the entrance. The rear facade, facing a fjord, accommodates the living room – which doubles as an art gallery lit by continuous, high-level strip windows – a dining room and semi-circular study. Successfully uniting the articulated forms into a harmonious whole, the concept was taken through into the interior, with much of the furniture also specially designed by Korsmo. Like Le Corbusier, he believed in the ability of a fully-designed environment to transform the way people lived and to solve the problems of society.

☞ Aalto, Asplund, Doesburg, Fehn, Fry, Lubetkin

240

Arne Korsmo. b Oslo (NOR), 1900. d Lima (PE), 1968. **Villa Damman**, Oslo (NOR), 1932.

Krier Leon

Krier House

In a town of towers, this house stands tallest. Leon Krier, a leading proponent of the 1980s New Urbanist movement to return to traditional towns and architecture, was an advisor in the early stages of planning Seaside, the famous new resort community in the Florida Panhandle. He decided to build a house of his own there which has become a landmark in more ways than one. It is a small house on a compact site, but rises high in the air to its 'temple' top that affords a fine view of the Gulf of Mexico. By regulation, all Seaside houses have white picket fences, and this one is no exception. Krier has spent most of his career in the theoretical realm of architecture, writing and drawing, and this house represents his first built work. It is a craftsman's house, intricately assembled as if built by a ship's carpenter. Krier is also known for his planning of the neo-traditional UK town of Poundsbury in Devon, under the instruction of the Prince of Wales.

☛ Duany Plater-Zyberk, Graves, Jencks & Farrell, Terry

Leon Krier. b Echternach (LX), 1946. **Krier House**, Seaside, FL (USA), 1985–7.

Kropholler Margaret House VI (*Meezennest*)

This masonry house with a sculpted, thatched roof was one of seventeen country houses built in the artists' colony of Park Meerwijk, in a verdant coastal town in northern Holland. One of the first realized Dutch Expressionist projects, this colony was supervised by Amsterdam School architect Jan Frederick Staal with Piet Kramer, G F La Croix, C J Blaauw and Margaret Kropholler – Staal's young assistant who later became his second wife, and the architect of House VI. *Meezennest* (Tom-Tit's Nest) is actually a double-house with its mirror image, *Meerlhuis* (Blackbird House) on the opposite side. As one of the most evocative schemes in the colony, this house draws from a combination of Japanese, Indonesian and Dutch vernacular sources, as well as the ideals of the English Arts and Crafts movement. Kropholler is considered to be Holland's first female architect and the Park Meerwijk designs were profoundly influential in Japan through the writings of Sutemi Horiguchi.

☛ **Horiguchi, Shirakawa Farmers, P Webb**

Margaret Kropholler. **b** Haarlem (NL), 1891. **d** Amsterdam (NL), 1966. **House VI** (*Meezennest*), Park Meerwijk, Bergen (NL), 1916–18.

Kyoto Merchants   Ikegaki Residence

Traditional Kyoto merchant houses, or *machiya*, are famous for their small courtyard gardens, typically equipped with a stone lantern, a Zen-style rock arrangement and bamboo plants. These houses often have a store-front facing onto the street with the living quarters at the back, between which the garden is created. Established as an Imperial capital in AD 794, Kyoto is one of only a few Japanese cities created on the ancient Chinese-style plan, and it is still characterized by its north-south boulevards and east-west avenues. Large city blocks created by these crossing streets were originally occupied by aristocratic mansions and large temples, as well as markets. However, by the end of the sixteenth century, these blocks were reorganized to accommodate much smaller and narrower houses, sometimes referred to as 'a bed for an eel'. Still popular in Kyoto, *machiya* have influenced the work of many contemporary architects, such as Tadao Ando.

☞ **Ando, Horiguchi, Pompeii Romans, Toshihito & Toshitada**

Kyoto Merchants. Active (JAP), nineteenth century. **Ikegaki Residence**, Kyoto (JAP), circa nineteenth century.

Kyrgyz

Yurt

To the nomadic Mongolian tribes of the central Asian Steppe, the *yurt* is a 'sanctified shelter under the protection of which life proceeds'. Its circular structure and domed roof combine the minimum structure with maximum strength, and it can be dismantled in an hour, loaded onto pack animals and relocated as grazing patterns dictate. Although the name and outer detailing may differ between tribes, all *yurts* have a lattice willow framework, linked together with rawhide nails. Roof poles slot into a wooden ring and are lashed to the frame, and a woven band is tied around the top of the wall to hold the structure together. As many as eight layers of felt may be used as covering, the outer layer being oiled for waterproofing. The entrance faces south, away from prevailing winds, opposite which is an altar or family shrine. Today, three-quarters of the Mongolian population still live in *yurts*, although they are more likely to be factory-produced than hand-made.

☞ **Blackfoot, Moors, Qashqai, Sami**

244

Kyrgyz. Active (AFG, IR, KAZ, KYR, MNG, TKM), c200 BC to present day. **Yurt**, Xinjiang (CHN), as built today.

Laan Dom Hans van der   Naalden House

Dom Hans van der Laan – an architect and a monk – devoted his life to a quest to discover the primitive origins of architecture. He believed there was a fundamental link between the act of building and the human need to order the space around us. The commission for this house arose when van der Laan visited his friend, Jos Naalden, at his house designed by the Dutch functionalist architect, J B Bakema (c1970). He was enthusiastic about the layout of the glass-walled courtyard house, but felt that it lacked strength and solidity and offered to design Naalden a house that would demonstrate the space-forming function of walls. The result is an articulated, masonry, three-sided court, bounded by a cloistered gallery; the three wings are expressed as distinct articulated volumes, using the walls to define and enclose the common space. This design undoubtedly influenced van der Laan's published thesis *Architectonic Space* (1977).

☛ Bijvoet & Duiker, Breuer, Brinkman & van der Vlugt, Kahn

Dom Hans van der Laan. **b** Leiden (NL), 1904. **d** Vaals (NL), 1991. **Naalden House**, Best (NL), 1978–82.

Lacaton Vassal House at Lège Cap-Ferret

This unusual house, raised on stilts beside the Bassin d'Arcachon, is clad in corrugated aluminium, allowing what would otherwise be a dark underbelly to be illuminated by the sun's rays reflecting off the water. The shimmering effect gives the house an almost magical presence among the pine trees which is enhanced by the fact that six trees actually grow through the otherwise simple, box-like structure. To keep the building watertight, the trunks pass through plastic sheet-covered skylights, to which they are held with rubber strips, allowing movement without damaging the structure. The house is built out of everyday, industrially-produced materials, yet at the same time embodies a dream of living in communion with nature; not least with living tree trunks forming part of the internal space. Thus it fuses modernist and romantic ideals, continuing a body of work by the architects that features a number of unusual private houses.

☛ **Hara, Jersey Devil, Le Corbusier, Patkau Architects**

Lacaton Vassal. Anne Lacaton. b (FR), 1955. **Philippe Vassal**. b (FR), 1954. **House at Lège Cap-Ferret**, Bordeaux (FR), 1997–8.

Landaise Farmers
Landes Farmhouse

The coastal region of south-west France, though once covered by enough vegetation to graze sheep (*landes* means heather), is in fact a vast sand dune. The Landaise farmhouse, one of the most enchanting forms of French vernacular architecture, is timber-framed, with clay and wattle filling, and a three-sloped canal-tiled roof, and entered via a recessed veranda or *estantade*. This opens on to a big square room, dominated by a huge fireplace, with as many as six rooms opening off it. The farmhouse was part of a complex, called an *aerial*, including a domed bake oven, a bergerie and a fanciful wooden chicken-house raised high on stilts. In 1857, the Landes' ecology was suddenly transformed when the region was planted with pine trees designed to stabilize the shifting sand floor and give employment in turpentine production. However, soon turpentine prices dropped and there were devastating forest fires, causing massive emigration from this once pastoral area.

☛ **Bernese Farmers, Shirakawa Farmers, Weobley Yeoman**

Landaise Farmers. Active (FR), early nineteenth century. **Landes Farmhouse**, Ecomusée de la Grande-Lande, Marquèze, Sabres (FR), c1820s.

Larsson Carl   Lilla Hyttnäs

'Cosy Corner' is one of the most famous watercolour illustrations by Larsson for his book, *Ett hem* (*A Home*). This shows his young family enjoying the idyllic country cottage which he and his wife, Karin, gradually extended, furnished and decorated themselves. Larsson was an artist rather than an architect, and produced large-scale paintings for public buildings, as well as smaller watercolours. This drawing room is seen as one of the most quintessentially Swedish of all his rooms, although it is more formal than many at Lilla Hyttnäs. It epitomized a revival of the 'Gustavian' style, from the late eighteenth-century Gustave III, but interpreted through the rural elegance and relative simplicity of small manor houses.

The extraordinary success of *Ett hem* popularized a broader vision of Swedish Style, incorporating light colours, painted surfaces, traditional textiles and the influence of folk art and nature; influences that remain strong in our homes today.

☞ **Asplund, Erskine, Gallén-Kallela, Isidore**

248

Carl Larsson. b Stockholm (SWE), 1853. d Falun (SWE), 1919. **Lilla Hyttnäs (Little Furnace)**, Sundborn (SWE), 1890–1919. 'Lathörnet' or 'Cosy Corner' is one of a series of watercolours published in *Ett hem* (*A Home*), 1899.

Laugier Abbé

Primitive Hut

Just as Rousseau's hypothetical noble savage represented a natural human being, unspoilt by the complexities of civilization, this image illustrates a dismissal of the social roots of architecture and a return to pure structure and form. The Primitive Hut, presented as an idealized prototype, had a huge impact on architectural thinking when the engraving

was published in Abbé Laugier's *Essai sur l'architecture* in 1755. The Muse of Architecture, amid Classical ruins, is explaining the origins of architecture to Cupid and points to an idealized primitive hut formed by four trees which have grown in a perfect square to a height exactly double their spacing. The upper branches are growing inwards to form a

pedimented roof and an entablature is formed by horizontal branches. It illustrates Laugier's theory, in line with the scientific mood of the Enlightenment, that architecture emerged as a pure and logical progression of the natural order.

☞ **Ledoux, Schinkel, Soane, Viollet-le-Duc**

Abbé Marc-Antoine Laugier. b Manosque (FR), 1713. **d** Paris (FR), 1769. **Primitive Hut**, engraving, 1753. 'Allegory of Architecture Returning to its Natural State', frontispiece, *Essai sur l'architecture*, 2nd ed., Paris, 1755.

Laurana Luciano

Palazzo Ducale

The fifteenth-century courtier, Baldassare Castiglione, described Federigo da Montefeltro's Ducal Palace as 'a city in the form of a palace'. Set in the heart of the medieval walled city of Urbino, the imposing walls of the palace bear reliefs of arms and armour, commemorating Federigo's reputation throughout Europe as a great soldier. Beyond these walls,

Laurana's work is revealed further in the delightful arcaded courtyard, the state and private apartments with superimposed loggias, and a hanging garden overlooking the city walls to the undulating hills beyond. Federigo, who was also a patron of the arts (most notably of the painter, Piero della Francesca), directed a series of other architects to complete the palace over

a number of stages, so individual contributions are sometimes difficult to distinguish. However, it is the enlightened Renaissance culture of its ducal patron, most evident, perhaps, in Federigo's *studiolo*, that leaves the strongest mark.

☞ **Alberti, Maiano, Michelozzi, Sangallo**

Luciano Laurana. **b** Zara (CRO), c1420. **d** Pesaro (IT), 1479. **Palazzo Ducale**, Urbino (IT), 1466–79.

Lauterbach Heinrich

Villa Schmelowsky

Combining ocean-liner imagery with clear, cubic forms, this house reflects the Modernist tradition at both a superficial and a profound level. The short cantilevers and open, high-level terrace stake a claim to their space in a consciously Cubist manner, while the porthole lends a nautical air. These two strands come together in the living room, with its balcony resembling a captain's bridge, and its asymmetrical curved roof. Lauterbach's composition deals with the same generic problem of a site which slopes steeply away from a road as Mies van der Rohe addressed at his Tugendhat House (1930). Mies may have achieved greater elegance, but Lauterbach was a friend of the organic apostle, Scharoun, and his design has a certain consistency in its awkward compositional devices. Its long, narrow form is essentially self-contained, like a ship, and its connection to its surroundings – a bridge from the road – is the static equivalent of a gangplank.

☛ Koninck, Scharoun, Tait, Terragni, Žák

Heinrich Lauterbach. b Breslau (GER), 1893. d Mid to late twentieth century. **Villa Schmelowsky**, Jablonec nad Nisou, (CZ, was Bohemia), 1931.

Lautner John   Sheats House

Nearly thirty years after its construction, John Lautner remodelled, or in his own words 'perfected', his original vision for the Sheats House, using modern construction methods. By replacing the 1963 mullions with frameless silicon-sealed glazing, he produced an invisible curtain of air between the living area and its view over the city, which emphasized its almost cave-like quality, a debt to his mentor Frank Lloyd Wright. Lautner was apprenticed to Wright after graduating and became the first of the Taliesin Fellows, before going on to set up his own practice. He revered Wright, although Henry-Russell Hitchcock, the architectural critic, considered that his work could 'stand comparison with that of his master.' It is arguable which of Lautner's houses is the most iconic; but it is indicative that many of them have been featured in films. Others equally celebrated include the 'Chemosphere' residence of 1960 and the Arango House in Acapulco (1977).

☛ Breuer, Ellwood, Goff, Neutra, Niemeyer, Wright

John Lautner. b Marquette, MI (USA), 1911. **d** Los Angeles, CA (USA), 1994. **Sheats House (Sheats-Goldstein House)**, Los Angeles (CA), 1963, remodelled 1989–96.

Lavenham Clothier

Little Hall

Lavenham is famed for its fourteenth- and fifteenth-century, timber-framed houses, built from the profits of the local weaving industry. Little Hall is typical of these and, thanks to restoration, graphically demonstrates the arrangements of a two-part hall-house. The central, round-arched entrance leads to a passage that runs across the end of the hall, which comprises the section to the right. This is open to the rafters with a hearth in the middle; the large, two-tiered window lights the upper end of the hall where a table, set on a dais, provided a formal place for dining and family life. The gabled cross-wing, on the left, has two storeys; the lower floor contains two service rooms, a buttery for jugs, bottles and barrels, and a pantry for dry food. The projecting upper floor contains solar chambers, private rooms for sitting and sleeping. The closely-set vertical timbers and curved angled brackets are largely decorative, as the oak-framed structure is immensely strong.

☛ **Ludlow, Moreton Family, Weobley Yeoman**

Lavenham Clothier. Active (UK), early fourteenth century to mid-sixteenth century. **Little Hall**, Lavenham (UK), late 1390s.

Le Breton Gilles   Château de Fontainebleau

Nowhere better demonstrates the resurgence of the French monarchy after the Middle Ages than the Château de Fontainebleau, which achieved a significant architectural marriage between Renaissance classicism and French traditions. In 1528, King Francis I decided to improve what was no more than a hunting lodge and commanded his master mason, Gilles Le Breton, to undertake the works. The king soon became more ambitious, so what began as alterations became a piecemeal transformation, with a new entrance, galleries and ranges, including the facade of the Cour du Cheval Blanc shown here. The resulting picturesque irregularities, in particular the lack of symmetry, are at odds with the overall style, but it works as a naturalization of Classicism into the French idiom. This is shown in the plainness of the decoration, with rusticated window surrounds sometimes taking the place of pilasters and an entablature.

☞ J le Breton, Cecil, Cerceau, Cortona

Gilles Le Breton. **b** Paris (FR), c1500. **d** Paris (FR), 1552. **Château de Fontainebleau**, Fontainebleau (FR), 1528–40.

Le Corbusier Villa Savoye

The Villa Savoye is an icon of functionalist, machine-age symbolism, embodying many of Le Corbusier's revolutionary concepts including the 'Five Points of a New Architecture'. The use of the slender columns, *pilotis,* to support the main living accommodation above the ground, gives the house a striking elegance and lightness, while the strip windows on all sides unify the design. Made possible by the development of reinforced concrete technology, the *pilotis* enabled Le Corbusier to separate stationary living space from a ground zone given over to moving objects, or traffic. Inside, a ramp leads from ground level up towards the rooftop solarium, dramatizing a sense of movement through the house, while also distilling associations with the industrial era. This house is an eloquent expression of Le Corbusier's influential vision of a rationalized architecture for the twentieth century, which would lift its inhabitants into a realm of light, air and order.

☛ **Breuer, Gray & Badovici, Mies van der Rohe, Yamada**

Le Corbusier (**Charles-Edouard Jeanneret**). **b** La Chaux-de-Fonds (SW), 1887. **d** Cap Martin (FR), 1965. **Villa Savoye**, Poissy (FR), 1929–31.

Le Vau Louis & Hardouin-Mansart Jules

Palace of Versailles

A hunting lodge transformed into an extravagant, monumental palace, Versailles is – perhaps more than any other building – the symbol of France. It was the royal residence and seat of government from 1682 until the French Revolution in 1789, when Louis XVI and his family fled Versailles. The original hunting lodge was built by Louis XIII in 1624, but his son Louis XIV was responsible for the various stages of its redevelopment. In 1661, Le Vau began to transform the relatively simple château into a Baroque masterpiece. In strict axial form, he created a twenty-five bay facade adding two vast wings on either side of the existing château, set at the top of a flight of terraces. In 1678, after Le Vau's death, Jules Hardouin-Mansart took over further enlargements bringing the total length of the facade to almost half a kilometre (1,640 ft). He also created Versailles' most famous room, the Hall of Mirrors, as well as the Grand Trianon and the Orangerie.

☞ Cerceau, Gabriel, Pöppelmann, Rastrelli

Louis Le Vau. b Paris (FR), 1612. d Paris (FR), 1670. **Jules Hardouin-Mansart**. b Paris (FR), 1646. d Marly (FR), 1708. **Palace of Versailles**, Versailles (FR), 1624, ongoing additions until 1789.

Ledoux Claude-Nicolas House of the Surveyors of the Loüe River

This engraving of the dramatic mountain landscape of the Franche-Comté shows the plunging waterfall of the Loüe River cascading through the central elliptical opening of this highly-geometric building. Designed to act as a combined bridge and watercourse, as well as a home for the river surveyors, its form makes an analogy with the occupation of its inhabitants and celebrates the taming and harnessing of water. It is one of several building types dreamed up by the visionary eighteenth-century architect, Ledoux, to populate his partially-realized utopian project for an ideal community in the heart of the French countryside, at Chaux. Inspired by Rousseau's call for a return to origins, he intended the Neo-Classical forms and arrangement of the buildings to regulate the moral behaviour of its inhabitants. He had already constructed a salt works at Arc-et-Senans in 1775–9, but had to complete his designs while imprisoned in the Bastille as an enemy of the new Republic.

☞ I Jones, Laugier, Nash, Palladio, Soane

Claude-Nicolas Ledoux. b Dormans (FR), 1736. d Paris (FR), 1806. House of the Surveyors of the Loüe River, engraving, c1790. First published in *L'Architecture considerée sous le rapport de l'art, des moeurs et de la législation*, 1804.

Legorreta Ricardo   Greenberg House

The use of the wall as a canvas for the interplay of light and shadow, sun and shade, is emphasized in this house designed by the Mexican architect, Ricardo Legorreta. An heir to the Arab-Hispanic tradition of Luis Barragán, Legorreta utilizes the thickness and variation of massive walls to create a place of privacy and refuge from the outside world. The two towers, one containing a studio, the other a library, contribute to this sense of seclusion. A feeling of calm expansiveness is achieved through the use of a combination of interior atria and exterior terraces; while the desert tones of external ochre-coloured plaster are contrasted on the inside by walls painted in magenta, lavender or cherry. This sculptural style, working in harmony with the desert climate, is a noticeable departure from the steel skeleton and lightweight skin of the modern, domestic California architecture of Rudolph Schindler and Richard Neutra.

☛ **Barragán, Bofill, Fathy, Predock, Schweitzer**

Ricardo Legorreta. b Mexico City (MEX), 1931. **Greenberg House**, Los Angeles, CA (USA), 1991.

Lescaze William

Lescaze House

The facade of this radically remodelled brownstone house appears to be a white frame with large areas of glazing, rather than a stone wall with windows punched into it. Swiss-born and trained Lescaze sought to reverse every convention of his neighbours' houses. Built just after Henry-Russell Hitchcock and Philip Johnson had sanitized Modernism for American consumption as the 'International Style', this house remains one of its finest examples in New York. A discreet ground-level entrance leads to the studio (brownstone entrances tend to be slightly below street level), while the living quarters are above, reached via a flight of steps under the cantilevered canopy. Internally, Lescaze created a remarkable series of spaces in the long, thin site, creatively using rooflights, lightwells and terraces, and culminating in a roof garden. With this, his own house and studio, he demonstrated that modern living was compatible with existing urban form.

☞ **Architecture Studio, Chareau, P Johnson, Rudolph**

William Lescaze. **b** Geneva (SW), 1896. **d** New York (USA), 1969. **Lescaze House**, New York, NY (USA), 1934.

Lever William Hesketh — Houses in Cross Street, Port Sunlight

The houses of the garden village of Port Sunlight demonstrate the particularly British tradition of combining the artistic qualities of the Picturesque with a benevolent desire to provide a high standard of housing to those who could not afford it. These feelings prompted William Hesketh Lever, a successful grocer-turned-industrialist famous for Sunlight Soap, to employ over thirty different architects to design cottages for his workers, close to the factory where they worked. The ones shown here are by the architects, Grayson and Ould. Other designs have half-timbering, decorated plasterwork, tile hanging and all the features of the vernacular idiom known as the Old English style. As well as houses, there are shops, a school, a girls' club (now the residents' club), a nursing home and a church, all laid out within one square mile, creating a green and pleasant village for the fortunate factory workers.

☛ Lutyens, Parker & Unwin, Pugin, Shaw

William Hesketh Lever (later First Viscount Leverhulme). **b** Bolton (UK), 1851. **d** London (UK), 1925. **Houses in Cross Street, Port Sunlight**, Merseyside (UK), 1896.

Leverton Thomas   Bedford Square

The restrained, Palladian elevations of this Georgian terraced housing in a Bloomsbury square in London lend uniformity to what was, in fact, a speculative development by individual leaseholders. The fifty-three plots were developed from 1775–83 by builders to a standardized facade design, constructing the interior to each client's specification. Each of the four terraces surrounding the oval-shaped garden has a stucco-fronted and pedimented centre, which breaks the austerity of the predominant brickwork and leans towards the Regency period. The north terrace, seen here, shows the architectural 'fault' of a pilaster occurring directly beneath the pediment's apex – probably resulting from the collation of a general design by a builder on site. The overall design is generally attributed to Thomas Leverton. He was undoubtedly responsible for several interiors in the square and lived at number thirteen from 1795 until his death.

☛ Kent, Malton, Nash, Soane, Wood

Thomas Leverton. b Essex (UK), 1743. d London (UK), 1824. **Bedford Square**, London (UK), 1775–83.

Libera Adalberto   Casa Malaparte

In building the inter-war Casa Malaparte, Rationalist architect Libera, together with his client, the writer Curzio Malaparte, reinforced something of the myth of the writer in his solitary study on this bare rock of his Capri island exile. Conceived as a simple stone house, the design was soon developed to incorporate a broad, ritualistic flight of tapering steps that lead to the plain roof terrace. This detail ties the house to its rocky setting, demonstrating how a building can be treated as a geographical accent, part of the landscape itself. This relationship with nature is continued inside by a series of small windows framing intense views along the dramatic coastline or glimpses of rocks and waves in the distance. Although more modern than classical in its architectural heritage, Casa Malaparte manages to evoke an antique ruin; indeed, it was built almost in sight of Tiberius' Villa Iovis which had, at the time, just been excavated.

☛ Coderch, Portoghesi, Rossi, Terragni, Tiberius

Libera Adalberto   Casa Malaparte

Adalberto Libera. **b** Trento (IT), 1903. **d** Rome (IT), 1963. **Casa Malaparte**, Capri (IT), 1938–41.

Loess Han

Cave House

On the dry Loess Plain in north-eastern China, cave houses have been a traditional form of dwelling for nearly two thousand years. With cool summers and cold winters, the earth insulation provides comfortable living conditions; indoor temperatures can be up to 15° C (59° F) cooler in summer and 10° C (50°F) warmer in winter than outside. In addition, construction costs are minimal while, most importantly, land available for crop-growing is maximized. The facade is constructed of a wooden frame faced with white paper to admit light. The single-arched chamber allows for a bedroom to the rear and living area at the front, furnished with a stove whose flue punctures the cultivated fields above. The cave houses in Ya'an have more recently become a pilgrimage site for visitors to the *de facto* capital of the Communist Party. Mao Zedong ended the infamous Long March here in 1935, and set up his Revolutionary administration in these cave dwellings.

☛ **Anchorites, Coober Pedy Miners, Gitano, Tiwa Indians**

Loess Han. Active (CHN), c2000 BC to present day. **Cave House**, Ya'an, Shanxi Province (CHN), circa AD 500 to present day.

LOOS Adolf

Steiner House

The curved metal roofline of the street front of this house masks its scale and the fact that it is built on three levels; more importantly, that the rear facade is rectilinear and flat-roofed, evidence of Loos' perception of architecture as spatial sequences, or *Raumplan*. One of the first houses to be constructed of reinforced concrete, the Steiner House is also one of few built works by Loos, a famous polemicist against the elaborate decoration of the Art Nouveau and Vienna Secessionist movements. Apart from the curved roof, the geometric form and rear garden facade of the house anticipate later Modern characteristics, such as functional interior spaces, solid white cubic forms and horizontal fenestration.

Loos, influenced by a visit to America where he encountered the severity of Louis Sullivan's work, fought against ornamentation; his famous essay 'Ornament and Crime' was published in 1908.

☞ **Morris, Olbrich, Sullivan, Wagner, Wright**

264

Adolf Loos. **b** Brno (CZ), 1870. **d** Vienna (AUS), 1933. **Steiner House**, Vienna (AUS), 1910.

L'Orme Philibert de   Château de Chenonceau

Chenonceau is perhaps the most sublime of all the French châteaux, with its five-bay bridge building apparently leaping over the gently flowing River Cher. Its delicate grace testifies to the taste of its successive female owners, who transformed the once modest manor and watermill into an unrivalled Renaissance pleasure palace. Between 1556–9, L'Orme, at the behest of Henri II's mistress Diane de Poitiers, united the two banks with his imaginatively conceived bridge. The three-storey, Italianate Grande Galerie above was added by the Mannerist, Jean Bullant, in 1576, after the redoubtable Catherine de Medici took possession. Inside, Catherine Briçonnet introduced the first straight staircase in France.

Classical simplicity contrasts with exuberant sculptured balustrades, roofs and dormers which, combined, radiate a charm that is reflected in the surrounding waters. Chenonceau is, as Flaubert described, 'floating on air and water'.

☛ Berthelot, Cerceau, Cortona, Le Breton

265

Philibert de l'Orme. b Lyon (FR), c1508. d Paris (FR), 1570. **Château de Chenonceau**, Indre-et-Loire (FR), 1556–9.

Lubetkin Berthold   House A at Whipsnade

As this house was for himself, Lubetkin took the opportunity to experiment. It was designed for maximum outdoor living, and built on a platform cut into the hill to make the most of the views. The bedrooms are provided with outdoor sleeping porches, and there is also an outdoor fireplace. Lubetkin was not a strict functionalist and he worked in an intuitive way, as demonstrated in the two highly-expressive curved elements of the building. First, on the roof is an extended parabolic screen which, below, makes a room-within-a-room for dining, and focuses this space on the view across the valley; second, the entrance is screened by a semicircular 'sun-catch'. Lubetkin came to England in 1931 and set up Tecton (1932–48) with young admirers of his work who had studied at the Architectural Association in London. Although best known for the Penguin Pool (1934) at London Zoo, his deeply held socialist views led him to concentrate most of his career on public housing.

☞ **Chermayeff, Connell, Fry, Goldfinger, Tait**

Berthold Lubetkin. **b** Tiflis (RUS), 1901. **d** Bristol (UK), 1990. **House A at Whipsnade**, Bedfordshire (UK), 1933–6.

Luckhardt Hans & Wassili   House II at Rupenhorn

Flat-roofed and essentially regular cuboid forms with traces of Corbusian influences, the Luckhardt brothers' three houses at Rupenhorn are archetypal Modernist images. Using a similar design language and identical construction, the houses mark the triumph of *sachlichkeit* over the Expressionism which characterized their earlier work. Objectivity becomes an aesthetic, achieving that elusive goal of uniting art and everyday life. Internal details proclaim these values, with plain polished stone walls, radiators treated as sculptural objects, books as decorative patterns. Pragmatic things like cars, servants and cooking are banished from the principal floor. The billowing terrace of House II perhaps shows the merest hint of the architects' Expressionist heritage but it also establishes a clear, abstract plane from which the living and sleeping quarters of the house arise; being *sachlich* did not necessarily mean *existenzminimum*.

☞ **Connell, Fry, Gropius, Lauterbach, Lubetkin**

Wassili Luckhardt. b Berlin (GER), 1889. **d** Berlin (GER), 1972. **Hans Luckhardt. b** Berlin (GER), 1890. **d** Bad Wiessee (GER), 1954. **House II at Rupenhorn**, Berlin (GER), 1929–30.

Ludlow Laurence de   Stokesay Castle

In the late twelfth century, Stokesay Castle was begun with just a simple stone tower, seen here behind the tree to the right. The de Saye family added a hall in the 1270s, with four prominently gabled windows down its length, and it was only in the 1290s that a rich wool merchant, Laurence de Ludlow, obtained a licence to erect the crenellated tower at the far end. This at last gave it some semblance of a castle, although he probably intended it as no more than a fashionable status symbol. Stokesay has a particularly lucid internal medieval arrangement of hall and attendant service rooms, solar (a private room on the upper floor of a medieval house), chambers, and a magnificent framed roof. To the left, the pretty, late sixteenth-century framed and jettied gatehouse, built on a stone base, gives the lie to any defensive intention, the upper part being filled with the decorative foiled panels so admired in the West Midlands of England.

☛ Compton, Lavenham Clothier, Moreton Family

268

Laurence de Ludlow. Active (UK), mid to late thirteenth century. **d** (UK), 1296. **Stokesay Castle**, Shropshire (UK), late twelfth century, with later additions.

Ludwig II

Schloss Neuschwanstein

Rising out of trees rather than parting clouds, and lacking a rainbow bridge, Schloss Neuschwanstein is nevertheless the fabled Valhalla made real. At the command of Ludwig II, King of Bavaria, the design attempted to give living form to the composer, Richard Wagner's epic operas of Norse and German mythology. Already obsessed with the majesty of Louis XIV,

Ludwig demonstrated his fascination with Wotan and the gods of German legend at Neuschwanstein. The design was realized by Eduard Riedel (1813–85), who had designed Ludwig's Schloss Berg in Bavaria in the domestic Gothic style. However, the precariously-sited castle was completed by another favoured architect, Georg von Dollmann, in the Romanesque Revival

style, its extravagantly turreted exterior being largely finished by 1881. Julius Hofmann (1840–96) designed the later interiors, including endless murals depicting the Wagnerian legends, and culminating with a throne room worthy of *Parsifal*.

☞ Dollmann, Eschwege, L'Orme, MacNeilledge

Ludwig II, King of Bavaria. b Munich (GER), 1845. Reigned Bavaria (GER), 1864–86. **d** Schloss Berg, nr Starnberg (GER), 1886. **Schloss Neuschwanstein**, nr Füssen, Bavaria (GER), 1868–86.

Lutyens Sir Edwin   Deanery Gardens

A large, long roof presides over the vertical features of this house, which combines formal principles with a response to function. The two-storey bay window declares the importance of the hall within, while presenting an axial relationship with the dominating roof. Lutyens was the pre-eminent British architect of the early twentieth century. His fascination with axial compositions would later take him towards Classicism, but at Deanery Gardens essentially vernacular elements are arranged on axes to create one of the most sophisticated houses in the Arts-and-Crafts tradition. Hidden from the public by an ancient wall, the house is orientated towards this, its most private side. Comfort and privacy override public ostentation: the Edwardian taste was for impressing ones peers, rather than dominating peasantry, but this house exudes an enduring image of domesticity that suited the client, *Country Life* magazine founder, Edward Hudson.

☛ **Baillie Scott, Mackintosh, Shaw, Voysey, P Webb**

Sir Edwin Landseer Lutyens. **b** London (UK), 1869. **d** London (UK), 1944. **Deanery Gardens**, Sonning (UK), 1902.

Maasai

Enkang Hut

The Maasai *enkang*, a circle of about twelve lozenge-shaped huts, can be entirely built by the women for themselves and their children in two weeks. It also contains separate huts for the headman and young warriors, again built by the women. The *enkang* accommodates two or three families, each male head having more than one wife, and the enclosure it forms is used as a corral for their cattle. The walls are constructed using stakes of euphorbia, incorporating small vents, but no windows; and low-vaulted roofs are woven from willow-like *leleshwa* wands. The hut entrance, at a right-angle to the wall with a projecting porch, is designed to repel marauders or wild animals. The buildings last for about eight years, after which the group will seek a fresh location. The Maasai, a cattle-herding people, do not like to dig into the soil or to use mud. Instead, they daub their buildings with a plaster of cattle-dung, which does not smell when dry and it is easy to obtain and apply.

☛ **Dogon, Mousgoum, Syrian Farmers, Tihama Farmers**

Maasai. Active (KEN and TAN), early seventeenth century to present day. **Enkang Hut** (KEN and TAN), as built today.

Mackintosh Charles Rennie   Hill House

Hill House is an extraordinary assembly of unusually detailed features. Windows of all shapes and sizes, stumpy chimney-stacks and round turrets – arbitrarily scattered about blank patches of plain walling and finished with traditional Scottish 'harling' or rendering – give the house an ungainly lop-sided appearance. More greatly admired on the European continent than in his own country, Mackintosh had won second prize in a German competition for the design of 'A House for a Connoisseur'. For Hill House, he returned to a similarly asymmetrical design resulting from the novel layout of internal spaces building up into simple cubic volumes dominated by solid, unornamented shapes and a dash of the Scottish baronial style. Today, this house, his famed Glasgow School of Art and his exquisitely-detailed, much reproduced furniture and stylized ornament ensure his position as Scotland's most celebrated architect.

☞ **Hoffmann, Loos, Morris, Olbrich, Voysey, Wright**

Charles Rennie Mackintosh. b Glasgow, Scotland (UK), 1868. **d** London (UK), 1928. **Hill House**, Helensburgh, Scotland (UK), 1902–3.

MacNeilledge Charles Scotty's Castle

Albert Johnson, a wealthy Chicago insurance magnate, was drawn to Death Valley when his gold-mining interests brought him into contact with the legendary prospector, Walter Scott, better known as 'Death Valley Scotty'. In 1924, Johnson purchased 1,500 acres of desert land and asked Frank Lloyd Wright to design a ranch complex. While Johnson was impressed with the 'indigenous purity' of Wright's proposal, he favoured a grander hacienda style. MacNeilledge, who had remodelled Johnson's home in Chicago, was subsequently commissioned to design the ranch on a Spanish-Mediterranean theme. With MacNeilledge's professional guidance, Johnson and Scott were free to indulge their whims and preferences. The castle is the exuberant result of the two men's life-long friendship and common passion for the desert. Although paid for by Johnson's millions, the house was to become universally known as Scotty's Castle.

☛ Delano & Aldrich, Gill & Mead, Hunt, Mizner, Morgan

273

Charles Alexander MacNeilledge. Active (USA), early to mid-twentieth century. **d** Los Angeles, CA (USA), 1958. **Scotty's Castle**, Grapevine Canyon, CA (USA), 1931.

Ma'dan

Mudhif

The Ma'dan have inhabited a vast marshy wilderness between the rivers Euphrates and Tigris in southern Iraq for over two thousand years. Here they have traditionally built the *mudhif*, or guest house. These great arched structures, based on tall tapering bundles of reeds, have served their needs for accommodation. Four reed columns frame each end and arches, formed from two bundles bent together, span the interior, which may measure up to 30 x 4.5 m (100 x 15 ft). The walls and roof are made of reed matting, which becomes latticework at each end to aid ventilation. Each settlement has several of these large *mudhifs*, as well as numerous smaller versions to serve individual families. They are all built on islands made of reed, which raise them a little above water level. In these conditions, a *mudhif* may last for ten or twenty years before rot claims it. However, the *mudhif* illustrated here is built on dry land and would have a longer life.

☛ **Abelam, Hutu, Tihama Farmers, Toda, Tukanoan, Zulu**

274

Ma'dan (Marsh Arabs). Active (IRQ), c3000 BC to present day. **Mudhif,** Marshlands, Lower Tigris and Euphrates (IRQ), from circa first millennium BC to present day.

Maiano Benedetto da   Palazzo Strozzi

Palazzo Strozzi rises like a forbidding fortress in the middle of Florence. Its rusticated stone walls are penetrated by a monumental arched entrance and divided into three storeys by string courses, which are surmounted by uniform arched windows. The over-sized, shade-giving cornice, which is unfinished on the Via Strozzi side, was designed separately by Simone Pollaiuolo, known as Il Cronaca. Beyond the austere facade is an unexpectedly airy courtyard, renowned for its light-filled, elegantly-proportioned loggia. Filippo Strozzi wanted his palace, attributed to Benedetto da Maiano, to be larger and finer than any other in Florence, without offending the powerful Lorenzo de' Medici (Lorenzo the Magnificent). The story goes that the banker shrewdly presented for approval a much-simplified proposal to the duke, who urged Strozzi to build a grander residence, one worthy of the Strozzi family – and Lorenzo himself.

☛ **Alberti, Laurana, Michelozzi, Sangallo**

275

Benedetto da Maiano. b Maiano (IT), 1442. **d** Florence (IT), 1497. **Palazzo Strozzi**, Florence (IT), 1489–c1536.

Maiuri Amadeo

Casa del Mosaico di Nettuno e Anfitrite

The small town of Herculaneum, on the shore of the Bay of Naples, was destroyed by the eruption of Mount Vesuvius in the first century AD, and buried under metres of solidified mud. In the 1930s, the excavator, Maiuri, uncovered this house, named after the mosaic of the mythological characters, Neptune and Amphitrite, in the small open-air dining room. The marble-faced platforms are for the placing of cushions for dining in a reclined position, while water flows soothingly from the mosaic fountain on the rear wall; painted garden scenes are still just visible on the walls to either side. The arrangement of rooms was such that a visitor could catch sight of the mosaic, first along a vista across the atrium of the house, and then framed by the window of the main reception room (the tablinum to the left of the photograph). All these delights reveal, on a small scale, the pleasures enjoyed in the many larger villas built by wealthy Romans on the Bay of Naples.

☞ **Minoan, Pompeii Romans, Tiberius**

276

Amadeo Maiuri. b 1886. d 1963. **Casa del Mosaico di Nettuno e Anfitrite**, Herculaneum (IT), third quarter of first century AD (excavated 1930).

Mallet-Stevens Robert   Villa de Noailles

Rendered in flat, unadorned stucco, the street façade of this sprawling villa expresses a monumentality that is not compromised by the playful composition of its geometrical volumes and bold windows. Situated on a hillside, the massive façade hides a luxurious retreat with extensively landscaped terrace gardens, a covered swimming pool, gymnasium and squash courts. The original project, a five-bedroom weekend home for film enthusiast and modern art collector, Viscount Charles de Noailles, was expanded to eventually include over sixty rooms; some of which were specially designed by other architects, including an open-air room by Pierre Chareau and a flower room by Dutch artist Theo van Doesburg. The client originally intended to commission Mies van der Rohe or Le Corbusier for this project, but settled on the untested Mallet-Stevens whose architectural reputation at the time, aged thirty-seven, was based only on inventive movie set designs.

☛   Bijvoet & Duiker, Chareau, Doesburg, Le Corbusier, Perret

Robert Mallet-Stevens. **b** Paris (FR), 1886. **d** Paris (FR), 1945. **Villa de Noailles**, Hyères (FR), 1924–33.

Malton Thomas

Georgian Perspective

Although a trained architect, Thomas Malton was also a topographical artist of commendable skill. He exhibited a few designs for rather vaguely-defined buildings at the Royal Academy of Art, but is chiefly remembered for his series of aquatint views of Sir Robert Taylor's buildings in which he was among the first to exploit this new process of perspective illustration. In 1792–1801, he published another series of aquatint views, *A Picturesque Tour through the Cities of London and Westminster*. Among the one hundred views is this one of a staircase, with the open strings and plain balusters typical of the late Georgian style, its two landings lit by large Venetian windows and the ceilings adorned with panelled plasterwork.

The gridlines and vanishing points demonstrate the extent to which proportion governed the design of Georgian interiors, and the way in which the size of the elements relate to each other and to the scale of the human figure.

☞ Adam, Leverton, Nash, Soane, Taylor, Wood

Thomas Malton. b London (UK), 1726. d Dublin (IRE), 1801. **Georgian Perspective**, engraving, 1775. Published in *A Picturesque Tour through the Cities of London and Westminster*, 1792–1801.

Mandan Indians Earth Lodge

A large, round, Mandan earth lodge, built on a framework of four sturdy posts and willow branches and covered with thick grass mats and earth, might measure up to 15 m (50 ft) in diameter and house twenty to thirty people. Mandan women gathered the building materials from their native Missouri River Valley (an area now part of North Dakota in the USA) and built the lodges. The women also owned, maintained and inherited the dwellings, along with any family land. A typical Mandan village consisted of more than one hundred lodges built in a circle around a sacred cedar tree or cedar post. The dwellings disappeared after the Mandan Indians were almost eradicated by smallpox in the 1830s, although reconstructions were made based on first-hand accounts and sketches from surviving Mandan and on the detailed paintings of American artist-adventurers, such as George Catlin.

☛ Blackfoot, Maasai, Maori, Tiwa Indians

Mandan Indians of North America. Active (USA), c8000 BC to present day. Earth Lodge, Missouri River Valley, ND (USA), as built c1500–1838.

Manrique César   Taro de Tahíche

This dramatic white room is inside a volcanic bubble. It is one of five such spaces in the home which César Manrique built for himself in the black torrents of lava formed by the volcanic eruption of 1730 on the island of Lanzarote. The house has two interconnected levels: an upper outdoor level inspired by traditional local architecture and this lower level of colourful volcanic bubbles (red, white, yellow, black and avocado), invisible from the outside. This house and studio are considered to be the work that most exemplifies the artist and sculptor's harmonious synthesis of the acts of man with nature. Manrique was born in Lanzarote but left the island at a young age, returning in 1968 at a time when it was being developed heavily for tourism. His passion for the island's inherent beauty, its traditional heritage and architecture were important factors in the works of architecture and landscape that he created over thirty years, leaving a lasting legacy on the island.

☛ **Anchorites, Le Corbusier, Senosiain, Soleri**

César Manrique. b Arrecife, Lanzarote (CI), 1919. d Tahíche, Lanzarote (CI), 1992. **Taro de Tahíche** (now César Manrique Foundation), Teguise, Lanzarote (CI), 1968–72.

Maori

Marae

The Maori *marae* is a cluster of individual dwellings organized around a central space, the focus of which is the meeting house, or *whare nui*, the symbolic centre of the tribe. The *whare nui* is distinguished by its beautifully-carved and painted side-posts and barge-boards representing the genealogical history of the tribe. Other buildings, including sleeping, learning and eating houses, are placed in relation to one another according to sacred laws or *tapu*. Their slightly inclined side walls are covered with a layer of bulrush thatch, secured by poles to protect against wind damage. Inside, they are commonly lined with bracken stalks, darkened by the smoke of a continually burning fire. Apart from mats on the earth floor and a sling for firewood, the dwellings typically contain no furniture. A Maori renaissance in the twentieth century has seen a significant rise in the number of *marae* – a testament to the strength of contemporary Maori culture.

☞ **Mandan Indians, Sa'dan Toraja, Samoan, Tukanoan**

Maori. Active (NZ), circa AD 1000 to present day. **Marae**, Te Kumi Village, Walkato, King County (NZ), circa AD 1000 to present day.

Marmillion Edmond Bozonier   San Francisco Plantation

At its core, this elaborate plantation house is a Louisiana 'raised cottage', its living quarters set above a basement. In execution, however, it is much more than that; its fanciful rendition of plantation architecture is inspired by the picturesque Stick Style and, even more, the Gothic styling of the sternwheeler paddleboats that plied the Mississippi River. Its oversized *piano nobile* includes an open veranda accessed by an external flight of steps; on the roof are two cupolas and a 'widow's walk', more typically found in the houses of seafarers. The interiors feature hand-painted ceilings and numerous *faux* finishes, including marbling and wood graining. Built by Edmond Bozonier Marmillion in 1856, a Louisianan of French descent, the house passed through several other owners before being privately restored in 1977. Its distinctive architecture was to inspire the author, Frances Parkinson Keyes, to write *Steambook Gothic* about an imaginary family living in the house.

☛ Calrow, Hoffman & Chalfin, Pender, Potter

Edmond Bozonier Marmillion. Active (USA), nineteenth century. **San Francisco Plantation**, Garyville, LA (USA), 1856.

Mather Rick

Hampstead House

Shafts of light bounce off the walls and illuminate the basement pool of this classic Modern Movement-style house. Lying in the water, one can look up through the glass ceiling to the double-height living space and through a further roof light to the rooms above. To allow light to penetrate so deeply into the house, the building is organized around a series of large voids, supported by a solid concrete-frame structure. Mather's ingenious use of structural glass – for the stairs and some of the floors – compounds the impression of lightness and transparency. Mather's design came a very close second in the competition for the 1998 Stirling Prize, commended by the judges for its skilful manipulation of light and for the dramatically interconnected volumes of the interiors, within its cool, white-painted exterior. Mather's pioneering use of glass can be seen in an earlier all-glass extension for an eighteenth-century house, also in Hampstead, of 1994.

☞ Bo Bardi, Chipperfield, Pawson Silvestrin, Winter, Yoh

Rick Mather. b Portland, OR (USA), 1937. **Hampstead House,** London (UK), 1992–5.

Mathey Jean-Baptiste Château Troja

This château, planned in a distinctly French way, is actually on the outskirts of Prague. When the Thirty Years War ended in 1648, central Europe was in ruins and desperately in need of architects. Italians were greatly favoured in the south, but Johann Friedrich, Archbishop of Prague, commissioned his own architect who was both French and originally a painter.

Between 1675 and 1694 Jean-Baptiste Mathey enjoyed a remarkable career in which his French planning and devotion to Classical rationality (as opposed to the luxuriance of Italian Baroque) were a conscious artistic challenge to established taste. The Château Troja has a typically French *corps-de-logis* as its centrepiece, with wings attaching it to terminal pavilions,

right and left. The facades, moreover, are articulated in the French style, with a giant order of pilasters, set on pedestals in the centre so as to embrace its third storey, all very much in the manner of Louis Le Vau and Jules Hardouin-Mansart.

☞ Fischer von Erlach, Guarini, Le Vau & Hardouin-Mansart

Jean-Baptiste Mathey. **b** Dijon (FR), c1630. **d** Paris (FR), c1696. **Château Troja**, Prague (CZ), 1679–96.

Maybeck Bernard   Roos House

Designed by the architect of the Piranesian, Neo-Classical Palace of Fine Arts in San Francisco, the Roos House takes on a more medieval character. A facade of ornamental, half-timber framework of redwood, infilled with white-painted stucco, supports quatrefoil tracery, reflecting Maybeck's early experience in furniture design and adding an overall sense of whimsy to the house. That which appears ornamental on the exterior becomes structural on the interior, with the heavy redwood beams demonstrably supporting the double-storey living room in the manner of an Art and Crafts manor house. The house has an innovative raft-like foundation, which permits the structure to rock with the movement of the earth during quakes and eliminates the need for heavy foundation walls. The overall composition of the Roos House is, at once, whimsical and baronial, setting the tone for the informal fantasy of Bay Area styles to come.

☛ Carrère & Hastings, Greene & Greene, Lutyens, P Webb

Bernard Maybeck. b New York, NY (USA), 1862. d San Francisco, CA (USA), 1957. **Roos House**, San Francisco, CA (USA), 1909.

McCoskrie Edward & Greenfield Joseph

W H Lyon House

To engage in the layered detailing of the W H Lyon House is to journey into the eclectic opulence of the Victorian era. McCoskrie and Greenfield imbued each level of this house with its own decadent array of ornament: the veranda with its hand-turned spindles; the first storey with its balcony and cornice work; the second storey with its pedimented dormer windows; the mansard roof with its finials and iron-cresting; and even the cupola, with its own mansard roof and crested cap. Although now demolished, the Lyon House is still one of the most elaborate examples of Second Empire homes. This strain of Classic Revivalism – like its forefather, the Italianate manner – drew its stylistic inspiration from the Italian Renaissance. Appealing to Victorian society's desire for a visible representation of prestige, sophistication and history, Second Empire houses enjoyed a wide-ranging popularity throughout the era.

☛ Calrow, A J Davis, Marmillion, Mora, Pender, Potter

286

Edward McCoskrie. b (CAN), 1821. d (CAN), 1893. Joseph Greenfield. b 1845. d (CAN), 1910. W H Lyon House, Winnipeg, MB (CAN), 1881.

McKim Mead & White

William G Low House

Charles McKim designed this now-demolished house on a site overlooking Narragansett Bay for a New York lawyer living in Brooklyn. This vast, triangular house was dominated by its great gabled roof sloping close to the ground and spanning 42 m (140 ft). It was covered, top-to-bottom, in square-cut cedar shingles and had a mostly flat facade, interrupted by a series of bay windows. At one end, tucked under the gable roof, was a deep covered porch. The Beaux-Arts trained McKim designed the interiors to be spare, with little ornamentation, but the rooms were arranged on six different levels offering a certain amount of spatial complexity. The simplicity of the architecture gave the house a great coherence; McKim's early Shingle Style work reflected his passion for clarity and geometric order. Although it was torn down in the 1960s, scholar Richard Guy Wilson terms the William G Low House one of McKim Mead & White's 'most original' designs.

☞ **Furness, Greene & Greene, Potter, Richardson, Sullivan**

McKim Mead & White. **Charles Follen McKim. b** Pennsylvania, PA (USA), 1847. **d** St James, NY (USA), 1909. **William Rutherford Mead. b** Brattleborough, VT (USA), 1846. **d** Paris (FR), 1928.
Stanford White. b New York, NY (USA), 1853. **d** New York, NY (USA), 1906. **William G Low House**, Bristol, RI (USA), 1887.

Mecanoo   House and Studio in Rotterdam

Built next to typical nineteenth-century brick rowhouses, the sheer luminosity of this house makes a strong break with the tradition of its neighbouring structures. With views of a canal to the rear and onto a lake at the front, the house's interior space opens to its magnificent setting with an abstract facade of clear glass, steel frame and a concrete panel, arranged in a composition reminiscent of a De Stijl painting. A solid wall-enclosed ground floor, containing the entrance, studio and garage, gives way to the single unit of the two upper storeys – a double-height space with a stairway connecting the library on the first floor with the dining and living areas situated above to take maximum advantage of the views. Designed by Dutch architects Erick van Egeraat and Francine Houben of Mecanoo for themselves, the house also includes Asian influences, such as the metal-framed bamboo sun-screen and a Japanese garden.

☛ Doesburg, Koolhaas, Myers, Rietveld & Schröder

Mecanoo. Henk Döll. b Haarlem (NL), 1956. **Erick van Egeraat. b** Amsterdam (NL), 1956. **Francine Houben. b** Sittard (NL), 1955. **Chris de Weijer. b** Wageningen (NL), 1956. **House and Studio in Rotterdam** (NL), 1989–91.

Mehmed II

Topkapi Palace

Shortly after his conquest of Constantinople in 1453, the Sultan, Mehmed II, began building a palace on the site of the original acropolis of ancient Greek Byzantium. The palace would remain the administrative centre of the Ottoman Empire for almost 400 years, until a new palace was built further north on the shore of the Bosphoros. Spectacularly sited, standing on a high promontory surrounded on three sides by water – the Golden Horn, the Bosphorus and the sea of Marmora – and with views in every direction, the complex was organized as a series of courts and gardens with pavilions set within them. The palace contained ceremonial apartments for an elaborate court, as well as the more private areas, including the *harem*, or female quarter, which remained the residence of female pensioners until early in the twentieth century. Today, Topkapi Palace is a famed museum housing a collection of art and artefacts from the Ottoman Empire.

☛ Akbar, Jai Singh I, Kröpülü Family, Ming Dynasty

Sultan Mehmed II. Reigned Constantinople (TRK), 1444–81. **Topkapi Palace**, Istanbul (TRK), begun 1459, last addition 1840.

Douglas House is situated, almost precipitously, high above Lake Michigan on a steeply sloping site. Meier designed this house early in his career, at a time when his ideas of form and colour (or the absence of colour, Meier's trademark), were drawn largely from his study of the purist work of Le Corbusier. Here, against the background of blue of the lake and sky and the green of the trees, Meier sought a 'dramatic dialogue' that would offer a contrast between the natural and the manmade, enhanced by the vivid whiteness of the house. Entered at roof level via a walkway, the house is arranged so that the lakeside view opens up as one descends to the living and dining areas, with the private spaces facing away from the lake. One of the New York Five group of architects, Meier's strength is in his consistency of an architectural philosophy, demonstrated in his early houses as well as his later public buildings, such as the Getty Museum in Los Angeles (1997).

☛ Acayaba, Eisenman, Graves, Groote, Gwathmey

Richard Meier. b Newark, NJ (USA), 1934. **Douglas House**, Harbor Springs, MI (USA), 1971–3.

Melnikov Konstantin   Melnikov House

A remarkable fusion of two masonry cylinders, Melnikov's house and studio, in its traditional street setting, is a strong statement recalling formal Constructivist experiments. Its interior arrangements, however, show how awkward such forms are to adapt for occupancy, even for the bohemian lifestyle of a revolutionary artist. The spaces are most successful on the upper floor, when the whole form is incorporated, or where freestanding screens do not compromise the volume. Below are irregularly-shaped storage rooms with hexagonal windows, a visual incongruence from the mystic components of Russian Constructivism, alongside the revolutionary and *sachlich* elements. Somehow, during the New Economic Policy, Melnikov procured this site in Moscow in the once lively district around the Arbat, an area which had attracted artists under the Tsars. He managed to build this extraordinary house and remain in it, throughout the Stalinist terror, for almost fifty years.

☛ **Apyshkov, Behrens, Le Corbusier, Lubetkin, Raymond**

Konstantin Stepanovich Melnikov. **b** Moscow (RUS), 1890. **d** Moscow (RUS), 1974. **Melnikov House**, Moscow (RUS), 1927.

Mendelsohn Erich   Mendelsohn House

A composition of simple white boxes, ribbon windows, flat roofs and abstract white walls places this house as decidedly Modern, but in a quieter, less histrionic fashion than many of its contemporaries. Built at the height of his fame, the architect's own house was a surprising retreat from the exhilarating, expressionist architecture of the 1920s which had made him so famous. The entrance is approached along a meandering path through the woods that reaches a series of outdoor terraces. The interiors are surprisingly cosy and relaxed, opening up at the rear to views of Lake Havel. But the Jewish Mendelsohn's success – and even his life – was threatened by the rise of the Nazis in Germany. The day after Hitler's accession to power, less than three years after having completed this house, Mendelsohn emigrated to England, before moving to Palestine in 1936, where he designed many buildings. He eventually settled in the USA.

☛ Behrens, Chermayeff, Gropius, Mies van der Rohe

Erich Mendelsohn. b Allenstein (GER), 1887. d San Francisco, CA (USA), 1953. **Mendelsohn House**, Berlin (GER), 1929–30.

Michelozzi Michelozzo   Villa Medici

This intimate, irregular courtyard and loggia that Michelozzi added to a farmhouse-style villa in the country shows a slight relaxation of the perfect symmetry typical of Renaissance fenestration and wall openings. Framed by three arches, the loggia offers a stately transitional zone between indoors and out, domesticity and nature. The irregular windows above admit the sights, sounds and aromas of country life to the occupants grateful for a break from busy Florence. The villa is one of several Medici family country retreats. Cosimo di Medici hired Michelozzi to alter this fourteenth-century villa, which had been a meeting place for the Florentine Platonic Academy, frequented by leading artists and architects such as Alberti and Brunelleschi. Michelozzi went on to design the Palazzo Medici-Riccardi, one of the most influential houses of fifteenth-century Florence. Cosimo died here, at the villa that became his favourite residence, as did Lorenzo the Magnificent.

☛ **Alberti, Bigio, Giulio Romano, Laurana, Sangallo**

Michelozzo Michelozzi (Michelozzo di Bartolommeo). b Florence (IT), 1396. **d** Florence (IT), 1472. **Villa Medici**, Fiesole, Tuscany (IT), c1433.

Mies van der Rohe Ludwig   Farnsworth House

The view of the Farnsworth House through the trees is one of the supreme delights of Modern architecture. The most exquisite of the glass-box houses, it hangs from a steel frame, its travertine floor suspended well above ground level, which is liable to heavy (sometimes devastating) flooding from the nearby Fox River. Designed as the perfect weekend retreat, it is a single volume completely open to view, with an elegant, timber-veneered service core enclosing a fireplace on one side, kitchen and services on the other and a bathroom at each end. Its open entrance porch occupies one-third of the entire floor space. As the ultimate example of International Style minimalism applied to domestic living, it has been much debated – not least by the client whose relationship with Mies deteriorated into legal action as the estimated price rocketed. The house has been widely quoted and inspired Philip Johnson's later designed, but earlier completed Glass House.

☞ Bo Bardi, Eames, Ellwood, P Johnson, Koenig, Lautner

294

Ludwig Mies van der Rohe (Ludwig Mies). b Aachen (GER), 1886. **d** Chicago, IL (USA), 1969. **Farnsworth House**, Plano, IL (USA), 1946–50.

Ming Dynasty

Forbidden City

The strict regular layout, seen in this aerial view, and indeed the very name of the Forbidden City, suggest the harsh rule of the two dynasties that dominated China from the fourteenth century until their demise in 1911. Yet the human scale of its pavilions and courtyards, and the trees and statuary that adorn every view, partly belie this. Following their conquest in 1368,

the emperors of the Ming dynasty transformed the old Chinese capital into Beijing and in 1420 inhabited their palace which occupied the innermost enclosure of three rectangles that made up their new city. From its centre, running down towards the formal entrance, are the three halls and buildings that make up the political centre of the City. To the north are the residential

quarters, with the Emperors' and Empress' houses set within a walled courtyard. They are surrounded by a dense, symmetrical arrangement of smaller courtyards and houses, all alive with brightly-coloured figurative carving and moulded tiles.

☞ **Hadrian, Loess Han, Minoan**

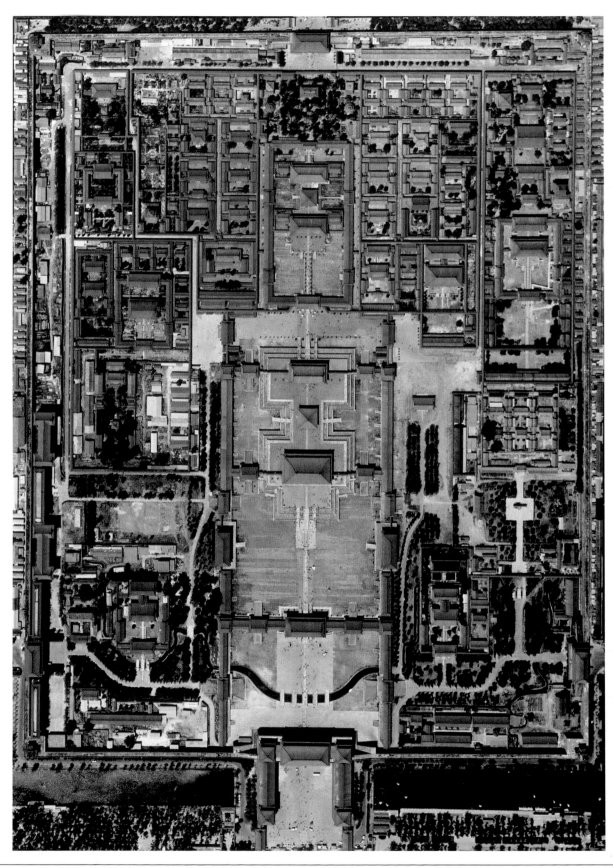

Ming Dynasty. Reigned (CHN), 1368–1644. **Forbidden City**, Beijing (CHN), aerial view, 1368–1420.

Minoan

Palace of Knossos

The prehistoric palaces of Crete, of which the Palace of Knossos is the largest and most famous, served as religious and administrative centres for the Minoan civilization, named after its legendary King Minos. Originally laid out with entrances from all four sides to a central stone-paved court, the Royal quarters and administrative areas, with vast underground storage, were kept separate. What the visitor sees today, however, is largely the creation of the 1930s excavator, Sir Arthur Evans, who, with a succession of architects, rebuilt much of the 3,500-year-old palace. However, his restoration was not based on the strongest evidence, and may well have been influenced by fashions of the day. The tapering columns, shown here, were modelled on those in Minoan paintings, and the fresco of a charging bull was recreated from very few fragments, yet it is interesting to note an almost Art Nouveau quality to the finished restoration.

☞ **Hadrian, Maiuri, Pompeii Romans, Tiberius**

Minoan. Active (GR), 2600 BC to 1100 BC. **Palace of Knossos**, Crete (GR), c1600 BC, reconstructed 1923–30.

Miralles Enric & Tagliabue Benedetta   Casa La Clota

Miralles came to international recognition in the early 1990s, with the completion of several highly-acclaimed buildings in the Catalan region of Spain. This unusual house in La Clota, a dilapidated fringe area of Barcelona, was designed to unite two existing houses to create a single new house, relying on the juxtaposition of old and new for its aesthetic identity. The dramatic design concept was to cut away the floors from the existing small dark rooms to reveal an entirely new spatial arrangement. Half of the new house (one of the existing houses) is now occupied by a double-height, light-filled library, fitted with structural shelves that slot into the old corroding shell. The architects have deliberately made no attempt to beautify the existing concrete frame, preferring to rely on the dramatic interplay of materials and textures to create an undeniably modern aesthetic that nonetheless exemplifies an ongoing tradition of craftsmanship in Spanish architecture.

☛ Campo Baeza, Gaudí, Gehry, Ungers & Kinslow

Miralles Enric & Tagliabue Benedetta   Casa La Clota

Enric Miralles. b Barcelona (SP), 1955. d San Feliu de Codinas (SP), 2000. Benedetta Tagliabue. b Milan (IT), 1963. Casa La Clota, Barcelona (SP), 1997–9.

Mizner Addison   Casa Nana

Sprawling and grand, the Casa Nana – the last of Addison Mizner's large-scale Palm Beach houses – was designed for a Danish immigrant whose fortunes came from a chain of Midwestern American grocery stores. Mizner, a Californian, arrived at Palm Beach at the end of World War I and quickly became the innovator of an architectural style that would become synonymous with Palm Beach. His form of Mediterranean Revival architecture drew on Moorish, Spanish, French, Italian Renaissance, Venetian and Central American sources combined to create an evocative 'old world' atmosphere. The focal element of this house is a rounded stair tower which has an open arcade that paces the spiralling rise of the stairs. The tower not only provides ascent, but is also the main entrance to the house. The fact that it was separate to the house itself gave rise to the legend that Mizner had actually forgotten to include it, although that was not the case.

☞ **MacNeilledge, Morgan, Nasrid Dynasty, Vaux & Church**

Addison Mizner. **b** Benicia, CA (USA), 1872. **d** Palm Beach, FL (USA), 1933. **Casa Nana**, Palm Beach, FL (USA), 1926.

Mockbee Coker House at Shiloh Falls

Set on the banks of the Tennessee River, this striking house is the result of an unusual but successful collaboration between client, architect and builder. Built as a weekend retreat for two brothers and their families, the house also accommodates an extensive collection of contemporary photography and pre-Columbian artefacts, requiring it to be part-gallery and part-home. The architects – known as much for their painting and sculpture as for their buildings – worked closely with the builder to elaborate the design and refine the details. Arranged on a linear axis running down the steep site, the house contrasts sharply with the wooded slopes, its angled and irregular geometry jutting through the trees. With its references to local vernacular, including agricultural and industrial motifs in the steel structure and roof, the house embodies the design approach of Mockbee Coker which stresses the importance of making and thinking simultaneously.

☛ **Bohlin Cywinski Jackson, Rural Studio, Scogin Elam & Bray**

Mockbee Coker. **Samuel Mockbee. b** Meridian, MS (USA), 1945. **Coleman Coker. b** Memphis, TN (USA), 1951. **House at Shiloh Falls**, Hardin County, TN (USA), 1996.

Moore Charles

Moore House

One of the most prolific and influential architectural practitioners, writers and teachers of his time, Charles Moore invested the many houses he designed for himself with his original, and often whimsical artistry. Despite tight budget constraints, this small house near San Francisco – one of his early projects – displays all the artistic invention for which

Moore became renowned. Two groups of massive, solid timber Tuscan columns form the dramatic primary structure and planning nucleus of the house. Above each cluster (one defining the living space, the other a sunken bath), a white-painted pyramidal skylight floods the interior with daylight. The juxtaposition between the heavy structure and the

lightweight external envelope is emphasized by the fact that the walls never meet at the corners, where you would expect to find structural support. Instead, sliding glass panels open the building up to views of the oak forest beyond.

☛ Barnes, Gwathmey, Outram, Turnbull, Venturi

300

Charles Willard Moore. b Benton Harbor, MI (USA), 1925. d Austin, TX (USA), 1993. Moore House, Orinda, CA (USA), 1962.

Moors

l-khayma

The Arabic-speaking nomads of the western Sahara, more widely known as Moors, occupy the region from the River Noun in south-west Morocco to the River Senegal including Mauritania and West Sahara. This cotton tent, *l-khayma*, from Chinguetti in central Mauritania, is typical of those used in the southern provinces, where the export of livestock has made supplies of the more traditional tent materials of goat-hair and wool scarce. Although less durable, two or three layers of cotton in narrow strips are light to transport, and deflect the sun's rays more than the earlier coffee-coloured goat- and camel-hair tents. The characteristic peak is due to a very small wooden ridge-piece into which two raking poles fit, on the front–rear axis, allowing standing room at the centre. The wooden props at the sides, only 1.5 m high, allow only sitting room on most of the undivided floor area. Light storage racks can be inverted to make camel-litters when on migration.

☛ **Blackfoot, Kyrgyz, Qashqai, Sami**

Moors. Active (MAU and MOR), circa AD 100 to present day. **L-khayma**, Chinguetti (MAU), as built today.

Mora Bernardo

Villa Carmela

Havana today, even in bad repair, owes a measure of its distinctive charm to a scattering of ornamental houses of the early years of the Republic. Their idiosyncratic, additive style was arrived at not by trained architects, but by mostly anonymous master craftsmen. Mora was well-versed in the manner of artfully arranging a richly decorated facade and interior from the wide choice of historicist architectural elements and details then newly available to the capital's builders. This family house, embellished with ready-made corbels, arches, columns, florid tiles and lacey ironwork, inspired Cuba's most famous daughter, the artist Amelia Pelaez (1896–1968), to work many of these architectural fancies into her coveted modernist paintings. The house, still lived in by a surviving sister, enshrines the studio and many artworks by Cuba's beloved Amelia, which accounts for its preserved, near-vintage condition.

☛ **Apyshkov, Calrow, Havana Creole, Roper**

Bernardo Mora. Active (CU), early twentieth century. **Villa Carmela**, Havana (CU), 1912–14.

Moreton Family

Little Moreton Hall

The epitome of half-timbering at its most decorative, Little Moreton Hall was built in three stages for three successive generations of the Moreton family. The south range was built in the last phase when, in 1559, William Moreton employed the carpenter Richard Dale to remodel the living quarters. Its small-panelled framing is exuberantly decorated with trefoils, herringbone, circles and quatre-foiled stars, a speciality of Cheshire carpenters of the time. The immense three-tiered windows, at a time when glass was a very expensive commodity, are another sign of opulence. To the right, a great brick chimney-stack appears to be supporting this elaborate timber structure, and is balanced on the far side by a timber garderobe tower containing privies which discharged into the moat. With its almost continuous band of windows, the Long Gallery is further evidence of the stylistic and structural self-confidence of the Elizabethan age.

☛ Compton, Ludlow, Smythson, Weobley Yeoman, Wolsey

303

Moreton Family. Active (UK), fifteenth and sixteenth century. Little Moreton Hall, Cheshire (UK), c1450–1550.

Morgan Julia

Hearst Castle

'La Cuesta Encantada', the Enchanted Hill, was how William Randolph Hearst described this audacious retreat he had built overlooking the Pacific Ocean. Resembling a flamboyant Spanish mission church, the castle appears to be designed as a stage-set for the Hollywood stars who were among Hearst's frequent guests. Built over twenty years, the complex grew to 130 rooms, with decorative elements and artworks drawn mainly from southern Europe and inserted into a reinforced concrete structure. Besides the main house, there are guest cottages, outdoor and indoor pools, greenhouses, a zoo and a pergola encircling the hill for over a mile. Tycoon Hearst was the inspiration for the movie, *Citizen Kane*, and his castle, in turn, a model for Kane's fictional house, Xanadu. Trained at the Ecole des Beaux-Arts in Paris (the first woman to be admitted), Morgan's knowledge of Classical architecture and engineering enabled her to supervise every aspect of this enormous project.

☛ Gill & Mead, Hoffman & Chalfin, MacNeilledge, Mizner

Julia Morgan. b San Francisco, CA (USA), 1872. d San Francisco, CA (USA), 1957. **Hearst Castle**, San Simeon, CA (USA), 1919–47.

Morphosis

Crawford Residence

The diverse mixture of materials and elements of this ocean-view house makes it an 'architecture of fragments'. The house is divided into two components, forcefully split down the centre by the lap pool: one wing for the living, dining and kitchen facilities, and the other for bedrooms. The two are united by a north-south, skylighted 'cosmic' axis on the far side of the house, with only its first storey visible on the street level. Built with the conviction that European Functionalism is unsuited to the unpredictable, chaotic world of southern California, the house expresses Morphosis' contention that the 'Modernist penchant for unification and simplification must be broken'. Headed initially by Thom Mayne and Michael Rotondi (both associated with the inauguration of the rebellious 'SCI-ARC' school of architecture in Los Angeles), the firm sought an architectural pluralism appropriate to its local, cultural and historical setting.

☛ Donovan Hill, Gehry, Israel, Moss, RoTo Architects, Zapata

Morphosis. **Thom Mayne**. b Danbury, CT (USA), 1943. **Michael Rotondi**. b Los Angeles (USA), 1949. **Crawford Residence**, Montecito, Santa Barbara, CA (USA), 1987–92.

Morris William

Kelmscott Manor

An artist, poet, designer and political theorist, William Morris founded the Arts and Crafts movement, putting fresh life into the various crafts associated with building. He had a romantic passion for the Middle Ages and a belief in a simple, honest approach to design. When he bought Kelmscott Manor in 1871, it exemplified all that he held dear, both for its architecture and as a setting for the furniture and fittings that fulfilled his ideal of traditional design. The Tapestry Room, shown here, features Belgian tapestries that have hung there for over two hundred years. Beyond is Morris' bedroom, with an early seventeenth-century oak four-poster bed, with embroidered hangings made by his wife and daughter. In the foreground is a much-reproduced Sussex chair, designed by Morris as a prototype of hand-crafted, yet easily reproducible furniture. Today, the house is a museum, containing many of Morris' belongings, as well as mementos of his friends in the Arts and Crafts circle.

☛ **Greene & Greene, Lutyens, Mackintosh, Shaw, Voysey**

William Morris. b London (UK), 1834. d London (UK), 1896. **Kelmscott Manor**, Kelmscott (UK), 1570, additional wing built in 1665, renovated by Morris in 1871.

Moss Eric Owen

Lawson-Westen House

The spiralling staircase at the heart of the Lawson-Westen House offers a dramatic moment of architectural abstraction. It is symbolic of the intricacy and disjunction not just of this house, but of much contemporary Californian architecture. The clients for this house said they wanted 'room to breathe', and they had a preference for high-ceilinged living rooms. The architect's interpretation of this brief was to create a split between 'limited and limitless, known and unknown'. The house form is generated by the circular kitchen, which is literally the central hearth where cooking and entertaining take place. Above this, the open staircase has balconies looking back down on to the kitchen and double-height living space, as well as views out through the irregular, strangely-shaped windows. With the Lawson-Westen House, Eric Owen Moss has created a house of enormous spatial complexity and unexpected architectural anomalies.

☛ **Gehry, Israel, Koning Eizenberg, Morphosis, RoTo Architects**

307

Eric Owen Moss. b Los Angeles, CA (USA), 1943. **Lawson-Westen House**, Brentford, CA (USA), 1988–93.

Mourier Jean   George Larue House

The simplicity of this typical Quebecois house, with its white-washed walls, pitched roof and shuttered windows, conjures up picturesque images of rural life centuries ago; a time when the central chimney provided the only source of heat, and the dormer windows the only source of light for the wooden spaces of the second storey. Although formally a paradigm of European medieval peasant architecture, the insular quality of the stucco-like facade, and the specific materials used in its construction (limestone and pine) betray its Canadian setting. The development of New France in the sixteenth and seventeenth centuries was very much a product of its settlers' desire to transplant the life they had known on the shores of Normandy to the unknown banks of the St Lawrence River. However, an ocean away from its motherland, New France developed its own specific identity, within which the Norman house became the prototypical image of Quebec's early beginnings.

☞ **Carter, Hebridean Crofter, Lavenham Clothier**

308

Jean Mourier. Active (CAN), late seventeenth century. **George Larue House**, St Jean, QC (CAN), c1700.

Mousgoum

Parabolic Domed House

A dome built in parabolic form (like a section through the narrow end of an egg) is both beautiful and practical, its wall having the strength of the top of an egg, relative to its size. Living near the Logone River in northern Cameroon, the Mousgoum built parabolic huts as great as 10 m (33 ft) high and 7 m (23 ft) in diameter. A thin wall of blue clay mixed with straw would be raised without scaffolding or formwork; small moulded buttresses allowed the builders to climb up the dome as it tapered to the top. There, a ventilation and chimney hole was made, which could be plugged during the rainy season. Moulded surrounds, both outside and inside the building, emphasized the 'key-hole' entrance. A traditional Mousgoum house comprised a circle of domes linked by a low earthen wall used for sleeping, cooking and storage; but by the 1950s, new parabolic domes were smaller in size, as pictured here. Regrettably, today, they are no longer built.

☛ **Dogon, Maasai, Syrian Farmers, Tihama Farmers**

Mousgoum. Active (CAM), twentieth century, origin unknown. **Parabolic Domed House**, Logone River (CAM), circa mid-twentieth century.

Muche Georg   Haus am Horn

The Haus am Horn, designed by the winner of a Bauhaus student competition, Georg Muche, was the centrepiece of the Bauhaus exhibition of 1923. The house, intended to be part of a Bauhaus estate, was to have a profound effect on domestic architecture for decades to come. At the centre of the innovative, rational plan was a double-height living space with clerestory windows, surrounded by smaller functional rooms. The furniture and fittings, all designed and manufactured at the Bauhaus, were as radical as the house itself. Marcel Breuer, then a Bauhaus student, designed a startlingly modern kitchen; for the first time, visitors to the exhibition saw an integrated kitchen with separate upper and lower cupboards, continuous worktops and built-in appliances. The house, a great success despite the troubled political and economic conditions in Germany at the time, proved to be the ultimate expression of the Bauhaus ideal of *Gesamtkunstwerk*, or total work of art.

☞ **Breuer, Doesburg, Gropius, Hoff, Mies van der Rohe**

310

Georg Muche. **b** Querfurt (GER), 1895. **d** (GER), 1987. **Haus am Horn**, Wiemar (GER), 1923.

Murcutt Glenn

Marika-Alderton House

Designed for a well-known Aboriginal artist and her extended family, this lightweight, timber-frame house is raised one metre above the ground, not only to allow cooling air currents to pass underneath, but also to protect the interior from wild dogs, insects, reptiles and monsoon floods. This prefabricated system consists of opening, slatted wall panels, which ensure good ventilation and protection from the harsh sunlight, a function shared with the dominant over-hanging roof. The client's request for a 'healthy building' fitted with the architect's long-standing interest in developing an architecture that responds to landscape, climate and local cultures. Murcutt is renowned for his fusion of vernacular and modernist forms and materials: he was once described as 'a timber and tin Miesian'. Marmburra Marika has suggested that the building might be a 'bridging house' between the culture of the Aboriginal community and that of the dominant white settler.

☛ Andresen O'Gorman, Grose Bradley, Poole, Rural Studio

Glenn Murcutt. b London (UK), 1936. **Marika-Alderton House**, Yurkalla Community, NT (ASL), 1994.

Muthesius Hermann   Haus Freudenberg

In his capacity as technical attaché to the Imperial German Embassy in London, between 1896 and 1903, Muthesius studied and published work on the English country house and architects of the late nineteenth century. Webb, Shaw, Lutyens, Voysey and others had developed a style of domestic building for a new middle class, adapted from the vernacular of the English countryside. Muthesius so admired this style that he sought to emulate it when he began his own architectural practice on his return to Berlin. The Haus Freudenberg, built near Muthesius' own house in Nikolassee, is one of the most obviously influenced by the English model. Its butterfly-shaped plan, embracing the entrance courtyard on one side and the garden to the rear, is taken directly from that of The Barn (1896) in Exmouth, Devon by E S Prior. However, the steep roofs, with their eyebrow dormers, reflect a middle European rather than an English vernacular.

☛ **Behrens, Lutyens, Shaw, Voysey, P Webb**

312

Hermann Muthesius. **b** Groß-Neuhausen (GER), 1861. **d** Berlin (GER), 1927. **Haus Freudenberg**, Berlin (GER), 1907–8.

Myers Barton   Myers House

The framed reflections in the first-storey windows of this geometric facade locate both the intention and position of this late-Modernist Toronto house within its deeply urban context. Myers' design ideals can be seen in the exposure of structure and extrapolation of visual lines on the exterior, and in the industrial details surrounding the glazed courtyard of the interior. He sought to explore and further the Modernist ideals of a frank expression of function, material and form, as well as imbricate the house into the vernacular of its traditional row house setting. In his houses of the late 1950s and 1960s, Myers not only furthered the Modernist tradition but in his aggressive pursuit of individualism, also identified an aesthetic that foreshadowed the High-Tech movement of the next decade. Furthermore, his consideration of tradition and vernacular foreshadowed this characteristic of Post-Modern architecture.

☛ Bolles & Wilson, Eames, Kahn, Kishigami, Rogers, Rudolph

Barton Myers. b Norfolk, VA (USA), 1934. **Myers House**, Toronto, ON (CAN), 1970–1.

Nash John

Cumberland Terrace

'Acrid putrescences' was Thomas Carlyle's cry against Nash's scenographic architecture, where terraced houses were grouped, composed and manipulated into the form of Italianate palaces. 'Nash neglected detail in preference for breadth of treatment', was Sir Albert Richardson's drier assessment. As urban scenery, Nash's spectacular creations surrounding Regent's Park in central London, have stood the test of time. Immaculately maintained by the Crown Estates Commission, they convey a convincing idea of an urban life set in a park, which Nash was one of the first to introduce. There is also variety in his ensembles: in between the great lengths of palace facades, smaller houses are grouped around courtyards which lead to a 'village' of stuccoed villas. The idea of a city within a park has inspired many modern architects, including the young Le Corbusier in his urban theories, the 'maisons à redents', of the early 1920s.

☞ **Apyshkov, Burlington, Leverton, Thomson, Wood**

John Nash. b London (UK), 1752. **d** Isle of Wight (UK), 1835. **Cumberland Terrace**, Regent's Park, London (UK), 1826.

Nasrid Dynasty Alhambra Palace

The Court of Lions, named for its bestial fountain, is arguably the most enchanting in the sequence of canopied open spaces comprising the Alhambra, the royal palace of the last Muslim stronghold in Spain. Constructed as a fortified castle on a hill overlooking Granada's Vega plain, it was surrendered in 1492 without incident to Ferdinand and Isabella, and subsequently altered by Christian rulers. However, little has changed within the old medieval walls; nothing but sky is ever visible from inside, no earthly sights intrude on its gossamer interiors. Senses are lulled by the pierced and decorated architecture, by the insubstantial columns that lead the eye up to sumptuous ceilings and honeycombed vaults, by the slim channels of water that criss-cross its floors and by the heavenly light. It is said that illusion was the goal of the Moors who designed it; they wished to create an unworldly refuge, a literal Koranic paradise in the guise of an invincible fort.

☞ al-Haddad, Eschwege, Isabella I & Ferdinand II, Tarifa

Nasrid Dynasty. Reigned (SP), 1232–1492. **Alhambra Palace**, Granada (SP), 1334–91.

Ndebele

Decorated Houses

The Transvaal Ndebele decorate their houses with wonderfully colourful abstract patterns. In doing so, they contradict the architectural theory that decoration should grow from architectural form, not simply adorn the surface. This inspired graffiti originated from the patterns that adorn the clothing and furnishings of the neighbouring Sotho-Tswana tribes. The Ndebele took these up and applied them, in sombre earthen colours, to their traditional round houses made of poles and clad in wattle and daub. Later on, these were replaced by rectangular-plan houses and the Ndebele enlarged their palette by adding the full range of primary colours. The result was much more vivid decoration which they applied to both the walls of their houses and of the enclosing courtyards, or *lapa*. The brilliant colour highlights semi-figurative patterns, suggesting plants, animals and buildings, arranged with a fine sense of balance rather than complete symmetry.

☛ Abelam, Dogon, Hausa, Sa'dan Toraja

316

Ndebele. Active (SA), early seventeenth century to present day. **Decorated Houses**, nr Pretoria, Transvaal (SA), 1940s to present day.

Neolithic Orkney Islanders

Skara Brae

Skara Brae is a remote point on the windbattered Orkney Islands, off the coast of Scotland. The earliest surviving remains of a Neolithic (late Stone Age) village were discovered here, preserved under drifting sand dunes, and consisting of small, rectangular, dry-stone huts. Each one was complete with stone box bunks built around a hearth stone, partitioned with hewn Caithness stone slabs, and with recessed squares above forming cupboard spaces and a 'dresser' of two shelves. The roofs no longer exist, but it was likely they were formed by heaped midden material held by retaining walls. Some of the huts even had drains running into a main sewer. These findings also point to the start of the Bronze Age, when people started domesticating animals and cultivating the land. The builders of these houses had to be fairly skilled stone-workers with access to tools, but it is likely they were also stock farmers who lived off the land.

☞ Galician Celts, Provençale Farmers, Shetland Island Celts

Neolithic Orkney Islanders. Active Scotland (UK), from circa fourth millennium BC. **Skara Brae**, Orkney Islands, Scotland (UK), c2000 BC onwards.

Neumann Balthasar   Residenz

Of the all-powerful prince bishops of Würzburg, none showed more artistic patronage than Johann Philipp Franz Schönborn and his successors. He gave the greatest of German Baroque architects, Balthasar Neumann, his first important commission in 1719. This was for a new palace, modestly known as the Residenz, in which two wings, each embracing a pair of courtyards, flanked a further, open courtyard, behind which lay the central range of the palace. Bishop Karl Phillip von Greiffenklau later obtained the services of the Italian painter, Giovanni Battista Tiepolo, to paint the Kaisersaal, shown here, with a depiction of Emperor Barbarossa's marriage to Beatrice of Burgundy. In typically Baroque fashion, the painting merges into *trompe-l'œil*, which then merges into Antonio Bossi's ornate plasterwork, all in remarkable contrast to the red marble columns and pilasters that articulate the room.

☛ **Fischer von Erlach, Guarini, Hildebrandt, Vanbrugh**

Johan Balthasar Neumann. b Eger, Bohemia (now Cheb, CZ), 1687. **d** Würzburg (GER), 1753. **Residenz**, Würzburg (GER), 1719–44.

Neutra Richard

Kaufmann Desert House

Designed as a pavilion for inhabiting and encountering the arid desert of Palm Springs, the Kaufmann Desert House radiates out from its centre like a pin-wheel, with each wing only one room wide in order to maximize the views of the surrounding mountains and landscape. The house sensitively adapts the International Style to this hot, harsh climate, using strong horizontal lines to contrast with the mountainous landscape. Working in the California regionalist tradition of Rudolph Schindler, Neutra combines a Modernist vocabulary with a distinctive American accent, evocative of Frank Lloyd Wright's Taliesin West. Here, however, the steel-frame house retains an intrusive presence, unlike Wright's organicism.

The house closely interacts with its setting, and fulfils Neutra's aspiration that his architecture combine 'the goal of building environmental harmony, functional efficiency, and human enhancement into the experience of everyday living'.

☞ P Johnson, Le Corbusier, Mies van der Rohe, Schindler

Richard Josef Neutra. b Vienna (AUS), 1892. d Wuppertal (GER), 1970. **Kaufmann Desert House**, Palm Springs, CA (USA), 1946–7.

Nevisian Creole Chattel House

Sunny and colourful, this Creole chattel house bespeaks the Caribbean. Although the architecture varies from island to island, a common British heritage does link them. The houses are typically wooden, have steep-pitched roofs – most often corrugated metal to shed the torrential rains of the tropics – and typically broad galleries or verandas to afford both outdoor living and shading from the sun inside. Chattel houses often feature elaborately carved gingerbread ornament, along eaves, cornice lines, balustrades and columns. Paint was not generally available in the Caribbean until the 1920s, when brilliant hues of turquoise, pink, yellow, coral, blue and lavender – generally used two or three at a time – began to adorn the houses. The term chattel house derived from the word for a family's movable belongings: these houses could be dismantled, section by section, stacked on a mule cart and relocated to wherever there was work.

☞ **Airstream Co., Carter, Havana Creole, Kyrgyz**

Nevisian Creole. Active Nevis, West Indies (FKN), circa late seventeenth century to present day. **Chattel House**, Nevis, West Indies (FKN), circa late nineteenth century.

Niemeyer Oscar — Canoas House

The free, curving roofline is the intuitive gesture that sets the organic organization for Niemeyer's own house, whose fluid spaces revolve freely around a natural boulder. The house's unassuming nature and embracing patio confirm Niemeyer as one who is recognized for a humility born of his love for the customs and people of his native country. While influenced by Le Corbusier, with whom he worked early in his career, in 1936, Niemeyer nonetheless continues to draw his primary inspiration from the spirit and imagery of Brazil. 'The straight line, hard, inflexible, created by man, does not attract me,' he wrote. 'What does draw me is the free and sensual curve... The curve I find in the mountains of my country, in the clouds of the sky, and the waves of the sea.' This plasticity inspires Niemeyer even in his famous, large-scale projects, such as the many public buildings of the new city of Brasilia, 1957–60.

☛ Bo Bardi, Le Corbusier, Scharoun, Seidler, Sert, Yamada

Niemeyer Oscar

Oscar Niemeyer. b Rio de Janeiro (BR), 1907. **Canoas House**, Rio de Janeiro (BR), 1953–4.

Nikitin Nikolai   Pogodinskaya Izba

As a transplant from the Russian countryside into central Moscow, this coloured and highly-decorated version of the traditional peasant log hut, or *izba,* has the air of being someone's personal manifesto, and so it was. The young Nikitin created this house for the historian, artist and writer, Mikhail Petrovich Pogodin (1800–75), who was a passionate and pioneering Slavophile, a believer in peasant rights and cultural values as a foundation for the future Russia. Here sympathizers gathered, among them such fellow writers as Gogol, Aksakov, Zagoskin and Ostrovsky. Nikitin's later work largely comprised churches, but as a propaganda statement for the revival of folk traditions and populist values, this house became the model for a wave of rural schools, hospitals and other community buildings across Russia. This nationalistic 'Pseudo-Russian' style was to be spread further by Gartman, Ropet and others.

☞ **Gartman, Peter the Great, Tolstoy, Vesnin**

322

Nikolai Vasilevich Nikitin. b (RUS), 1828. **d** Moscow (RUS), 1913. **Pogodinskaya Izba**, Moscow (RUS), 1856.

O'Donnell & Tuomey   Courtyard House

The core of this two-block house was the shell of a basement workshop situated in a long, narrow back garden, which had been used as an open-air dining room for the clients' adjacent restaurant. One block contains the kitchen and living room, and is separated from the restaurant by a small courtyard and from the bedroom tower (shown here) by another, larger sunken courtyard. The bedroom block refers to the ancient tower houses of Ireland, one of many historical architectural references used in this project. It accommodates the distinct desires of its occupants: the parents' bedroom is large and sunken (they work late and avoid morning sun); above them, one daughter sleeps in a skylit alcove with a view of the stars; above that, another daughter has a balcony with a long view across fields to the town skyline. The architects first came to prominence with work on a much larger scale, including their regeneration of the run-down Temple Bar area of Dublin.

☛ **Ando, Kikutake, Myers, TEN Arquitectos**

O'Donnell & Tuomey. **Sheila O'Donnell**. **b** Dublin (IRE), 1953. **John Tuomey**. **b** Tralee (IRE), 1954. **Courtyard House**, Navan (IRE), 1997.

Ogawa Shinichi   Cubist House

This 6 m (20 ft) glass cube house, in a typical residential neighbourhood in Japan, stands in stark contrast to its surrounding chaotic urban context. However, the simple repetition of the steel grid facades, each one divided into thirty-six square glass panels, emphasizes the house's neutrality, and the images reflected on the glass surface helps its substantiality to vanish into its surroundings. Within the cube is an inner, more private solid structure, set back behind the glass wall, containing most of the accommodation. A gallery and a continuous ramp which connects to the first-floor level where an open workspace is situated create a buffer between the two. The overall effect is that of a jewel placed in a monochromatic, free-flowing setting. The contradictory features of the building's mass suggest an unconventional relationship between a house and its urban context, while providing its owner, an industrial designer, with a home and an office within one setting.

☞ Ban, Hara, Kishigami, Yoh

Shinichi Ogawa. b (JAP), 1955. **Cubist House**, Yamaguchi (JAP), 1991.

O'Gorman Juan — Diego Rivera and Frida Kahlo House and Studio

Later in his life, O'Gorman turned away from his early enthusiasm for Le Corbusier's Modernism – his own house, built some twenty-five years after this one, is a sequence of mosaic- and relief-encrusted, cave-like spaces. But here, at the house and studio built for his friends, the artists Diego Rivera and Frida Kahlo, the abstractions of Le Corbusier's early houses are precisely re-expressed. If anything, O'Gorman's expressed functionalism is even more ideological; the concrete frame is more strongly stated (and restated in the entrance gateway with its cactus fence) than in Le Corbusier's otherwise very similar Ozenfant Studio of 1923, for example. Indeed, ideological commitment seems to have led to O'Gorman's withdrawal from architecture for over ten years, and to the very different, architectural concerns of his later practice, where his work as a painter, and that of his artist friends, led to a more local and personal expression.

☛ Brinkman & van der Vlugt, Doesburg, Perret

Juan O'Gorman. b Mexico City (MEX), 1905. d Mexico City (MEX), 1982. **Diego Rivera and Frida Kahlo House and Studio**, Mexico City (MEX), 1930–2.

Okada Satoshi & Tomiyama Risa   Villa Manbow

This weekend house for a video-art producer and his family is built on a steep hill in Atami, a scenic seaside town with commanding views over the Pacific Ocean. The dwelling has been created by the juxtaposition of two contrasting volumes, an ellipsoid egg shape and a rectangular box, that are raised to avoid moisture seeping in from the ground. Copper plates protect the exteriors from salty sea breezes, while adding a 'foreign' element to the house's appearance. Horizontal windows arranged on the upper side of the ellipsoid allow panoramic views while heightening a sense of flotation within the living space. The architects' intention to create an 'infinite' space is realized in the seamless, curved interior by the use of a white-paint finish throughout. With its conspicuous exterior and elaborate interior arrangement, this building provides a fantastical weekend home that is detached from contextual reality, giving it the aura of a spaceship.

☛ Kiesler, Suuronen, Ushida Findlay, Yamashita

Satoshi Okada. b Hyogo (JAP), 1962. Risa Tomiyama. Active (JAP), late twentieth century. Villa Manbow, Atami (JAP), 1997.

Olbrich Josef

Grosse Glückert Haus

A characterful building set in the leafy suburbs of Darmstadt, the Glückert Haus is the best-preserved of the many houses Josef Olbrich built after he was invited to join an artists' colony there. Like all his buildings in Darmstadt, the house is a total work of art: the exterior was highly decorated (you can just see the stylized trees on the gable end, but the mural above the porch was never completed); the interior, heavily embellished. Julius Glückert, who commissioned the house, used it as a furniture showroom and Olbrich went on to build him a second home to live in. Darmstadt was at the heart of the Secessionist movement – the Austro-German equivalent of Art Nouveau – of which Olbrich was a leading exponent. Indeed, the movement is named after the Secession exhibition building in Vienna, designed by Olbrich in 1898 as a radical alternative to the more traditional Academy of Fine Arts.

☛ **Behrens, Hoffmann, Plečnik, Schönthal, Wagner**

Josef Maria Olbrich. b Troppau (GER), 1867. **d** Düsseldorf (GER), 1908. **Grosse Glückert Haus**, Darmstadt (GER), 1901.

Oliveira Mateus Vicente de   Palace of Queluz

At once Palladian and Rococo, the Facade of the Ceremonies is part of the second phase of reconstruction that transformed a sixteenth-century country house into a palace for King Pedro III of Portugal. The works were begun in 1747 by the architect, Mateus Vicente de Oliveira, but following the destruction of Lisbon caused by the earthquake of 1751, he was called back to the city to supervise its reconstruction. He began this facade, with its giant pilasters and central pediment, in 1761, but its carved decoration of shells and garlands was supervised by the French immigrant Jean-Baptiste Robillion in 1764–7, who later went on to succeed Vicente de Oliveira as architect. The facade, an epitome of grace, overlooks the Upper Gardens, laid out in the French style with terraces, parterres and statuary. Low box hedges, forming regular geometric patterns, frame a blue-and-white tiled canal and its bridge, complementing the ranges of the palace set around it.

☛ **Fischer von Erlach, Le Vau & Hardouin-Mansart, Neumann**

Mateus Vicente de Oliveira. b Barcarena (POR), 1706. **d** (POR), 1785. **Palace of Queluz**, Sintra (POR), 1747–58, with later additions, 1760–86 and 1786–92.

Otto Frei

Atelier Warmbronn

Two years in a World War II prisoner-of-war camp rebuilding bombed bridges led Frei Otto to investigate structures requiring minimal materials to achieve maximum strength and span. The majority of Otto's work, and that for which he is most famous, concentrates on large-span structures for public buildings, such as the elegant roof for the Munich Olympic Stadium of 1972. For his own house and studio at Warmbronn, however, he adopted a more domestic scale that nonetheless relies on structure for its architectural expression. The house consists of two separate buildings dug into the slope of the site. The upper section contains living and sleeping spaces, the lower a studio and workshop. Two angled timber frames support a south-facing glass skin over the entire building, with cable winch-operated doors opening it up to the landscape. Despite his inauspicious introduction to architecture, Otto has enjoyed a genuinely innovative career now spanning half a century.

☛ Azuma, Herzog + Partner, Ritchie, Rogers

Frei Otto. b Siegmar (GER), 1925. **Atelier Warmbronn**, Warmbronn, nr Stuttgart (GER), 1969.

Outram John   New House

Like a set design for Mozart's *The Magic Flute*, John Outram's New House suggests strength and power, with a touch of melodrama. The entrance courtyard has virtually no windows, drawing attention to the wide central doorway, while the armillary sphere seems to indicate a place for some kind of ritual enactment. Although they may not be explicit, the house carries many levels of symbolism through which Outram likes to bring his work to life. This is expressed in the hierarchy of materials which, as with many of Outram's buildings, includes coloured concrete. The interior has many finely-crafted details, creating patterns in floors and on walls, continuing the richness of colour from the exterior. Outram is no ordinary Post-Modernist, but one of the most original contemporary architectural thinkers, with an ability to communicate successfully to non-architects through his unrestrained decorative designs.

☛ **Graves, Jencks & Farrell, Moore, Terry, Venturi**

John Outram. b Taiping (MALAY), 1934. **New House**, Wadhurst Park (UK), 1978–86.

Palladio Andrea   Villa Rotonda

Palladio was probably more influential than any architect had been before his time – and possibly since – both for his *Four Books of Architecture*, published in 1570, and his many built villas; the Villa Rotonda being his most famous. This villa is remarkable for being symmetrical about both axes, with four identical pedimented porticoes leading into a central domed hall. Palladio described the site, on a small hill just outside Vicenza, as being like a theatre with 'the most lovely views on all sides, some screened, some more distant, and others reaching to the horizon'. The villa's centrality and symmetry, governed by classical rules of proportion, give the house a quality of abstraction, which may have been what led Goethe to describe it as being 'habitable rather than homely'. The subsidiary rooms are pushed to the four corners of the plan; it is the hall and porticoes that are the essence of the building, a concept that has been much duplicated over the centuries.

☞ **Adam, Burlington, Jefferson, I Jones, Terry**

Andrea Palladio (Andrea della Goledola). b Padua (IT), 1508. d Vicenza (IT), 1580. **Villa Rotonda (Villa Capra)**, nr Vicenza (IT), c1566–70.

Parent Claude   Maison Drush

The tilt of this Modernist, rectilinear house at a 120-degree angle is intended to blow apart the restrictions of straight-lined, static architecture. Designed in 1963, the Maison Drush was the first house built by the radical French architect, Claude Parent, who, in his formative years, had worked with Le Corbusier. Parent advocated rejecting the conventional form of buildings to open up new freedoms: roofs tilted for walking over; walls only built in order to stop people walking into others who are sleeping. But the Maison Drush was also designed as a comfortable home for an engineer and his family, who originally wanted a traditional building. The house itself is composed of two separate parts, the tilted bedroom block anchored by the three-storey living accommodation block. Although the house itself is a pragmatic realization of an idea, the overwhelming impression of it falling over – with its suggested dynamism and instability – remains.

☞ **Domenig, Eisenman, Erickson, Le Corbusier**

332

Claude Parent. b Neuilly (FR), 1923. **Maison Drush**, Versailles (FR), 1963–5.

Parker & Unwin
Letchworth Garden City

Half-timbering, tall chimneys and sweeping roofs are as characteristic of Parker & Unwin's work as any other Arts and Crafts architect's. Their image of domesticity drew on romanticized medievalism in architectural form and social relations, but several elements separate them from their peers. Using the principles of Ebenezer Howard's book, *Tomorrow: A*

Peaceful Path to Real Reform of 1898, they sought an idealized social balance for the community they planned at Letchworth, and their internal plans were almost as radical as their exteriors were conservative. A generation earlier than the Modernists, they defined spaces for specific functions rather than providing separate rooms. This proto-functionalism relied

on an aggressive use of traditional devices, like inglenooks. Their gentle questioning of social relations had far-reaching corollaries. This image of a girl, dressed for tennis, hints more at the intended social programme than does the house itself.

☛ **Baillie Scott, Lever, Lutyens, Shaw, P Webb**

333

Parker & Unwin. Richard Barry Parker. b Ashover (UK), 1867. **d** Letchworth (UK), 1947. **Raymond Unwin**. **b** Whiston, Rotherham (UK), 1863. **d** Lyme, CN (USA), 1940. **Letchworth Garden City**, Letchworth (UK), c1903–4.

Patkau Architects

Barnes House

The angular geometry of this house is a response to the landscape in which it is sited: a rocky outcrop on Vancouver Island overlooking the Strait of Georgia. The architects describe it as 'a landscape focusing device … through which the experience of this place is made manifest'. The 'prow' marks the entrance, at the end of a gentle ascent through the trees. The pervasive presence of the woodland is evoked inside the house by tree-like columns rising to support a heavy timber roof, and timber is also used for the frame structure of the building envelope, rendered with stucco. John and Patricia Patkau are always keen to emphasize the pragmatic nature of their approach, which rejects any notion of an architectural ideal. They are happy to mix different materials together and most of their buildings have assumed unusual, asymmetrical forms developed out of the particular characteristics of the site.

☞ Lacaton Vassal, Mockbee Coker, Scogin Elam & Bray

334

Patkau Architects. John Patkau. b Winnipeg, MB (CAN), 1947. **Patricia Patkau. b** Winnipeg, MB (CAN), 1950. **Barnes House**, Nanaimo, BC (CAN), 1993.

Patwon

Patwon-ki-Haveli

The exquisitely carved sandstone *jali* work of this Jaisalmer *haveli*, or townhouse, was all the rage with the eighteenth to nineteenth-century urban elite in prosperous cities across India. Rich merchant classes adopted the court styles of Mughal and Rajput architecture, mixing Jain and Hindu figural themes with rich floral and geometric details that are clearly Islamic in inspiration. Focus was placed on the decorative detail and impact of the house's street facade – the optimal display area of the owner's prestige – rather than the home's functional layout. Increasing numbers of storeys, prominent and highly ornate balconies, veranda screens, elaborate brackets, cusped arches, oriels and small rooftop kiosks (*chattri*) were used to define the many windows, porches and patios creating a composite style frontage. The rooftop terrace was reserved for the men of the house, where they would retire to take the pleasures of women and music within shimmering pavilions.

☛ **Akbar, al-Haddad, Amar Singh II, Jai Singh I**

335

Pawson Silvestrin

Neuendorf House

A spectacular, shimmering swimming pool projects from the terrace of this holiday house for a German art dealer, out towards the horizon and the rugged, red landscape of southern Majorca. The house stands like a square medieval fortress, rendered with local earth-coloured stucco, with local limestone used throughout for the floors and for massive tables, benches and basins. Despite its precision and geometric purity, the whole composition is conceived to allow architecture and nature to interact and enhance one another. The outer walls have only narrow openings, and the brightness of the interior courtyard contrasts with the still calm of the interiors. Pawson and Silvestrin are the primary exponents of architectural Minimalism, eliminating all applied ornament from their architecture, but creating a sense of austere luxury through the use of expensive natural materials. Silvestrin sees his work as 'strong but not intimidating … elegant but not ostentatious'.

☛ Ando, Barragán, Chipperfield, Laan

Pawson Silvestrin. Practiced 1987–9. **John Pawson**. b Halifax (UK), 1949. **Claudio Silvestrin**. b Milan (IT), 1951. **Neuendorf House**, nr Santanyi, Majorca (SP), 1989.

Pender John   Belltrees Homestead

Henry Luke White, the grandson of an English immigrant farmer, was a renowned ornithologist who made significant contributions to the understanding of Australia's unique bird species. In 1907, he commissioned the architect, John Wiltshire Pender, to build Belltrees Homestead, one of the finest Australian Federation-style homes in New South Wales.

This style is a derivation of the English Edwardian style with its Art Nouveau influence, adapted to reflect the Australian climate and availability of building materials. Belltrees has symmetrical facades with shady verandas on both ground and first level. The richly-decorated balustrades incorporate both timber and 'lace' ironwork, typical of this style. The interiors,

in contrast to the dark colours of the preceding Victorian taste, were light and airy, providing a dramatic backdrop to the richly-decorated, baroque timber staircase, one of the grandest residential staircases in the country.

☛ **Calrow, McCoskrie & Greenfield, Potter, Sloan**

John Wiltshire Pender. **b** Tobermory, Scotland (UK), 1833. **d** Maitland, NSW (ASL), 1917. **Belltrees Homestead**, Scone, NSW (ASL), 1907.

The facade of this residence and studio, designed for the Cubist sculptress Chana Orloff, abstractly suggests a face – eyes, brow, nose and mouth. Located in an intimate Parisian street expressly built for artists, the house stands in contrast to its neighbours, the white, purist studios by André Lurçat. Its internal organization is expressed externally by the use of a reinforced concrete frame, in-filled with glass and entrance doors at the ground-floor studio level, and bricks laid in a rough, rhythmical chevron pattern at the first-floor apartment level. Containing two studios (one serving as a gallery), the house is one of several which Auguste Perret designed for artistic clients, including the painters Marc Chagall, Georges Braque and Maurice Denis. The use of concrete which Perret helped pioneer, the unique handling of materials and the precision of the finish (such as the fine line of the cornice), are all characteristic of Perret's attentive craftsmanship.

☞ **Goldfinger, Le Corbusier, O'Gorman, Perriand, Raymond**

338

Auguste Perret. b Brussels (BEL), 1874. **d** Paris (FR), 1954. **Residence and Studio for Chana Orloff**, Paris (FR), 1926–9.

Perriand Charlotte　Chalet at Méribel-les-Allues

The expansive windows opening onto a scene of pine trees in the snow, the rough-hewn stone, and the timber beams and overhang immediately identify this, Perriand's own house, as a mountain retreat. Yet also evident is the profound influence of Japanese culture on her: the calm ordering of materials, the simplicity of the table and stools, the refinement of timber detailing and the symbiotic relationship between nature and the chalet's interior. Perriand, who worked as a furniture and fittings associate in Le Corbusier's studio until 1937, became interested in the synthesis of traditional design with the functionalist intentions of the International Style. As she explained, 'As long as I had to do a chalet traditional in techniques because of the specifications of the resort, I wanted to investigate the merits of the valley's indigenous housing ... I unite peasant traditions with the Japanese house. Who would believe this possible?'

☛ Chareau, Gray & Badovici, Le Corbusier, Perret

Charlotte Perriand. b Paris (FR), 1903. d Paris (FR), 1999. **Chalet at Méribel-les-Allues**, Savoie (FR), 1960–3.

Peruzzi Baldassare

Villa Farnesina

The Villa Farnesina's U-shaped courtyard, incorporating a north-facing loggia, took full advantage of its setting on the banks of the River Tiber. Far enough from the city of Rome to be a considered a suburban retreat for its owner, the Sienese banker Agostino Chigi, it was the scene for elaborate entertainments and dinner parties. The exterior, plain on the entrance facade, was originally decorated by the architect himself using terracotta-coloured stucco, with herms and satyrs flanking the windows. The interior, also, was elaborately painted with illusionary scenes: the story of Cupid and Psyche by Raphael in the loggia and, on the *piano nobile*, the main *salone* was decorated again by the architect, with perspectival views suggesting that the viewer was standing in an open loggia overlooking Rome – or an idealized version of it – from the hills above. Naturally, Peruzzi took the opportunity to include the Villa Farnesina in the scene.

☛ **Giulio Romano, Palladio, Raphael, Sangallo**

Baldassare Peruzzi. **b** Siena (IT), 1481. **d** Rome (IT), 1536. **Villa Farnesina**, Rome (IT), 1509–11.

Peter the Great   Izba

At first sight, this enlarged version of the Russian peasant hut or *izba*, looks unremarkable: crossed logs, a simple pitched roof, a porch with steps to the raised floor. But its very large, mica-filled windows refer, ambiguously, to the city. Moreover, a peasant rich enough to afford such a house would have raised it by a full storey to shelter his animals, and displayed his status by the use of elaborate decoration. These are clues as to the *izba*'s unusual client, and indeed to its unique purpose. It was built in 1702 for Tsar Peter the Great, skilled carpenter as well as passionate developer of Russia's maritime trade and defences, so he could personally supervise construction of the fortress that would defend his growing northern port of Archangel.

Except for their tiled Russian stoves, the four rooms inside are ship-like in their universal use of timber and low ceilings. As a rare relic of the great Tsar's life, this *izba* was brought to the Kolomenskoe Outdoor Museum in Moscow in 1933.

☞ **Fontana & Schädel, Gartman, Nikitin, Tolstoy, Vesnin**

341

Peter the Great (Peter I), Tsar of Russia. b Moscow (RUS), 1672. Reigned (RUS), 1682–1725. d St Petersburg (RUS), 1725. **Izba**, Markov Island, nr Archangel (RUS), 1702. (Relocated to Kolomenskoe Outdoor Museum, Moscow in 1933.)

Pietilä Reima & Raila   Vesterinen House

During the 1960s, Kauko Vesterinen worked as a carpentry supervisor on the Pietiläs' celebrated Dipoli Student Residence in Helsinki (1967). He developed both a working relationship and a friendship with the architects, and decided to ask them to design his house. The Pietiläs used the opportunity – and Vesterinen's carpentry skills – to experiment with design and construction methods that they would later implement in other projects. The two-storey house is finished, both inside and out, with white-painted timber boards, mostly constructed by Vesterinen himself. The ceiling, with its complex joinery and angles, is particularly noteworthy. The ground-floor entrance, office and workshop open up, via a winding stair, to the light-filled open space of the sculpturally complex main living areas above. The overall design, like all of the Pietiläs' work, celebrates Finnish design traditions, reinterpreting them in a Modern idiom.

☛ **Aalto, Gunnløgsson, Holscher, Sirén**

Reima Pietilä. b Turku (FIN), 1923. d Helsinki (FIN), 1993. **Raila Pietilä**. b Pieksaemaeki (FIN), 1926. **Vesterinen House**, Jollas, Helsinki (FIN), 1989.

Plečnik Jože

Langer House

A rhythmic, textile-like pattern covers the undulating, rendered facade of the first house Plečnik was commissioned to work on. As his client, builder Karl Langer, had already started the foundations, Plečnik was restricted by the ground plan, but completely modernized the facade and the staircase. The window of the main salon, on the top left, inventively rests on an organically-shaped pillar, as the curved oriel window form could not be taken down to the straight ground level foundations. In later years, Plečnik was to draw on his native Slovenian roots, which, combined with Classical forms, create a highly idiosyncratic architecture and which, in retrospect, have been seen as a precursor to Post-Modernism.

However, this turn-of-the-century house is much closer to contemporary Vienna Secessionist works, such as the city's new underground stations and the work of Otto Wagner, with whom Plečnik had studied.

☛ Guimard, Horta, Schönthal, Viollet-le-Duc, Wagner

343

Jože Plečnik. b Ljubljana (SLO), 1872. d Ljubljana (SLO), 1957. **Langer House**, Vienna (AUS), 1900–1.

Pompeii Romans

House of the Vetii

An elegant colonnade, or peristyle, of fluted Doric columns surrounds the courtyard garden of this luxurious and stylish Pompeiian villa, giving us a glimpse of the sumptuous interior spaces within a wealthy Roman single-family house, or *domus*. Carved stone water basins and fountains are dispersed around this central garden court amidst colourful flowerbeds and planters. The most distinguishing features of the *domus* plan were the *atrium*, where columns lined the open vestibules, and the adjacent garden courtyard. The rooms were typically situated around the *atrium*, which provided interior lighting and ventilation and served as a gallery where wall paintings, mosaics and statuary of the family's ancestors were displayed. As privacy was paramount to the Roman upper classes, the street frontage would have had windowless walls, adding to the seclusion, hidden beauty and security within the compound.

☞ **Hadrian, Maiuri, Michelozzi, Minoan**

344

Pompeii Romans. Active (IT), c600 BC to AD 79. **House of the Vetii**, Pompeii (IT), c200 BC.

Poole Gabriel

Poole House

The main living space of this house in the Australian bush opens onto an expansive north-facing veranda, screened from the sun by tensioned PVC fabric awnings. Awnings are used as an integral part of the overall roof structure that covers the three separate pavilions that make up the house. The awnings are stretched across an inner layer of polycarbonate sheeting to create a 'cushion of cool air' between the two, while allowing light to filter through into the interior. They are also stretched across the open decks connecting the pavilions. The architect and his wife had occupied 'about fifteen houses' before building this one, using each opportunity to develop further the principles of an environmentally-responsive architecture. Poole maintains his house design makes living in the heat more bearable; the Poole House represents an advance on his earlier 'tent' house, based on the form of old railway settlers' tents.

☛ Andresen O'Gorman, Fagan, Jourda Perraudin

345

Gabriel Poole. b Ipswich, QSL (ASL), 1934. **Poole House**, Lake Weyba, QLD (ASL), 1996.

Pöppelmann Matthaeus Zwinger Palace

Conceived as a royal playground, the setting for festivals and tournaments, by Augustus the Strong, Elector of Saxony (1694–1733), the Zwinger Palace evolved under Pöppelmann's direction into a boisterous, grandiloquent Baroque showpiece. However, the arcaded enclosure, with its tall, fenestrated galleries of one and two storeys, its platforms and stairways, and rounded pavilions (the Wall Pavilion, built against the former rampart, or *zwinger*, is visible here) were the only portions of his masterplan that Pöppelmann saw completed. Still, the union of structure and sculptural decoration in the ensemble is evidence of both the seamless collaboration between the architect and the sculptor, Balthasar Permoser (1651–1732), and the extravagance and self-aggrandizement of their patron. Augustus is immortalized at the apex of garlands, urns, masks and caryatids ornamenting the central opening of the Wall Pavilion, in the figure of Hercules holding up the globe.

☛ Fischer von Erlach, Hildebrandt, Neumann

Pöppelmann Matthaeus Zwinger Palace

Matthaeus Daniel Pöppelmann. b Herford (GER), 1662. d Dresden (GER), 1736. **Zwinger Palace**, Dresden (GER), 1709–22, destroyed 1945, rebuilt 1963.

Porta Giacomo della

Villa Aldobrandini

The hilltown of Frascati, built below the ancient site of Tusculum, where Cicero, Cato and Lucullus once lived, is encircled by a dozen Renaissance villas which look back across the *campagna* towards Rome, some 20 km (12 m) away. Set wide yet shallow against the hillside, the Villa Aldobrandini's oversized broken pediment dominates the villa's facade and gestures across to the town below, from where it is approached by an avenue of hedges, now grown to form a solid tunnel. The first-floor *piano nobile* is at the same level as the rear terrace, which is carved into the hillside and leads upwards to a sequence of fountains, grottoes and cascades. Although the house and gardens are organized axially, the visitor must continually step to one side to climb the slope, revealing at each new level an unfolding sequence of surprises. This processional route links the realm of the town below with the shadowy world of trees and statues above.

☞ Bigio, Gabriel, Raphael, Vignola

347

Giacomo della Porta. **b** Porlezza (IT), c1532. **d** Rome (IT), 1602. **Villa Aldobrandini (Villa Belvedere)**, Frascati (IT), 1594–1603.

Portoghesi Paolo   Casa Baldi

Bound to the earth by its use of native tufa (a soft, porous rock) interspersed with thin lines of red brick, the Casa Baldi has been described as an 'archaeological fiction' due to its self-conscious allusions to other architectural periods; especially the Baroque. A precursor of the Post-Modern movement, the house loosely borrows the forms of Guarini or Borromini, with its undulating concave curves – with gaps in-between for windows overlooking the River Tiber. Three spatially fluid storeys are separated by a string course cornice: a lower ground floor, a grander main level and a smaller second level much like the roof terraces of the Modernists. A professor of architectural history, Portoghesi reacted against the Rationalist school of thought and, working with his collaborator, Vittorio Gigliotti, advocated an architecture which 'listens' to its site: 'Listening architecture tends to put the building in key with the place, making it grow out of the place like a plant.'

☛ **Connell, Guarini, Reichlin & Reinhardt, Rossi, Siza**

Paolo Portoghesi. b Rome (IT), 1931. **Casa Baldi**, Rome (IT), 1959–61.

Potter Edward — Mark Twain House

The author Samuel Clemens, better known as Mark Twain, purchased two parcels of land in Hartford, an area known for its community of writers, artists and musicians. He then commissioned the popular architect, Edward T Potter, to design this house, which is arguably the most spectacular example of the Stick Style, so popular in America between 1860 and 1880.

Loosely based on medieval architecture, the style, like Clemens himself, was unusually flamboyant, and has been described as 'the avoidance of plain walls at all costs'. It is most evident in the curving porch-support braces, the steeply-pitched gabled roof with overhanging eaves and the horizontal wall-banding raised from the surface for emphasis. As soon as funds

permitted, Clemens employed the brilliant designer, Louis Comfort Tiffany (1848–1933), to decorate the interior. The result is one of the best surviving examples of Aesthetic design, a reactionary response to overblown Victorian design.

☛ **Hunt, McKim Mead & White, Richardson, Vaux & Church**

Edward Tuckerman Potter. **b** Schenectady, NY (USA), 1831. **d** New York, NY (USA), 1904. **Mark Twain House**, Hartford, CT (USA), 1874.

Powell-Tuck Connor & Orefelt

Villa Zapu

The siting of the Villa Zapu, squarely on the prow of a hill, reflects the tradition of the villa in the manner of Palladio and Jefferson, while its specific form and details deconstruct and oppose its country house heritage. This duality takes on a different form in the interior, with the ground floor detailed and furnished in the manner of an eighteenth-century French château, while the first floor is in the style of 1930s Moderne. Designed in 1984 by the English architect, David Connor, for a Californian client, the house duly reflects it schizophrenic nature. Similarly, the landscaping, by George Hargreaves, cleaves the line between nature and artifice by using a palette of indigenous plantings to create compelling, but unnatural patterns. The house created a sensation in the California wine country when it was first built, and a drawing of the house graced the label of the wine produced by this modern-day *seigniorial* manor.

☛ **Graves, Jefferson, Meier, Morgan, Palladio**

Powell-Tuck Connor & Orefelt. Julian Powell-Tuck. b Birmingham (UK), 1952. **David Connor. b** Birmingham (UK), 1950. **Gunnar Orefelt. b** Stockholm (SWE), 1953. **Villa Zapu,** Napa Valley, CA (USA), 1984.

Predock Antoine

Turtle Creek House

The stepped roof of Antoine Predock's Turtle Creek House, resembling the local geology, is designed to be part of the prehistoric trail along a limestone formation, where woodlands, prairie and stream converge. Designed for enthusiastic bird-watchers, the limestone ledges are planted with indigenous vegetation to encourage bird habitats. The network of roof terraces is part of a series of viewing spaces extending across the site, which lie under the major north–south route of migrating birds. The central 'fissure' of the house's rock-like form reveals the entrance foyer, with access to the north wing, containing the main living area, and the south wing, for formal social gatherings; a gallery zone links the wings. Above the entrance, a sky ramp of tensile steel projects into the canopy of trees. Predock's blunt, often windowless architecture is reminiscent of the prevalent adobe house-building traditions of Arizona and New Mexico.

☛ Ando, Domenig, Legorreta, Tiwa Indians

Antoine Predock. **b** Lebanon, MS (USA), 1936. **Turtle Creek House**, Dallas, TX (USA), 1993.

Prince Bart

Price House

A shimmering swimming pool is at the heart of the living core of this spectacularly creative ocean-front home. Three structurally autonomous timber pods connect to create a fantastical composition full of hidden rooms and unexpected treasures, in some ways recalling a Japanese teahouse. The wooden shingle cladding, traditionally associated with the seaside, is here taken to a new level. Following his mentor, Bruce Goff, who was one of the more imaginative of Frank Lloyd Wright's students, Prince refuses to fall into any of the conventional categories of architecture. He works closely with his clients and his projects are often constructed with a variety of materials, colours and textures that reflect his interest in organic forms. The client for this house, Joe Price, is well known among architects for convincing his father to commission Frank Lloyd Wright to design the Price Tower in Bartlesville, Oklahoma in 1956.

☛ Gaudí, Goff, H Greene, Mockbee Coker, Predock, Wright

352

Bart Prince. b Albuquerque, NM (USA), 1947. **Price House**, Corona del Mar, CA (USA), 1984–9.

Prouvé Jean

Prototype House

Insofar as prefabricated houses can achieve apocryphal status, this one has. The house was designed by the hugely influential and innovative manufacturing designer, Jean Prouvé, of whom Le Corbusier said, 'Everything he touches and conceives immediately assumes an elegant plastic form while offering brilliant solutions with regard to strength and manufacture.'

Prouvé's prolific work – which includes furniture as well as buildings – is often overlooked or has vanished. Designed and produced in six weeks in 1955 in response to L'Abbé Pierre's controversial condemnation of the French housing crisis, the prefab houses were funded by the public sending in tokens from packets of washing powder. A demonstration model was shipped to Paris and erected in seven hours, the kitchen and bathroom pod craned into place with saucepans already in the cupboards. Prouvé trained as a blacksmith and produced his own furniture and building components in his workshop.

☛ Eichler, Fuller, Goodman, Le Corbusier, Perret

Jean Prouvé. **b** Paris (FR), 1901. **d** Nancy (FR), 1984. **Prototype House**, demonstration model erected in Paris (FR), 1956.

Provençale Farmers

Dry-Stone Borie

Bories, or dry-stone beehive huts, are among the earliest forms of stone architecture. Found in many countries and called by many names, they are both practical and relatively easy to build. By stacking limestones in diminishing circles when clearing farm land, a dry snug shelter is created, and its corbelled roof is the oldest known form of vault construction.

In the Iron Age, bories were often dwellings with interior wall niches and even rudimentary chimneys; the first century BC writer, Strabo, describes them in use in Ancient Gaul. But more recently they have been built as improvised shelters: shepherds' huts, tool sheds and bergeries. The borie shown here, however, is part of a rare village of bories located in the French Vaucluse region of Provence. Built between 200 and 500 years ago, it comprises some twenty buildings grouped round a central communal oven. Inhabited until the nineteenth century, the village's history remains a mystery.

☞ Finistère Farmers, Girolamo II, Neolithic Orkney Islanders

354

Provençale Farmers. Active (FR), tenth century. **Dry-Stone Borie,** Gordes, Vaucluse (FR), circa fifteenth to eighteenth century.

Pueblo Indians   Cliff Palace

Cliff Palace, the spectacular, prehistoric 200-room village carved into steep stone cliffs in Colorado, has long been a source of wonder. The Pueblo Indians are thought to have occupied the canyon country we now call Mesa Verde since AD 300; however, the magnificent and mysterious carved cliff dwellings are estimated to date from AD 1200. They were only occupied for a mere one hundred years and were abandoned for centuries. The remarkable Cliff Palace and other cliff dwellings were made by excavating around caves and other openings and adding rooms – typically 2 m x 3 m (6 ft x 8 ft) – of sandstone block with mortar made of mud and water. These monumental structures remained undiscovered by the Western world until W H Jackson, a famous pioneer photographer, came upon them in 1874. Thanks to the USA National Park system, Mesa Verde and its cliff dwellings have been preserved as a national park since 1906.

☞ **Anchorites, Coober Pedy Miners, Gitano, Loess Han**

Pueblo Indians. Active (USA), circa AD 300–1300. **Cliff Palace**, Mesa Verde National Park, Canyon de Chelly, CO (USA), circa AD 1100–1300.

Pugin A W N

The Grange

Pugin, the greatest architect of the English Gothic Revivalist style, built The Grange (which included St Augustine's church) as an expression of his vision of a Gothic and Catholic medieval community. He equated the pre-industrial past – especially the virtues of Gothic architecture – with his faith. To Pugin, Gothic was more than just a style; it represented truth and embodied Christian morality because it was rational, rigorous and clearly expressed structure without any unnecessary concealment. In Pugin's hands, the Revivalist style was embellished with rich and intensely patterned interiors and asymmetrical planning, and The Grange became a source of inspiration for much nineteenth-century domestic architecture. It was from his home here that Pugin produced his prodigious output of work, including designs for furniture, plates, tiles and stained glass, as well as his most famous work, the Houses of Parliament, London (1840–70), with Charles Barry.

☞ **Morris, Shaw, Viollet-le-Duc, Voysey, P Webb**

Augustus Welby Northmore Pugin. b London (UK), 1812. d Ramsgate (UK), 1852. **The Grange**, Ramsgate (UK), 1843–4.

Qashqai

Bohun

Following a tradition used for centuries, black goat-hair is hand woven by the nomadic Qashqai tribe into broad cloth panels, stretched across framing poles, and anchored with rope and wooden stakes to create a rectangular tent. The average interior space is 20 sq m (215 sq ft) and the plan is divided into three main areas: the women's quarters for childcare, storage and cooking; the men's area for receiving guests and sleeping; and a central dining, reception and lounge area. Bathing and toilet facilities are located outside the tent. Colourful rugs and kilims line the interior walls to provide insulation, and woven reed mats are used to clad the exterior for security. During the rainy season, the roof is pitched up using wooden poles, and a narrow ditch is dug around the tent to channel rainwater away. In the summer months, the sides are raised for ventilation and most domestic activities are done outside.

☛ **Blackfoot, Kyrgyz, Moors, Sami**

Qashqai. Active (IR), present day. **Bohun (Black Handwoven Tents)**, Nomadic – Central Isfahan to Fars Province (IR), still built and used today.

Raphael

Villa Madama

While being one of the three giants of High Renaissance painting, along with Leonardo da Vinci and Michelangelo, Raphael was also a practical – and learned – architect. The Villa Madama was started towards the end of Raphael's life, for Cardinal Giulio de' Medici, later Pope Clement VII, on the slope of Monte Mario, looking east to the River Tiber. In a letter to a friend, Raphael made clear his intention to emulate antiquity, in particular the villas described by the Roman writer, Pliny the Younger, where, as here, sequences of gardens and fountains are as important as the internal spaces. The garden loggia decoration was completed after Raphael's death by his colleagues and pupils, Giovanni da Udine and Giulio Romano, assisted by Baldassare Peruzzi, and captures perfectly the character of an Ancient Roman interior, such as the contemporaneously discovered Golden House of Nero, where stucco, painted mythological scenes and structure all combined to form a whole.

☞ **Giulio Romano, Maiano, Peruzzi**

Raphael (Raffaello Santi). b Urbino (IT), 1483. d Rome (IT), 1520. **Villa Madama**, Rome (IT), c1516.

Rastrelli Bartolomeo   The Winter Palace

Only as 'Empress of All the Russias', perhaps, could a client commission such an enormous palace in the heart of the city, the vast Smolny Convent and Church in a similar style nearby, and an almost identical palace in the countryside at Tsarskoe Selo. The Winter Palace, for the Empress Elisabeth, became the backdrop to a vast military parade-ground, which also held great outdoor church services. Its other long elevation dominates a stretch of the River Neva to the north. These complexes for the Empress were Rastrelli's main works. His Italian origins enabled him to create a Baroque style that was feminine yet powerful, before the more sober Catherine the Great imported Classicism in the 1780s. By the time the Bolsheviks entered this building during the 1917 Revolution to depose the remnants of the Tsar's government, it was mainly offices. Today, it forms part of the Hermitage Museum, one of the largest and finest art galleries in the world.

☞ **Cameron, Fontana & Schädel, Hildebrandt, Oliveira**

Bartolomeo Francesco Rastrelli. b Paris (FR), 1700. d St Petersburg (RUS), 1771. **The Winter Palace**, St Petersburg (RUS), 1754–62.

Raymond Antonin — Reinanzaka House

This exposed reinforced concrete house was the first of its kind in Japan. Raymond was a Czech-born architect, educated in America, who was sent to Japan by Frank Lloyd Wright to work on the Imperial Hotel in 1919. On completion, he and his wife, the designer, Noémi Pernessin, decided to stay in Tokyo, and build this house. It was Raymond's first break with the Wrightian style, choosing plain surfaces and cubic forms to draw out the similarities between Modern architectural concepts and those of traditional Japanese architecture. Both the interior and exterior walls are exposed concrete and all of the rooms are orientated towards the south, opening onto a private garden. The Raymonds also developed an interest in local artefacts, which was reflected in their integration of traditional Japanese objects, like rice paper lanterns, with modern furniture and textiles to achieve stylish compositions that were sensitive to their settings.

☛ Horiguchi, Lauterbach, Le Corbusier, Perret, Schindler, Žák

Antonin Raymond. **b** Kladno (CZ), 1888. **d** New Hope, PA (USA), 1976. **Reinanzaka House**, Tokyo (JAP), 1924.

Reichlin Bruno & Reinhart Fabio   Casa Tonini

Unabashedly obtrusive in a mountain village, this house is deliberately and elaborately provocative. It is simply too grand; its windows and openings too large, their arrangement too different to fit in. And it is perfectly symmetrical on four sides and centrally organized, which is also expressed in the roof. The square windows allude to the ground plan, which is also square, its geometry becoming a motif throughout the house. Only the freestanding arch signifies any hierarchy – here is the entrance. The Casa Tonini is didactic to even a casual observer, but it goes further by self-consciously quoting from Palladio's Villa Rotonda. By referring so blatantly to such a famous precedent, while intensifying its strict geometry, the architects are making a radical argument for the value of the social and cultural dimensions of a house over its economic or even functional ones, thereby criticizing the values by which we live and build.

☛ Botta, Palladio, Portoghesi, Stern, Vacchini, Venturi

361

Bruno Reichlin. b Lucerne (SW), 1941. **Fabio Reinhart. b** Bellinzona (SW), 1942. **Casa Tonini**, Toricella (SW), 1972–4.

Rewal Raj

Sham Lal House

Brickwork infuses this house with a complex texture. Rewal's attention to detail and sensitivity to material are evident in the brick *jali* (lattice or screen work), which act as parapets for roof terraces, and the formwork marks left exposed on the balcony ceilings. Wall planes wrap around rooms and protect the deep-set windows from sun and rain. Vertical emphasis disappears in the fastidiously cornered brickwork, favouring the horizontality of the land. Brick-on-edge cornices, plastered fascias and an unobtrusive transition from floor to flora are gestures that reconcile house and garden. These finer details explain why such functionalism in brick – also seen in Rewal's houses for the painter, Satish Gujral, and for himself – was popular among Rewal's generation. Inspired by Jeanneret's Chandigarh and Le Corbusier's Primitivist *œuvre*, this fresh aesthetic happily marries Enlightenment-style Rationalism with India's labour-intensive building technologies.

☞ **Correa, Doshi, Kahn, Le Corbusier, Patwon**

Raj Rewal. b Hoshiarpur (IN), 1934. **Sham Lal House**, New Delhi (IN), 1973–5.

Reynolds Michael   Nautilus Earthship

Michael Reynolds has been building houses from what he describes as 'nuisance resources' for over twenty years and has attracted international attention for his passive solar Earthship buildings. Started in 1994, a development of 130 Earthships, called the 'Greater World Community', is still under construction. One of the houses, overlooking a deep gorge in the rolling mesa, is the Nautilus Earthship. Based on a seashell form, the building is made from discarded car tyres packed with earth and adobe-plastered to form a thermal mass storage heater, absorbing heat during the day and re-radiating it during the night. Rainwater tanks on the roof and photo-voltaic cells on the south facade allow the house to operate independently of mains water and power supplies. Although Reynolds' building forms are unorthodox, they are exemplary in their superior climatic and structural performance and, most importantly, their imaginative use of recyclable resources.

☛ Day, Droppers, Herzog + Partner, Tiwa Indians, Vale

Michael Reynolds. b New Albany, IN (USA), 1945. **Nautilus Earthship**, Taos, NM (USA), 1996.

Richardson Henry Hobson   Watts Sherman House

With its extraordinary texture and balance, the Watts Sherman House alludes to America's nineteenth-century tendency to imitate historic house styles, as well as anticipating the influence of the Arts and Crafts style to come. It is arguably the first Shingle Style house, and although designed by Henry Hobson Richardson, it was at a time when Stanford White (largely considered to be the premier Shingle Style architect) was employed by the Richardson office. Indeed, Richardson recommended that White finish the interiors, and the client, Sherman, subsequently commissioned White to design the 1881 addition to the house. The building materials included stone, wood, brick and stucco, as well as the identifying shingles. The house makes strong references to early English architecture, with its large chimneys and half-timbering, and scholars believe that it was Richardson's tribute to the revivalist English architect, Norman Shaw.

☞ McKim Mead & White, Potter, Shaw, Sullivan

Henry Hobson Richardson. b Priestley Plantation, LA (USA), 1838. d Brooklyn, NY (USA), 1886. **Watts Sherman House**, Newport, RI (USA), 1874–5.

Rietveld Gerrit & Schröder Truus   Schröder House

The open-plan spatial organization of this 1924 house was remarkable for its time. The first floor was occupied by a large living and dining area, with sliding panels for partitioning off smaller rooms arranged around it. It was also innovative in its use of huge windows, strong blocks of colour and built-in furniture. The design programme was developed by the client, Truus Schröder, in collaboration with Rietveld, as an expression of her desire for a house where she could live closely with her children and entertain a constant flow of visitors and liberal ideas. Rietveld started his career as a furniture designer with links to the radical Dutch De Stijl art movement. The Schröder house is celebrated as the first architectural embodiment of De Stijl principles of colour and abstraction, with its white and grey intersecting planar walls and coloured windows and railings, and is a landmark in the history of modern house design.

☞ **Doesburg, Gropius, Hoff, Kikutake, Raymond**

Gerrit Thomas Rietveld. **b** Utrecht (NL), 1888. **d** Utrecht (NL), 1964. **Truus Schröder**. **b** Utrecht (NL), 1900. **d** Utrecht (NL), 1985. **Schröder House**, Utrecht (NL), 1924.

Ritchie Ian

Eagle Rock

This exuberant structure plays with its construction, clearly expressing every strut, tie and truss. At the client's request, the house has a strong narrative content: it is based on the form of a bird, with two large steel A-frames as the central body, from which are suspended the head and tail (the head, to the left of the picture, is used as a car port) and two accommodation 'wings'. The bird analogy is carried through to the louvred blinds, which have been described as feathers which ruffle in the wind. Influenced by the work of the 1960s design group, Archigram, and being part of the High-Tech *œuvre*, the house gives the impression that it could be mass-produced and relocated as necessary. It is, however, a one-off, highly-crafted, site-specific holiday house. It was assembled from prefabricated elements, much of the work being carried out by the architect, Ian Ritchie, himself.

☛ Domenig, Eames, D Greene, Rogers, M Webb

366

Ian Ritchie. b Hove (UK), 1947. **Eagle Rock**, Budlett's Common (UK), 1982–3.

Rogers Richard & Su   Rogers House

One glass box seen from another was the unexpected Rogers' response to a brief to design a retirement house for his parents, set in a leafy suburb of London. It was built in the Californian tradition of post-war Case Study Houses, in which cheap, steel-framed boxes supported plain panels and a flat roof to form an adaptable machine for living in. This experimental style reached a new generation of British architects in the 1960s, who developed a new type of technologically expressive architecture. Here, Rogers worked very much in collaboration with his parents, allowing for a separate consulting room for his doctor father, and incorporating a strong use of colour which appealed to both his artist mother and himself. Although in this case, very occupier-specific, Rogers did envisage this simple and comparatively cheap design as a prototype to be replicated in the thousands.

☛ Cook, Eames, Ellwood, Koenig, Soriano, Team 4, Winter

Richard Rogers (Lord Rogers of Riverside). b Florence (IT), 1933. Su Rogers. b 1940. Rogers House, London (UK), 1968–9.

Roland Family   Roland House

As stoic as the logs they placed side by side to make their home and shelter, the Roland Family poses proudly before the entrance to their Canadian prairie house. The front door and single window – which open onto the main room of the house accommodating both kitchen and living room – are the only elements that break up the stark facade. The unusual vertical positioning of the logs arose from necessity, as the only available logs were too short to lay horizontally. Building out of necessity with only the limited resources of the immediate surroundings became the common trait of all late nineteenth-century building techniques in this part of Canada. The nineteenth-century settlers, drawn by the allure and promise of 'The Last Best West', put in place the ethic and aesthetic of the Canadian Prairies through their ingenuity and dedication.

☛ Bohlin Cywinski Jackson, J Davis, Peter the Great

Roland Family. French settlers, active (CAN), late nineteenth and early twentieth century. **Roland House**, Alix, AB (CAN), c1903.

Roosevelt James & Franklin D   Springwood

Springwood started out as a clapboard farmhouse, was later transformed into a summer house befitting a future American president, and was witness to portentous moments in history and numerous important visitors, among them Winston Churchill and King George VI. The house was built in 1826 in the US Federal style and purchased by James Roosevelt in 1867, who then began what was to be more than three decades of improvements and enlargements that transformed it into the Victorian style. Still later enlargements and adaptions by his wife, Sara, produced the sober, classicized stone and stucco mansion, with its wood-panelled rooms, that it is today. In 1882, their son, Franklin D Roosevelt, was born at Springwood and lived there throughout his life. In the grounds, his wife Eleanor built her own cottage, Val-Kil, and in 1938, Roosevelt continued the family tradition and commissioned work for a presidential library.

☛ **Carrère & Hastings, Hoban, Jefferson, Walpole**

James Roosevelt. b (USA), 1828. **d** (USA), 1900. **Franklin Delano Roosevelt. b** Hyde Park, NY (USA), 1882. **d** Warm Springs, GA (USA), 1942. **Springwood (Franklin Delano Roosevelt House)**, Hyde Park, NY (USA), 1826–1915.

Roper Robert William

William Roper House

Built in the American Greek Revival style, William Roper House is a graceful yet imposing sight along East Battery Street in downtown Charleston. Bold, classically simple elements are found throughout the house, such as the five-column Ionic portico, interior and exterior mouldings and friezes, pediment gables, a full entablature and heavy cornices. They were often painted white to replicate the white marble Greek ruins, although these had, in fact, originally been brightly-coloured. The Greek Revival style flourished in the US – as nowhere else – during the 1830s and 40s, and expressed America's aspiration to represent the new Republic and the nation's foundation in Ancient Greek democratic ideals. Alexander Jackson Davis complained that Greek temple-front buildings were so prevalent in American towns that it was difficult for visitors to distinguish between a church, a bank or a courthouse.

☛ Bulfinch, A J Davis, Hoban, Jefferson, Rousseau

Robert William Roper. Active (USA), early to mid-nineteenth century. **William Roper House**, Charleston, SC (USA), 1838.

Rossi Aldo

Pocono Pines House

Symmetrical and boasting twin gables, the Pocono Pines House is Aldo Rossi's rational response to American vernacular domestic architecture. Most of the work he did in his lifetime drew on Italian prototypes, but when an American developer commissioned him to design three houses in a mountain resort area of Pennsylvania, Rossi looked to other sources. His work is always evocative, an architecture of memory and distant allusion, and this house is no exception. With its formal, geometric twin gable-ended dormers and symmetrical windows, it reinterprets an array of early American house styles, from clapboard farmhouses to Cape Cod cottages. Rossi was a principal exponent of Rationalist architecture, as expressed in his highly influential book *The Architecture of the City* (1966), whether designing an apartment building in the bustling city of Milan, or a single-family home in the forests of Mount Pocono.

☛ **A J Davis, Graves, Libera, Stern, Venturi**

Aldo Rossi. **b** Milan (IT), 1931. **d** Milan (IT), 1997. **Pocono Pines House**, Mount Pocono, PA (USA), 1988.

Rothery John Mount Ievers Court

Although far from the fashionable city of Dublin, this Irish Georgian dwelling is considered a regional jewel among the great Palladian-style country houses built by the Anglo-Irish aristocracy. The steeply-pitched roof, pair of tall chimneys and slight narrowing of the facade as it rises contribute to a desired sense of height. The influence of seventeenth-century Dutch house design can be seen at Mount Ievers Court, notably in its roof design and thick north facade, constructed inside and out of brick imported from Holland. Architect Rothery's records state that thirty-four tons of oak harvested for roof timbers were brought by boat, then carted twenty miles to the Ievers family house in County Clare. When Rothery died in 1736, the house was unfinished; it was later completed by his son, Isaac, who was also an architect.

☞ **Adam, Campen, Fortrey, I Jones, Kent, Palladio**

372

John Rothery. Active (IRE), late seventeenth and early eighteenth century. **d** (IRE), 1736. **Mount Ievers Court**, Sixmilebridge (IRE), c1730–7.

RoTo Architects Carlson-Reges Residence

Formerly the machine shop for the city's first power station, this Neo-Classical pavilion has been converted into an unusual urban residence near downtown Los Angeles. Surrounded by railyards and a major freeway, it presented the architects with the challenge of providing a hospitable living environment, as well as a semi-public garden gallery. Gathering inspiration and a variety of materials from the client-builder's own scrapyard, RoTo successfully combined the simplicity of the existing structure with a series of large-scale interventions that work both with, and against, the logic of the original 1920s building, creating infinite opportunities for unexpected juxtapositions. Perhaps the most inventive addition is an old steel gasoline tank, found on the site, that was cut in half and welded together end-to-end for use as an elevated lap pool. Michael Rotondi had previously been part of Morphosis, with Thom Mayne, until 1991 when he founded RoTo Architects with Clark Stevens.

☛ **Miralles & Tagliabue, Morphosis, Moss, UN Studio**

RoTo Architects. Michael Rotondi. **b** Los Angeles, CA (USA), 1949. **Clark Stevens. b** Ann Arbor, MI (USA), 1963. **Carlson-Reges Residence**, Los Angeles, CA (USA), 1996.

Rottier Guy

Arman House

More a social philosopher and artist than an architect in the conventional sense, Rottier has spent much of his career investigating the potential of buildings to express what he refers to as 'arTchitecture'. Many of his projects investigate temporary, environmentally-considered structures that could be relocated or, in some cases, destroyed after use. The Arman House, designed for an artist as a living and studio space, is a built expression of some of these ideas, although without the budget or technical innovation to bring the ideal to full fruition. Following on from the theoretical Cable Village of 1965, in which temporary living pods were hung from a spider's web, the Arman House fits neatly into a small hollow, implying by its form that it has been dropped into place and could just as easily be removed. The nylon rope web suggests a structural capability, but is essentially a sculptural gesture in this dramatic and intriguing house.

☛ Fuller, D Greene, Hübner-Forster-Hübner, Prouvé, Smithson

374

Guy Rottier. b Sumatra (IND), 1922. **Arman House**, Venze (FR), 1968.

Rousseau Pierre   Hôtel de Salm

The strict geometric order and symmetry of Greek temple architecture inspired this balanced composition for a Neo-Classical mansion's courtyard facade: a central portico, with Corinthian entablature and columns, flanked by matching Ionic colonnades. The colonnades provide a formal but permeable screen between the private courtyard and public street. A product of the Age of Enlightenment and the German Prince of Salm's ardent desire for social standing in Paris, the Hôtel de Salm is considered a masterpiece of French Neo-Classicism. Strong horizontal and vertical elements are perfectly balanced; ornament is minimal. By contrast, on the rear elevation that overlooks the River Seine, Rousseau designed an ornate facade with a domed rotunda. Napoleon arranged to buy this mansion for the Legion of Honour, and today it houses the Legion's museum and offices.

☛ Cortona, Gabriel, Hadrian, Palladio, Thomson

Pierre Rousseau. **b** Nantes (FR), 1751. **d** Amiens (FR), 1810. **Hôtel de Salm**, Paris (FR), 1782–6.

Roy Victor

Ravenscrag

The asymmetric composition, along with the presence of the tower, or *campanile*, identify the Italian villa style of this urban estate. Although removed stylistically from its country of origin, Ravenscrag is typical of the Victorian architecture of this region inasmuch as it is the product of a nineteenth century, mainly British solution to the reconsideration of urban dwellings. As industrialization pulled more and more people into the city, a demand was created for appropriate accommodation for the upper-class members of society. The solution was to build houses from catalogues that prescribed various single dwelling types – like the Italian villa. One of the first, and by far the most extravagant of its type built in Canada – particularly after its 1872 additions of a new ballroom, conservatory and billiard room – Ravenscrag became a stopping point for international royalty, nobility and leaders, and was often referred to as a second government house.

☞ Bigio, Elliot, McCoskrie & Greenfield, Sloan, Vaux & Church

376

Victor Roy. **b** (CAN), 1837. **d** (CAN), 1902. **Ravenscrag**, Montreal, QC (CAN), 1861.

Rudolph Paul

Rudolph House

The sleek urbanity of this interior in a transformed New York brownstone townhouse little resembles the aggressiveness and unrefined New Brutalist aesthetic of Rudolph's earlier Boston Government Center or Yale Architecture School. Rather, the Rudolph House invites one to move through the four floors of this intricately planned space, where transparency and verticality are the main themes. From the main living area on the ground floor, one's eye is unexpectedly drawn ever upwards by the dynamics of the space: a mixture of shifting levels, materials and light creates a dematerialized translucence. Clear plastic flooring, screens of pale raw silk and a silver reflective finish on the structural elements, as well as a clear plastic jacuzzi in the main bathroom, augment this iridescence. Rudolph embraces the Manhattan cityscape by emphasizing a startling panorama on the constructed terrace – the whole ensemble suggesting an elegant cocktail party.

☛ Kahn, Lescaze, Meier, Williams & Tsien

Paul Rudolph. b Elkton, KY (USA), 1918. d New York, NY (USA), 1997. **Rudolph House**, New York, NY (USA), 1973–97.

Rural Studio

Bryant House

Protected by the embrace of a large front porch, the Bryant family watches night fall from their home in rural Alabama. This family, two grandparents and their three young grandchildren, used to live in a shack without plumbing or heating before this house was designed and built for them, free of charge, by a group of students from Auburn University.

It was the first project for Rural Studio, an educational and sociological initiative, founded by architect, Samuel Mockbee, that brings students to impoverished Hale County as part of their architectural training. They are responsible for every step of the process, from meeting with the clients and completing the design, to choosing materials and working as

the construction crew. In an effort to reduce costs, the walls of this house are made of 80-pound hay bales rendered in stucco, and the floor is a concrete slab covered with bricks. The entire 80 sq m (850 sq ft) house was built for only $15,000.

☛ **Fernau & Hartman, Mockbee Coker, Murcutt**

Rural Studio, Auburn University, founded by Samuel Mockbee. b Meridian, MS (USA), 1945. **Bryant House (Haybale House)**, Hale County, AL (USA), 1993.

Saarinen Eero
J Irwin & Xenia Miller House

Eero Saarinen, the son of Finnish architect, Eliel Saarinen, already had a longtime familial connection with J Irwin Miller when he was asked to design this house on the Flatrock River in Columbus. This classically modern house is actually four separate structures arranged into one unit under a skylighted metal roof and has been likened to a modern version of Palladio's Villa Rotunda. On the interior, Saarinen used marble for walls and travertine for the floor, which extends out onto an all-round veranda; the furnishings included rugs and chairs that Saarinen designed himself. The Millers commissioned two of only four built single-family residences by Saarinen, who is better known for his more famous public buildings, such as the TWA terminal at Kennedy Airport (1956–62) with its wing-like vaulting roofs. In this building, he used form in an abstract and highly symbolic manner quite different to the contained and geometric form of the Miller House.

☛ **Eames, Gesellius Lindgren & Saarinen, Palladio**

Eero Saarinen. **b** Kirkkonummi (FIN), 1910. **d** Ann Arbor, MI (USA), 1961. **J Irwin & Xenia Miller House**, Columbus, IN (USA), 1953–7.

Sa'dan Toraja

Tongkonan

Few vernacular buildings are more impressive than the *tongkonan*, or ancestral house of the Toraja. The Sa'dan Toraja, who live in the highlands of southern Sulawesi, cultivate rice which they store in barns that are smaller versions of the *tongkonan*. Both building types have a saddle-backed roof which soars above each end of the building to a height of 10 m (33 ft) or more – the form symbolizing the horns of the water buffalo. They are arranged hierarchically with the north-facing *tongkonan* standing in line opposite a row of rice barns. Covered with a thick thatch of split bamboo rods, the roof protects a row of rooms on different levels, floored with thick planks; the water buffalo are kept in a pen below. This heavy structure is supported by posts and beams, and the front gable end is boarded with richly-decorated panels, painted in red, black and white. The horns from the sacred buffalo are mounted on the house-pole and denote the rank of the occupiers.

☛ **Abelam, Maori, Ndebele, Toba Batak**

380

Sa'dan Toraja. Active (IND), from sixteenth century to present day. **Tongkonan**, south Sulawesi, nr Borneo (IND), as built today.

Safdie Moshe

House in Jerusalem

The ancient and the modern combine in the house that Moshe Safdie designed for himself in the Old City of Jerusalem. Set on an escarpment with panoramic views across to the Dead Sea, the house reads like a history of the city: its lower levels date from the Crusades, its second floor from the Ottoman era, its top floor was added by Safdie in the 1970s. Each strata is identifiable, yet all blend effortlessly together in a manner which exemplifies Safdie's work. He formerly worked with Louis Kahn in Philadelphia and was catapulted to fame by Habitat 67, his design for Expo '67 in Montreal. This was an apartment block in which the flats were stacked up on top of each other in the seemingly random manner of a medieval hill town. The design was the result of Safdie's exploration of how the lessons of ancient architecture can be applied to contemporary buildings.

☛ Bawa, Eldem, Fathy, Kahn, Rewal

Moshe Safdie. b Haifa (IS), 1938. **House in Jerusalem** (IS), 1973.

Saitowitz Stanley   Transvaal House

This assemblage of industrial, prefabricated building materials – such as cold-rolled trusses, cellular metal decking and off-the-shelf details – form an intriguing whole. Inspired by an outcrop of rocks on the site, the house becomes an outcrop of habitable forms; its columns are placed in line with the contours of the site, and the outline of the house is an approximation of the rock formation. The house has been designed to reside between oppositions: landscape and construction, earth and sky, rigid system and free-flowing spaces. The roof, made from galvanized metal tiles, steps down to the ground and can be climbed, like a cliff, blurring the boundaries between natural and manmade. Meanwhile, the low brick walls contain space while allowing it to flow from inside to out. The house looks unfinished, ready to revert back to natural forms, and deliberately so. Saitowitz wanted the act of habitation to be the final element in his design.

☞ Eames, Future Systems, Holl, Morphosis, Murcutt

Stanley Saitowitz. b Johannesburg (SA), 1949. **Transvaal House**, Transvaal (SA), 1978.

Sami

Goatte

Often incorrectly referred to as Lapps, the Sami people inhabit the inhospitable northernmost part of the European continent, which they refer to as Sapmi. These hardy nomadic people, identified by their rights to herd reindeer rather than by nationality, on the whole, no longer live in the traditional *goatte,* or *lavvu*, pole-frame tents, except for the short periods in summer when their herds graze along the coast. The age-old form of the *goatte* is constructed from stripped poles, readily obtained from the abundant birch and fir forests, which are closely grouped and embedded into the ice to form a rigid cone. These act as a skeleton to support the hides, bark and furs which are then tightly wrapped around the frame.

Inside, warmth is generated from a central stone hearth from which the smoke escapes via the open apex. Today, the resurgence of Sami traditionalists who wish to return to their former nomadic life is gaining momentum.

☛ **Blackfoot, Inuit, Kyrgyz, Moors, Tihama Farmers**

Sami. Active (FIN, NOR, RUS, SWE), c8000 BC to present day. **Goatte**, Finmark Plain, Lappland (FIN), as built today.

Samoan

Fale Tele

This traditionally designed Samoan *fale tele* (great house) uses locally sourced materials and construction techniques that have been maintained for thousands of years throughout Polynesia, although rarely seen today. Coconut branches or sugarcane is used for thatch roofing, and stone is used for the base and flooring. Coconut fronds are woven to form walls, protective screens, blinds and sleeping mats. Wooden posts, purlins and rafters provide the structural support of the building, tied together with coconut fibre cord. The Samoan house is not a single multi-roomed structure, but rather, part of a compound made up of separate, usually circular or elliptical, freestanding functional rooms. The *fale tele* is situated at the front of the residential compound, and is used to house guests as well as for occasional meetings. The size of the house historically indicated the social rank of the owners; the largest *fale tele* recorded covered 16 m (53 ft) in diameter.

☛ Hutu, Ma'dan, Maasai, Maori, Sa'dan Toraja, Zulu

384

San Gimignano Comune di

Torres Meliandi and Rognosa

The walled hilltown of San Gimignano was self-governing through a Commune from the twelfth century until it was annexed to Florence in 1353. It was during this period that the many tower houses, which give the town its characteristic profile, were built by the wealthy San Gimignano families as part of their palazzi. One explanation is that, built for defence, the imposing towers reflected a rivalry both with surrounding cities, as well as between the citizens themselves. Another explanation is that the towers served a purpose in the mercantile economy that led to the growth of the town; the saffron-dyed wool cloth produced there may have been hung, protected from sun and dirt, within the towers. In either case, the competitive tower-building led to the introduction of a statute to prohibit any private building exceeding the height of the public ones, such as the 51 m (167 ft) Torre Rognosa, pictured on the right, which formed part of the Governor's Palace.

☛ **Santorini Islanders, Vallibus, Yemeni**

Comune di San Gimignano. Active (IT), c1100–1353. **Torres Meliandi and Rognosa** (left, Torres Meliandi, poi Aldobrandini, and right, Torre Rognosa, Palazzo del Podestà), San Gimignano (IT), 1255.

Sangallo the Younger, Antonio da   Palazzo Farnese

Allesandro Farnese, later Pope Paul III, employed all the best architects and artists of the time to build and decorate his magnificent Roman palace. Sangallo began the work in 1514, in the High Renaissance style, with windows set in tabernacles on both ground and upper floors. He treated the inner court with arches and engaged columns, just like those of the ancient Colosseum, following the most advanced taste of his day. However, when Michelangelo (1475–1564) came to add a third storey some thirty years later, Sangallo's original design seemed very tame to him – as Michelangelo had famously broken the chains of Classical usage by introducing forms that were both free in their use of detail and much more bold. Michelangelo designed a very deep, almost over-sized cornice above the top storey, to unify the proportion of all three storeys seen together, and the details of the tabernacle surrounds to his windows deliberately flaunt the Classical precepts of the earlier work.

☛ **Alberti, Laurana, Maiano, Porta**

Antonio da Sangallo the Younger (Antonio Cordiani). b Florence (IT), c1483. d Rome (IT), 1546. **Palazzo Farnese**, Rome (IT), begun 1514, continued by Michelangelo Buonarroti, 1546 and completed by Giacomo della Porta, 1589.

Santorini Islanders

Houses on Santorini

Tourists and architects alike join in their admiration of Santorini (Tera), the most southerly of the Greek Cycladic Islands. The distinctive crescent-shaped island was formed by the eruptions of a now inactive volcano in 1500 BC. On the western side of the island, white houses perch on the cliffs which plunge abruptly into the sea and define the coastline, while at the northern end the dramatic village of Oia clings to the edge of the caldera. Steep flights of steps lead to small walled courtyards and the cubic, white-washed walls of the houses. While some of these have the flat roofs typical to the Cyclades, many of the Santorini houses are spanned with elongated barrel vaults, which owe their prevalence on the one hand to a widespread lack of timber, and on the other to a tradition of functional simplicity. These primary forms, relieved with chimneys and ovens in a multitude of levels, angles and precarious sites, have an eternal visual appeal.

☛ Anchorites, Girolamo II, Libera, Tiwa Indians, Yemeni

Santorini Islanders. Active (GR), c3200 BC to present day. **Houses on Santorini**, Cyclades (GR), c1850–1900.

Sauvage Henri

Villa Majorelle

The almost animalistic, organic carved fireplace, naturalistic painted friezes and ornate wrought ironwork are features of this *Gesamtkunstwerk* created by the atelier of the owner, Louis Majorelle, a successful cabinet-maker and wrought ironworker. The design also brought together the Parisian painter, Francis Jourdain, and ceramic artist, Alexandre Bigot, all working under the direction of Henri Sauvage, one of the major figures in the Nancy School of Architecture. The interior detailing of the house is a superior example of the Art Nouveau style. The stained glass and ironwork were the work of two Nancy artists, Jacques Gruber and Victor Prouvé. Sauvage worked in practice with Charles Savarin between 1898 and 1912 and was later to collaborate with the French architect and urban designer Tony Garnier on proposals for social housing for *cités-jardins* (garden cities). He realized some social housing in Paris, as well as a pavilion for the Universal Exhibition in Paris, 1900.

☛ **Cauchie, Guimard, Horta, Olbrich, Strauven**

Henri Frédéric Sauvage. **b** Rouen (FR), 1873. **d** Paris (FR), 1932. **Villa Majorelle**, Nancy (FR), 1902–3.

Scarpa Carlo   Villa Ottolenghi

As in the work of Frank Lloyd Wright, to whom Scarpa is often compared, the structural elements of this house appear like the strata of natural rock; as demonstrated in the columns of alternating rings of coloured natural stone and smooth polished concrete, shown here. The plan of the house is hinged on a series of nine of these columns, arranged in three clusters, from which groups of rooms fan out towards the landscape, each with its own separate series of views of the gardens, pools and roof-terraces set into a vineyard above Lake Garda. Scarpa's method of work is such that each event is separately conceived and studied, and related to the whole loosely and thematically (rather than rigidly and formally). This gives rise to buildings which are hard to understand from plans or photographs, but offer the inhabitant, or visitor, an orchestrated succession of delights.

☞ **Asplund, Le Corbusier, Sert, Snozzi, Wright**

Scarpa Carlo   Villa Ottolenghi

Carlo Scarpa. b Venice (IT), 1906. **d** Sendai (JAP), 1978. **Villa Ottolenghi**, Verona (IT), 1974–8.

Scharoun Hans

Schminke House

The canted relationship between the north-south orientation of the central block of this house and its two side wings, which follow the site boundaries at a 26-degree angle, gives an inherent dynamism to this design. Scharoun exploits this characteristic with transparent walls and double-height spaces. His architecture depended on interpretation of site (note the cantilever off the garden wall), and of the functions which a building would accommodate, in opposition to preconceived Corbusian forms. The imminent Nazi regime – during which Scharoun remained in Germany – repressed the consummation of the refined relationship between form and function he achieved here. After World War II, Scharoun became Director of the Building and Housing Department for Greater Berlin, setting the stage for his greatest works and public buildings, and giving him free rein to influence the next generation of German architects.

☛ Gropius, Lauterbach, Niemeyer, Yamada

Hans Scharoun. b Bremen (GER), 1893. d Berlin (GER), 1972. Schminke House, Löbau (GER), 1933.

Schindler Rudolph Kings Road Studios

The soothing palette of this experimental house reflected the independent lifestyle chosen by its adventurous inhabitants. Designed by Schindler for himself, his wife and another couple, this unusual architectural composition consisted of four individual studios and a shared kitchen. Arranged in pairs, each L-shaped set of studios framed a private outdoor patio with a fireplace that served as a traditional living room in the warm climate of southern California. The couples slept on the roof in open-air sleeping lofts and ate food grown in their own garden. A student of Otto Wagner's in Vienna, Schindler began working for Frank Lloyd Wright in Chicago in 1917. While in California on a project, he became captivated with the warm climate, lifestyle and the many opportunities he found there, so he and his wife settled in Los Angeles. They subsequently sponsored fellow Austrian architect, Richard Neutra, to join them and their families shared the Kings Road Studios from 1925 to 1928.

☞ Gill & Mead, Gray & Badovici, Hoff, Neutra, Wright

Rudolph Michael Schindler. b Vienna (AUS), 1887. d Los Angeles, CA (USA), 1953. **Kings Road Studios**, Los Angeles, CA (USA), 1921–2.

Schinkel Karl Friedrich   Schloss Charlottenhof

At Charlottenhof, Schinkel transformed an existing manor house, set in a meadow on the edge of the royal park at Sanssouci, into an idyllic home for Crown Prince Wilhelm of Prussia and his Princess. The house was reclad in the Italianate manner developed by French architects following their travels in Italy, but Schinkel's most important change was to provide a new garden terrace running at first-floor level, linked to the former manor house by a central portico and, beyond, a double-storey entrance hall with a bubbling square fountain. Schinkel's achievement at Charlottenhof was to combine carefully controlled axial sequences of space with changing perspectives of the royal park, bringing the suggestion of sunny Italian summers to the flat meadowland of north Germany. Schinkel spent his early career as a stage designer and painter, and only later did he become Prussia's leading architect, often commissioned by its royal family.

☞ Burlington, Cameron, Nash, Palladio, Roper, Rousseau

392

Karl Friedrich Schinkel. **b** Neurappin (GER), 1781. **d** Berlin (GER), 1841. **Schloss Charlottenhof**, Sanssouci, nr Potsdam (GER), 1826–33.

Schönthal Otto

Villa Vojczik

Otto Schönthal graduated from the Academy of Fine Arts in Vienna at a time when Otto Wagner was at his most influential in his role as professor. Many of Wagner's students went on to create a distinct Viennese style and influence an entire generation of post-Secession designers. Schönthal's work characterized this pre-Art Nouveau period, which is exemplified in his villa for Dr Vojczik. The house features a classical ground plan with a central mass crossed lengthwise by an access corridor. The facade is where Schönthal makes his definitive statement. Classical, symmetrical organization and a simple structure – overlayed with rich ornamentation – betray his exploration of the three-dimensional articulation of planes, a common preoccupation of the Wagner School. The entire house, including details such as balconies and rainwater pipes, has been carefully attenuated in accordance with the Wagnerian principle of 'Art in Everything'.

☛ Cauchie, Loos, Olbrich, Wagner

Otto Schönthal. b Vienna (AUS), 1878. d Vienna (AUS), 1961. **Villa Vojczik**, Vienna (AUS), 1902.

Schweitzer Joshua   The Monument

Three asymmetrical, brightly-coloured cubes stand, like an oasis, on the edge of the Joshua Tree National Park outside Los Angeles. Built as a weekend retreat for the architect, the small, Neo-Primitive compound is made up of an olive-green living area, a blue bedroom suite and an orange outdoor pavilion. The blocks are set in the landscape like manmade boulders, cut with openings at uneven angles to make the scale and composition both abstract and mysterious. While they appear to be freestanding volumes from the outside, the rooms are interconnected and flow freely. The oddly-angled windows expressively frame fragments of the extraordinary landscape. Even though the colours have been inspired by the intense hues of the local vegetation of lichen and cactus flowers, the house still contrasts dramatically with its natural setting, while the angular, irregular forms provide a sharp but not dissonant divergence from the rounded rock formations.

☞ Arquitectonica, Barragán, Coderch, Gehry, Legorreta

394

Joshua Schweitzer. b Cincinnati, OH (USA), 1953. The Monument, Joshua Tree National Park, CA (USA), 1988–90.

Scogin Elam & Bray   Chmar House

As it soars skyward, this house exults in nature while, at the same time, showing deference to it. It is at once a *tour de force* and yet, somehow, quite unassuming. The Chmar House sits on a two-and-three-quarter acre site next to a nature preserve; thus the bucolic nature of the setting in the rolling wooded Atlanta countryside, is well-protected. The actual placement of the house was selected after a tree fell here, naturally providing a clearing. The house is raised above the ground on tree-like columns to cause as little disruption to nature as possible; the living areas form one wing, and the guest quarters another. The design draws inspiration from Japanese architecture and ritual (the clients are practicing Buddhists), so that the spaces unfold as a ceremonial passage. The interiors, clad in birch and plywood panels, with windows of varying shapes and sizes, connect inside once again to nature outside.

☛ Edmond & Corrigan, Mockbee Coker, Patkau Architects

Scogin Elam & Bray. Mack Scogin. b Atlanta, GA (USA), 1943. Merrill Elam. b Nashville, TN (USA), 1943. Lloyd Bray. b Atlanta, GA (USA), 1951. Chmar House, Atlanta, GA (USA), 1988–9.

Scott Tallon Walker

Goulding House

Jutting out alarmingly over the River Dargle, Ronald Tallon's Goulding House might seem more suited to the hills of Los Angeles than the rural backwater of Enniskerry in Ireland. This extraordinary summerhouse was built for Sir Basil and Lady Goulding, who wanted a place in their back garden to hold parties and conferences. Tallon, of Dublin architects Scott Tallon Walker, came up with a Mies-influenced single-storey design, just ten metres long. Two bays of the steel-framed structure, diagonally braced on the exterior, are anchored to the hillside while the remaining three cantilever out over the river. The final two are fully glazed, the rest clad in cedar, which softens the otherwise crisp, high-tech styling.

Scott Tallon Walker was better known for its larger industrial and public buildings, and the practice has won RIAI Gold Medals for several projects including the GEC Factory in 1959 and Caroll's Factory in Dundalk in 1973.

☞ Eames, Mies van der Rohe, Murcutt, A Williams, Zenetos

Scott Tallon Walker. **Michael Scott. b** Drogheda (IRE), 1905. **d** Dublin (IRE), 1989. **Ronald Tallon. b** Dublin (IRE), 1927. **Robin Walker. b** Waterford (IRE), 1924. **d** Dublin (IRE), 1991. **Goulding House,** Enniskerry (IRE), 1972.

Segal Walter

Self-Build Housing

This is one of fourteen houses built to a design by Segal to minimize costs by using full-size, mass-produced sheet materials, standard timber cross-sections and simple foundations. The prototype was built in his own back-garden in the mid-1960s, and he developed a system of easily understandable drawings and basic construction techniques: a counterpoint to the highly sophisticated systems of an increasingly industrialized construction business. This Lewisham project was remarkable because the houses were all built by their future owners, who ranged from retired men to single mothers. One of them wrote of the enormous benefits the project brought to the community: 'Segal taught us to think for ourselves … he literally changed our lives'. The scheme inspired many more self-build projects, and was seen by architects as a criticism of the way Modernism had alienated individual end-users from the design process.

☞ Day, Eichler, Gehry, Goodman, Suuronen

Walter Segal. **b** Ascona (SW), 1907. **d** London (UK), 1985. **Self-Build Housing**, London (UK), 1977–80.

Seidler Harry

Rose Seidler House

Graduating from Harvard University in 1946, where he was taught by ex-Bauhaus members, Walter Gropius and Marcel Breuer, Seidler left for Australia to design a house in Sydney for his parents. The Rose Seidler House, one of a small group of dwellings which Seidler designed for his family and friends, was the first building of a prolific career, now spanning over fifty years and ranging from small domestic projects to high-rise apartments and office towers. A hollowed-out, floating white box, the house is anchored to the ground by a series of elements that extend from the main volume, such as the garden retaining walls and the visually dominant ramp. The open terrace, with its mural painted by Seidler, links the living and bedroom spaces. In 1988, the Historic Houses Trust opened the house to the public, reinforcing its status as an important work of Modernism and one of the most influential houses in Australia.

☞ Breuer, Gray & Badovici, Gropius, Mies van der Rohe

Harry Seidler. b Vienna (AUS), 1923. **Rose Seidler House**, Sydney, NSW (ASL), 1948.

Sejima Kazuyo — Villa in the Forest

The client of this house, a scientist who also deals in paintings, commissioned this as a second home to accommodate artists visiting from abroad. The house consists of two circular walls that each have different centres; the outer wall delineates a profile of the house while the inner wall divides the house into two parts, an atelier and a dwelling space. Due to its forest location in a cold climate, the house has a thick concrete perimeter wall. Sejima, whose earlier projects had emphasized a continuity between inside and outside, wanted to create a self-contained continuity within the building's substantial walls. The continuous space between the two eccentric circular walls gently diminishes and extends in width and height, demonstrating her almost obsessive preoccupation with circular movement. Here Sejima offers a simple yet evocative response to the demands of the forest environment and her client's practical requirements.

☛ Hara, Herzog & de Meuron, Ito, Koolhaas

Kazuyo Sejima. b Ibaraki (JAP), 1956. **Villa in the Forest**, Tateshina, Nagano (JAP), 1994.

Senosiain Javier · Mexican Whale House

The undulating, swelling outline of this house is generated by a highly unusual construction technique. A pneumatic structure was inflated on a concrete base and sprayed with polyurethane foam, which was allowed to harden before the internal armature was deflated. The interior and exterior surfaces were then plastered with cement mixed with metal fibres and, on the outside, embedded with decorative polychrome broken tiles. The mosaic effect owes much to the Spanish architect, Gaudi, but the organicism of the whole is primarily generated by the architect's belief that curved spaces represent the natural habitat of humans. Window openings are limited to reduce solar glare, while filtered daylight enters the interior through blowhole-like openings in the upper surface of the building. The whale form offers an effective shelter from harsh environmental conditions, and is a model of architecture that coexists in harmony with nature.

☛ Gaudi, Grataloup, D Greene, Kiesler, Okada & Tomiyama

Javier Senosiain. b Mexico City (MEX), 1948. **Mexican Whale House**, Mexico City (MEX), 1992–4.

Serlio Sebastiano Château d'Ancy-le-Franc

The Italian painter and architect, Sebastiano Serlio, was called to France in 1541 at the King's command. Here, he produced several designs and built two houses, only one of which, the Château d'Ancy-le-Franc, survives to show off his particularly austere Italian style. Begun in 1546 for the Count of Tonnerre, brother to Henri II's mistress, it has a typically Italian square courtyard formed by equal ranges, articulated on each of the two storeys by a triumphal arch motif taken from the Belvedere Courtyard in the Vatican. The external facade employs the flat pilasters more familiar to French taste, as are the corners, emphasized by square towers with pyramidal roofs. Despite this, all the flamboyance typical of French architecture only a generation beforehand, has been swept away for plainer, more disciplined detailing. Serlio was later to expound this type as an exemplary design in his treatise on classical architecture, *Tutte l'opere d'architettura* (1584).

☛ Cerceau, J le Breton, Maiano, Peruzzi

401

Sebastiano Serlio. b Bologna (IT), 1475. d Fontainebleau (FR), 1554. **Château d'Ancy-le-Franc**, nr Tonnerre, Burgundy (FR), 1541–50.

Sert Josep Lluís

Sert House

This tightly-organized courtyard is the heart of the house that Catalan-born architect, Josep Lluís Sert, built for himself near Boston in 1958, during his tenure at Harvard. Although the open atrium plan was used in ancient Roman houses, it takes on a thoroughly Modern image when carried out in Sert's rigid, highly-rational language. Instead of symmetry and axial sequences, the architect created off-centred alignments of sliding doors and square windows. The furnishings are deliberately minimal; a simple Japanese 'butterfly' stool by Sori Yanagi takes on great visual and symbolic stature when seen against such an austere backdrop. Sert was an alumnus of Le Corbusier, one of Modernism's founding figures. He emigrated to the USA during the Spanish Civil War, and succeeded Bauhaus master, Walter Gropius, at the helm of Harvard's Graduate School of Design from 1953 to 1969.

☞ Coderch, Gropius, Le Corbusier, Lubetkin, Niemeyer

Josep Lluís Sert. b Barcelona (SP), 1902. **d** Barcelona (SP), 1983. **Sert House**, Cambridge, MA (USA), 1958.

Shah Jahan

Royal Tent Palace

This portable cloth palace of the Emperor Shah Jahan is one of the most impressive monuments to have survived from the Mughal period. Elegantly lobed velvet arches and sumptuous cloth panels embroidered with foliate patterns in gold and silver surround this inner chamber and throne room. For several months each year, the royal entourage and legions lived in the cool airy splendour of their tents as they travelled to distant parts of the Mughal Empire to hunt and campaign. The design of such elaborate tents is undoubtedly rooted in the semi-nomadic lifestyle of the pre-Mughal tribes of Persia and the Turkoman regions. Many structural elements and decorative details are evident in Mughal garden palaces and pavilions of Delhi, Agra and Fatehpur Sikri. Rediscovered in Meherangarh Fort, Rajasthan after more than 300 years, this well-preserved tent would have served as the Hall of Public Audience accessed by a network of formal avenues.

☛ **Akbar, Amar Singh II, Jagat Singh II, Nasrid Dynasty**

Emperor Shah Jahan. Reigned (IN), 1628–57. **Royal Tent Palace**, by the Imperial Textile Workshop, Agra (IN), mid-seventeenth century.

Shaw Richard Norman   Bedford Park

Bedford Park in London is *the* prototypical garden suburb. Its picturesque appearance, leafy street layout, even its architectural styling, taken individually, were not particularly innovative: however, together they were a sensation. From 1877, Norman Shaw, and later his assistant, E J May, designed the houses in irregular rows, with pleasing variations. Red brick and tile-hung walls are set off by white-painted doors with prominent wooden hoods, and tall, bowed windows. The gables are curved, double-curved, sometimes pilastered and pedimented, occasionally tile-hung and often set off by adjacent dormer windows. In short, this is the Queen Anne style. London's suburbs are at their best when they preserve the intimate scale of the villages on which they are founded. Bedford Park's countless imitators have characterized many areas of outer London, and given many Londoners the idyllic homes they most desire in the midst of the metropolis.

☞ **Lutyens, Parker & Unwin, Voysey, P Webb**

Richard Norman Shaw. b Edinburgh, Scotland (UK), 1831. d London (UK), 1912. **Bedford Park**, London (UK), begun 1877.

Shekhtel Fedor

Ryabushinsky House

The organic detailing of its great windows and the wild lilies of its mosaic frieze are only the prelude to an extraordinary sinuous staircase that rises through the heart of this house. The ponderous porchway leads through a screen of two vast dragonflies to the great baluster whose lamp is a dripping octopus. The white marble stair ascends symbolically from the underwater world to the sunshine under the pyramidal rooflight. The Ryabushinsky family were bankers of vast wealth and cultural influence in Moscow and it was here that Stepan Ryabushinsky hung his unique collection of icons. His family had belonged to the banned Old Believer sect of the Russian Orthodox church; a secret chapel was only discovered in the house in the late 1980s. Shekhtel, a great friend of Chekhov, was the leading architect of Russian Art Nouveau, although later his work was to evolve into a more free-style Classicism.

☛ Geisler & Guslisty, Hoffmann, Horta, Olbrich

405

Fedor Osipovich (Frants Adolf) Shekhtel. b St Petersburg (RUS), 1859. d Moscow (RUS), 1926. **Ryabushinsky House**, Moscow (RUS), 1900–2.

Shetland Island Celts   Mousa Broch

The prehistoric hillfort settlements built by the Celts were first described by the Romans around AD 297; it is possible, however, that this form of defensive dwelling, the broch, was built as long ago as 600 BC. One can imagine from the ruins existing today that the broch was an imposing sight, its circular, slightly funnelled central tower rising up to 12–15 m (40–50 ft) high. Its dry-stone walls could be up to 4 m (13 ft) thick, constructed of rubble and stone; in later developments, galleries were built within the thickness of the wall, in order to reinforce them so they could be built higher still. A circular enclosure surrounded the broch, accessed by low tunnels, with its own in-built defence features to prevent attacks by marauders. Inside the walls, families or tribes would occupy huts or lean-to timber structures built around hearthstones. Some of the larger brochs had up to five or six mezzanine timber floors and stairs rising through the galleried walls.

☛ Galician Celts, Girolamo II, Provençale Farmers

Shetland Island Celts. Active Scotland (UK), c1000 BC to AD 850. Mousa Broch, Shetland, Scotland (UK), c600 BC to the Middle Ages.

Shinohara Kazuo   House in White

Space appears to expand horizontally and vertically within this square-plan, two-storey wooden house. With its double-height living area and compacted bedroom spaces stacked on top of each other, the house expresses Shinohara's dual pursuit of abstraction and reinterpretation of traditional Japanese residential architecture. While the minimal elements of white walls, wooden floor and tile roof render abstract space, the central polished cedar column refers to quintessential, or almost mythic aspects of Japanese rural dwellings. Shinohara was completing a doctorate on the spatial composition of Japanese architecture at the Tokyo Institute of Technology under Kiyosi Seike at the time of this house's design, and went on to pursue further abstraction of space, both in residences and larger public works. His work has been profoundly influential on the 'Shinohara-school' architects, which include Toyo Ito and Itsuko Hasegawa.

☛ Hasegawa, Ito, Shirakawa Farmers

Kazuo Shinohara. b Shizuoka (JAP), 1925. **House in White**, Suginami Ward, Tokyo (JAP), 1967.

Shirakawa Farmers

Gassho-Zukuri Farmhouse

This type of farmhouse, with its high ridge and steep thatched roof, is found only in Shirakawa and a few other villages of the mountainous Hida region of central Japan. Its unique construction method, using giant logs that are tied together with thick ropes and tree branches to support itself, is known as *gassho-zukuri* (hand-joining style). The ground floor is used as the living and working space while the upper floors are used to farm silkworms. To maintain the silkworms at the optimum warm temperature, the heat and steam from the ground floor central hearth rise to the upper floors through a screened opening in part of the ceiling which aids the circulation of warm air. The farmhouses of Shirakawa village, along with the Katsura Imperial Villa and Ise Shrine, were praised by Bruno Taut in the 1930s as the best examples of simple and rational Japanese architecture. The village has also been designated a World Heritage site by UNESCO.

☞ **Bernese Farmers, Kyoto Merchants, Landaise Farmers**

Shirakawa Farmers. Active (JAP), eighteenth century to present day. **Gassho-Zukuri Farmhouse**, Shirakawa, Gifu Prefecture (JAP), circa eighteenth century, still lived in today.

Shuttleworth Ken   Crescent House

The main space of this house is the garden room, a single, 36 m (118 ft)-wide volume accommodating all the communal activities of Shuttleworth's young family: cooking, eating, relaxing and playing. However, despite this open planning, the building is surprisingly restrictive; for example, the over 4 m (13 ft)-high, concave glass wall bathes the room in light, but has no opening sections to allow immediate access to the garden, so as not to detract from the simple geometric form. A partner of the High-Tech firm Foster and Partners, Shuttleworth wanted a home which was 'spacious and airy yet utilitarian and functional', and not 'lavish, profligate or precious'. All the surfaces are white, apart from the raw concrete of the chimney and end wall. Colour is provided by furnishings and objects which are changed over each season: towels, cushions, bed linen, tablecloths, table mats, vases, etc. are all blue in winter, yellow in spring, green in summer and red in autumn.

☞ Diller & Scofidio, Future Systems, Rogers, Team 4

Kenneth Shuttleworth. **b** Birmingham (UK), 1952. **Crescent House**, Winterbrook (UK), 1997.

Sirén Kaija & Heikki   House on Lingonsö Island

Located on a previously uninhabited island, this group of simple log buildings was designed by the Siréns as a holiday home. Wanting to make the most of the dramatic setting, the architects decided to familiarize themselves with the climatic conditions before designing their house. The first stage, starting in 1966, was to build a harbour basin and breakwater, a small sauna and a living space. In 1967, they built an adjacent kitchen and dining pavilion linked by a wooden veranda. Finally, in 1969, they added a sleeping pavilion and covered patios to form a protected courtyard. To ensure a unified aesthetic, despite the long, drawn-out construction, all of the buildings were built using pre-cut, machine-planed logs.

Intended as a humble stage for human activities, as well as for observing nature, the Siréns have followed a tradition of Finnish architecture, capturing the simple drama of the pine-forested landscape through the frame of the building.

☛ **Aalto, Gunnløgsson, Hølmebakk, Holscher, A Jacobsen**

Kaija Sirén. b Kotka (FIN), 1920. **d** Helsinki (FIN), 2001. **Heikki Sirén. b** Helsinki (FIN), 1918. **House on Lingonsö Island**, Barösund Archipelago (FIN), 1966–9.

Siza Álvaro

Alcino Cardosa House

Set in a former vineyard at the mouth of the River Minho in Portugal, two small agricultural buildings have been transformed and combined to form a single house by the introduction of a new triangular block of bedrooms. Low, largely glazed and partly sunken behind a dry-stone wall, the addition succeeds in tying the disparate elements together.

The three buildings, each at a different angle, fan outwards, stepping down towards the valley below, the terracing continued in the rows of vineyards and the splayed forms of a swimming pool. The fanning geometry, the natural stone walls, the refined detail of the new bedrooms, and the rows of vines all suggest an inevitable natural growth. Since the

1950s, Álvaro Siza has built extensively both in Portugal and internationally. Fundamentally Modernist, yet rooted in Portugal's heritage, his work reveals a unique sensitivity to the rural or urban context to which it belongs.

☛ Dewes & Puente, Doshi, Portoghesi, Souto de Moura

Álvaro Siza Vieira. b Matosinhos (POR), 1933. **Alcino Cardosa House**, Moledo do Minho (POR), 1964–8, with later additions, 1971–3.

Sloan Samuel   Longwood

With a finial rising from its ornate Byzantine cupola, Longwood is the folly to end all follies. An octagonal residence of elaborate proportion, dimension and detailing, the house's eclectic mix of Corinthian fluted columns and Victorian 'Carpenter Gothic' capitals are worthy of particular note. (Carpenter Gothic is a style featuring exterior woodwork with Gothic motifs.) It was begun in 1859 with a design by the Philadelphia society architect, Samuel Sloan, and built in 1860–61 for Haller Nutt, a physician, and his wife Julia. The dates themselves are significant in that the American Civil War was by then under way, and the South was increasingly becoming a battleground. Indeed, Dr Nutt dismissed the carpenters so they could return to Pennsylvania to fight for the North, and the house was never completed. Only nine of the planned thirty-two rooms were finished, although those are still intact today, along with their original furniture.

☛ A J Davis, Elliot, Roper, Weeks

Samuel Sloan. b Beaver Dam, nr Honeybrook, PA (USA), 1815. **d** Raleigh, NC (USA), 1884. **Longwood**, Natchez, MS (USA), 1860–61.

Smithson Alison & Peter   House of the Future

This ergonomic, plastic-moulded bath, and its companion shapes equally attuned to the physical form, embodied the new direction for house design, so the architects believed. The house formed part of the Ideal Home Exhibition of 1956, and its free-flowing spaces, furniture and lighting presented a new vision of domesticity. Both the Smithsons, and their contemporary, the painter Richard Hamilton, were fascinated by America's economic boom-driven consumer society, especially as represented in magazines, such as *Life*. And the development of new materials, like the plastic impregnation of fibrous plaster that would make these organic shapes mass-producible, meant their rhetorical ideas could become reality. However, by the time such devices did become affordable, taste had moved on. What made the Smithsons such an enduring influence was their perception that architecture could come out of 'ordinary' products and quotidian experiences.

☛ D Greene, Grimshaw, Suuronen, M Webb

Alison Smithson. b Sheffield (UK), 1928. d London (UK), 1993. **Peter Smithson**. b Stockton-on-Tees (UK), 1923. **House of the Future**, Ideal Home Exhibition, London (UK), project, 1956.

Smythson Robert   Hardwick Hall

Immortalized in the refrain 'Hardwick Hall, more glass than wall', this house is regarded as one of the finest flowerings of Elizabethan architecture. The dynamic massing and height of the building, combined with its profusion of expensive, glittering windows – which bend the rules of Classicism by increasing in size towards the top of the house – has an exhibitionist quality reflecting the personality of its owner, Elizabeth, Countess of Shrewsbury. The six towers are crowned triumphantly with her initials and, although Smythson was one of the leading architects of the English Renaissance, she is thought to have played a major role in its design. The plan is significant for its transformation of the traditional medieval hall into a two-storey space running through the centre of the house, heralding the emergence of the conventional entrance hall, and for the Baroque drama of the stone staircase located to its right.

☞ Compton, Hawksmoor, I Jones

414

Robert Smythson. b Crosby, Ravensworth (UK), c1535. d Wollaton (UK), 1614. Hardwick Hall, Derbyshire (UK), 1590–7.

Snozzi Luigi   Casa Bernasconi

Seen from the pergola, the house and garden of the Casa Bernasconi seem to converge: the green lawn transforms into the flat, blue surface of the swimming pool, which itself seems to be an extension of the skylit staircase, along the highly polished floor and through the large glass opening. It is built in the mountains of Italian-speaking Switzerland, Ticino, a famous enclave of Modern Rationalist architecture, of which Snozzi is a leading proponent. The house itself is a series of habitable terraces, set against its steep backdrop. It is entered at the top level, where the bedrooms are, via a long stair that cuts across the steeply-sloping hill. The living room and kitchen are at pool level, with a pergola leading you still further down the hill. Snozzi's houses, always in exposed concrete and using the language of Modernism, draw on the elemental stone architecture of what was traditionally a poor region, but today is a popular tourist destination.

☛ Botta, O'Donnell & Tuomey, Reichlin & Reinhardt, Rossi

Luigi Snozzi. **b** Mendrisio (SW), 1932. **Casa Bernasconi**, Carona (SW), 1989.

Soane Sir John   13–14 Lincoln's Inn Fields

The spatial inventiveness of Sir John Soane's own house remains unequalled and hugely influential in the history of British architecture. Using his characteristic eccentric variant of Classicism, with his experimental use of light and strategically placed grooves, he remodelled two 1740s terraced houses to produce this architectural manifesto, which remains a museum today. Applying shallow segmental arches and flat saucer domes, and liberally sprinkling his surfaces with mirrors, rectangular and round, he melted the boundaries of each room and merged it into its neighbours. This spatial dissolution dematerializes his architecture to the point of weightlessness, as here, in his Breakfast Parlour. A saucer dome carries a lantern ringed by mirrors, and more mirrors are set into the soffits of the flat arches that carry it. In the spandrels of the dome, there are yet four more mirrors, this time convex, which reflect the whole room in reduced perspective.

☛ **Aitchison, Laugier, Ledoux, Leverton, Malton**

Sir John Soane. **b** Goring-on-Thames, nr Reading (UK), 1753. **d** London (UK), 1837. **13–14 Lincoln's Inn Fields (Sir John Soane Museum)**, London (UK), No.13, 1812–13, No.14, 1823–4.

Soleri Paolo

Dome House

Imagine sleeping comfortably under the stars in the Arizona desert, free to gaze at a 360-degree view of the sky. This was the challenge for Paolo Soleri and Mark Mills when they were asked to build a home for Nora Woods on a site near Phoenix, in 1949. The dwelling is composed of two contrasting parts; a solid masonry base carved into the hillside, containing a studio and the cool sleeping quarters for the hot summer months, and the transparent, light-filled main living area, shown here. The rotating glass dome is constructed of two intersecting half-domes, one transparent and the other aluminum-painted to reflect the heat. A copper tube sprays water along its base as a further defence against the desert heat. Since building the Dome House, Soleri's continued interest in an ecologically responsive architecture and lifestyle led to his most ambitious project, an experimental prototype community in Arizona called Arcosanti, which he has been building since 1970.

☛ Droppers, Fuller, D Greene, Prince, Reynolds

Paolo Soleri. b Turin (IT), 1919. **Dome House**, Cave Creek, AZ (USA), 1949.

Soriano Raphael   Case Study House

Blurring the boundaries between interior and exterior, this austere California home was an experiment in residential, light steel-frame construction, and marked Soriano's shift from Bauhaus white cubes to more informal structures. Designed for the Case Study House Program – sponsored by *Arts & Architecture* magazine to showcase the work of young architects – all of the structural building components were prefabricated and assembled on site in three days. Soriano delighted in working with off-the-shelf materials, such as plywood partitions and window panels, which fitted into a standardized grid system, the fundamental ordering principle behind all his work. By leaving portions of the roof grid open, he created interior patios and allowed light to penetrate unexpectedly into the living spaces. Soriano began his career in the office of Richard Neutra, whose Lovell House (1927–9) was an early example of domestic steel construction.

☛ **Breuer, Eames, Eichler, Ellwood, Koenig, Neutra**

Raphael Soriano. **b** Rhodes (GR), 1907. **d** Los Angeles, CA (USA), 1988. **Case Study House**, Pacific Palisades, CA (USA), 1950.

Souto de Moura Eduardo   Casa Moledo

Architectural critics have identified a 'School of Oporto' – which includes Souto de Moura and Álvaro Siza among others – united in a non-doctrinaire response to the complexities of a country in a sometimes difficult transition from its agricultural past. Here, granite walls, like those of the surrounding vineyards of northern Portugal, step up the hillside to form a series of flat terraces. Where the walls become higher, they split to reveal a simple house form – comprising a single row of rooms, glazed both front and back. The topmost terrace is a flat roof which appears almost to float above the live rock of the hillside. Beyond this is a spectacular view over the valley and towards the Atlantic Ocean. The Casa Moledo demonstrates a theme common in Souto de Moura's buildings; the fusion of traditional and modern, of using vernacular architecture without resorting to artifice. The simplest possible means are used, with the richest possible results.

☞ Dewes & Puente, Doshi, Geyter, Siza

Eduardo Souto de Moura. b Oporto (POR), 1952. Casa Moledo, Caminha (POR), 1998.

Starck Philippe   Kit House for 3 Suisses

Apocryphally, Abbé Laugier's classical peristyle was a rough construction of tree trunks. Here, it reappears as the elemental timber porch, complete with classically stepped podium – or steps. The usual references of this entirely generic, mass-produced house – classical, *dacha*, pavilion, pagoda – are treated straightforwardly, but knowingly, by *enfant terrible* designer Philippe Starck, more famous for his rocket-shaped lemon squeezer and range of fashionable, slightly cheeky hotel designs. The house kit is an economic house, purchased from the furnishing company, 3 Suisses, by catalogue and erected by them, using the balloon-frame construction that colonized much of North America. 'Here I'm only interested in the small qualities of life … the nice kitchen that lights up when you're having breakfast, the proximity of the bathroom, the log fire,' said Starck. However, he does add touches of kitsch and essential high architecture for those in the know.

☛ **Arad, Eichler, Laugier, Prouvé, Segal**

Philippe Starck. b Paris (FR), 1949. **Kit House for 3 Suisses**, prototype, 1993.

Stein Seth

House for a Classic Car Collector

Commissioned as a *pied-à-terre* in a London mews, where space is at a premium, this structure contains all the usual functional spaces necessary for a small family, but also houses and displays the owner's two classic cars. Stein responded to the unusual brief ingeniously by designing a double-deck elevator that is capable of turning garage space into living space, and vice-versa. When the elevator is in the upper position, its lower deck is at street level and is able to receive a car, while the space below is freed to become extra living space. When the elevator is in the lower position, the car on the deck is displayed at the basement level, as if in a glass case, while the upper deck is ready to receive a second car.

This celebration of movement and flexibility is a nod towards the innovative work of the Archigram group of 1960s London, and the use of frosted and clear glass enhances the fetishistic voyeurism of a true classic car enthusiast.

☞ Bolles & Wilson, Geyter, D Greene, Koolhaas, M Webb

Seth Stein. b New York, NY (USA), 1959. **House for a Classic Car Collector**, London (UK), 1998.

Stel Simon van der   Groot Constantia

With its simple symmetrical form, single-room-deep plan and all ornament concentrated in the gables, Groot Constantia set the pattern for the Cape Dutch tradition, which lasted nearly a century and a half. Built for the Cape Colony's first governor, it uses basic architectural skills to make a little corner of Europe in Africa. Its models are many, including seventeenth-century Dutch urban, a touch of Classical and something of peasant building, mediated through a Protestant sensibility and a sublimated but powerful sense of the vastness of Africa. It is, therefore, an early example of what became a major theme of European colonial architecture. At this date, decades before Palladianism overtook northern Europe, the urge for decoration distantly mirrored the licensed ornament of a burgher's ruff in a Hals portrait. In later Cape Dutch houses, however, the *naïveté* becomes subsumed within ornament which more obviously refers to architectural tradition.

☞ **Berringer, Carter, Fagan, Mourier, Villiers**

422

Simon van der Stel. b 1639. **d** 1712 (SA), Governor of Cape Colony, 1679–88. **Groot Constantia**, Constantia, Cape Province (SA), 1685, revised 1778.

Stern Robert A M   Lawson House

The Lawson House is a hybrid. Although built in the Shingle Style and scaled as if it were a large and important house, it also draws on the American beach cottage – not the grand cottages of Newport fame, but the simple 'shack by the sea' tradition. Situated on top of a sand dune, the house is approached via an ascending walkway and then a wide, monumentally-scaled stairway leading to a shaded porch. The roof is a dominant architectural element, steeply pitched and penetrated by a Roman thermal window. Inside, the living room looks out to sea, while the master bedroom is tucked in the attic under the capacious roof. Robert A M Stern, widely acknowledged as a key theorist and originator of the Post-Modern movement, was influential in reintroducing the Shingle Style and reviving interest in historical American domestic architecture. He describes the Lawson House as a 'marriage of high Classicism with grandma's house'.

☛ **Graves, Jencks & Farrell, Rossi, Venturi**

Robert A M Stern. **b** New York, NY (USA), 1939. **Lawson House**, East Quogue, Long Island, NY (USA), 1979–81.

Strauven Gustave   Maison Saint-Cyr

A long-time collaborator of Victor Horta, Gustave Strauven went on to develop his own distinctly flamboyant style of second-generation Art Nouveau. The Maison Saint-Cyr, Strauven's most exuberant design, is characterized by its extraordinary, narrow street facade. Despite the restricted width of the site, Strauven used its extreme proportions to celebrate his artistry. The sculptural relief of the surface, while providing decorative embellishment, is also very successful in introducing light and external space into the building via its full-width balconies and full-height windows. All of this creates a general impression of lightness, emphasized by the dramatic, filigree 'crown' at the top of the building. Strauven allowed himself to be almost carried away by the potential of this project, pushing both the materials and his artistic expression to the limit. In doing so, he undoubtedly created one of the most seductive buildings of his time.

☞ **Cauchie, Horta, Kishi, Schönthal, Wagner**

Gustave Strauven. b 1878. **d** 1919. **Maison Saint-Cyr**, Brussels (BEL), 1900.

Studio Atkinson
Zachary House

This house in Zachary, Louisiana – the very first project built by Stephen Atkinson – is a variation on a humble housing type common throughout the southern USA, known as the 'dogtrot'; two rooms separated by an open breezeway. The house seems almost childlike in its simple profile, rustic corrugated metal exterior and freestanding masonry chimney. However, the typical metal roof of Atkinson's dogtrot is exaggerated by a 45-degree pitch and corrugated metal siding – recalling the exteriors of nearby farm structures – the architect's own embellishments. Corrugated shutters at the ends of the house conceal glazed double doors. The breezeway between the two internal rooms opens onto a long deck extending at a right-angle from the house. This home, built for Atkinson's parents in the region where he grew up, shows how powerful even the most modest buildings can be.

☛ J Davis, Herzog & de Meuron, Murcutt

Studio Atkinson. Stephen Atkinson. b Baton Rouge, LA (USA), 1967. Zachary House, Zachary, LA (USA), 1999.

Studio Granda   House in Vordertaunus

The house that Margret Hardardottir and Steve Christer – collectively known as Studio Granda – built in Vordertaunus, near the German city of Wiesbaden, is really two buildings: a timber-clad pavilion and a red-painted box. Taken together, the two create a rich mix of spaces – those in the former are light and airy (the roof terrace, in particular, has fantastic views), the latter are more intimate and cosy. It is typical of this young Icelandic practice to approach a house design in this way. Its best-known work to date – the competition-winning design for the city hall in Reykjavik (1987–92) which launched their career – has an equally complex combination of private and ceremonial spaces. In the face of much contemporary architecture, which stresses the need for light and open-plan living, Studio Granda recognize that people need different spaces to suit their moods.

☛ **Baumschlager & Eberle, Katsalidis, Kishigami, Klotz**

Studio Granda. **Steve Christer**. b Blackfyne (UK), 1960. **Margret Hardardottir**. b Reykjavik (ICE), 1959. **House in Vordertaunus**, nr Wiesbaden (GER), 1989–92.

Sullivan Louis

Bradley House

One of the most influential forces of the Chicago School and mentor to the young Frank Lloyd Wright, Louis Sullivan designed some of the finest houses in turn-of-the-century North America. In the Bradley House, his most complex and mature domestic work, Sullivan employed a cross-shaped plan using the heavy-walled entry vestibule as the symbolic heart of the house. From this space, the two axes radiate out into a sequence of rooms. On the exterior, the dominant volume containing the main living and sleeping areas, is intersected by a smaller block, which is more expressively articulated and features a semicircular study. Any impression of heaviness is alleviated by cantilevered porches at each end of the building, and long strips of windows down the side elevations. The house is a vibrant example of Sullivan's philosophy that form should follow function; an approach he always inflected with his sensitive employment of Beaux-Arts organic ornamentation.

☛ **Furness, Greene & Greene, Potter, Wright**

427

Louis Henry Sullivan. b Boston, MA (USA), 1856. **d** Chicago, IL (USA), 1924. **Bradley House**, Madison, WI (USA), 1910.

Suuronen Matti   Futuro House

Thirty years after its design, the UFO-like Futuro House is receiving renewed attention from a new generation. It was designed in 1968 as the ideal holiday house, using the ratio of 1:2 to give it its perfect symmetrical and elliptical shape. This prefabricated, glass-fibre bubble house could be built by four men in an afternoon and transported to any site by helicopter, with its fully equipped kitchen, bathroom, two bedrooms and lounge already installed. Some 600 models were made by the plastics factory, Polykem AB of Helsinki, even though its price was too high for mass production, and only two houses were to remain in Finland. However, its fashionable, space age design was exhibited around the world and influenced many other types of building developed using the same system of construction; including kiosks, service stations and hotel complexes. The oil crisis in 1973, however, resulted in the cancelling of an order for more than 15,000 modules.

☞ Berglund, Eames, Future Systems, D Greene, Prouvé

428

Matti Suuronen. b Lammi (FIN), 1933. **Futuro House**, prototype, 1968.

Syrian Farmers Idlib Houses

For thousands of years, adobe-covered, mud-brick domed houses like these have dotted the semi-arid steppes of northern Syria. In the Idlib region, groups of these beehive-shaped earthen cupolas cast dramatic shadows across the landscape. Constructed from sun-dried bricks, laid to slope gently to the apex, the section of the dome is egg-shaped and immensely strong. The concentric layers of brick are bound together with a render of mud and straw. Small, regularly-spaced gaps are left allowing ventilation, and stones are inserted in the exterior surface of the curve making it possible to climb the dome for repairs. A single entrance is formed using a wooden lintel supported by adobe pillars. The interior contains a hearth near the entry and a wall niche cupboard. The houses are sometimes placed together, side-by-side, and joined by an exterior layer of render, making them appear to be a continuous structure.

☞ **Girolamo II, Inuit, Provençale Farmers, Tiwa Indians**

Syrian Farmers. Active (SYR), c6000 BC to present day. **Idlib Houses**, Idlib, Steppes of Northern Syria (SYR), c6000 BC to present day.

Tait Thomas

House at Silver End

The flat roofs and white rendered walls of the new Modern Movement took a long time to take root in Britain, if indeed they ever did. Among its promoters was Lord Braintree; he saw a social purpose in the new architecture, and also a means of promoting the windows made in his Crittall steel window factory. He commissioned Thomas Tait to design

Silver End, one of the earliest British housing estates in the International Modern style, incorporating individual houses, terraced housing and even a Welfare Club house. While built to provide homes for the Crittall workers, Silver End also served to promote the product. The angled oriel window rising above a cantilevered balcony, which is also a porch, has

all the style of Art Deco, although on closer inspection the anachronistic chimney stacks and white-painted, conventional brickwork reveal the compromise of the Modern design intent.

☞ Behrens, Connell, Fry, Gropius, Lescaze

Thomas Tait. b Paisley, Scotland (UK), 1882. **d** Aberfeldy, Scotland (UK), 1954. **House at Silver End**, Rivenhall (UK), 1927–8.

Talman William   Chatsworth House

Chatsworth House is better known as the seat of the Dukes of Devonshire than for its architecture; perhaps because the house grew in stages and is not particularly showy. Its south front was built to the design of William Talman and, for the first time for an English country house, makes use of a Classical Giant order. This embraces the two main floors, which are set over a rusticated basement and, at the centre, support a pediment in the best Classical tradition. The grand west front is visible to the left, built later in 1700–3 after Talman had been dismissed, and thought to be designed by Thomas Archer, who had built a fantastic cascade house close by. The park, laid out by Capability Brown in the 1760s, frames the house and its gardens in the natural way he so favoured, and this embraced a new approach by way of a three-arched bridge, handsomely designed by James Paine.

☛ **Hawksmoor, I Jones, Palladio, Vanbrugh**

William Talman. b West Lavington (UK), 1650. **d** Felmingham (UK), 1719. **Chatsworth House**, Derbyshire (UK), 1686–96, continued by Thomas Archer, 1700–3.

Tarifa Marqués de   Casa de Pilatos

With its elaborate mix of Moorish, Gothic and Renaissance architectural elements, geometric motifs and Greco-Roman sculptures, this courtyard helped make the Casa de Pilatos the prototype for sixteenth-century Andalusian palaces. Moorish Gothic-style galleries surround this large patio, where smooth marble columns contrast with richly textured walls and archways. Intricate pattern upon pattern is juxtaposed in the *Mudéjar*, or Moslem, style as built by the Spanish Christians. This is evident from the tiled marble floor and *azulejos* (glazed tiles) to the bas-relief plaster walls that stretch up to Gothic-style stone balustrades. Credit for this high style goes to Don Fadrique, first Marqués de Tarifa. The Casa de Pilatos takes its name from the purported house of Pontius Pilate in Jerusalem, which influenced Don Fadrique when he visited it in 1519. It later became the ducal palace for the Medinaceli family, which has helped preserve it.

☛ **Eschwege, Isabella I & Ferdinand II, Nasrid Dynasty**

432

Marqués de Tarifa (Fadrique Enríquez de Ribera). b Seville (SP), 1476. **d** Seville (SP), 1539. **Casa de Pilatos**, Seville (SP), 1519–70.

Taylor Sir Robert   Heveningham Hall

With its three-bay pavilions flanking a seven-bay central block, linked by simplified wings, Sir Robert Taylor's exterior follows the formula of English Palladianism, and details, such as the attached columns and the rusticated and blank arched base, reinforce the effect. However, the central block's decorated attic with four sculptural figures, and surmounted by two vases, echoes the composition of Roman triumphal arches. This device, probably influenced by Robert Adam's Kedleston Hall, justifies entering at ground level rather than through an elevated portico. James Wyatt's interiors, especially the entrance hall, show Adam's influence more explicitly, with screens of columns along either end. Heveningham may be, as the critic Nicolaus Pevsner claimed, Suffolk's grandest Georgian mansion, but the Vanneck family was not old landed gentry. Its fortune derived from business, and architecture was a means of consolidating their elevated social position.

☛ Adam, Burlington, Kent, Ledoux, Leverton

Sir Robert Taylor. b Woodford (UK), 1714. d London (UK), 1788. **Heveningham Hall**, Sylly (UK), 1778.

Team 4
Creek Vean

Constructed from humble materials – predominately concrete blocks which are worked to an extraordinary level of precision – Creek Vean is a response to the steep and uneven landscape, and the particular requirements of the client. The central steps are a major organizational element in this seemingly simple house; they both separate and unite the two sleeping and living wings, while connecting the different levels and providing a static external space from which to enjoy the view. Team 4 comprised the young Richard Rogers and Norman Foster and their respective architect wives. It is said that the difficulty they had in achieving their required level of detail with the wet trades (concrete, mortar, plaster) used here, put them off working with traditional techniques. All their later work uses industrial prefabricated elements, a predominant feature of the uncompromising High-Tech architecture for which they have both become known.

☛ Aalto, Atelier 5, Le Corbusier, Mies van der Rohe, Rogers

Team 4. **Norman Foster**. b Manchester (UK), 1935. **Wendy Foster**. b (UK), 1935. d (UK), 1989. **Richard Rogers**. b Florence (IT), 1933. **Su Rogers**. b (UK), 1940. **Creek Vean**, Cornwall (UK), 1964–6.

TEN Arquitectos

Casa RR

The luminous, aquamarine glass stairtower, smooth stone wall and shimmering, reflecting pool of this courtyard house suggest a sleek townhouse. In fact, it is a suburban family home outside Mexico City that draws on the time-honoured courtyard house of colonial Latin America. Designed by local architect, Enrique Norten of TEN Arquitectos, who favours sophisticated forms and materials over historical ones, the house has an inwardly-focused paved courtyard that screens out the surrounding neighbourhood. The stairs, encased in translucent glass which is incised with clear strips, lead to a catwalk that provides access to the bedrooms, screened by a smooth stone wall. Below the stone is a band of clear glass that looks into a double-height living room. With its composition of various masses and materials, the house suggests an abstract version of the individual buildings which ring Mexico's colourful *zócalos*, or public plazas.

☞ **Barragán, Bo Bardi, Dewes & Puente, Kikutake**

TEN (Taller de Enrique Norten) Arquitectos. Enrique Norten. b Mexico City (MEX), 1954. **Casa RR**, Mexico City (MEX), 1998.

Terragni Giuseppe   Villa Bianca

While an indebtedness to Le Corbusier is evident in the cubic volumetric form and horizontal stripped fenestration of the Villa Bianca, Terragni's own brand of Rationalism is also apparent. Architect of the infamous, rather static office building, Casa del Fascio, and the unbuilt Danteum museum project of the same period, Terragni, in contrast, here exhibits an obsession with sliding planes, protruding volumes and floating canopies. The conflicting dynamics of the villa's structure constrain and, at the same time, extend the building beyond its proper enclosure, producing an active and fluid series of spaces, both inside and outside its shell. This concern for the displacement of mass is characteristic of Terragni and his Rationalist comrades, who sought to synthesize the values of Italian Classicism and the dynamism of the machine age. Contrary to its name, the villa is painted not white, but a pale pink, named instead after a beloved lost child of the original owner.

☞ **Le Corbusier, Libera, Lubetkin, Rossi, Vacchini**

Giuseppe Terragni. b Meda (IT), 1904. **d** Meda (IT), 1943. **Villa Bianca**, Seveso (IT), 1937.

Terry Quinlan

Pin Oak House

Is this the elevation of an English Palladian villa of the mid-eighteenth century? It looks like one, in composition, style of drawing and with the elegant horses in front; but it is actually a house of the 1980s in Kentucky, built for the Texan owner of a stud farm by Quinlan Terry, the leading English classical architect of the late twentieth century. Terry finds the compactness of Palladian plans well adapted to modern living, and the Pin Oak House is smaller than it looks, with only three bedrooms, a main living floor on the *piano nobile* and housekeeper accommodation in the basement. As a student in the 1950s, Quinlan Terry reacted against modern architecture and went to work for Raymond Erith (1903–73) who recreated Classicism in post-war England. Terry has received many commissions for houses in England, including the Riverside development at Richmond, and increasingly in the USA.

☛ Burlington, Cameron, Jencks & Farrell, Krier, Palladio

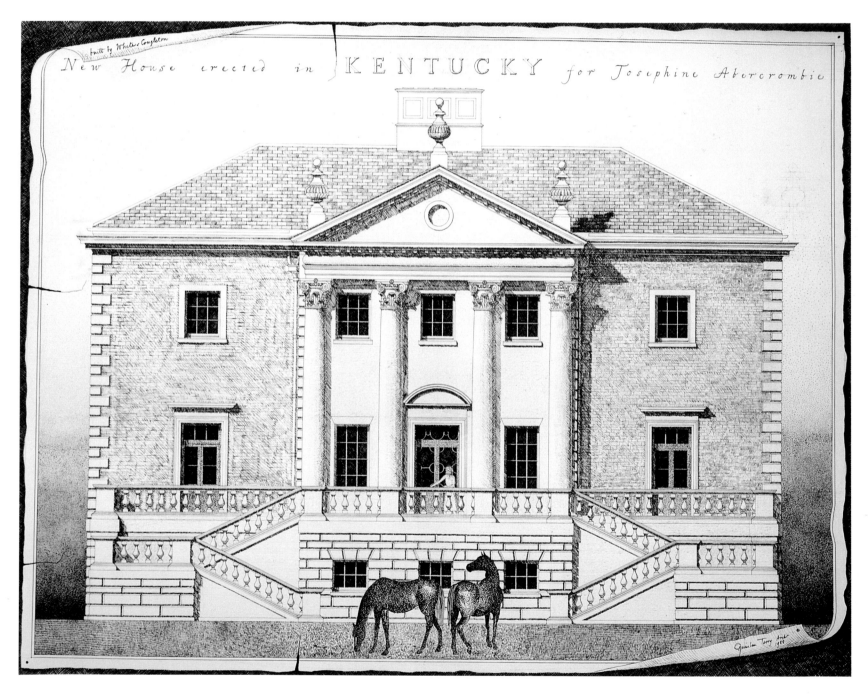

John Quinlan Terry. b London (UK), 1937. **Pin Oak House (Abercrombie House)**, Versailles, KY (USA), 1986–8.

Testa Clorindo

Green House

This retirement house by Clorindo Testa and his collaborator Juan Fontana rises defensively above the rough scrub of the pampa. It is a solid building, with small white window openings and grilles, which fulfils the client's prescriptive brief of protection from floods and earthquakes (neither particularly prevalent in the area) and a tranquil space for her family. Its distance from Buenos Aires could also be seen as a protective buffer from the proximate dangers of living in a city. A strongly-expressed double ramp forms an entire wing of the house, providing wheelchair access for a family member. Although there is also a lift, the ramp becomes a dominant architectural feature, a real link between outside and inside.

Testa's Bank of London in Buenos Aires, 1960–6, is thought by many to be one of the most important buildings of its time. His architecture stems from a love of expressing form through art, often producing graphic art or sculpture of his projects.

☞ Le Corbusier, Rossi, O M Ungers, A Williams

Clorindo Testa. b Naples (IT), 1923. **Green House (House R)**, Exaltación de la Cruz, Provincia de Buenos Aires (ARG), 1999–2000.

Thom Ron & Merrick Paul   Fraser House

With the organic planes of its cedar-shingled roof and the vertical thrust of its brickwork, the Fraser House appears to grow out of the natural setting in which it is so deeply embedded. Overlooking a broad ravine at the edge of Toronto's downtown area, the house is infused with both the natural logic of the site and the tailored needs of a receptive client. With no right angles or parallel walls, the three storeys of the house are arranged around an open stairwell, with the main entrance at middle level. The attention to the relationship between form and site is rooted in the West Coast background shared by Merrick and Thom. Thom, a self-taught architect, is primarily known for his definitive West Coast domestic architecture and industrial work in Ontario. However, it is his deep understanding of site and programme and his ability to translate this into built form that has won him his place in architectural history.

☛ Barnes, Erickson, Hariri & Hariri, Patkau Architects

Ron Thom. b Penticton, BC (CAN), 1923. d Toronto, ON (CAN), 1986. Paul Merrick. b (CAN) 1938. Fraser House, Toronto, ON (CAN), 1967.

Thomson Alexander 'Greek'　Holmwood House

This classical villa is actually closer to Glasgow than Greece. Its Scottish-born architect never even made the Grand Tour of Europe – but he still acquired the epithet 'Greek' from his mannered style of architecture. For Thomson, a practising Presbyterian, the architecture of Egypt and Greece was sacred; after all, Greek civilization had prepared mankind for the coming of Christ. In buildings such as Holmwood (widely considered his finest house), and in churches and monuments across Scotland, he created a new and distinctive architecture that blended classical Greek design with elements from Egyptian and other Eastern styles. Writing of Holmwood, the critic Thomas Gildard commented: 'If architecture be poetry in stone-and-lime this exquisite little gem, at once classic and picturesque, is as complete, self-contained and polished as a sonnet'. Its strong horizontal lines have been said to anticipate later houses by Lutyens and Frank Lloyd Wright.

☛ Leverton, Lutyens, Palladio, Soane, Wright

Alexander 'Greek' Thomson. b Balfron (UK), 1817. d Glasgow, Scotland (UK), 1875. Holmwood House, Cathcart, Scotland (UK), 1857–8.

Thule

Qammaq

The remains of this Thule winter dwelling haunt the east Canadian arctic landscape that at once engulfs and rests beneath it. The lichen-covered stones encircling this reconstructed whale-bone structure of a *qammaq* bespeak the age and grace of this dwelling type, which has been documented as early as the sixteenth century. The Thule people of the Canadian arctic region lived a nomadic lifestyle, governed by the hunt for food and the change of seasons, and these *qammaq* dwellings provided shelter through the harsh winters. The living space was dug out of the earth and lined with stones, sod and skins for insulation. The roof was also made of skins and sod, often with a stretched gut window for light and ventilation. As the ancestors of modern-day Inuit, many traces of Thule culture remain; however, dwelling types such as this *qammaq*, were gradually abandoned with the decline of whaling and the introduction of European influence.

☛ Inuit, Kyrgyz, Sami, Zulu

Thule. Active (CAN), AD 1000 to 1820s. **Qammaq**, Kekerten Island, Nunavut (CAN), circa sixteenth century (reconstruction).

Tiberius

Villa Iovis

The island of Capri had been a favourite resort of the Emperor Augustus. His adoptive son and successor, Tiberius (said to have owned twelve villas on the island) retired to this one, the Villa Iovis, perched on a sheer cliff edge a thousand feet above the sea, after the foiling of Sejanus' coup. Suetonius, Tiberius' ancient biographer, records scenes of both debauchery and cruelty taking place here; the condemned were said to have been flung over the cliff onto the rocks below. A more recent commentator noted that, while it is impossible that all the stories could be true, it is incredible that all should be false. The villa, built over vast cisterns for the storage of rainwater, is arranged around a central courtyard. The state rooms were to the east, the Emperor's private apartments overlooking the sea to the north, baths to the south and service rooms to the west. Clifftop walks gave views across the panorama of the Bay of Naples, from the island of Ischia to the Cape of Sorrento.

☛ **Libera, Maiuri, Minoan, Pompeii Romans**

442

Emperor Claudius Nero Tiberius. b Rome (IT), 42 BC. d Misenum, now Miseno (IT), AD 37. **Villa Iovis**, Capri (IT), AD 14–37, excavated 1932.

Tichborne William   Beaulieu House

One of the finest and best preserved country houses of seventeenth-century Ireland, Beaulieu House was, unusually for its time, built without fortifications. This was rare until William of Orange defeated the Catholic King, James II, in the Battle of the Boyne in 1690, establishing what was to be a stable, if strained, peace for the following hundred years. This stability led to the abandonment of the old castle strongholds and the beginning of the more predominant unfortified dwelling. The style of the house is 'artisan mannerist', a less sophisticated version of the Classicism introduced by Inigo Jones to England not long before. The two large chimneys dominate the house, which is faced in rendered stone with finely-wrought brick door and window surrounds. Very few alterations have been made to the house, which is probably accounted for by the fact that it still belongs to descendants of the family that built it almost 350 years ago.

☞ Cerceau, Hawksmoor, I Jones, Rothery

William Tichborne. Active (IRE), mid-seventeenth century. **Beaulieu House**, Drogheda (IRE), 1667.

Tigerman Stanley   Daisy House

Perched on a sand dune high above Lake Michigan, this whimsical house challenges the traditional perception of Classical symmetry. Tigerman conceptualized the design as analogous to the form of the human body, symmetrical on the outside and asymmetrical on the inside. In addition, its plan and elevation refer, subtly, to male and female anatomy. The undulating walls are constructed of vertical cedar boards, accented by an inset doorway and the soft flow of the concrete stairs. Inside, the sleeping quarters are located on either side of the central volume, allowing maximum privacy for children and parents. Post-Modern *enfant terrible* of the Chicago architecture scene since the 1960s, Stanley Tigerman is known for his sculptural expression and playful, sometimes controversial approach to design, in particular his earlier Hot Dog House of 1974.

☛ **Barnes, Gwathmey, Saitowitz, Starck**

Stanley Tigerman. b Chicago, IL (USA), 1930. **Daisy House**, Porter, IN (USA), 1975.

Tihama Farmers

Usha

The *usha* hut was recorded as early as 1500 BC in the hot and humid Tihama region, one of the richest agricultural areas in Saudi Arabia, extending down the Arabian Peninsula into Yemen. Grouped in walled stockades to prevent attacks from wild animals, each hut is about 4 m (13 ft) in diameter, with the circular base formed by curved and mud-rendered branches.

This is topped with a conical roof of sorghum thatch held down by tightly drawn ropes running from a central pole projecting from the roof. Two rectangular doors are placed on opposite sides to encourage cooling breezes to circulate through the hut. Inside, the walls are covered with mud plaster up to head height, above which is a timber shelf. All the interior surfaces are painted white and colourfully decorated by the women. Today, the *ushshash* (pl.) – once so prevalent in the Tihama region – are only found in Yemen where, unlike Saudi Arabia, a lack of prosperity has led to their preservation.

☛ **Girolamo II, Hutu, Kyrgyz, Syrian Farmers**

Tihama Farmers. Active (SAU), c1500 BC to present day. **Usha**, Jīzān (SAU), first recorded c1500 BC, still found in (YEM) today.

Tiwa Indians

Taos Pueblo

When the Spanish conquistadors occupied these permanent Native American settlements in the mid-sixteenth century, they described them as '*pueblos*' (villages), a name which stuck. Today, thirty *pueblos* survive in Arizona and New Mexico, some as much as a thousand years old. Taos, below the Sangre de Cristo mountains, is the largest of these, comprising two clusters of dwellings. Up to five-storeys high, the stepped blocks house some 1,500 Tiwa–speaking people. Entry to the dwellings was formerly through openings in the roofs, the ladders being drawn up afterwards. Today they have doors and windows in the mud-plastered adobe walls, with *vigas* (roof-poles) extending from them. Un-named and multi-functional, the rooms are used differently according to the season. Outside there are domed ovens for baking and, hidden from view, the *kivas* or underground ceremonial chambers essential to the annual cycle of fertility dances and rituals.

☞ C Johnson, Mandan Indians, Pueblo Indians

Tiwa Indians. Active (USA), thirteenth century to present day. Taos Pueblo, Taos, Sangre de Cristo, NM (USA), thirteenth century to present day.

Toba Batak

Ruma Gorga

Located along the shores of Lake Toba, the Toba Batak people are the most populous of the seven Batak subgroups. According to their culture, the *ruma gorga*, or decorated house, is a physical manifestation of the universe. They believe that the earth is set upon posts and humans inhabit the middle layer of a three-tiered universe, and they apply the same principle to their houses. This arrangement provides both physical and spiritual protection for the family, and the house is built according to strictly prescribed rituals. The essential features of the house, which is constructed from local hardwood, are the stilts, the canoe-shaped side walls and the spectacular saddle-shaped roof. This is covered in a thatch of sugar-palm fibres and projects over the gabled ends shading those working beneath. The finest houses are carved and painted with elaborate designs, all of which is undertaken exclusively by the men of the tribe, and contributes to the house's spiritual power.

☞ **Abelam, Maori, Sa'dan Toraja**

Toba Batak. Active (IND), circa AD 200 to present day. **Ruma Gorga**, Sumatera (IND), as built today.

Toda

Mund Hut

The polyandrous Toda tribe's hamlets, or *munds*, have changed little since 1603, when the Jesuit priest Fenicio first recorded their existence. Home to around twenty persons, each *mund* is located near pastures, running water and forestry, where the Toda can enact the rites and sacrifices associated with their belief that cattle are sacred. The dairy building of the *mund* is the equivalent of a temple; alongside calf-sheds and stone-walled pens, it occupies the most sacred space of the settlement. But the sacred/secular versus pure/impure distinction is spatial, not formal, therefore a standard built-form has sufficed. The original *mund* hut – seen here in the foreground – is a half-barrel vault of bamboo covered with thatch, beneath which nestle the endwalls made of upright planks or stone gables. A mere hole provides entry to their dark homes, yet the Toda still resist the sunny bungalows of modernity, preferring their own ancient sustainable habitat.

☞ **Abelam, Hausa, Hutu, Samoan**

Toda. Active (IN), circa seventeenth to present day. **Mund Huts**, Nilgiri Hills, Tamil Nadu (IN), early seventeenth century to present day.

Toffinou

Pile Houses on Lake Nokwé

The houses that the Toffinou tribe build along the northern shores of Lake Nokwé are raised on piles which are set into the bottom of the lake. The piles need to be tall and strong so as to support the floors of the houses well above the tidal waters. The adjacent mangrove forests of the hinterland provide the timber for this, as well as bamboo for filling the framed panels of the walls and palm leaves for thatching the roofs. These Toffinou settlements, particularly the town of Ganvié which has a population of some 10,000, are perhaps no more than 150 years old. This is because the mildly salt waters of the lake are a recent creation brought about by a sandy spit that has partly blocked the mouths of Benin's rivers So and Ouémé and formed a tidal lagoon. This is full of fish, which the men catch from their canoes – the only form of transportation and communication on the lake – and the women take to market and trade for all the necessities of life.

☛ **Annamese, Ma'dan, Tukanoan**

Toffinou. Active (BEN), early seventeenth century to present day. **Pile Houses on Lake Nokwé**, Ganvié (BEN), c1850 to present day.

Tokugawa Yorinobu Rinshunkaku

This villa is one of the finest examples of seventeenth-century residential architecture that was built for the powerful Samurai, or warrior, families who ruled Japan from 1603 to 1868 under the Tokugawa Shogunate. The villa consists of three separate buildings set in a garden, connected to each other in a zigzag pattern. Its buildings feature a typical Shoin-style interior characterized by *tatami*-covered floors (a system of sized mats), decorative alcoves and translucent *shoji* sliding doors. Decoration was limited to the alcoves and the finely-carved wooden screens above the *fusama* sliding doors which divide the spaces. These doors were adorned with paintings of natural scenery and ancient Chinese motifs, in shimmering colours, by the celebrated Kano School artists of the same period. The Rinshunkaku was commissioned by Yorinobu, who established the Kishu branch of the Tokugawa clan in 1619. It was originally built in Wakayama in 1649 and moved to its current site in 1917.

☛ Horiguchi, Ishikawa, Schindler, Toshihito & Toshitada

450

Yorinobu Tokugawa. b Yamashiro (JAP), 1602. **d** Kishu (JAP), 1671. **Rinshunkaku**, Wakayama (JAP), 1649, relocated to Yokohama (JAP), 1917.

Tolstoy Count Leo   House at Yasnaya Polyana

This comfortably human-scale house, with its casual extensions and spreading wooden verandas, was the only part of his grand family residence which Count Leo Tolstoy retained in the mid-1850s, when he sought to live a philosophically and practically simpler life. It was here that he wrote *War and Peace* in the 1860s and *Anna Karenina* in the 1870s, with his wife Sophia making repeated fair copies of his day's work every evening. It was on this estate that Tolstoy applied his progressive views on peasant freedom and education, before the state's official liberation of the serfs in 1861; and it was in this house that he endeavoured to live like a peasant himself. The whole culture of pacifism and Christian humanism which he preached is expressed in the utter simplicity of the house and its environment. 'Without Yasnaya Polyana,' Tolstoy wrote, 'I can hardly think about Russia or my attitude to her.'

☞   Gartman, Nikitin, Peter the Great, Potter, Vesnin

Count Leo Tolstoy. **b** Yasnaya Polyana (RUS), 1828. **d** Astapovo (RUS), 1910. **House at Yasnaya Polyana**, nr Tula (RUS), c1800.

Torres & Lapeña

House in Cap Martinet

Located just across the street from a house by the famous Spanish architectural master, Josep Lluís Sert, this sculptural design by the contemporary team of Torres & Lapeña is both hidden from its neighbours while, at the same time, open to the spectacular views of the sea. The series of folded and angled white-washed walls define spaces within the house, while propelling the viewer from the entrance, via framed vistas back onto the house itself, through to the panorama of the Mediterranean sea beyond. Such seemingly free and open plans express the exuberant spirit of Spanish design, particularly as seen in the works of the Catalan architects Jujol and Coderch, both of whom are sources of inspiration to Torres & Lapeña. While the use of white-washed stucco walls refers to traditional vernacular building on the island of Ibiza, their crisp, regular edges announce the architects' allegiance to true Modernism.

☛ **Coderch, Junquera & Pérez Pita, Scarpa, Sert**

Torres & Lapeña. **Elías Torres Tur**. b Ibiza (SP), 1949. **José Antonio Martínez Lapeña**. b Tarragona (SP), 1941. **House in Cap Martinet (Gili House)**, Ibiza (SP), 1987.

Toshihito & Toshitada Princes Hachijo — Katsura Rikyu

The Katsura Rikyu was first built as a modest princely retreat on the banks of the Katsura River by Prince Hachijo Toshihito and subsequently expanded by his son, Toshitada. Epitomizing the relaxed yet elegant *Sukiya-shoin* style of domestic architecture of the period, the complex consists of the main palace building of four staggered volumes, which overlook a central pond, and five tea ceremony pavilions sited within the surrounding stroll garden. The translucent *shoji* screens which partition the buildings modulate the admission of daylight and frame the garden views. The studied informality of the Katsura Rikyu and its gardens – in particular, its minimalist exterior and the use of modular planning (a result of the coordination between the *tatami* floor mats, doors and wall panels) – has long been considered the epitome of Japanese architectural aesthetics and has influenced Modernist architects such as Walter Gropius and Le Corbusier.

☛ **Gropius, Ishii, Le Corbusier, Tokugawa**

Prince Hachijo Toshihito. b Kyoto (JAP), 1579. **d** Kyoto (JAP), 1629. **Prince Hachijo Toshitada. b** Kyoto (JAP), 1619. **d** Kyoto (JAP), 1662. **Katsura Rikyu (Katsura Imperial Villa)**, Kyoto (JAP), 1617–62.

TR Hamzah & Yeang   Roof-Roof House

Much environmental design has an earthy, naturalistic feel to it, but not that of TR Hamzah & Yeang. The Roof-Roof House, built for Ken Yeang in 1985, has a sharp-edged slickness befitting Malaysia, a country whose burgeoning cities bristle with new skyscrapers. Although trained in Britain, Yeang and his business partner, Hamzah, have practiced from Malaysia for more than two decades. The country's climate (searingly hot and humid in summer) informs all their architecture. With the Roof-Roof House they pioneered what they called an 'environmental filter' – a louvred parasol on columns that oversails the whole complex, minimizing its exposure to the sun. It is aligned in such a way as to gain maximum benefit from the prevailing winds, while the rooftop swimming pool acts as a heat barrier. Many of the lessons learned in designing this house have been applied to their much larger buildings, such as the Menara Mesiniaga building in Selangor (1989–92).

☛ **Herzog + Partner, Powell-Tuck Connor & Orefelt, Safdie**

454

TR Hamzah & Yeang. **Tengku Robert bin Tengku Mohd Hamzah**. b Kota Bahru, Kelantan (MALAY), 1939. **Ken Yeang**. b Penang (MALAY), 1948. **Roof-Roof House**, Selangor (MALAY), 1985.

Traquair Earls of Traquair House

Traquair House, the oldest continuously inhabited house in Scotland, could easily be thought to be heavily influenced by French architecture from the same period. It is likely, though, that Scottish masons had simply arrived at the same logical development of historical traditions. The house today is more of a manor house, having developed from its earlier forms of heather hut (circa AD 950), through timber Royal Hunting Lodge (1100s), restoration by the Crown (1300s) until it finally became the home of James Stuart, the second son of the Earl of Buchan in 1491. At this point it was a tower house, and Stuart had plans to develop it, until he fell at the Battle of Flodden in 1513. It was much later, circa 1642, that the First Earl of Traquair remodelled the house in a more symmetrical style. James Smith completed this task, creating two pavilions to either side of the main front and enclosing the courtyard with elaborate wrought ironwork.

☞ Le Breton, L'Orme, Shetland Island Celts

Earls of Traquair. First Earl, active Scotland (UK), seventeenth century, descended from the Lairds of Traquair, circa mid-fifteenth century. **Traquair House**, Innerleithen, Scotland (UK), circa AD 950, remodelled c1642.

Tukanoan

Maloca

In the West, we usually think of each house as the home of a separate family, but in western Amazonia whole clans of related families may live in one large community house. Tukanoan clan houses, called *maloca*, may be more than 30 m (100 ft) long, half as wide and a third as high. Rectangular in plan – sometimes with a rear semi-circular apse – their immense, leaf-thatched roofs are supported by pairs of posts and cross-beams forming a centre aisle. Families live in enclosures to the rear of the *maloca*, the middle and front spaces being the male area. The complex spirituality of the Tukanoan people is expressed in the form of their houses. Symbolically, the domestic area represents the female womb, the frame is the male skeleton and the roof the skin and hair. Important rituals are held within this cosmic space, and symbolic decorations, inspired by visions, are painted on the front gable.

☞ **Annamese, Ndebele, Toba Batak, Toffinou**

Tukanoan. Active (COL), from late eighteenth century to present day. **Maloca**, Vaupes River basin, Amazonia (COL), as built today.

Turnbull William   Zimmermann Residence

A simple redwood, lattice timber frame encloses an Escher-like labyrinth of smooth white interiors. The main living spaces are accommodated in the freestanding white 'inner house' encircling a central atrium and rising up to a series of roof decks. Between the lattice frame, which is roofed in corrugated polycarbonate sheeting, and the inner house are a number of porches which add to a feeling of being not quite indoors, while providing a cool respite from the heat in summer. Built on a ridge overlooking hayfields on the flood plane of the Potomac River, and surrounded by oaks and maples, the house appears barn-like; however, its simple form belies its complex layering. William Turnbull was one of the founders of the Berkeley-based firm of Moore Lyndon Turnbull Whitaker (MLTW, founded in 1962), and with his partner, Charles Moore, was architect of the Sea Ranch condominiums in northern California, a seminal example of Bay Area Modernism from 1964.

☞ Barnes, Eisenman, Gehry, Gwathmey, Moore

William Turnbull. b New York, NY (USA), 1935. d Sausalito, CA (USA), 1997. **Zimmermann Residence**, Fairfax County, VA (USA), 1972–5.

UN Studio

Möbius House

Glass and concrete continually interplay in this elegant house, seamlessly transforming between interior and exterior, structure and partition; walls even twist and become bookshelves or seating. Built in a suburban enclave outside Utrecht, the house is organized conceptually around the Möbius band, the mathematical model of a continuous single-sided surface, that gave the house its name. The circulation is based on the double-locked torus, two loops that move independently, meeting and folding back onto each other at various points along their path, using complex geometries only made possible in architecture by the use of computer. This movement is embedded in the changing patterns of use as the family enacts its daily routine over each twenty-four hour period, shifting between zones of public and private activities, between studios, bedrooms and social spaces, all of which are fluidly integrated into a single formal composition.

☛ **Hariri & Hariri, Koolhaas, RoTo Architects, Zapata**

458

UN (United Net) Studio. **Ben van Berkel**. b Utrecht (NL), 1957. **Caroline Bos**. b Rotterdam (NL), 1959. **Möbius House**, Het Gooi (NL), 1998.

Ungers House III

The purity of the form and the exterior wall are so severe, and the detailing so invisible, that we cannot be sure if this is a wall or the image of a wall; a house or a household object; made of concrete or of paper. There is no main entrance; any of the equally placed doors will do. It sits on a delicate stone plinth, like a Classical temple, and its use of repetition and symmetrical arrangement reinforce this analogy. But more than an abstracted Classicism, the house reflects Ungers' interest in finding the essence of architecture. Like most of his work, the house becomes the built declaration of his theoretical interests. An influential writer and teacher in Europe and the USA for over forty years, and a key exponent of Rational architecture in the 1960s and 70s, his work has moved from rough materiality and asymmetry, through Rationalism and now, late in his career, to purity.

☞ Laugier, Loos, Mies van der Rohe, Rossi, Schinkel

Oswald Mathias Ungers. b Kaisersesch, Eifel (GER), 1926. **Ungers House III**, Cologne (GER), 1958.

Ungers Simon & Kinslow Thomas   T-House

The dominant T-shape of this house contains both residential accommodation and a workspace and library for its owner, a writer who needed space to store his 10,000-volume collection. The two storeys of the bar of the T are divided horizontally into solid and void. The solid top half houses the stacks of books on a mezzanine and the transparent lower half, with views out to the woods, is for working and reading, with direct vertical access to the bookshelves. Visitors enter the house across a promenade deck above the residential part of the house, which is a low-slung pavilion that emerges from the slope of the site. The only external clue to the presence of the lower volume is a funnel-like chimney. The dramatic orange colour of the cladding comes from the effect of the weathering steel shell, which is further dramatized by the regular spacing of black, vertical glazed slots. It is an abstract composition, difficult to read without any sense of scale.

☞ Acayaba, Schweitzer, Vicens Ramos Architects, Winter

460

Simon Ungers. b Cologne (GER), 1957. **Thomas Kinslow**. Active (USA), late twentieth century. **T-House**, Wilton, NY (USA), 1988–92.

Ushida Findlay
Soft and Hairy House

A one-storey, concrete spiral tube surrounds a courtyard that is linked to a roof garden covered with plants amid projecting skylights. The linear interior space within the tube is articulated ambiguously so that it maintains an organic continuity. However, the interior is also uniquely designed to establish a series of theatrical spaces, such as a perforated, blue, egg-shaped bathroom, a cosy study surrounded with bookshelves and spiral drapes, and a bedroom softly lit by a skylight above the bed. The architects, quoting Salvador Dalí's words literally, intended to make a 'soft and hairy house' where a personal illusion could be explored and realized within various dream-like settings. The house both reflects and encourages the expression of diversity in its inhabitants' lifestyle. Its highly subjective character, however, precludes any objective criticism.

☛ Grataloup, Okada & Tomiyama, Senosiain, Yamashita

Ushida Findlay. **Eisaku Ushida**. **b** Tokyo (JAP), 1954. **Kathryn Findlay**. **b** Scotland (UK), 1953. **Soft and Hairy House**, Tokyo (JAP), 1993.

Vacchini Livio   House at Tenero-Contra

Crisp geometries float against the mountain landscape, the full-height, sliding glass windows inviting you to step out into mid-air. But the shrill, stridently artificial yellow floor and raw concrete walls and roof bring you dramatically back to the reality of this house. The precast, reinforced concrete roof is supported by three columns (painted black) on the end elevations, giving the impression that this huge room has no vertical structure, but is rather sandwiched between the floor and the ceiling. The long concrete wall subdivides the rectangular space and screens the bathroom, kitchen and a dining alcove on the other side; these functions are not integral, but inserted like furniture. The building is trying to be a pure, uncompromising piece of architecture rather than fulfil a specific function, and is an almost rhetorical development of a classic Modernist building by Mies van der Rohe, the Farnsworth House (1946–50).

☞ Botta, Le Corbusier, Mies van der Rohe, Snozzi, Yoh

Livio Vacchini. b Locarno, Ticino (SW), 1933. **House at Tenero-Contra** (SW), 1992–3.

Vale Brenda & Robert   Autonomous House

'It breaks architects' hearts,' says Brenda Vale 'when they have to leave out the architecture and keep the insulation. But somebody has to do it.' Unlike fashionable, High-Tech style eco-houses, with their drag-coefficient streamlining, the Vales' Autonomous House in Southwell often gets mistaken for a farmhouse conversion. It is an object lesson in how to design ecologically to the point where no outside energy is used at all. There is one small narrowboat stove, yet the house saves its own heat with shredded newspaper insulation, small windows and living rooms on the upper, warmer floors. In the basement, second-hand orange juice vats filter its water supply off the roof. Sewage is treated in a very large composter which takes four years to move effluent from lavatory to orchard – which, say the Vales, makes conventional sewage treatment seem 'rather disgusting'. The Vales have since moved to New Zealand where their work in low-energy living continues.

☛ Day, Grataloup, Grose Bradley, Herzog + Partner

Brenda Vale. b Gants Hill (UK), 1949. Robert Vale. b Banstead (UK), 1948. Autonomous House, Southwell (UK), 1994.

Vallibus Sir John   Little Wenham Hall

Built during the reign of Edward I, Little Wenham Hall is a remarkably well-preserved example of a medieval knight's house. The height, scale and form of this structure make it clear that Sir John Vallibus was a man of standing for whom financial limitations were not a consideration. This is particularly demonstrated in the vaulting, imported stone, high quality workmanship and generous accommodation. The ground floor consists of two domestic chambers, with a stair leading to a large hall on the first floor used as the family's private retiring chamber, complete with heating and built-in seating. The windows, while narrow on the outside, splay deeply inwards to light the interior. The tower contains the chapel and one chamber above it, while the turret houses a circular staircase. The brick construction is rare for this period, and the quality and completeness of the building contribute to its unique value in the study of high medieval architecture.

☞ **Ashburnham, Ludlow, Shetland Island Celts, Traquair**

Sir John Vallibus. Active (UK), early to mid-thirteenth century. **d** 1286. **Little Wenham Hall**, Little Wenham, nr Ipswich (UK), 1265–80.

Valsamakis Nicos   Lanaras Residence

The Lanaras residence was designed as a vacation house for a family of four. The generative principle for its design was that of obtaining unobstructed views from the main living area towards the Saronic Gulf, above which the house is located. The living and dining rooms are situated in the glazed volume contained between the two concrete slabs cantilevered out over the sloping site. The slabs, supported by slender steel columns, extend to create a large covered terrace which provides shelter from the sun. The design of the house is a sensitive and playful response to its context by establishing a dialogue between the internal spaces and the setting, and is, in many ways, reminiscent of the 1950s Case Study Program houses of California. Functionalism, compositional clarity and, at the same time, clear references to context are typical qualities of the architecture of Nicos Valsamakis, as is his attempt to adapt Modernism to Greek regional culture.

☛ Atelier 66, Eames, Koenig, Neutra, Mies van der Rohe

Nicos Valsamakis. b Athens (GR), 1924. **Lanaras Residence**, Anavyssos, Attica (GR), 1961–3.

Van der Merwe Miszewski

Tree House

The prevalent Umbrella Pines on the wooded slopes of Table Mountain near Cape Town suggested the conceptual design solution for this house. Five enormous tree-like structures anchor the roof, which sails over and shelters the spaces below. Underneath, the house relies on an ordering system of layers – starting with a monolithic masonry wall running the length of the house – to establish scale and privacy. Beyond this, a three-storey void drops behind a secondary glass layer, allowing light down into the deepest recesses of the house. Crossways, another series of layers and screens begins with the terrace opening up to the landscape, followed by the semi-private living room and, finally, the private bedrooms, bathrooms and kitchens stacked at the rear. The house conveys the architects' preoccupation with environmental design and *genius loci* (spirit of place) in a way that brings the house and its occupants into a direct dialogue with nature.

☛ **Acayaba, Eames, Harvey, Lacaton Vassal, Murcutt, Poole**

Van der Merwe Miszewski Architects. Anya Van der Merwe. b Cape Town (SA), 1960. **Macio Miszewski**. b Cape Town (SA), 1961. **Tree House**, Cape Town (SA), 1998.

Vanbrugh Sir John   Castle Howard

Castle Howard's winged plan derives from Palladio's villas, but has all the heady excitement of Vanbrugh's Baroque style. Being a poor draughtsman, he engaged the help of Nicholas Hawksmoor, his colleague in the Royal Office of Works. The main front has the close-set pilasters that they both favoured, and a triumphal arch motif for emphasis. The wing on the left is part of the original design and houses the kitchen court; the wing on the right was built to the design of Sir Thomas Robinson in 1753–9, when the style had changed to a more chaste Classicism. The dome rises over a magnificent entrance hall, flanked by staircases and a gallery which give dramatic views in all directions. The dome itself, and much of the left-hand side of the garden front, was burnt out in 1940, the latter still unrestored, and now housing an exhibition to remind visitors of when the house was featured in the UK television film of *Brideshead Revisited*.

☛ Fischer von Erlach, Hawksmoor, Hildebrandt

Sir John Vanbrugh. **b** London (UK), 1664. **d** London (UK), 1726. **Castle Howard**, nr York (UK), 1699–1712, with later additions, 1753–9.

Vasari Giorgio   Villa Giulia

Built for Pope Julius III in a side valley of the River Tiber, just outside the walls of Rome, this retreat is as well-known for its gardens as it is for the villa itself. Vasari oversaw the building of the whole complex of gardens, terraces, hemicycles and villa, but many other architects were involved. The *casino* of the villa, by Giacomo Vignola, consists of only three rooms on each of its two floors, but its semicircular arcade forms a backdrop to the series of three walled gardens by Bartolomeo Ammannati. The first garden (shown here) opens via a central colonnaded portal with stucco reliefs onto a sunken water garden, or *nymphaeum*, shaded by four plane trees (to remind learned visitors of the fountain court of the ancient writer, Pliny). The sound of birds in two aviaries added to the effect of the cool splashing of the fountains. Across the *nymphaeum* could be glimpsed the third garden, the *giardino segreto*, which could only be reached by concealed staircases on either side of its loggia.

☛ **Giulio Romano, Porta, Vignola**

Giorgio Vasari. **b** Arezzo (IT), 1511. **d** Florence (IT), 1574. **Villa Giulia**, Rome (IT), 1551–5.

Vaux Calvert & Church Frederick   Olana

Vaux, the re-settled Englishman who was the co-creator of New York City's majestic Central Park, drew the plans and supervised the building of Olana, but the credit for the conception of the picturesque Orientalist villa goes to its owner, the artist Frederick Church. America's foremost painter of enormous landscapes, a true artist of the exotic and the sublime, Church obsessed over every detail of what he called his 'feudal castle', choosing the coloured bricks and tiles that pattern its walls, calibrating every one of its pointed arches and limning the decorative stencilling around the doors. While manipulating elements of Italian, French and Moorish architecture, he made sure there were views over the Hudson River from every room. He also combined styles in the interiors, filling its rooms with the collections of a lifetime of travel. Built at a time when his career was waning, Church made Olana his last great, romantic work of art.

☛ Aitchison, Hoffman & Chalfin, Hunt, Morgan, Raphael

Calvert Vaux. b London (UK), 1824. d New York, NY (USA), 1895. Frederick Edwin Church. b Harlford, CT (USA), 1826. d Hudson, NY (USA), 1900. Olana, Hudson, NY (USA), 1870.

Velde Henry van de   Villa Bloemenwerf

To the contemporary eye, the Villa Bloemenwerf appears far from radical, but it was ground-breaking in its time. 'Art is beginning anew because society is beginning anew,' wrote Henry van de Velde in 1895, the year of its completion. Like William Morris and British exponents of the Arts and Crafts movement, van de Velde believed art was not something you hung on the walls, but an approach to be applied to all objects. The house that he designed in Uccle, near Brussels (the first of a string of homes for his family) was a complete artistic environment for which he designed not just the building, but all the furniture, light fittings and cutlery (he even designed his wife's clothes). It established him as one of the leading figures of Belgian Art Nouveau, and he went on to become a founder member of the Deutsche Werkbund in 1907, an organization of artists and craftsmen whose aim was to improve the quality of designed products.

☛ Behrens, Cauchie, Horta, Morris, Muthesius

Henry van de Velde. b Antwerp (BEL), 1863. **d** Oberagen (SW), 1957. **Villa Bloemenwerf**, Uccle, nr Brussels (BEL), 1895.

Venturi Robert

Vanna Venturi House

The flat, overstated, metaphorical facade of this house has become an icon of late twentieth-century Post-Modern domestic architecture. Venturi designed this house – his first built work – for his mother while he was still young. She had asked for comparative simplicity, yet did not want a modern house that would be incompatible with her antique furniture. This now-famous facade makes reference to classical architecture, but does so using overscaled elements. It has a skewed symmetry and is primarily an oversized gable with a chimney set slightly off-centre, rising above it. The interior offers a similar mix; it fulfils familiar domestic expectations, while at the same time important elements, such as the fireplace and chimney, have a competitive rather than compatible relationship. Venturi refined his notions of complexity and contradiction over the years in increasingly large projects, not least the National Gallery extension in London (1991).

☞ Jencks & Farrell, Outram, Palladio, Rossi, Stern

471

Robert Charles Venturi. **b** Philadelphia, PA (USA), 1925. **Vanna Venturi House (Mother's House)**, Chestnut Hill, PA (USA), 1959–64.

Vesnin Leonid

Dacha

For an urbanized Russian, the soul comes alive at 'the country place', or *dacha*. Whether it is the primitive cabin of a working family, or the grand holiday home of a princely one, the *dacha* represents the warm and trusted sanctuary for family and friends. Here, one reconnects to the rhythms of nature and the spirit of Russia. For a brief period before World War I, as

again today, architect-designed *dachas* were an accessible accoutrement of Russia's business and professional classes. This early design by the eldest of the three Vesnin brothers has all the originality of response to function that later characterized their work as leaders of the Russian Constructivist group of architects in the 1920s. A vast dining table, focus of hospitality,

dominates the main floor which is raised and entered by a traditional enclosed stair or *kryltso*. Timber construction and rural forms express the romance of 'escape' and are heightened by the tense distortions of Art Nouveau.

☛ **Gartman, Nikitin, Peter the Great, Shekhtel, Tolstoy**

472

Leonid Alexandrovich Vesnin. b Nizhny Novgorod (RUS), 1880. **d** Moscow (RUS), 1933. **Dacha**, nr Moscow (RUS), project, c1908.

Vicens Ramos Architects
House at Las Matas

This dramatic house takes advantage of a large unencumbered site to explore the sculptural potential of the client's brief. By separating the functional spaces into clearly defined volumes, Vicens Ramos have achieved a dynamic, and at the same time very practical and comfortable family home. A long rectilinear plane containing bedrooms for six children spreads across the landscape, overlapping with the centralized cuboid core of the living and dining rooms. Above, the master bedroom and study are separated from the rest of the house for privacy. As a result of the volumetric rigour, the internal plan is geometrically complex, generating a dynamic play of ramps, voids and catwalks, all enhanced by carefully placed windows for natural light. Oxidized steel and rendered concrete external walls change hue and texture with the passage of time, serving to dramatically enhance each component of the house, adding to the overall sculptural effect of the design.

☞ Le Corbusier, Rietveld & Schröder, Ungers & Kinslow

Vicens Ramos Architects. Ignacio Vicens y Hualde. b Madrid (SP), 1950. José Antonio Ramos Abengózar. b Alcázar de San Juan (SP), 1958. House at Las Matas, Madrid (SP), 1992.

Vignola Giacomo   Villa Farnese

Built on the pentagonal plan begun by Antonio da Sangallo and Baldassare Peruzzi in the 1520s, this sumptuous palace by Vignola dominates the hilltown of Caprarola. From the originally open loggia on the *piano nobile*, decorated with scenes from the life of Hercules, Cardinal Farnese could survey his possessions beyond the impressive series of terraces and sweeping stairs of the approach to the villa. A central, circular arcaded courtyard opened up the plan within, and separate winter and summer apartments on two sides of the pentagon led to their respective winter and summer gardens, terraced out of the hill behind. Beyond, through chestnut plantations rising up the hillside, was an open-air dining room, the *casino*, approached by a staircase with water cascading down its centre. As in many *cinquecento* villas, scholars advised the Cardinal on the themes and meanings of the paintings he commissioned to decorate the wall and vault surfaces.

☞ **Alberti, Porta, Vasari**

Giacomo Vignola (Jacopo Barozzi da). b Vignola (IT), 1507. **d** Rome (IT), 1573. **Villa Farnese**, Caprarola (IT), 1559–73.

Villiers Paul de

Boschendal Manor House

A spreading, white-walled house with an elaborate gable set against the Drakenstein mountains of the Franschhoek Valley, Boschendal encapsulates the late Cape Dutch tradition. Its Huguenot builder's religion demanded simplicity; necessity dictated the H-shaped plan – as local timbers could only span one room – as well as the white lime-plastered walls, a process essential to prevent rain damage. The rectilinear white walls made these houses very distinctive in the African landscape, while the gables, a highly-specific derivation of European Classicism, recall architecture and humanity's dominance over nature. Coming at the end of the Cape Dutch tradition, Boschendal shows subtle refinements. With its half columns and urns, the gable shows the influence of Neo-Classicism – brought to the Cape in 1783 by architect Louis Michel Thibault, who studied with Ange-Jacques Gabriel in Paris – and which superseded the earlier designs based solely on curves.

☞ Burnett, Fagan, Mourier, Stel

Paul de Villiers. Active (SA), late eighteenth and early nineteenth century; descendant of Abraham de Villiers, one of the first Huguenot settlers to be granted land by Cape Governor, Simon van der Stel, in 1685. **Boschendal Manor House**, Groot Drakenstein, Franschhoek Valley, Cape Province (SA), 1812.

Viollet-le-Duc Eugène-Emmanuel House from the *Dictionnaire raisonné*

This illustration, published in Viollet-le-Duc's *Dictionnaire raisonné de l'Architecture* – a ten-volume, encyclopedic treatise on architecture – represents one of many variations on the theme of Gothic house construction. The flat masonry facade with contrasting heavy timber scaffolding could just as easily be a real or an imagined exemplar. Viollet-le-Duc was a celebrated architectural historian and restorer of monuments and was responsible for a renewed interest in French medieval architecture. He was also a great champion of the Gothic style as a relevant, contemporary structural system that would become the basis for an emerging, mature, nineteenth-century architecture. Choosing to remain outside the traditional education system of the Ecole des Beaux-Arts, he instead pursued his interest in the past through the restoration of historic monuments; most famously, the Notre-Dame Cathedral in Paris which he began with Jean-Baptiste Lassus in 1844.

☛ **Guimard, Pugin, Walpole, Wyatville**

Eugène-Emmanuel Viollet-le-Duc. **b** Paris (FR), 1814. **d** Lausanne (SW), 1879. **House from the *Dictionnaire raisonné de l'Architecture***, published in 1868.

Voysey C F A   The Orchard

It is the sweeping roofs, asymmetrical composition and traditional, economic materials (slate and roughcast render) which give this house its initial vernacular feel. But closer inspection reveals tell-tale details that place this modest house at the cusp of Modernism: an emphasis on the horizontality of windows; bare, almost abstract planes of render at the gable ends; and minimal flush detailing at window reveals. Designed by the Arts and Crafts architect, Voysey, as his family home, the light and sparse interior is carefully planned around their functional requirements for living. Voysey was heavily influenced by the ideas of John Ruskin and William Morris, but his lightness of touch and acceptance of the role of the machine gave his work a more contemporary and relevant edge. Voysey's legacy can be traced in the craft approach to Modern architecture and, albeit in a diluted form, in early British local authority housing schemes.

☛   Baillie Scott, Lutyens, Parker & Unwin, P Webb

Charles Francis Annesley Voysey. b Yorkshire (UK), 1857. d London (UK), 1941. The Orchard, Chorleywood (UK), 1899–1901.

Wagner Otto

Villa Wagner II

With its simple geometry, hierarchical rows of narrow windows, smooth walls and restrained ornamentation, this house reflects Wagner's insistence on rationality as the basis for architectural beauty. A loggia on the right side overlooks a garden. Set off by a stepped frame, the front door is wood, but faced with a modern building material: aluminium. The decorative glazed tiles that underscore the design's geometric logic are held in place with aluminum bolts that declare their presence via large round heads. Wagner delighted in juxtaposing traditional materials with new ones, expressiveness with economy of means. This house is considered among his purest modernist statements and influenced younger architects, such as Adolf Loos and Richard Neutra. It contrasts with its next-door neighbour, the larger Villa Wagner I, a grand, ornate *palais* that proved too expensive for Wagner to maintain.

☛ Hoffmann, Loos, Mackintosh, Neutra, Olbrich, Schönthal

478

Otto Wagner. b Penzing (AUS), 1841. **d** Vienna (AUS), 1918. **Villa Wagner II**, Vienna (AUS), 1912–13.

Walpole Horace   Strawberry Hill

Many visitors to this house have thought it to be a stunningly well-preserved vestige of England's medieval architecture – but they have all been wrong. Strawberry Hill was in fact built in the eighteenth century by the great antiquarian and writer, Horace Walpole. At the age of thirty, Walpole acquired a very ordinary little house on the banks of the River Thames and set about turning it into one of the greatest examples of Gothic Revival architecture, incorporating an asymmetrical form with many turrets, battlements and gables. Although no architect himself – he employed a number of architects over the course of the house's transformation – the inspiration and direction was his, and it is to him that the house is generally credited. His great achievement was to put Gothic design on the map at a time when the Middle Ages was widely considered to be an era of England's past devoid of artistic merit.

☛ A J Davis, Kazakov, Vanbrugh, Wyatville

Horace Walpole, 4th Earl of Orford. b London (UK), 1717. d London (UK), 1797. **Strawberry Hill**, Twickenham (UK), 1753–76.

Washington George Mount Vernon

From this view, the field-side facade of America's most famous house, it is clear to see where George Washington lost his way when expanding the family estate into a formal seat for a country gentleman. The symmetry is askew, the oversized entry fails to line up with the cupola and the windows are disordered. Although Mount Vernon appears to be built of stone, it is in fact constructed of cut blocks of wood disguised under paint mixed with sand to create a gritty surface. However, Washington, the father of his country and the very first to assume the US presidency, made up for these shortcomings when he planned the Potomac River facade in 1787. He added a piazza and the two-storey, square-columned porch, so widely reproduced in American buildings that it is both icon and cliché. Yet, despite an overload of imitations, Mount Vernon stands as a potent symbol of national idealism; the dream house, the emblem of patriotism.

☞ Burlington, Hoban, Jefferson, I Jones, Kent

George Washington. b Westmoreland County, VA (USA) 1732. **d** Vernon, VA (USA), 1799. **Mount Vernon**, Fairfax County, VA (USA), 1757–87.

Webb Mike

Drive-in Housing

This is a proposal for a system of housing, a solution for modern living, where the concern is not about aesthetics, but about service requirements. The scheme combines the perceived advantages of the car – freedom of mobility and status – with our living needs. Mobile, personalized living areas are designed to be driven around and plugged into fixed service points which contain washing and cooking machines. The Drive-in Housing project prompts us to question what we want from our homes – a sense of permanence of location, or an emphasis on replaceable products? Designed by Mike Webb, part of the infamous Archigram group, the scheme was not physically realized (the infrastructure required would demand political, or even revolutionary input), but its prophetic influence can be seen in contemporary work practices, where 'hot desking' and the effects of a mobile phone culture are having a huge impact on our office environment.

☛ **Airstream Co., Fuller, Future Systems, D Greene, Rogers**

Mike Webb. b Henley-on-Thames (UK), 1937. **Drive-in Housing**, project, 1964–5.

Webb Philip

Red House

Its simple use of common red brick, its external expression of the convenient arrangement of rooms inside, and its simplification of past styles into a styleless expression of utility make The Red House a radical departure from fussy, over-elaborate Victorian England, and a pointer towards the rational architecture of the Modern movement. The rambling yet tautly balanced outline is at once poetic and functional, qualities enhanced by the detailing of doors, windows and chimney-stacks; part Gothic, part Georgian, partly simply traditional. The Red House, built for Webb's friend, the newly-married William Morris, symbolizes the beginnings of the earthy yet sentimental aestheticism of the Arts and Crafts movement. The furniture and embroideries designed for the house led to the setting up of Morris Marshall Faulkner & Co. in 1861, where Webb, with his talent for design simplicity and proportion, was put in charge of the furniture production.

☛ **Lutyens, Mackintosh, Morris, Shaw, Voysey**

482

Philip Speakman Webb. **b** Oxford (UK), 1831. **d** Worth (UK), 1915. **Red House**, Bexleyheath (UK), 1858–9.

Weeks David

Shadows-on-the-Teche

On the shores of the Bayou Teche sits this graceful antebellum plantation house, built in the Greek Revival style so favoured in the early nineteenth-century American South. However, it is distinguished in that the red brick facade was left unpainted; most such Greek Revival houses were conceived as white temples on a hill. The house has a strikingly proportioned facade, with its two-storey portico and six prominently proportioned columns. Built by a wealthy planter, David Weeks, four generations of the same family lived there amid the live-oak trees and Spanish moss, except for a brief period of occupation by the Union Soldiers from the north during the American Civil War. In 1958, William Weeks Hall, a great-grandson, bequeathed Shadows-on-the-Teche to the National Trust for Historic Preservation. The interior, restored with original furnishings, provides a glimpse of life in early nineteenth-century America.

☛ **Burnett, Calrow, Jefferson, Marmillion, Roper**

David Weeks. Active (USA), late eighteenth and early nineteenth century. **d** CT (USA), 1834. **Shadows-on-the-Teche**, Bayou Teche, New Iberia, LA (USA), 1831–4.

Weobley Yeoman
Cruck-Frame Cottage

With the weight of its roof transmitted, independently of the walls, directly to the ground through a cranked A-frame, this cottage uses one of the simplest medieval techniques for framing a building. It comprises pairs of curved or elbowed timbers, known as crucks, joined together at the apex and braced by a collar to form the A. The origin of this vernacular architecture is unclear: cruck-frames are hardly known in eastern England, yet are very common in the west, particularly in Herefordshire, where oaks with great curving branches abound. Crucks are best suited to low buildings, but they provide an immensely strong, stable frame that can be reused many times either by removing them to a new site, or by simply renewing the walls or floors. This cottage may only be a few hundred years old, but the crucks are probably much older and may have framed a barn for many centuries before the cottage was built within their span.

☛ Lavenham Clothier, Moreton Family, Mourier

484

Weobley Yeoman. Active (UK), late fifteenth to nineteenth century. **Cruck-Frame Cottage**, Weobley (UK), late thirteenth to early nineteenth century.

Williams Amancio   House over the Brook

This house represents a dynamic synthesis of Le Corbusier's principles with Latin American imagination and daring. Williams, who worked as an aviator for a number of years before studying architecture, designed and built the house for his father, a well-known musician. Located in Mar del Plata, some 500 km (310 m) from Buenos Aires, the house takes advantage of the bucolic natural setting by spanning a small brook that runs through the property. The bridge-like house is entirely constructed of formed, exposed concrete, with the flat floor slab and curved supporting slab below forming an integral whole, so that 'form, structure and quality are thus here the same thing', says Williams. With the uninterrupted glazing and rooftop terrace, every advantage is taken of the views of this idyllic setting. The most complete of only a handful of built designs by Williams, the house embodies his innovative and meticulous approach to architecture.

☞ Ando, Hølmebakk, Le Corbusier, Mies van der Rohe, Testa

Amancio Williams. b Buenos Aires (ARG), 1913. **House over the Brook**, Mar del Plata (ARG), 1943–5.

The transparency of the glazed rear facade of this house in uptown New York contrasts with a more discreet elevation onto the street, in which a large screen of limestone presents a barrier to curious eyes. The building is a rare phenomenon – one of very few new townhouses built in the city in the last half century, replacing two nineteenth-century brownstones on the site. Just as the exterior shows a clear departure from the traditional, the internal layout represents a move away from cellular rooms to a more open, interconnected series of generic spaces. These are filled with daylight entering both laterally and from above, through a large skylight set above a glass-balustraded, five-storey central stairwell. To maximize the available space, the terraced garden is excavated to basement level and accessed via a bridge. The house represents the architects' commitment to the regeneration of the city, to stem the flight of families to suburban areas.

☛ Lescaze, Rudolph, Shuttleworth, UN Studio

486

Tod Williams Billie Tsien Associates. **Tod Williams**. b Detroit, MI (USA), 1943. **Billie Tsien**. b Ithaca, NY (USA), 1949. **New York City House**, NY (USA), 1994–6.

Winter John

Winter House

With its clearly-defined grid of steel and glass, this controlled, anonymous object does not immediately bring to mind a house. It is a perfect flush box – there are no traditional projections, such as cills or eaves – with more window than wall. The structure is clad in Corten, purposely rusted steel sheets (the rust stabilizes the steel and protects it from further oxidization), a maintenance-free material more usually found in industrial situations. In contrast to the regular facade, the interiors are fluid, with free-plan living areas on the ground and top floors, and cellular bedrooms on the middle floors. The house relates to the outside in a variety of ways; there is an enclosed private garden, and long vistas over the neighbouring Highgate cemetery. Designed by John Winter for his family, the house is strongly influenced by the work of Mies van der Rohe and industrial architecture, and shares some ideals which emerge in later High-Tech works.

☞ Kahn, Mies van der Rohe, Rogers, Vicens Ramos Architects

John Winter. b Norwich (UK), 1930. **Winter House**, London (UK), 1968–9.

Wolsey Cardinal

Hampton Court Palace

Begun in 1520 for Cardinal Wolsey, Hampton Court was the greatest palace of its day, outshining royal works, just as Wolsey himself appeared to outshine Henry VIII. An original small manor was extended to a great courtyard house, entered through this turreted gateway, and intended for Wolsey's household of well over four hundred. All this magnificence was achieved in Tudor Gothic, although the terracotta medallions set half way up the turrets, made in 1521 by Giovanni da Maiano, add a Renaissance touch to the style. Within ten years, the palace had no rival, which incensed Henry VIII so greatly that Wolsey was forced to make a gift of it to his royal master. However, he acted too late, and was soon stripped of all his extensive powers. Henry VIII went on to add a great hall and other buildings, some of which were swept away for the new works designed by Sir Christopher Wren for King William and Queen Mary in the late seventeenth century.

☞ Compton, Cortona, Henry VIII

Cardinal Wolsey. b Ipswich (UK), c1473. d Leicester (UK), 1530. Hampton Court Palace, Hampton Court (UK), 1520–22.

Wood the Elder, John   The Circus

This elegant, unified, Bath-stone facade gives scale and grandeur to, what would otherwise be, thirty-three relatively ordinary townhouses; a device much replicated to this day. Loosely based on an inverted form of the Coliseum in Rome, this circular terrace employs both Classical form and pagan detail: three Doric orders and a parapet decorated with acorn finials – a knowing reference to the legend of King Bladud who, with his pigs (who ate the acorns), supposedly founded Bath. The Royal Circus forms part of John Wood the Elder's plan for Bath, most of which was built under his control and completed by his son. As became typical of such developments (in London and Edinburgh, for example), the architect/developer focused his energies on the site plan and facade – from the front the separate houses are indistinguishable, but the rear elevations, which were constructed by different builders, reveal an *ad hoc*, more individual story.

☞   **Adam, I Jones, Leverton, Nash, Palladio**

John Wood the Elder. b Bath (UK), 1704. **d** Bath (UK), 1754. **The Circus**, Bath (UK), begun 1754.

Wright Frank Lloyd   Fallingwater

With its dramatic, horizontal concrete slabs cantilevered over the roaring crescendo of a waterfall, Fallingwater symbolizes both the romance of nature and the triumph of man. At first glance, the horizontal emphasis is reminiscent of the prevalent International Modernism of the time; however, the natural materials and hand-crafted details – evident in the stacked stone walls – betray its roots in the Arts and Crafts tradition, while the plan is derived from Wright's earlier Prairie House-type, with volumes developing from a central core. Inside, the contrast between man and nature continues: the polished flagstone floor appears as though a river had flowed over it for centuries, yet the recessed ceilings float overhead as manmade works of art. Arguably the most important twentieth-century house in the USA, Fallingwater was built towards the latter part of Wright's extraordinarily prolific and influential career.

☛ Donovan Hill, Goff, Groote, E F Jones, Neutra, Schindler

Frank Lloyd Wright. b Richland Center, WI (USA), 1867. d Phoenix, AZ (USA), 1959. **Fallingwater (Kaufmann House)**, Bear Run, PA (USA), 1935–9.

Wyatville Sir Jeffry   Endsleigh Cottage

Endsleigh Cottage is one of those delightfully English understatements; hardly a cottage, more a whole hamlet of cottages. It was designed for the sixth Duke of Bedford, at the instigation of the Duchess, as a convenient country residence from which they could oversee their extensive estates in Devon and Cornwall. In the foreground, a gabled Tudor wing, conveniently out of sight and sound from the main house and separated by a long corridor, contains the childrens' play room and school house. The castellated Tudor main house itself has separate suites for the Duke and Duchess and, at an angle beyond that, a more rustic Tudor-style wing for the extensive kitchens and servants quarters. Tall chimney-stacks, a multiplicity of dormers and gables, and rendered walls outlined to look like rough masonry, provide the essential Picturesque style, enhanced by the sweeping views over the grounds towards the Tamar estuary laid out by Humphry Repton.

☛ A J Davis, **Moreton Family, Pugin, Walpole**

Sir Jeffry Wyatville. b Burton-on-Trent (UK), 1766. **d** London (UK), 1840. **Endsleigh Cottage**, Milton Abbot (UK), 1810.

Yamada Mamoru

Mamoru Yamada House

As a unique expressionist transformation of the traditional Japanese house, Yamada's own house and studio brings together a curvilinear freedom – similar to that of Hans Scharoun or Oscar Niemeyer – within the context of Japan. Yamada sought to create a new urban dwelling in this three-level, reinforced concrete house that was built in a section of Tokyo formerly dominated by single-level dwellings. The main living space, which is lifted off the ground by *pilotis* and accessed via a spiral stair, retains *tatami* mats and *shoji* screens, but has subtly different proportions and lacks the customary *tokobashira* symbolic wooden columns in the traditional decorative alcove. Yamada was the only Asian architect featured in the 1932 *International Style* book, and like Sutemi Horiguchi, his co-founder of the Bunriha Japanese Secessionist Movement of 1920–7, sought to create a new, Modern architecture.

☛ **Horiguchi, Niemeyer, Saitowitz, Scharoun**

Mamoru Yamada. **b** Gifu Prefecture (JAP), 1894. **d** Tokyo (JAP), 1966. **Mamoru Yamada House**, Tokyo (JAP), 1959.

Yamashita Kazumasa Face House

A funny, yellow, grinning face suddenly interrupts a row of conventional houses in downtown Kyoto. This building's painted concrete facade is embellished with two round windows, a projected cylindrical ventilation opening and recessed glass entrance doors. It accommodates two studios for a graphic designer on the street level, and family living space on the second and top levels. In designing this house, Kazumasa Yamashita applied his 'separate parallel plan', in which the residential space is arranged to the south and service space to the north, with a circulation area between them. Owing to a directional inconsistency, the interior arrangement does not correspond to the east facade that attracts attention from the street. Playfully treated as a signboard, the front facade of the Face House demonstrates an early post-modern tendency, while the interior arrangement expresses the architect's commitment to an alternative living environment.

☛ Bolles & Wilson, Okada & Tomiyama, Ushida Findlay

493

Kazumasa Yamashita. b Aichi (JAP), 1937. **Face House (Ka no Ie)**, Kyoto (JAP), 1974.

Yazdi

Wind-Catcher House

Since the tenth century, Yazd, a city on the central plateau of Iran, has been extremely prosperous, profiting first from silk manufacturing and then in the mid-nineteenth century from the trade in opium. Most of the city, famous for its distinct mud-brick architecture, originated after AD 900 and buildings from this period have been preserved today due to the hot, dry climate. The general form of the Yazdi house has varied little over the centuries and is arranged around three or four sides of a courtyard which contains gardens and pools. The most striking characteristic is the rooftop *badgirs*, or wind-catchers, which have a vent facing towards the prevailing wind that funnels breezes into the interiors. In this dry desert location, where temperatures reach 40°C (104°F), the courtyard form and the *badgirs* significantly help to cool the inhabitants although, with the advent of air conditioning, these magnificent wind-catchers are no longer built.

☞ al-Haddad, Tiwa Indians, Vale, Yemeni

494

Yazdi. Active (IR), circa AD 900 to present day. **Wind-Catcher House**, Yazd (IR), circa ninth century to mid-twentieth century.

Yemeni

Tower Houses

The spectacular form of the traditional mudbrick tower houses of the Yemen, some of which are over eight storeys high, developed for reasons of self-defence against attackers, as well as for protection against the harsh climate. The lower floors are used for storage, with a single entrance door in an otherwise impenetrable facade. In San'a, the capital of Yemen, the houses are grouped in clusters around a tight network of streets, generating extensive shading at street level and to the interior spaces. The accommodation is divided into separate quarters for men and women; the men's quarters on the middle floors represent a more public zone in which business transactions and entertainment take place. The women's quarters are on the more private top floors, and roof terraces with open arcade parapets are common. The baked mudbrick construction, waterproofed and decorated with plaster, is a highly skilled craft carried out by local master-builders now in short supply.

☞ **Dogon, San Gimignano, Tiwa Indians, Yazdi**

Yoh Shoei

Another Glass House Between Sea and Sky

Parallel concrete walls set into the hillside support two cantilevered, shelf-like slabs between which enclosing glass walls define the interior space while providing maximum views. With this house, located on a steep hill site in Fukuoka overlooking the Sea of Japan, Yoh explores an idea of 'levitation' which he realizes by contrasting the apparent instability and lightness of the building with the solidity and weightiness of the site. With its vertical anchorage and horizontal cantilever, this structure can be understood not only as a technological innovation, but also as an expression of the unique relationship between the building and its surroundings. Yoh believes the most beautiful structures are those which, deceptively, do not look strong, and he has produced many transparent designs, from furniture to museums. As a result, he is well-known for his attention to light in his buildings, as perfectly demonstrated here.

☞ Ban, Mies van der Rohe, Ogawa, Vacchini

Shoei Yoh. b Kumamoto (JAP), 1940. **Another Glass House Between Sea and Sky**, Itoshima, Fukuoka (JAP), 1991.

Yoshimura Junzo   Summer House

Junzo Yoshimura, the designer of many celebrated post-World War II houses, is known for his superb handling of what is termed the 'Japanese Modern House'. Apprenticed to the Czech-born architect, Antonin Raymond, in the US, Yoshimura's architecture combined western Modernism with traditional Japanese materials and construction methods.

Located in a mountain forest, this villa was designed to be used all year round by the architect and his family. A light, timber-framed living space, topped with an attic containing a study and *tatami* room, sits on a contrasting solid concrete base. The living and sleeping quarters are highly adaptable, despite their small size. As in traditional Japanese houses, screens and panels divide and open up the spaces as function, mood and weather dictate. The central fireplace provides the architectural and spiritual focus at the heart of this simple house, designed as a place in which to experience nature.

☞ Hara, Raymond, Sejima, Van der Merwe Miszewski

Junzo Yoshimura. b Tokyo (JAP), 1908. d (JAP), 1997. **Summer House**, Karuizawa (JAP), 1962.

Žák Ladislav

Villa Herain

As seen from the street, this modest house has an unassuming presence, with its two long bands of windows set in a plain white, rectilinear facade. By contrast, the garden elevation takes advantage of the scenic hillside site overlooking Prague, with large expanses of glass looking onto the garden and beyond, and a rounded, glazed stair tower. Built as one of twenty original houses at the Baba housing exhibition of 1932, the Villa Herain was one of three designed by the young Ladislav Žák. The estate was built for a series of individual clients, in this case the art historian, Karel Herain, who moved in after the exhibition closed to the public. The exhibition was sponsored by the Czechoslovak Werkbund and based on the model of the successful Stuttgart-Weissenhof housing estate in Germany organized by Mies van der Rohe in 1927, which sparked the construction of twelve other housing exhibitions across Europe.

☞ Brinkman & van der Vlugt, Lauterbach, Raymond

498

Ladislav Žák. b Prague (CZ), 1900. d Prague (CZ), 1973. Villa Herain, Prague (CZ), 1932.

Zanuso Marco

Zapper House

One side of this vacation house has only a few tiny windows punched in its walls, which form a crisp wedge that virtually mirrors the shape of the Alps directly across Lake Como. One of Zanuso's priorities is siting and designing his buildings in harmony with their natural surroundings. Its appearance softened by wood-shingled siding, this steel-framed wedge discourages intrusions on privacy and focuses attention from within the house to the spectacular panorama. When the house is seen from the lake, however, it reveals a markedly different personality: a voluminous L-shaped dwelling with two, glass-enclosed wings under steeply pitched roofs. The wings, which are equal in size and provide separate accommodations for the children and their parents, embrace the nearby landscape and distant views. In the 'elbow' of this L-shaped house, Zanuso created an enclosed common room to provide a retreat from the glazed living areas.

☛ **Atelier 66, Eames, Snozzi, Vacchini**

Marco Zanuso. b Milan (IT), 1916. **Zapper House**, Musso (IT), 1972–3.

Zapata Carlos

Golden Beach House

The entry facade of this beach-front house, just north of Miami Beach, signals the architect's desire to break the box of Modernism. Sensual materials, such as the translucent wall panels of veined onyx, and crisply cut forms are a radical departure from the 1920s Spanish colonial house – Franklin Roosevelt's former winter retreat – that was demolished to make way for this dramatic ensemble. The new 576 sq m (6,200 sq ft) house sits atop the existing foundations and follows its H-shaped plan almost exactly, with a soaring, double-height entry hall and living space separating the two wings. Its walls, however, take on a whole new life. No two meet at right angles; they are treated as dynamic planes that convey a constant sense of motion and discovery, with suggestive slivers of glass scored into their surface to let in light. Zapata's design recalls the fluid, non-rectilinear designs of contemporaries, such as British-based, Iraqi-born architect, Zaha Hadid.

☛ **Koolhaas, Morphosis, Moss, UN Studio**

Carlos Zapata. **b** Rubio (VEN), 1961. **Golden Beach House (Landes House)**, Miami, FL (USA), 1993.

Zenetos Takis

Single-Family House

Central to the dramatic, cantilevered design of this house is the architect's philosophy of approaching every project from a new angle in order to achieve a unique solution. In this particular case, the relationship between the building and the site was, naturally, of great importance. The living area is raised above the ground, by means of concrete columns, and is part of a daring cantilever which projects both the interior living space and the adjacent terrace into the surrounding pine trees. The balustrade of the terrace is articulated as a bench and establishes an experiential threshold between the built and the natural environment, while providing dramatic views towards the sea. Takis Zenetos was distinguished as the most radical, Modernist post-war architect in Greece during the 1960s and 1970s and was dedicated to the idea of progress through technology in architecture.

☛ Lubetkin, Niemeyer, Perret, Prouvé, Valsamakis, Wright

Zenetos Takis

Single-Family House

Takis Zenetos. b Athens (GR), 1926. **d** Athens (GR), 1977. **Single-Family House**, Kavouri, Attica (GR), 1959–61.

Zulu

Indlu

From Rome to Greenwich, domes have featured famously in Western architecture – but some of the most beautiful domes have been built by the Zulu in Shakaland and the Drakensberg mountains of Natal. The women construct the rigid dome framework of the *indlu* in concentric half-hoops of slender withies, using a cross-piece held by forked posts as a central internal support. Over this, a covering of grass mats or layers of light but finely-combed grass thatch would be placed, secured by a net of braided straw. An entrance arch of woven and stitched grass displays the owner's skill, and is closed by a wickerwork door. In recent times, walls of wattle and daub, or mud brick, have become common, although many roofs are still carefully thatched. Internally, the space is zoned for the women to the left and the men to the right, but the traditional hierarchical arrangement of the *indlu* in a great circle has been replaced by groups in homestead clusters.

☛ **Hutu, Maori, Samoan, Thule**

502

Zulu. Active (SA), 1816 to present day. **Indlu**, Shakaland or Drakensberg Mountains, Natal (SA), circa mid-twentieth century.

Zumthor Peter

Gugalun House

A family of mountain farmers needed to remodel their tiny wooden home to make it more appropriate for modern living. The house, parts of which date from the early 1700s, was in an uncertain state of repair, but nonetheless quite charming, especially on its spectacular site overlooking a wooded ridge. The brief was to retain the character of the old building, so

Zumthor respected the coarsely repaired timbers, low ceilings and small windows and came up with the idea of 'knitting' a new building into the old. Under a new shared roof, which soars out over the end facade, a modern kitchen, bathroom and living room have been added behind the old house, contained in a new structure inserted into the hillside. The

new timbers will continue to darken with age, blurring the distinction between old and new. This materially-refined house follows on from Zumthor's critically acclaimed earlier works, including the Thermal Baths at Vals (1996).

☛ **Bernese Farmers, J Davis, Herzog & de Meuron**

Zumthor Peter

Peter Zumthor. b Basel (SW), 1943. **Gugalun House**, Versam (SW), 1990–4.

Glossary of terms, styles and movements

Adam Style

A **Neo-Classical** style of architecture and interior design based on the work of Robert Adam, an influential British architect known for his beautifully detailed interiors and furniture design. Adam's work dominated British taste in the late eighteenth century and was characterized by subtle detail, clarity of form and refined colour schemes.
☞ Adam

Adobe

An ancient building material made of unburned or sun-dried mud bricks, often mixed with straw. Adobe construction dates from the fifth millennium BC and is still used in Africa, Central Asia, Mexico and south-west America.
☞ C Johnson, Reynolds, Syrian Farmers, Tiwa Indians

Architrave

A beam or lintel extending from one column to another; the architrave is also the lower division of an **entablature**, below the **frieze** at the top of a column. (See Orders)

Art Deco

A style of architecture and design fashionable in Europe and America in the 1920s and 30s, also known as **Moderne**. A reaction to the curvilinear forms of **Art Nouveau**, Art Deco favoured rectilinear shapes, particularly stepped patterns and chevrons, and used rich materials and primary colours. The style takes its name from the popular Exposition des Arts Décoratifs et Industriels Modernes in Paris in 1925.
☞ Cormier, Mallet-Stevens

Art Nouveau

A highly decorative form of art, architecture and design, prevalent in Europe and America at the turn of the nineteenth century, which began as a deliberate move away from the imitation of classical forms, to embrace the new and the modern. It is characterized by flowing sinuous lines, taking inspiration from foliage, blooms, roots and stems, often in symmetrical but abstract compositions. The style included many regionally distinct manifestations: Jugendstil (Germany); Style Moderne (France); Stile Liberte (Italy); Modernisme (Spain); Nieuwe Kunst (The Netherlands) and Sezessionstil (Austria).
☞ Apyshkov, Cauchie, Doménech, Gaudí, Geisler & Guslisty, Guimard, Hoffmann, Horta, Olbrich, Velde

Arts and Crafts

An influential, late nineteenth-century English movement that sought to re-establish the ideals of craftsmanship which were increasingly threatened by mass production. William Morris was the key exponent of the movement, designing hand-crafted wallpaper, stained glass, printed textiles, carpets, tapestries and furniture. The aesthetic and social philosophy of the movement were inseparable and had a profound effect on many architects. The style was taken up in The Netherlands, Germany, Belgium, Austria and the USA, where regionalist variations developed.
☞ Baillie Scott, Gesellius Lindgren & Saarinen, Lutyens, Morris, Muthesius, Voysey, P Webb

Ashlar

Smooth-faced, square-edged masonry, laid in horizontal courses with vertical joints.

Atrium

An internal space rising through the full height of a building with rooms opening onto it, which developed from the Roman courtyard house. Widely used in modern architecture, it takes the form of a large, glass-covered, naturally lit space.

Balloon-Frame

Timber-frame construction used in American domestic architecture, in which the vertical structural wall elements rise from the ground through to the roof, past the intermediate floors.
☞ Kavanaugh

Baluster/Balustrade

A baluster is a row of vertical posts supporting a handrail. The balustrade is the entire handrail assembly, including all its constituent parts.

Baroque

A seventeenth- and eighteenth-century European style, based on **Classicism**, embracing an exuberant lack of restraint not previously seen. It is characterized by elaborate layers of detail, curved forms, theatrical illusionist effects, implied movement and complex spatial relationships.
☞ Brussels Guildsmen, Dollmann, Guarini, Le Vau & Hardouin-Mansart, Neumann, Pöppelmann, Rastrelli, Vanbrugh

Bauhaus

A German design school whose ideals and aesthetics had a profound influence on twentieth-century architecture. Founded in Weimar in 1919, the school became a focus for avant-garde and left-wing theories of architecture and design based on **Arts and Crafts** and **Deutsche Werkbund** principles of integrating art, design and architecture. The school moved to Dessau in 1926 into a new building designed by Walter Gropius. With the increasingly hostile political climate under the Nazi Party, the school closed in 1933. Many of the influential Bauhaus teachers, including Gropius, Marcel Breuer and Mies van der Rohe, emigrated to the USA, where their ideas found fertile ground in schools of architecture such as Harvard and Chicago's IIT.
☞ Breuer, Gropius, Mies van der Rohe, Muche

Beaux-Arts

A **Classical** style developed by the Ecole des Beaux-Arts in Paris in the nineteenth century. Characterized by grandness and a predilection for harmonious proportioning, the style dominated fashionable taste in France and the USA in the two decades prior to WWI. The school became an internationally renowned teaching centre and trained many important architects of the time.
☞ Cormier, Delano & Aldrich, Hunt, McKim Mead & White, Morgan, Richardson, Sullivan

Belvedere

A small room built on a roof or placed in a landscape specifically for the enjoyment of a view. Also called a gazebo or summerhouse.

Brownstone

Dark brown sandstone found in eastern USA. It was used extensively in the nineteenth century for the construction of New York terrace houses, called 'brownstones'.
☞ Lescaze, Rudolph, Williams & Tsien

Brutalism/New Brutalism (also Neo-Brutalism)

The term Brutalism was originally used to describe Le Corbusier's work in the period after 1950, where he used rough, exposed concrete finishes. In the UK, Alison and Peter Smithson – influential architects and theorists – used the term New Brutalism to describe their attitude of uncompromising rigour and intellectual clarity. By the 1960s, the term was used to refer to any concrete building deemed to be brutal in appearance, whether or not it had any conceptual similarity with the Smithson's theories.

Caisson

A structural element, or chamber, driven into the ground to facilitate building below water level. The term also refers to sunken ceiling panels.

Cantilever

A horizontal element, such as a balcony, canopy or eaves, projecting from the vertical face of a building, supported only by the wall to which it is attached.

Case Study Program

A programme established in 1945 by John Entenza, editor of the US journal, *Arts and Architecture*, to promote good innovative design. The Case Study experiment aimed to produce low-cost, steel-frame prototypes for houses in direct response to the post-war conditions and environment of southern California.
☞ Eames, Ellwood, Koenig, Soriano

Casino

A small country house or decorative pavilion used for recreation, often set in the grounds of a larger house.

Cast stone

Stone aggregate combined with cement and poured into a mould. It is often used in masonry construction in place of solid stone.

Chicago School

A group of architects working in Chicago in the late nineteenth century. They produced pioneering work with high-rise buildings using new technology and materials, such as the lift (elevator) and light-weight, steel-frame construction. A key exponent, Louis Sullivan's Schlesinger & Mayer Department Store (1899, now Carson Pirie & Scott) embodies the school's achievements, with its skeletal structure and horizontal windows.

Classical (also Classicism)

The term applied to architecture based on Greek and Roman antiquity. Prevalent during the Italian **Renaissance**, Classical theories of architecture were developed after the re-discovery of the treatises of Vitruvius (46–30 BC). In the seventeenth century, a more severe form of Classicism was evident, followed in the eighteenth century by a revival of Italian Renaissance architecture, including **Palladianism**. In the late eighteenth century, a reaction to the perceived excesses of **Baroque** re-established principles based on laws of nature and reason, and attention was again given to the use of archaeologically correct details. In the early nineteenth century, a freer, more picturesque style emerged in Europe and the USA, which was designed for effect rather than pursuit of a rule book perfection. By the early twentieth century, a reactionary movement once again changed the nature of Classicism and **Neo-Classicism** became the dominant style. From the mid-twentieth century, various forms of contemporary architecture based on classical precedence represented a reaction to the dominance of **Modernism**. (See Post-Modern)

Clinker brick

An economical and structurally efficient building brick made from the burnt and fused ash from a furnace.

Composite *see* Orders

Constructivism

An anti-aesthetic, anti-art, politically left-aligned ideology that evolved in the USSR around 1920, notably through the work of Konstantin Melnikov, Ivan Leonidov (1902–59) and the Vesnin brothers. Its ideas were taken up by the **Bauhaus** whose insistence on the value of machine manufacturing and the provision of affordable design had similar themes.

Corbel/Corbelling

A projection from the face of a wall to support a load such as an arch, beam or parapet. Corbelling is continuous courses of brick or masonry, where each course cantilevers over the one below to form an arch, vault or dome. (See Roof)

Corinthian *see* Orders

Cornice

The cornice forms the top projecting part of an **entablature**. The term is also used to mean any projecting ornamental moulding applied to the top of a wall, column or building. (See Orders)

Corten (also Cor-Ten, Weathering Steel)

A steel alloy which does not rust, rather it oxidizes slowly to a dull orange-brown colour, resulting in a high-wear, protective surface.

Craftsman

Following a nineteenth-century US tradition of bungalows (a single-storey house with an encircling porch), the Craftsman Style was developed by American architect brothers Charles and Henry Greene. The style reached its apogee in their work, which was typically of timber construction with elegant joinery and exposed beams, low-pitched **gabled** roofs and overhanging eaves, all designed and built with a concern for hand-crafted workmanship.
☛ Greene & Greene

Crenellation (also Battlement)

Real or decorative battlements, usually at the top of a building, composed of repeated indentations in the **parapet**. Historically, crenellations provided protection for archers in battle.

Cubism

An early twentieth-century style of architecture, based on the revolutionary art movement of the same name. Cubist painters, such as Pablo Picasso (1881–1973) and George Braque (1882–1963), used abstract methods of perspective and representation, with superimposed, interlocking and transparent planes depicting the different surfaces of an object simultaneously. In architecture, Cubism was practiced primarily in the Czech Republic, where it tended to extend no further than the treatment of facades with faceted, prismatic elements.
☛ Duchamp-Villon, Janák

Cupola

A small vaulted or domed space at the top of a larger dome, or a concave ceiling over a circular or elliptical room.

Curtain Wall

Historically, the side wall of a building, spanning between the buttresses of a church, or the protective towers of a fortification. In modern architecture, a non-load bearing wall or 'skin', often of steel and glass, covering the building's structural framework.

Deconstructivism (also Deconstruction)

Beginning in the 1980s and popular in Europe and the USA, Deconstructivism was an architectural experiment based on ideas from contemporary French philosophy. While sharing stylistic similarities with Russian **Constructivism**, Deconstructivism was concerned with ideas such as the fragmentation and dislocation of modern cities. Buildings are characterized by complex fractured shapes, the breaking of continuity between inside and out, a jarring use of superimposed grids and a general appearance of instability.
☛ Domenig, Eisenman, Gehry

De Stijl (The Style)

An influential Dutch art and architecture movement (and magazine) founded in 1917 by Theo van Doesburg, which advocated honest expression of structure, straight lines, planes and right angles, using primary colours and formal compositions based on cubes. Members included the painter Piet Mondrian (1872–1944) and architects Robert van 't Hoff and Gerrit Rietveld, whose Schröder House in Utrecht (1924) epitomizes De Stijl architecture.
☛ Doesburg, Hoff, Rietveld & Schröder

Deutsche Werkbund

A German organization founded in 1907 to improve the design of products through the co-operative integration of art, craft and manufacturing. The Werkbund was influential in industrial design, particularly after their Cologne exhibition in 1914 which featured buildings by Walter Gropius and Henry van de Velde. The experimental Weissenhofsiedlung housing estate in Stuttgart followed in 1927, showcasing houses by Le Corbusier and Mies van der Rohe, among others. By the 1930s, their ideas were taken over by Walter Gropius who used them as the intellectual corner-stone for the **Bauhaus** School. The organization disbanded in 1934.
☛ Behrens, Gropius, Le Corbusier, Mies van der Rohe

Domestic Revival

This nineteenth-century style saw a revival of **vernacular** English domestic architecture. Notable for its picturesque compositions, it is characterized by **mullioned** windows, timber-framing, lead-light glass, tall chimneys and **gabled**, tiled roofs. (See Old English)
☛ Lutyens, Richardson, Shaw

Doric *see* Orders

Dormer *see* Window

Dry-stone

Masonry construction in which stone is laid without mortar.

Elevation

An accurately scaled, two-dimensional drawing of any vertical surface of a building, internal or external. Also used to refer to the **facade** of a building. (See Plan & Section)

Elizabethan

The style of architecture prevalent during the reign of Queen Elizabeth I of England (1558–1603). Dominated by French and Flemish styles imported to England via pattern books and mixed with **Gothic** traditions, the style is characterized by grotesque ornamentation, elaborate vertical silhouettes using spires, chimneys and obelisks, and exuberant **facade** treatments including **mullioned** and **transomed** windows, mouldings and superimposed **Orders**.
☛ Smythson

Entablature

The upper part of an **Order** above the column, consisting of an **architrave**, **frieze**, and **cornice**.

Etruscan

In the eighteenth century, black and red antique vases were discovered in Etruria (now Tuscany, Italy) and were mistakenly thought to be Etruscan, but were in fact of Greek origin. The popularity of these vases inspired the Etruscan Style, which incorporated motifs such as griffins, lions and sphinxes, as well as Pompeii-inspired medallions, festoons and urns.

Facade

The exterior face or **elevation** of a building, commonly the front.

Faïence

Glazed earthenware – often decorated and coloured – used for face-work, usually as large, structural blocks.

Fascia

A plain horizontal band or stripe applied to the upper part of a wall.

Federal

Coinciding with the establishment of a Federal Government in the USA in 1789, the term refers to the architecture of this time until circa 1830. Essentially **Neo-Classical**, the style drew on the work of British architect, Robert Adam, and concurrent French styles.
☛ Bulfinch, Burnett, Dyckman, Hoban, Roosevelt

Five Points for a New Architecture: Le Corbusier

Le Corbusier's theoretical and publishing output was as prodigious as his architectural work and produced many **Modern Movement** epithets, including 'the house is a machine for living in'. His *Five Points for a New Architecture* set out the essential elements to be used in Modern architecture: *pilotis*; flat roofs used as terraces; the free plan; continuous, horizontal strip windows and free facade composition.
☛ Le Corbusier

Frieze

The frieze is the middle division of an **entablature**, between the **architrave** and the **cornice**. It is also any strip of decoration at the top of an interior wall below the **cornice**. (See Orders)

Functionalism

An architectural principle adopted by various twentieth-century groups, including the **Deutsche Werkbund** and the **Bauhaus**, which insisted that the form of a building should derive directly from its function. Functionalism was first promoted by Viollet-le-Duc and Louis Sullivan in the nineteenth century. While incorporating economic, social and political concerns to reform society through architecture, extremist interpretations of Functionalism insisted that artistic expression and aesthetic pleasure were to play no part in the design of a building. Buildings were characterized by white planar compositions and the extensive use of steel and glass.
☛ Brinkman & van der Vlugt, Loos, Sullivan, Valsamakis

Gable

The triangular upper part of a wall at the end of a pitched **roof**. A Dutch gable has curved or scrolled sides and a pediment at the top.

Garden City (also Garden Suburb, *Cité Jardin*)

An English architectural and urban design movement of the late nineteenth and early twentieth centuries that developed new, high quality, picturesque places to live and work, combining the healthy qualities and pleasures of the countryside with the facilities and employment opportunities of towns. Devised by Ebenezer Howard (1850–1928) in 1898, the idea was first brought to fruition at Letchworth, Hertfordshire by Parker & Unwin.
☛ Parker & Unwin, Shaw

Garderobe

A small room for clothes, or in a medieval building, a toilet.

Georgian

Architecture built during the reigns of the four King George's of England (1714–1830). The term is used to refer to stripped down, **Classical** domestic architecture characterized by plain **mullioned**, sashed windows and doorways topped with fanlights.
☛ Leverton, Malton, Rothery, Taylor

Gesamtkunstwerk

A German word meaning 'total work of art', first applied in the nineteenth century and later adopted by twentieth-century groups such as the **Bauhaus** and the **Deutsche Werkbund**. It is used to describe the synthesis of art, architecture and design, in which the separate parts of a building comprise a complete and artistic whole.

Giant Order (also Colossal Order)

Any **Order** that rises through more than one storey.

Gothic

A style of architecture also known as Pointed, that dominated European building from the twelfth to the sixteenth centuries. It is characterized by pointed arches, columns made up of clustered shafts, ribbed vaults, elaborate window **tracery** and most of all by an essentially vertical emphasis. In its five hundred years of prevalence, the style progressed through several distinct phases: First Pointed (or Early English); Second Pointed (or Decorated); and Third Pointed (or Perpendicular). Each stage had its own identifiable structural and decorative variations, but all conformed to the essential character of the style.

Gothick/Gothic Revival

Gothick architecture began in eighteenth-century England, as a result of a growing interest in the ruins of antiquity, and the rise in popularity of the Gothick novel, which incorporated a taste for ghosts, gloominess and a certain irrationality. Horace Walpole's house, Strawberry Hill (1753–76), is acknowledged as the exemplary architectural expression of the style. It owed little to historical **Gothic** and relied on a taste for the exotic rather than any attempt at a faithful rendition of precedent. A true Gothic revival based on scholarly study began with AWN Pugin and others in the 1840s, who saw in Gothic the purity and honesty of expression that matched their religious fervour. Their writings led to a spate of church-building and the restoration of medieval buildings.
☛ (Gothic Revival) Pugin, (Gothick) Walpole

Greek Revival

A phase of **Neo-Classicism** from the mid-eighteenth century that employed archaeologically correct details from ancient Greek architecture, which only became known in the west around 1750. At first regarded as primitive, early admirers saw an unblemished purity in the straightforward simplicity of the ancient buildings. The style was widely used, particularly in the USA and Britain.
☛ Ledoux, Schinkel, Soane, Thomson

Hemicycle

A semicircular room or recess, used in Roman architecture, town planning and landscape design for seating and debates.

High Renaissance

A brief period of the Italian **Renaissance** (c1500–1520), also called *Cinquecento*, when work by Leonardo da Vinci (1452–1519), Michelangelo (1475–1564) and Raphael was deemed to represent the highest artistic and intellectual achievements of the Renaissance.
☛ Raphael, Vasari, Vignola

High-Tech

An architectural approach that began in Britain in the 1970s, which emphasized the engineering aspects of contemporary building technologies. High-Tech buildings celebrate their services and structure by exposing them to view. Notable examples are the Waterloo International Terminal (1993) by Nicholas Grimshaw & Partners, and the Centre Georges Pompidou in Paris (1977) by Renzo Piano and Richard Rogers.

Hôtel

A French townhouse with a walled courtyard on the street side, and a garden at the rear.

Ionic *see* Orders

International Style (also International Modern)

The term 'International Style' (synonymous in the USA with the European **Modern Movement**) was first coined by Philip Johnson in 1932 in connection with an influential exhibition at the Museum of Modern Art in New York. The exhibition featured work such as Walter Gropius' Bauhaus (1925–6), Le Corbusier's Salvation Army Hostel (1929) and Mies van der Rohe's houses at the Weissenhofsiedlung (1927). The International Style was concerned with the development of a sophisticated aesthetic, which was characterized by the elimination of all decoration, smooth white planar surfaces, large expanses of glass and flat roofs.
☛ P Johnson, Mies van der Rohe, Neutra, Schindler

Italianate

A style of nineteenth-century architecture modelled on a type of **Classical** Italian palazzo with columns, such as the Palazzo Farnese in Rome (1517–89) by Antonio da Sangallo, the Younger. The style, used extensively in Britain, Germany and the USA, was characterized by plain **facades**, **quoins**, **stucco** ornamentation and the use of heavy exterior cornicing.
☛ L'Orme, Nash, Schinkel

Jacobean

Architecture built during the reign of King James I and VI of England (1603–25). The style fuses French, Italian and Flemish elements and employs superimposed **Orders**, obelisks and heraldic motifs, as well as Dutch **gables** and elaborate chimneys.
☛ Cecil

Jali

A perforated screen wall ubiquitously employed in Indian architecture, the *jali* was perfected during the **Mughal** era.
☛ Patwon, Rewal

Jugendstil *see* Art Nouveau

Loggia

A roofed arcade, gallery or colonnade, open to the air on one or more sides, serving as a protected place to sit or appreciate a view.

Louis XVI

A style of **Neo-Classical** architecture and interior design characterized by simplicity and sometimes severity that evolved during the reign of Louis XVI of France (1774–92).
☛ Ledoux

Mannerism

A style of sixteenth-century architecture that followed the **High Renaissance** and was a precursor to **Baroque**. The style used **Classical** motifs and forms in unexpected or illogical ways, often distorting and over-elaborating elements of a building, such as dropped keystones (the central stone of an arch) and columns inserted into wall recesses.
☛ Giulio Romano

Mashrabiyya (also Mashrabeyya)

Elaborate timber lattice-work screens used in Islamic domestic architecture.
☛ Aitchison, al-Haddad, El-Wakil

Mezzanine

A mid-height floor or storey inserted between two others.

Minimalism

Often confused with the 1960s art movement of the same name, architectural Minimalism is essentially an aesthetic style. Characterized by austerity, unadorned surfaces and a limited palette of materials and colours, it draws stylistically from various sources such as monastic buildings and Zen Buddhist gardens.
☛ Ando, Laan, Pawson Silvestrin

Modern Movement (also Modernism)

A twentieth-century movement that disconnected itself from links to the past by suppressing all forms of ornament and historical reference, in order to establish a style appropriate to modern living. Architects relied on a scientific, rational approach, with mass-produced building components and industrial construction methods preferred over craftsmanship and artistry. The Modern Movement emerged in Europe immediately prior to WWI and culminated in the architecture of the 1920s and 30s. Walter Gropius' Bauhaus building (1925–6) and the **Deutsche Werkbund**'s Weissenhofsiedlung housing estate

(1927) displayed the characteristic motifs of strip windows, flat roofs, cubic geometry and white planar surfaces punctuated by steel and glass. (See Bauhaus, Functionalism, International Style)
☛ Chermayeff, Fry, Gropius, Le Corbusier, Tait

Moderne

A term used in the USA in the 1930s, synonymous with **Art Deco**.

Modernisme *see* Art Nouveau

Moorish/Mooresque

Islamic architecture of the Moors who were prevalent in North Africa and Spain from AD 711 to 1492. The best example is the fourteenth-century Alhambra Palace in Grenada. Mooresque architecture, popular in the nineteenth century, is derived from that of the Moors and is characterized by interlaced ornamental foliage designs, called arabesque.
☛ Eschwege, Nasrid Dynasty, Tarifa

Mudéjar

A style of Spanish architecture and decoration that was developed by the Muslims who remained in Spain after the Christian re-conquest (circa mid-thirteenth century). It employs horse-shoe curves, stalactite work and arabesque decoration. (See Moorish)
☛ Gaudí, Tarifa

Mughal

A style of Indian architecture named after the ruling dynasty (1526–1828). The best example is the palace city of Fatehpur Sikri (1571–85), with its fusion of Persian, Islamic and Indian styles. The style is generally characterized by a combination of delicacy and monumentality, refinement of detail and opulent materials.
☛ Akbar, Patwon, Shah Jahan

Mullion

The vertical divisions between the panes of glass in a window.

Neo-Classical

An architectural movement prevalent from the eighteenth to the early twentieth centuries, that rejected the excesses of **Baroque** and **Rococo** architecture, and sought to rediscover the purity of **Classical** antiquity. An archaeologically correct application of Classicism was favoured, but there was also a preoccupation with the 'primitive' (for example, Abbé Laugier's Primitive Hut, 1753). This meshing of classical purity and primitivism produced a style that tended towards clear uncluttered forms, pure geometry, a rational approach to design, and, in some cases, a stripping away of ornamentation altogether. Neo-Classical architecture had a tendency toward severity, starkness and intellectual seriousness, however it also encompassed several styles (**Greek Revival**, Egyptian Revival and Empire Style), which had their own stylistic individualities but all springing from similar architectural roots. (See Neo-Primitivism)

Neo-Plasticism

The term refers to the artistic preoccupation of abstracting three-dimensional form into lines and planes devoid of any naturalistic references with a predilection for primary colours contrasted with black, white and grey. Piet Mondrian (1872–1944) explored these ideas in his paintings and through his connection with **De Stijl**, introduced the aesthetic to architecture.

Neo-Primitivism

A feature of late eighteenth-century **Neo-Classicism** whereby architectural theorists, notably Abbé Laugier, argued for a strict application of the Classical **Orders**, avoiding superfluous decoration. The basis for this approach was a re-examination of the first principles of architecture, which held up the example of the Primitive Hut – a structure of four tree trunks, with sawn logs and a pitched roof – as the prototype for all architecture.
☛ Laugier

Neo-Rationalism

Neo-Rationalism (also called Tendenza) was a late twentieth-century movement that evolved in the 1960s after Italian architect, Aldo Rossi, published *L'Architettura della città* (*Architecture of the City*) in 1966. The movement favoured historical continuity and embraced **Renaissance** theories and **Classical** principles. Rejecting functionalism and technology, Neo-Rationalists preferred to use the old fabric of the city as a source of inspiration and reference, rather than the total reinvention of architecture as **Modernism** had advocated.
☛ Botta, Reichlin & Reinhardt, Rossi, OM Ungers

Neo-Vernacular

Architecture which draws inspiration from **vernacular** building types. A twentieth-century reaction to the pervasive canons of **Modernism**, Neo-Vernacular architecture addresses specific aspects of site and culture, such as climate, availability of building materials, *genius loci* (spirit of place) and local tradition.
☛ Bawa, El-Wakil, Fathy, Murcutt

New Urbanism

A term coined in the 1980s and used in connection with the work of Andres Duany, Elizabeth Plater-Zyberk and Leon Krier, who promoted the idea of closely integrated urban communities with strong neighbourhood identities. The town of Seaside in Florida, USA (begun 1984) with its **Neo-Vernacular** timber buildings, human-scale streets and limited vehicle access, was a prototypical investigation into these principles.
☛ Duany Plater-Zyberk, Krier

New York Five

A loose association of five architects whose work was exhibited at the Museum of Modern Art in New York in 1962 and was published in the 1972 book, *Five Architects*. Also referred to as the 'Whites' (due to the absence of colour in their work), Peter Eisenman, Michael Graves, Charles Gwathmey, John Hejduk and Richard Meier all presented work that displayed a formal return to the **International Style** of the 1930s.
☛ Eisenman, Graves, Gwathmey, Meier

Oculus

A circular window or opening at the top of a dome.

Old English

A style of nineteenth-century English architecture which revived **vernacular** forms and formed part of **Domestic Revival**. Features include patterned tiles, steeply pitched **roofs**, exposed timber framing, ornamental brickwork and tall chimneys.

Oratory

A private chapel, or small room set aside for prayer.

Orders

Used in **Classical** architecture, an order is an assemblage of parts consisting principally of a column (base, shaft and capital) and an **entablature** (**architrave**, **frieze** and **cornice**), all proportioned and decorated according to one of the so-called Five Orders.
Doric: Characterized by a massive column placed on the ground without a base, terminating in a simple capital (crowning part of a column). The entablature consisted of a plain architrave and an ornamented frieze.
Ionic: The spreading scroll-shaped **volute** in the capital is the distinctive feature and the slender fluted shaft is used with a base. The entablature has a three-banded architrave and a frieze adorned with sculpture.
Corinthian: The most ornate of the Orders which, except for the distinctive capital decorated with acanthus leaves and volutes, is similar to the Ionic Order.
Tuscan: A simplified form of the Doric Order, the column has a simple base, and the capital and entablature above are stripped of ornament.
Composite: A variation of the Corinthian Order, the Composite Order is characterized by a capital which combines Corinthian foliage and Ionic volutes.

Organic Architecture

An elusive term that can and has been applied to widely diverse practices and forms. The early work of Frank Lloyd Wright and Alvar Aalto embodied a concept of organicism in which the parts of the building are inseparable from the whole, which in turn has an inseparable symbiotic relationship with nature. Conversely, architects in the late twentieth century have increasingly turned to scientific, mathematical and biological sources for inspiration, typically incorporating soft, flowing curvilinear shapes.
☛ Aalto, Senosiain, Ushida Findlay, Wright

Ottoman

Late Islamic architecture from the fourteenth century, prevalent in Turkey where it was influenced by Byzantium. Characteristics include domes, relief stone decorations, decorative tulips, arabesques, crescents and turbans, and lavish tilework. The Ottoman Style emerged in Europe in the eighteenth century, where the popularity of smoking rooms and Turkish Baths encouraged a style that incorporated many Ottoman motifs.
☛ Mehmed II

Palladianism

A **Classical** style based on the work of sixteenth-century Italian architect Andrea Palladio. Inigo Jones introduced the Palladian Style to England, but it wasn't until the eighteenth century that a full scale revival of Palladianism occurred, largely due to the efforts of Lord Burlington.
☛ Burlington, Cameron, Jefferson, I Jones, Palladio, Rothery

Parapet

A low protective wall set at the edge of a balcony or roof.

Pediment

A low-pitched **gable** front at the top of a Classical **Order**, often incorporating elaborate sculpture.

Peristyle

A range of columns surrounding a building or courtyard.

Perpendicular *see* Gothic

Piano Nobile

The principal floor of a building, accommodating the reception, entertaining and living spaces. It is usually located above the ground floor and entered via a staircase in the entry hall. External facade treatments, such as larger windows, indicate the importance given to the spaces within.

Picturesque

An eighteenth-century English concept that contrived to place buildings and landscapes in overtly painterly compositions. Picturesque compositions often incorporated real or contrived natural features, topographical decoration, pastoral scenes and real or sham ruins. (See Gothick & Romanticism)
☛ Lever, Wyatville

Pilaster

A rectangular, non-structural projection with the appearance of a column, attached to the surface of a wall, which in **Classical** architecture conforms to one of the **Orders**.

Pilotis

A French word for columns which raise a building above the ground creating an open space beneath. Used to great spatial and aesthetic effect by Le Corbusier and adopted by architects of the **Modern Movement** as a consistent motif.

Plan

An accurately scaled, two-dimensional drawing of a building seen from above, showing the arrangement of rooms and the thickness and composition of the walls. (See Elevation & Section)

Portico

A colonnaded roofed porch attached to the front of a building.

Post-Modern (also Post-Modernism)

A term used in the 1970s to refer to the work of architects who took a reactive stance against **Modernism** and the **Bauhaus**. Also known as POMO and P-M, Post-Modern architecture favoured a pluralist, eclectic aesthetic, often incorporating abstracted or simplistic references to **Classical** motifs, such as oversized columns, broken **pediments** and colourful mouldings.
☛ Graves, Jencks & Farrell, Moore, Outram, Stern, Venturi

Prairie Style (also Prairie School)

A style of architecture in the Midwestern USA between c1900 and 1916, named after designs by Frank Lloyd Wright such as the Robie House in Chicago (1909), which were inspired by the simple farm buildings of the American prairies. The style was characterized by low-pitched roofs with large overhanging eaves, a strong horizontal emphasis and the dominance of the hearth as the focus of the living spaces.
☛ Greene & Greene, Sullivan, Wright

Prefabrication (also Prefabs)

A construction system in which the components of a building are manufactured and partly assembled in a factory before being transported and erected on site.
☛ Goodman, Prouvé, Segal

Queen Anne/Queen Anne Style or Revival

English architecture built during the reign of Queen Anne (1702–14), when plainness and restraint were admired qualities. Buildings featured plain red brick, tall sash windows, canopied timber doors and flattened roofs hidden behind **parapets**. The Queen Anne Style emerged in the 1860s and incorporated eclectic motifs such as tall, white-painted sash windows, rubbed brick, terracotta embellishments, steeply pitched roofs, large chimneys, Dutch **gables**, **balustrades**, balconies and bay windows.
☛ (Queen Anne) Hawksmoor, (Queen Anne Style) Shaw

Quoin

The external corner of a building, formed by placing alternating small and large stones in a vertical stack, raised from the surface of the wall to turn the corner.

Rationalism

A movement founded in Italy in 1926 by Gruppo 7 (Group of 7) and associated with the rise of Fascism in Italy. Italian architect Giuseppe Terragni was the key exponent; his Casa de Fascio building in Como (1932–6) is arguably the defining building of the movement. An essentially **Modern** movement, Rationalism concerned itself with the pursuit of reason and encompassed a strong social, economic and political agenda, motivated by a desire to improve society through architecture. (See Neo-Rationalism)
☛ Terragni

Renaissance

Meaning 'rebirth', the Renaissance was a period in Italian architecture that rediscovered and celebrated the architecture of Ancient Rome, beginning with the work of Filippo Brunelleschi (1377–1446) in Florence in c1420. From this time, art and architecture based on Italian prototypes dominated Europe until

the mid-sixteenth century, followed by **Mannerism** and **Baroque**.
☛ Alberti, Laurana, Maiano, Michelozzi, Palladio, Porta, Serlio

Render

A finish applied to a surface, usually a wall. Render is applied wet and can be worked to a smooth or textured finish. Typical materials are plaster, concrete, mud and pebble-dash.

Rococo

An eighteenth-century style originating in France, Rococo was the last phase of **Baroque**, in which naturalistic forms were combined with coral and shell shapes, and S- and C-curves, achieving an elegant and delicate style of decoration.
☛ Dollmann, Oliveira

Romanesque/Romanesque Revival

A style of architecture (called Norman in northern France) that dominated western Europe from the tenth to the twelfth century. Buildings were characterized by massive walls and piers, semicircular arches and vaults, and geometrical planning. A Romanesque Revival occurred in the early nineteenth century and was particularly long-lived in Ireland where it remained popular well into the twentieth century.

Romanticism

A feature of late eighteenth- and early nineteenth-century architecture which appeared as the antithesis of rational **Classical** and **Neo-Classical** architecture. Romanticism emphasized emotion, instinct, the irrational and an interest in ruins and ghosts, over rationality and reason. Allied with **Picturesque** and **Gothic Revival**, Romanticism celebrated ivy-covered ruins, lost gardens and funerary environments, all of which was cultivated by a love of melancholy and the sublime.

Roof

The following examples represent a small number of the many types of roof.
Corbelled: Continuous layers of brick or masonry, where each course **cantilevers** over the one below to meet at the top forming a rough vault or dome.
Gable or Pitched: The most common type with sloping roof planes meeting at a top ridge and with **gables** at both ends.
Gambrel: In the USA, a gambrel roof is the same as a Mansard roof. Elsewhere, it is a hipped roof with a gable end at the apex.
Hipped: A roof with sloping ends rather than flat gable ends.
Mansard: Devised by French architect François Mansard (1598–1666) and particularly associated with **Second Empire**, the Mansard roof has a relatively flat top slope and a steeper lower slope on each side, allowing for a room, usually with **dormer** windows, within.

Secession (also Sezessionstil) *see* Art Nouveau

Sgraffito

A decorative stucco wall finish, composed of one layer of coloured plaster covered with another coat of white plaster. While the top coat is setting, it is scratched with a steel tool to expose the colour below, creating a *sgraffito* pattern.
☛ Cauchie

Second Empire

Architecture associated with the reign of Emperor Napoleon III (1852–70) in France. Characteristics include high mansard **roofs** with inset circular windows, **dormer** windows and ornamentation, all of which contributed to a general style of wealth and opulence.
☛ McCoskrie & Greenfield

Section

An accurately scaled, two-dimensional drawing representing a vertical slice through a building to show the arrangement of spaces, walls, windows, doors and roofs. (See Plan & Elevation)

Shingle Style

Named for its use of timber shingles, a domestic style of late nineteenth-century American architecture that developed as a nationalistic response to the celebration of the centenary of the American Revolution. Based on the traditional **Stick Style** and incorporating elements of the English **Queen Anne Style**, Shingle Style houses also employed ingenious open-plan interior arrangements which anticipated the later work of Frank Lloyd Wright and Greene & Greene.
☛ McKim Mead & White, Richardson

Shoin

A style of traditional Japanese residential architecture that developed from the Muromachi to Edo periods (1333–1868). Features include a decorative alcove (*tokonoma*), staggered shelves, a writing alcove (*tsukeshoin*) and decorative doors (*chôdaigamae*), together with **tatami**-mat floors, sliding screens (*shôji and fusuma*), verandas, square posts and a formal entryway (*genkan*).
☛ Tokugawa, Toshihito & Toshitada

Soffit

The underside surface of any part of a building. Commonly used to refer to the lower, exposed part of a ceiling, arch, vault or balcony.

Spandrel

In **Classical** architecture, the triangular space between an arch and the rectangular surround, or the space between two arches in an arcade. In contemporary architecture, spandrel panels form part of a **curtain wall**.

Stick Style

An American style of domestic timber architecture that evolved partly from **balloon-frame** buildings and other **vernacular** types, such as Swiss Chalets and French farm buildings. Popular in the nineteenth century, the style was characterized by timber framing and cladding, wide verandas, overhanging eaves, all giving a picturesque but angular, jagged appearance.
☛ Marmillion, Potter

String course

A horizontal band of moulding, such as brick or stone, on a **facade**.

Stucco

Slow-setting plaster used in Roman and **Renaissance** architecture to achieve a very smooth finish and three-dimensional surface decoration. It was used in early nineteenth-century English houses as an economical alternative to **ashlar**.

Sukiya

A seventeenth-century Japanese style of construction that combines the formal Shoin style with more rustic natural teahouse elements in a free and innovative arrangement. The term *suki*, from which the name derives, refers to the enjoyment of the tea ceremony ritual. (See Shoin)
☛ Horiguchi, Ishii, Kishi, Toshihito & Toshitada

Tabernacle

In a church, a receptacle where the sacraments are placed on an alter. Tabernacle work refers to richly carved screens and canopies, usually employed over choir stalls.

Tablinum

In Roman architecture, a room that opens onto the **atrium**.

Taliesin

Frank Lloyd Wright began construction of a new home and studio in 1911 near Spring Green, Wisconsin, calling it Taliesin after an ancient Celtic poet. When the house burned down in 1914 and again in 1925 and 1927, Wright's commitment to the house only

deepened and he continued to rebuild it. In 1932, he founded the Taliesin Fellowship, offering apprenticeships to young students to work in the Taliesin studio where they assisted with every aspect of the practice. From 1937 Wright decided to build a new home and studio in Paradise Valley, Arizona, called Taliesin West which became a permanent winter 'camp' for the Taliesin Fellowship. It was built over several years by Wright and his apprentices, and remained under construction until his death in 1959.
☛ Goff, E F Jones, Lautner

Tatami

A straw floor mat of a standard size (approximately 1.8 x .9 m or 70 x 35 in) in Japanese domestic architecture. Used in multiples, *tatami* mats determine the size and proportions of rooms.
☛ Tokugawa, Toshihito & Toshitada, Yamada, Yoshimura

Tracery

The decorative intersection between the **mullions** and **transomes** of a window or panel. Originating in Early **Gothic** churches of the late twelfth century, tracery became one of the principle decorative elements throughout the later Middle Ages.

Transom(e)

A horizontal bar dividing the panes of a **window**.

Truss

A timber frame placed at intervals to form the structural component of a **roof**.

Tuscan *see* Orders

Vernacular

A term for traditional building forms specific to a region or country, relying on indigenous building materials and methods of construction. (See Neo-Vernacular)
☛ Abelam, Bernese, Hutu, Maori, Sa'dan Toraja, Toda, Zulu

Volute

The scroll-shaped form found in the capital of the Ionic **Order**.

Weatherboard

External timber cladding made of overlapping horizontal boards.

Wiener Werkstätte

Founded in 1903, the Wiener Werkstätte (Vienna Workshop) was the Austrian equivalent of the English **Arts and Crafts** workshops. It grew from the **Secession** exhibition of 1900 and was the centre of contemporary design in Austria and Hungary until 1932.

Window

The following examples represent a small number of the many variations of window types.
Bay: A window projecting out from an external wall, forming a recess in a room.
Casement: A window where the framed glass is hung on hinges, and opens either inwards or outwards.
Dormer: A window projecting from the pitched surface of a roof, having its own roof which can be either flat or pitched.
Double-Glazing: A modern window in which two planes of glass are separated by an air space for thermal or acoustic insulation.
French: A casement window carried down to the floor so as to open like doors.
Oriel: Similar to a bay window but located only on an upper floor, it can be **cantilevered** or **corbelled** out from the wall.
Sash: A double- or triple-hung window where the framed glass panes are raised and lowered vertically by cords with counter-balancing weights.

Note: Biographical dates for architects in the glossary can be found under their individual entries in the book.

Directory of houses

Australia

Belltrees Homestead
Gundy Road, Scone, NSW
Homestead tours available to guests
of Belltrees. Contact for details
Pender, John Wiltshire

Dugout Houses
Contact Coober Pedy Information
Centre in Hutchison Street, Coober
Pedy, SA for tours of homes, churches
& mines
Open Mon to Fri, 9am to 5pm
Coober Pedy Miners

Rose Seidler House
Run by the Historic Houses Trust of
New South Wales, Clissold Road,
Wahroonga, Sydney, NSW
Open Sun, 10am to 5pm. Closed Good
Friday & Christmas Day
Seidler, Harry

Austria

Schönbrunn Palace
Vienna
Open Apr to Oct daily, 8.30am to 5pm;
Nov to Mar, 8.30am to 4.30pm
Fischer von Erlach, Johann Bernhard

Upper Belvedere Palace
Oberes Belvedere, 3rd District
Prinz Eugen-Strasse, Vienna
Open Tues to Sun, 10am to 5pm
Hildebrandt, Johann Lucas von

Barbados

St Nicholas Abbey
St Peter
Ground floor open Mon to Fri,
10am to 3.30pm
Berringer, Colonel Benjamin

Belgium

Hôtel Tassel
Rue Paul-Emile Janson, Brussels
Now the Mexican Embassy, the
interior can be viewed by advance
appointment only
Horta, Victor

Grand-Place
Brussels
Public urban spaces, open daily
Brussels Guildsmen

Maison Cauchie
Rue des Francs, Etterbeck, Brussels
Open first weekend of every month,
11am to 6pm
Cauchie, Paul

Bermuda

Carter House
Southside, St George's Parish
St David's Island
Now a museum, contact St George's
Historical Society for details
Carter, Christopher

China

Yurt
Contact NoviNomad who run eco
tours in Kyrgyzstan, including
visiting & staying in yurt
communities
Kyrgyz

Egypt

House of Abd al-Qadar the Smith
Gayer-Anderson Museum, Ibn Tulun,
Cairo
Open daily, 8am to 5pm
al-Haddad, Abd al-Qadar

Finland

Futuro House
A Futuro House is on display at the
Centraal Museum, Nicolaaskerkhof,
Utrecht, The Netherlands
Open Tues to Sun, 11am to 5pm
Closed Mon, 30 Apr, Christmas &
New Year's Day
Suuronen, Matti

Hvitträsk
Kirkkonummi, nr Helsinki
Open daily from June to Oct at
various times
Gesellius Lindgren & Saarinen

Kallela House & Studio
Ruovesi
Open to the public
Gallén-Kallela, Akseli

Summer House
Muuratsalo
Open by arrangement with the Alvar
Aalto Museum between June & Sept
on Mon, Wed & Fri, 1pm to 2pm. Prior
booking essential
Aalto, Alvar

France

Château d'Ancy-le-Franc
Nr Tonnerre, Burgundy
Open daily, Apr to mid-Nov
Serlio, Sebastiano

Château d'Azay-le-Rideau
Nr Tours, Indre-et-Loire
Open daily except New Year's Day
Berthelot, Gilles

Château de Chambord
Domaine National de Chambord,
Vieux chemin de la chaussée,
Chambord
Open daily, times vary throughout
the year
Cortona, Domenico da

Château de Chenonceau
Chenonceau, Indre-et-Loire
Open 16 Mar to 15 Sept, 9am to 7pm;
16 Sept to 15 Mar, 9am to 4.30pm
L'Orme, Philibert de

Château de Fontainebleau
Fontainebleau, Ile-de-France
Open in spring & summer daily, 8am

to 7.45pm. Autumn & winter daily,
9am to 5pm
Le Breton, Gilles

Château de Villandry
Nr Tours, Indre-et-Loire
Open daily, times vary throughout
the year
Breton, Jean le

Dry-stone Borie
Village des Bories
Gordes, Vaucluse, Provence
Open daily, 9am to 5.30pm
Provençale Farmers

Hôtel de Salm
Rue de Lille, Paris
Currently occupied by the Legion
d'Honneur. Open daily, 2pm to 5pm
Closed Mon
Rousseau, Pierre

Hôtel de Sully
Rue Saint-Antoine, Paris
Garden open 9am to 7pm. House open
by tour only on weekends. Closed on
selected days during the year
Cerceau, Jean du

Landaise Farmhouse
Ecomusée de la Grande-Lande,
Marquèze, Sabres
Contact the museum for details
Landaise Farmers

La Maison de Picassiette
Chartres
Open to the public. Contact the Office
de Tourisme Chartres, Place de la
Cathédrale, Chartres for details
Isidore, Raymond

Palace of Versailles
Open daily except Mon, May to Sept,
9am to 6.30pm; Oct to Apr, 9am to
5.30pm. Closed 1 May, 25 Dec & 1 Jan
*Le Vau, Louis & Hardouin-
Mansart, Jules*

Le Petit Trianon
Open daily except Mon & public
holidays, times vary throughout
the year
Gabriel, Ange-Jacques

Place des Vosges
Paris
Public urban spaces, open daily
Victor Hugo's house (now a museum)
is located at No. 6, Place des Vosges
Open from 10am to 5.40pm. Closed
Mon & public holidays
Henri IV

Villa E-1027
Currently undergoing renovation by
the French government & Friends of
E-1027. Due for completion in 2002
when it will be open to the public
Gray, Eileen & Badovici, Jean

Villa Majorelle
Rue Louis Majorelle, Nancy

Open May to Sept at weekends,
2.30pm to 3.30 pm; Oct to Apr on Sat,
2.30pm to 3.30pm. Guided tours in
French only. Advance reservations
advised from the Musée de l'Ecole
de Nancy
Sauvage, Henri

Villa de Noailles
Montée de Noailles, Hyères
Open daily, 10am to 12pm & 4pm
to 7pm. Closed Tues
Mallet-Stevens, Robert

Villa Savoye
Rue de Villiers, Poissy
Open daily except Tues, Apr to Oct,
9.30am to 12.30pm & 1.30pm to 6pm;
Nov to Mar, 9.30am to 12.30pm &
1.30pm to 4.30pm. Closd 1 Jan, 1 May,
1 & 11 Nov, & 25 Dec
Le Corbusier

Germany

Double House
The Master House, Ebertallee, Dessau
Open daily, Tues to Fri, 10am to 5pm.
Group tours can be arranged by
calling the Visitors Service of the
Bauhaus Dessau Foundation
Gropius, Walter

Haus am Horn
Weimar
Open to the public
Muche, Georg

Residenz, Würzberg
Open Tues to Sun, Apr to Oct, 9am
to 5pm; Nov to Mar, 10am to 4pm
Neumann, Balthasar

Schloss Charlottenhof
Park Sanssouci, nr Potsdam
Schinkel, Karl Friedrich

Schloss Linderhof
Nr Oberammergau
Open to the public
Dollmann, Georg von

Schloss Neuschwanstein
Nr Füssen, Bavaria
Open daily, 10am to 4pm
Closed 1 Jan, 1 Nov & 24–26 Dec
Ludwig II

Zwinger Palace
Zwinger, Dresden
Currently occupied by the
Mathematisch-Physikalischer Salon
Open daily except Thurs, 9.30am to 5pm
Pöppelmann, Matthaeus

Greece

Palace of Knossos
Crete
Open to the public
Minoan

India

Amber Palace
Jaipur, Rajasthan

Open daily, 9am to 5.30pm
Jai Singh I

Bari Mahal (Garden Palace)
City Palace Museum, Udaipur,
Rajasthan
Open daily except Sun, 10am to
4.30pm
Amar Singh II

Jag Nivas (Lake Palace)
Now a luxury hotel; some areas
are open to the public
Jagat Singh II

Patwon-ki Haveli
Jaisalmer, Rajasthan
Open to the public
Patwon

Raja Birbal's House
Fatehpur Sikri, Nr Agra, Uttar
Pradesh
Open to the public
Akbar

Tent Palace
Displayed in the Mehrangarh Fort
Museum, Jodhpur, Rajasthan
Open daily, 10am to 4.30pm
Shah Jahan

Italy

Cà d'Oro
Calle della Cà d'Oro, Cannaregio,
Venice
Now a museum, open to the public
Contarini, Marin

**Casa del Mosaico di Nettuno
e Anfitrite**
Herculaneum, nr Ercolano, Bay
of Naples
Open to the public
Maiuri, Amadeo

House of the Vetii
Pompeii
Open to the public
Pompeii Romans

Palazzo Carignano
Piazza Carlo Alberto, Turin
Now the Museo Nazionale del
Risorgimento Italiano
Open to the public
Guarini, Guarino

Palazzo del Tè
Mantua
Open to the public
Giulio Romano

Palazzo Ducale
Urbino
Now houses the Galleria Nazionale
delle Marche
Open daily, 9am to 2pm & Sun,
9am to 1pm
Laurana, Luciano

Palazzo Rucellai
Via della Vigna Nuova, Florence
Now houses the Ali Nari Museum of

Photography
Open Sun to Thurs, 9am to 1pm &
3pm to 8pm; Fri & Sat, 9am to 1pm &
3pm to 10.30pm
Alberti, Leon Battista

Palazzo Strozzi
Florence
Open to the public
Maiano, Benedetto da

Villa Adriana
Tivoli
Open to the public
Hadrian

Villa Aldobrandini
Frascati, Tivoli, Lazio
Open by appointment only, Mon
to Sat, 9am to 1pm
Closed public holidays
Porta, Giacomo della

Villa Farnese
Caprarola
Open Mon to Sat, Nov to Feb, 9am to
4pm; Mar, 9am to 5pm; Apr, May & Sept,
9am to 6pm; June to Aug, 9am to 7pm
Vignola, Giacomo

Villa Farnesina
Via della Lungara, Rome
Open daily except Sun, 9am to 1pm
Peruzzi, Baldassare

Villa Giulia
Rome
Open Tues to Sat, 9am to 7pm; Sun &
public holidays, 9am to 2pm
Vasari, Giorgio

510

Villa Iovis
Capri
Open to the public
Tiberius

Villa Medici
Via Mantellini, Fiesole, Tuscany
Open by appointment only
Michelozzi, Michelozzo

Villa Rotonda
Nr Vicenza
Villa open Wed only, 10am to 12pm &
3pm to 6pm; gardens open daily
except Mon
Palladio, Andrea

Japan

Gassho-zukuri Farmhouse
Gassho-zukuri Village in Shirakawa
is a World Heritage site
Open daily
Shirakawa Farmers

Katsura Imperial Villa
Kyoto
Visits with advance permission from
the Imperial Household Agency Office
*Toshihito & Toshitada, Princes
Hachijo*

Matsumoto Castle
Nagano, Honshu

Open to the public
Ishikawa, Kazumasa & Yasunaga

Rinshunkaku
Located in Sankeien Gardens,
Honmoku-Sankeien-mae, Yokohama
Open daily, 9am to 5pm
Closed 29–31 Dec
Tokugawa, Yorinobu

Mexico

**San Cristobal, Egerstrom
Residence & Stables**
Los Clubes, Mexico City
Open by appointment only
Barragán, Luis

The Netherlands

Mauritshuis
Korte Vijverberg, The Hague
Open Tues to Sat, 10am to 5pm; Sun &
holidays, 11am to 5pm
Closed Mon & Christmas Day
Campen, Jacob van

Schröder House
Prins Hendriklaan, Utrecht
Open Wed to Sat, 11am to 5pm; Sun,
12pm to 5pm or by appointment
Rietveld, Gerrit & Schröder, Truus

Sonneveld House
Annex of the Netherlands Architecture
Institute, Museumpark, Rotterdam
Open to the public
Brinkman & van der Vlugt

Portugal

Palácio de Pena
Estremadura, Sintra
Open in winter, 10am to 1pm & 2pm
to 5pm; summer, 10am to 1pm & 2pm
to 6pm. Closed Mon
Eschwege, Baron von

Queluz Palace
Queluz National Palace Square,
Sintra, nr Lisbon
Open daily, 10am to 1pm & 2pm
to 5pm. Closed Tues
Oliveira, Mateus Vicente de

Russia

Izba
Located at The State Art & Historical-
Architectural Museum-Reserve
Kolomenskoye, Moscow
Open to the public
Peter the Great

Melnikov House
Krivoarbatski Pereulok, Moscow
Open to the public
Melnikov, Konstantin

Menshikov Palace
Universitetskaia Naberezhnaia
(Embankment), St Petersburg
Open daily, 10.30am to 4.30pm
Closed Mon
*Fontana, Giovanni & Schädel,
Gottfried*

Pavlovsk Park & Palace
Nr St Petersburg
Open to the public
Cameron, Charles

The Winter Palace
Dvortsovaia Naberezhnaia
St Petersburg
Open daily, 10.30am to 5.30pm;
Sun, until 5pm. Closed Mon

Rastrelli, Bartolomeo

South Africa

Boschendal Manor House
Boschendal Winery, Groot
Drakenstein
Some areas open to the public
Villiers, Paul de

Decorated Houses
Ndebele Cultural Village of
Botshabelo, nr Middelburg, Orange
Free State
Ndebele

Spain

Alhambra Palace
Grenada
Open in summer, Mon to Sat, 9am to
8pm & Sun, 9am to 6pm; winter, 9am
to 6pm daily
Nasrid Dynasty

Casa de Pilatos
Plaza de Pilatos, Seville
Open daily. Ground floor, 10am to 2pm
& 4pm to 6pm; first floor, 10am to 2pm
& 4pm to 6pm
Tarifa, Marqués de

Casas Colgadas
Cuenca, Castilla-la Mancha
One of the hanging houses now
accommodates the Museum of
Abstract Art
Open Tues to Sun
Isabella I & Ferdinand II

Fundación César Manrique
Taro de Tahíche, Teguise, Lanzarote
Open daily, 9am to 6pm
Manrique, César

Palau Güell
Nou de la Rambla, Barcelona
Open Mon to Sat, 10am to 2pm & 4pm
to 8pm. Closed public holidays
Gaudí, Antoni

Turkey

Rahmi Koç Yali
Rahmi M Koç Museum, Istanbul
Open to the public
Eldem, Sedad

Topkapi Palace Museum
Kultur Bakanligi Anitlar ve Muzeler
Genel Mudurlugu II, Meclis Binasi,
Ulus, Ankara
Open daily, 9.30am to 5pm
Closed on Tues
Mehmed II

UK

Bedford Park
Turnham Green, London
Public urban spaces, open daily
Shaw, Richard Norman

Bedford Square
Nos. 34–36 house The Architectural
Association School of Architecture
which contains some public spaces,
including the ground floor gallery
Leverton, Thomas

Castell Coch
Glamorganshire, Wales
Open to the public, except when
booked for private functions
Burges, William

Castle Howard
Nr York
Open Mar to Nov daily, 10am to 4.30pm
Vanbrugh, Sir John

Chatsworth House
Chatsworth, Bakewell, Derbyshire
Open daily, 11am to 5.30pm
Talman, William

Chiswick House
Burlington Lane, London
Open Apr to Sept daily, 10am to 6pm;
first three weeks of Oct daily, 10am to
5pm; late Oct to March, Wed to Sun,
10am to 4pm
Burlington, Lord

The Circus
Bath
Exterior tours available
Wood the Elder, John

Endsleigh Cottage & Gardens
Milton Abbot, nr Tavistock, Devon
Open Apr to Sept, Fri to Tues, 11am
to 5pm
Wyatville, Sir Jeffry

The Grange
Currently undergoing restoration by
The Landmark Trust. Open to the
public on completion
Pugin, AWN

Hampton Court Palace
Hampton Court, Surrey
Open 25 Mar to 27 Oct on Mon, 10.15am
to 6pm & Tues to Sun, 9.30am to 6pm;
25 Oct to 24 Mar on Mon, 10.15am to
4.30pm & Tues to Sun, 9.30am to
4.30pm. Closed 24–26 Dec. Gardens
open all year round, 7am to dusk.
Wolsey, Cardinal

Hardwick Hall
Hardwick Park, Doe Lea,
Chesterfield, Derbyshire
Open Apr to Oct on Wed, Thurs,
Sat, Sun & Bank Holiday Mondays,
12.30pm to 4.30pm
Smythson, Robert

Hatfield House
Hatfield, Hertfordshire

Open 25 Mar to 12 Oct, Tues to Sat,
12pm to 5pm & Sun, 1pm to 4.30pm;
Easter, May Day, Spring & Aug Bank
Holiday Mondays, 11am to 4.30pm
Cecil, Robert

Hill House
Upper Colquhoun Street,
Helensburgh, Scotland
Open Apr to Oct daily, 1.30pm
to 5.30pm
Mackintosh, Charles Rennie

Holkham Hall
Wells-next-the-Sea, Norfolk
Open Sun to Thurs, 1pm to 5pm &
selected bank holidays
Kent, William

Holmswood
Netherlee Road, Cathcart, Scotland
Owned by the National Trust for
Scotland
Open Sat & Sun, 12pm to 4pm
Thomson, Alexander 'Greek'

Kelmscott Manor
Kelmscott, Lechdale, Oxfordshire
Open Apr to Sept on Wed, 11am to
1pm & 2pm to 5pm. Also open every
third Sat in Apr, May, June & Sept, &
the first & third Sat in July & Aug
Morris, William

**Kew Palace & Royal Botanical
Gardens**
Kew, Surrey
Gardens open daily, 9.30am to dusk
Closed 25 Dec & 1 Jan
Fortrey, Samuel

Leighton House
Holland Park Road, London
Open Mon to Sat, 11am to 5.30pm
Closed Sun & Bank Holidays
Aitchison Jr, George

Letchworth Garden City
The First Garden City Heritage
Museum, Norton Way South,
Letchworth Garden City,
Hertfordshire
Open to the public
Parker & Unwin

Little Hall
Market Place, Lavenham, Suffolk
Open Mon to Fri, 9am to 5pm & Sat,
10am to 4pm
Lavenham Clothier

Little Moreton Hall
Congleton, Cheshire
Open Mar to Nov, Wed to Sun & Bank
Holiday Mondays, 11.30am to 5pm;
restricted winter opening times
Special openings at other times for
booked parties
Moreton Family

Mousa Broch
Island of Mousa, Shetland Isles,
Scotland
Site managed by Historic Scotland

Open to the public
Shetland Island Celts

Port Sunlight
Merseyside
Public urban spaces, open daily
Lever, William Hesketh

Queen's House
Romney Rd, Greenwich, London
Open daily, 10am to 5pm
Closed 24–26 Dec
Jones, Inigo

Red House
Red House Lane, Bexleyheath, Kent
Open for guided tours on the first full
weekend of every month except Jan
Webb, Philip

Scotney Castle
Lamberhurst, Tunbridge Wells, Kent
Open at various times throughout
the year
Ashburnham, Roger

Sir John Soane's Museum
13–14 Lincoln's Inn Fields, London
Open Tues to Sat, 10am to 5pm. Also
open on the first Tues of every month,
6pm to 9pm. Museum tour on Sat at
2.30pm
Soane, Sir John

Skara Brae
Skara Brae Neolithic Settlement,
Mainland, Orkney, nr Stromness,
Scotland
Open to the public
Neolithic Orkney Islanders

Stokesay Castle
Craven Arms, Shropshire
Open Apr to Oct daily, 10am to 6pm
(5pm in Oct); Nov to Mar, Wed to Sun,
10am to 1pm & 2pm to 4pm
Closed 24–26 Dec & 1 Jan
Ludlow, Laurence de

Strawberry Hill
Twickenham, Middlesex
Open Easter to Oct on Sun
Walpole, Horace

Syon House
Brentford, Middlesex
Open Mar to Oct on Wed, Thurs, Sun,
Bank Holiday Mondays & Easter,
11am to 5pm
Adam, Robert

Traquair House
Innerleithen, Peeblesshire, Scotland
House & grounds open daily from 14
Apr to 31 Oct. House open, 12.30pm to
5.30pm, except for June, July & Aug
when the times are 10.30pm to 5.30pm
Grounds open daily, 10.30am to
5.30pm from Easter to end Oct
Traquair, Earls of

Turn End
Townside, Haddenham,
Buckinghamshire

Open at various times throughout
the year
Aldington, Peter

USA

Aluminaire House
Currently undergoing restoration by
the New York Institute of Technology
in Central Islip, NY
Open to the public on completion
Kocher, Lawrence & Frey, Albert

Bardwell House (now Allen House)
John Allen House is a museum run
by Historic Deerfield in Deerfield, MA
Open daily, 9.30am to 4.30pm. Closed
Thanksgiving & 24–25 December
Bardwell, Thomas

Biltmore
Ashville, NC
Open Jan to Mar daily, 9am to 5pm;
Apr to Dec, 8.30am to 5pm. Closed
Thanksgiving & Christmas Day
Hunt, Richard Morris

Boscobel
Garrison, Hudson Valley, NY
Open daily except Tues, Apr to Oct,
9.30am to 5pm; Nov & Dec, 9.30am
to 4pm
Dyckman, States Morris

Brevard-Mmahat House
First Street, Garden District, New
Orleans, LA
Walking tours of the Garden District
available at 10am & 1.30pm. Contact
www.neworleans.com for details
Calrow, James

Center Family Dwelling House
The house is part of the Shaker
Village at Pleasant Hill, Lexington
Road, Harrodsburg, KY
Open daily, 9.30am to 5.30pm
Closed 24–25 Dec
Burnett, Micajah

Cliff Palace
Mesa Verde National Park, Mesa
Verde, CO
Ranger-led tours available mid-Apr to
mid-Nov. Tickets for Cliff Palace must
be purchased from The Far View
Visitor Center which is open from
8am to 5pm. Closed in winter
Pueblo Indians

Eames House
Chataqua, Pacific Palisades, CA
This is a private residence, however,
self-guided visits to the exterior &
grounds are available to the general
public by appointment only, Mon to
Fri, excluding holidays, between the
approximate hours of 10am to 4.30pm
Eames, Charles & Ray

Earth Lodge
Knife River Indian Villages National
Historic Site in Stanton, IN operates
tours of earth lodge sites
Open summer, 7.30am to 6.00pm;

winter, 8.00am to 4.30pm. Closed
Thanksgiving, Christmas & New
Year's Day
Mandan Indians

Fallingwater (Kaufmann House)
Bear Run, PA
Open 1 Apr to mid-Nov daily except
Mon, 10am to 4pm; open weekends,
Dec & Mar. Closed Jan & Feb. Tours
available 10am to 4pm
Wright, Frank Lloyd

Farnsworth House
River Road, Plano, IL
Tours by appointment
Mies van der Rohe

Frick Residence
Now the Frick Collection, 1 East 70th
Street (between Madison and Fifth
Avenues), New York, NY
Open Tues to Sat, 10am to 6pm;
Sun, 12 Feb, Election Day & 11 Nov,
1pm to 6pm. Closed Mon, 4 July,
Thanksgiving, 24–25 Dec & 1–2 Jan
Carrère & Hastings

Gamble House
Westmoreland Place, Pasadena, CA
Open for tours, Thurs to Sun, 12pm
to 4pm. Closed national holidays
Greene & Greene

Harrison Gray Otis House
Cambridge Street, Boston, MA
Open Tues to Fri, 12pm to 5pm & Sat,
10am to 5pm
Bulfinch, Charles

Hearst Castle
Hearst Castle Road, San Simeon, CA
Open for tours daily, except
Thanksgiving, Christmas & New
Year's Day
Morgan, Julia

Henry Delamater House
The Beekman Arms/Delamater Inn
operates as a hotel & conference centre
Mill Street, Rhinebeck, NY
Davis, Alexander Jackson

**J Irwin & Xenia Miller House &
Garden**
5th Street, Columbus, IN
Open Apr to Sept
Contact for details
Saarinen, Eero

Kings Road Studios
Schindler House/MAK Center for
Arts & Architecture
North Kings Road, Los Angeles, CA
Open Wed to Sun. Tours available
on weekends
Schindler, Rudolph

Kykuit
Pocantico Hills, Sleepy Hollow, NY
Open daily except Tues, Apr to Nov.
Tours, 10am to 4pm at weekends &
10am to 3pm on weekdays
Delano & Aldrich

Longwood
Lower Woodville Road, Natchez, MS
Open daily, 9am to 4.30pm
Sloan, Samuel

Mark Twain House
Farmington Avenue, Hartford, CT
Open daily, Mon to Sat, 9.30am to 4pm;
Sun, 12pm to 4pm. Closed Tues from
Jan to Apr & Nov, 1 Jan, Easter
Sunday, Thanksgiving & 24–25 Dec
Potter, Edward

Monticello
Virginia Piedmont,
nr Charlottesville, VA
Open daily, Mar to Oct, 8am to 5pm;
Nov to Feb, 9am to 4.30pm
Jefferson, Thomas

Mount Vernon
Fairfax County, VA
Open daily, times vary throughout
the year
Washington, George

Nautilus Earthship
Greater World Community, Taos, NM
The Nautilus Earthship is available
for short-stay accommodation
Details on application
Reynolds, Michael

Olana
Hudson, NY
Open Apr to Oct, Wed to Sun. Times
vary throughout the year
Vaux, Calvert & Church, Frederick

Painted Ladies
Steiner St, San Francisco, CA
Pacific Heights Walking Tours on Sun
at 12.30. Contact the San Francisco
Tourist Office
Kavanaugh, Matthew

San Francisco Plantation House
Garyville, LA
Open daily. Tours, 10am to 4.30pm
Marmillion, Edmond Bozonier

Scotty's Castle
Grapevine Canyon, Death Valley, CA
Open daily. Tours, 9am to 6pm
MacNeilledge, Charles

Shadows-on-the-Teche
East Main Street, New Iberia, LA
Open daily. Guided tours, 9am to
4.30pm. Closed Thanksgiving,
Christmas & New Year's Day
Weeks, David

Springwood
Franklin Delano Roosevelt Home &
Library, Albany Post Road, Hyde
Park, NY
Open for guided tours daily, 8am
to dusk
Roosevelt, James & Franklin D

Taos Pueblo Houses
Taos Pueblo, World Heritage Site, NM
Open daily except for ceremonial

occasions. Call in advance for details
Tiwa Indians

Tipi
The Blackfoot Nation, Bear Chief's
Lodge, Browning, MT
Contact the Blackfoot Nation with
tourism enquiries
Blackfoot Indians

Villa Zapu
Mount Veeder Road, Napa, CA
Parts of the residence & vineyards
are open to the public
Powell-Tuck Connor & Orefelt

Vizcaya
South Miami Avenue, Miami, FL
Open daily, 9.30am to 4.30pm. Group
tours by appointment
*Hoffman Jr, Francis Burrall &
Chalfin, Paul*

The White House
Pennsylvania Avenue NW,
Washington DC
Open for tours in the mornings,
Tues to Sat. Closed Sun & Mon
Hoban, James

Wichita House
The house is now located at the Henry
Ford Museum & Greenfield Village,
Oakwood Boulevard, Dearborn, MI
Open daily, 9am to 5pm. Closed
Thanksgiving & Christmas Day
Fuller, Richard Buckminster

Yemen

Tower Houses
Dàr al-Haja Tower House, Al-Rawadh,
nr San'a
Now a museum, open to the public
Yemeni

House opening times may be subject
to change and access may be limited
during restoration work. It is
advisable to check the times and
dates of opening prior to visiting or
making travel arrangements. Private
houses and vernacular dwellings are
not listed, unless they are open to the
public.

Acknowledgements

Texts written by Peter Andrews, Iona Baird, Raul Barreneche, Sophia Behling, Karla Britton, Pamela Buxton, Catherine Cooke, Catherine Croft, Elsie Burch Donald, Talia Dorsey, Ellie Duffy, Beth Dunlop, Kimberly Elman, Martin Goalen, Jo Haire, Sarah Jackson, Ann Jarmusch, Helen Kohen, Virginia McLeod, Clare Melhuish, Jeremy Melvin, Aulani Mulford, Dung Ngo, Paul Oliver, Ken Tadashi Oshima, Alan Powers, Anthony Quiney, Kester Rattenbury, Tsuto Sakamoto, Torsten Schmiedeknecht, Jagan Shah, Steven Spier, Naomi Stungo, Douglas Wylie and Yasushi Zenno.

The publishers would like to thank Peter Buchanan, Edward Bosley, Haig Beck, Stephanie Bunn, Jackie Cooper, Gillian Darley, Beth Dunlop, Mark Fiennes, Patrick Nuttgens, Paul Oliver and Ken Tadashi Oshima for their invaluable advice.

And Atelier Works for the jacket design.

Photographic Acknowledgements

Aga Khan Trust for Culture/© Chant Avedissan: 118, 124; Aga Khan Trust for Culture/© Ahmet Ertug: 115; Airstream Inc: 8; AKG London/Hilbich: 386; AKG London/Erich Lessing: 264; Ole Akhøj: 167; Archivi Alinari: 151; Dimitris Antonakakis: 29; Peter Aprahamian: 143; Ron Arad Associates: 23; Arcaid/Richard Bryant: 9, 13, 39, 78, 97, 161, 283, 331, 336, 367, 421, 480; Arcaid/Jeremy Cockayne: 306; Arcaid/Nick Dawe: 82, 266, 430; Arcaid/Richard Einzig: 434; Arcaid/Lucinda Lambton: 366; Arcaid/Clay Perry: 176; Arcaid/Richard Turpin: 218; Arcaid/Alain Weintraub: 252, 352; Archigram Archives: 159, 481; Archipress: 219; Archipress/Franck Eustache: 74, 277, 292; Archipress/Pascal LeMaitre: 138; Archipress/M Loiseau: 327; Archipress/Michel Moch: 321; Arch Photo Inc/Eduard Hueber: 38, 460; Architectural Association/Marina Lathouri: 237; Architectural Association/E Smith: 40; Reproduced courtesy of The Architectural Review: 76; Architectural Studio/Gaston: 24; Architektur-Bilderservice Kandula/Günter Lachmuth: 169; Claire Arni: 88; Aspect Picture Library Ltd/© Bryan & Cherry Alexander: 383; Aspect Picture Library Ltd/© Tsune Okuda: 408; Aspect Picture Library Ltd/© Richard Turpin: 484; Atelier 5: 28; Paul Atterbury: 356; Axiom/James Morris: 100, 468; Axiom/Chris Parker: 54; Axiom/Peter Wilson: 62; Karl A Backus, AIA: 51; Morley Baer: 300; Ángel Luis Baltanás Ramirez – Fotógrafo: 87; Juvenal Baracco: 34; Edward Larrabee Barnes: 36; Alfonso Barrios: 58; © CH Bastin & J Evrard: 15, 60, 71, 186, 192, 235, 424, 446, 470; Bauhaus-Archiv Berlin/Hüttich-Oemler: 310; Courtesy of Belltrees Archive Collection: 337; Staffan Berglund Arkitektkontor AB: 42; P Berntsen: 188; Bildarchiv Foto Marburg: 73; Bildarchiv-Monheim.de/© Lisa Hammel: 392; Bildarchiv-Monheim.de/© Florian Monheim: 45, 89, 318, 346, 390, 479; Reiner Blunck Fotodesign: 96, 311, 345; Arquivo Lina Bo Bardi/Arnaldo Pappalardo: 49; Osvaldo Böhm: 83; Tom Bonner: 258; Bridgeman Art Library/John Bethell: 433; Bridgeman Art Library/Japan Information and Cultural Centre, London: 453; Steven Brooke Studios: 241; Anthony Browell/Oki-Doki: 104; Canadian Centre for Architecture, Montréal/Collection Centre Canadien d'Architecture: 86, 291; Canadian Centre for Architecture, Montréal /Collection Centre Canadien d'Architecture/© Richard Pare & Phyllis Lambert: 376; Lluis Casals Fotografia: 127; Martin Charles: 416, 477; © Richard Cheek for Hyde Park Historical Association: 369; Roberto Collovà: 411; Colorific/TCL/Lee Battaglia: 212; Colorific/TCL/John Bracegirdle: 200; Colorific/TCL/David Kjaer: 177; Colorific/TCL/David Levenson: 488; Colorific/TCL/Claus Meyer/Camara Tres: 150; Colorific/TCL/Pat & Baiba Morrow: 244; Colorific/TCL/John Moss: 130; Colorific/TCL/Tom Walker/Stock Boston: 273; Hans-Jürgen Commerell: 438; Contacts/Dick Sweeney: 16; The Conway Library, Courtland Institute of Art: 166; Corbis: 239, 475; Corbis/Yann Arthus-Bertrand: 289; Country Life Picture Library: 270, 464; Country Life Picture Library/Clive Boursnell: 194; Country Life Picture Library/Anne Hyde: 414; Country Life Picture Library/Julian Nieman: 7; The Czech Press Agency: 284; Richard Davies: 137; © James Davis Travel Photography: 210; Nick Dawe: 133; Christopher Day: 94; © Thomas Delbeck: 107, 215, 500; Design Press/Lars Hallén: 27, 120; Diller + Scofido: 98; Jacques Dirand: 420; Elsie Burch Donald: 129, 247, 354; John Donat: 487; Talia Dorsey: 313, 439, 441; Orestis Doumanis: 501; James Dow/Patkau Artchitects: 334; Melanie Eclare: 11; Edifice/Lewis: 397; Edifice/Schneebeli: 43; Edinburgh Photographic Library: 455; Edinburgh Photographic Library/P Davenport: 317; EHDD: 122; Electa Archive/Alessandra Chemollo: 245; © English Heritage Photo Library: 268; Erith & Terry Architects: 437; Esto/© Peter Aaron: 377, 469; Esto/© Wayne Andrews: 56, 287, 364, 370; Esto/© Mark Darley: 203; Esto/© Scott Frances: 290, 307; Esto/© Farrell Grehan: 296; Esto/© Bret Morgan: 64, 92, 109; Esto/© Roberto Schezen: 298, 305, 315; Esto/© Tim Street-Porter: 144; Eye Ubiquitous/David Cumming: 10; Eye Ubiquitous/Michael Reed: 227; Eye Ubiquitous/© Thelma Sanders: 301; Eye Ubiquitous/Julia Waterlow: 263; Gabriël Fagan: 123; Luis Ferreira Alves: 419; © Mark Fiennes: 95, 158, 185, 253, 272, 312, 330, 372, 489, 491; Museum of Finnish Architecture: 428; Museum of Finnish Architecture/Simo Rista: 140; First Garden City Heritage Museum, Letchworth Garden City, UK: 333; © Fondation Le Corbusier: 255; The Fort Abraham Lincoln Foundation, Mandan, North Dakota: 279; Foster & Partners/Nigel Young: 409; Dick Frank Studio: 114; Courtesy of the Freer Gallery of Art, Smithsonian Institution, Washington DC, F1986.7: 14; French Picture Library: 401; Mitsumasa Fujitsuka: 173; Tutsuo Fukaya: 302; Estate of Buckminster Fuller: 135; Nikos Georgiadis: 387; Paolo Giordano: 141; Glenbow Archives, Calgary, Canada (NA-648-2): 368; John Gollings: 18, 112, 164, 224; Luis Gordoa: 435; Daniel Grataloup: 155; Greatbuildings.com/Photo © Lawrence A Martin: 35; Anne Guernsey Allen: 384; Miguel de Guzman Garcia Monge: 220; John M. Hall/Hariri & Hariri: 171; T R Hamzah & Yeang: 454; Robert Harding Picture Library: 44, 260, 309; Robert Harding Picture Library/© C Bowman: 182; Robert Harding Picture Library/P Craven: 132; Robert Harding Picture Library/Nigel Francis: 183, 303; Robert Harding Picture Library/© R Frerck: 121; Robert Harding Picture Library/© Robert Frerck/Odyssey/Chicago: 65; Robert Harding Picture Library/Gascoigne: 347; Robert Harding Picture Library/T Gervis: 209; Robert Harding Picture Library/K Gillham: 138; Robert Harding Picture Library/Simon Harris: 225; Robert Harding Picture Library/Roy Rainford: 385; Robert Harding Picture Library/Geoff Renner: 77; Robert Harding Picture Library/Ellen Rooney: 359; Robert Harding Picture Library/Sassoon: 357; Robert Harding Picture Library/Michael Short: 328; Robert Harding Picture Library/V Theakston: 274; Robert Harding Picture Library/Guy Thouvenin: 55; Robert Harding Picture Library/Adina Tovy: 198, 265; Robert Harding Picture Library/Nedra Westwater: 254; Jerry Harpur: 72; Harvard University/Frances Loeb Library: 402; © Hearst Castle®/CA State Parks: 304; Lucian Hervé: 339; Todd Hido: 126; Hiroyuki Hirai/Shigeru Ban Architects: 32; Hiroyuki Hirai/Hirai Photo Office: 436; Knud Holscher: 189; Richard Horden Associates Ltd: 190; © Angelo Hornak Library: 63, 261, 431, 467; Timothy Hursley: 299, 378, 394, 395, 412, 425; Hutchison Picture Library: 84; Hutchison Picture Library/S Errington: 448; Hutchison Picture Library/John Hatt: 320; Hutchison Picture Library/Brian Moser: 456; Hutchison Picture Library/Christine Pemberton: 262, 422; Hutchison Picture Library/B Regent: 429; Hutchison Picture Library/Dr Nigel Smith: 196; Hutchison Picture Library/Tony Souter: 101; Hutchison Picture Library/Isabella Tree: 494; Images of Africa/David Keith Jones: 502; Index/A Pladevila: 102; Steven Inggs: 466; The Irish Architectural Archive: 443; Issaias & Papaioannou: 204; Darryl Jackson Pty Ltd: 206; Charles Jencks: 152, 213, 493; Jari Jetsonen: 342; Pierre Joly et Vera Cardot Photographes: 332, 374; Vasant Kamath: 223; Howard Kaplan/Architectural Photography: 444; Mitzuno Katsuhiko: 243; © Angelo Kaunat: 103, 221; A F Kersting: 81, 269; Kitazawa Architects: 360; Nelson Kon: 6; Balthazar Korab Ltd: 146, 149, 154, 195, 208, 216, 379; Roy Lewis: 403; Link Picture Library/Philip Scheder: 316; Ian Macdonald Smith: 70; Mahatta Madan: 362; © Duccio Malagamba: 452; Antonio Martinelli: 53, 389; Pedro Martinez de Albornoz: 280; Mitsuo Matsuoka: 17; Ned Matura, New York: 371; Norman McGrath: 156, 423; E Andrew McKinney: 33; © Nick Meers: 463; © Norbert Miguletz: 426; Jordi Miralles: 297; Ryuji Miyameto: 52; Kaneaki Monma: 497; Moon Studio/Batista: 363; David Moore: 19; Michael Moran: 486; P&G Morisson, The Hague, NL: 242; David Muench: 93, 355; Stefan Müller: 459; Musée de l'Ecole de Nancy/Cliché Claude Philippot: 388; Collection of the Museum of New Zealand Te Papa Tongarewa/Burton Brothers/C.10276: 281; Mario Mutschlechner: 400; National Archives of Canada/PA 38465: 286; The National Museum of Fine Art, Stockholm/Åsa Lundén: 248; National Technical Museum, Prague: 211; © National Trust for Historic Preservation/Ron Blunt: 483; National Trust Photographic Library/Dennis Gilbert: 153; National Trust Photographic Library/Ian Shaw: 26; Netherlands Architectural Institute: 47, 57; Netherlands Architectural Institute/© Stichting Beeldrech: 99; Dung Ngo/Anemic Design: 285; Norsk Arkitekturmuseum/Jim Bengston: 240; Norsk Arkitekturmuseum/Jiri Havran: 125; History Collection, Nova Scotia Museum, Halifax, Canada: 116; © Novosti/SCR Library: 226; Novosti (London): 341, 451; Paul Oliver: 91, 174; Paul Ott: 128; Atelier Frei Otto: 329; Frank den Oudsten: 184, 365; The Palace Museum, Beijing: 295; John Panikar: 105; Panos Pictures/Jean-Leo Dugast: 380; © R Perron: 282; Alberto Piovano: 232; Centre Pompidou: 108, 353; Professor Paolo Portoghesi: 348; Powerstock Zefa/Yann Arthus-Bertrand/Altitude: 256; Ramon Prat: 80; Claude Prevost: 202; Robert Reck: 351; Fabio Reinhart: 361; Patrick Reynolds: 85; Luisa Ricciarini: 293; Clark Richert: 106; Christian Richters: 163, 458; Simo Rista: 4; © Cervin Robinson: 136, 427; Paul Rocheleau: 172; RoTo: 373; Royal Commission on Historical Monuments: 404; Royal Institute of British Architects Picture Library: 111, 233, 257, 259, 278, 476; Philippe Ruault: 238, 246; Michal Ronnen Safdie: 381; Stanley Saitowitz: 382; Bill Sanders/Fort Lauderdale, Florida: 214; San Diego Historical Society: 148; Phil Sayer: 440; Daria Scagliola/Brakkee: 288; Scala: 165, 358; Scala/Luisa Ricciarini: 340; Deidi von Schaewen: 75; Schenkirz/Thomas Herzog: 181; Roberto Schezen/Gwathmey Siegel: 168; © Simon Scott: 119; Scott, Tallon & Walker: 396; SCR Photo Library: 22, 66, 131, 142, 145, 322, 405, 472; John Searle: 323; © Vaclav Sedy: 251, 498; Harry Seidler: 398; Shinkenchiku-sha: 30, 134, 170, 191, 199, 201, 205, 229, 230, 324, 326, 399, 407, 461, 492, 496, 503; Julius Shulman: 113, 117, 160, 217, 234, 319, 417, 418; Filippo Simonetti: 415; Sirén Architects: 410; Alison & Peter Smithson Archive: 157, 413; Courtesy of the Society for the Preservation of New England Antiquities/Photograph by Arthur Gaskell: 61; South American Pictures/Tony Morrison: 41; South American Pictures/Rolando Pujol: 175; Spectrum Stock/Ottmar Bierwagen: 308; AG Speranza/Giuseppe Carfagna: 442; AG Speranza/Sandro Vannini: 474; Margherita Spiluttini: 180, 343, 393, 478; © Stiftung Archiv der Akademie der Künste: 267; Ezra Stoller © Esto: 69, 222; © Tony Stone Images/Glen Allison: 335; Tim Street-Porter: 25, 37, 90, 110, 236, 350, 391; Richard Stringer/Clare Design: 79; Rob Super: 457; Hisao Suzuki: 68; Charles Tait Photographic: 406; Bill Timmerman: 59; Travel Ink/David Toase: 432; © Trip/Tibor Bognár: 67; © Trip/W Jacobs: 449; © Trip/K McLaren: 314; © Trip/R Nichols: 20; © Trip/Eric Smith: 5; © Trip/Trip: 445; © Trip/Viesti Collection: 197; © Trip/B Vikander: 271; The Ulster Folk and Transport Museum: 21; Union française pour le sauvetage de l'Enfance: 338; Nicos Valsamakis: 465; Serena Vergano: 50; Vicens & Hualde: 473; View/Peter Cook: 294, 490; Kjeld Vindum: 207; © Collection Viollet: 375; Tohru Waki/Shokokusha: 231; Paul Warchol Photography Inc: 187; © 2001 Matthew Weinreb, imagefind.com: 178; Guy Wenborne: 162; Werkfoto/Peter Hübner & Frank Huster: 193; Hans Werleman: 147; Werner Forman Picture Archive: 276, 344, 447, 450, 495; Whitney Museum of American Art/Bill Jacobson: 228; Claudio Williams: 485; Bertram D Wolfe Collection, Hoover Institution Archives, Stanford University: 325; Charlotte Wood: 31, 482; Yale Collection of Western Americana, Beinecke Rare Book and Manuscript Library/Photograph by Walter McCintock: 48; Jeff Yardis: 349; Alo Zanetta: 462; Courtesy of Marco Zanuso: 499

Jacket: Detail of Caimato Building, Lugano (SW), 1993 by Mario Botta/Photograph by Enrico Cano

All reasonable efforts have been made to trace the copyright holders of the photographs used in this book. We apologize to anyone that we have been unable to reach.